The
First & Final
Commandment

A Search for Truth in Revelation
within the Abrahamic Religions

Dr. Laurence Brown, MD

amana publications

First Edition
(1425AH/2004CE)

amana publications
10710 Tucker Street
Beltsville, Maryland 20705-2223 USA
Tel: (301) 595-5777 / Fax: (301) 595-5888
E-mail: amana@igprinting.com
Website: www.amana-publications.com

Copyright © 2004
Dr. Laurence B. Brown
All Rights Reserved
Author's website: www.Leveltruth.com
e-mail: LBrown@Leveltruth.com

Library of Congress Cataloging-in-Publications Data

Brown, Laurence B. (Laurence Bunting), 1959-
 The first & final commandment : a search for truth in revelation within the Abrahamic religions / Laurence B. Brown.
  p. cm.
 Includes bibliographical references (p.   ) and index.
 ISBN 1-59008-028-9 (alk. paper)
 1. Revelation--Comparative studies. 2. Judaism. 3. Christianity. 4. Islam. I. Title: First and final commandment. II. Title.

BL475.5.B76 2004
202'.117--dc22

2004018677

Printed in the United States of America by International Graphics
10710 Tucker Street, Beltsville, Maryland 20705-2223 USA
Tel: (301) 595-5999 Fax: (301) 595-5888
Website: igprinting.com
E-mail: ig@igprinting.com

To
The Lovers of Truth,
The
Friends of Free Inquiry;
To Those Who Dare,
In the Face of Church Establishments,
Of
Orthodox Denunciations,
And of
Lukewarm, Time-serving Christians,
To openly profess
What they believe to be true:
This volume is inscribed.[1]

---

1. Dedication by the Editor of *An Enquiry into the Opinions of the Christian Writers of the Three First Centuries Concerning the Person of Jesus Christ*, by Gilbert Wakefield, B.A. 1824.

The Peace Prayer of St. Francis

Lord, make me an instrument of your peace;
Where there is hatred, let me sow love;
Where there is injury, pardon;
Where there is doubt, faith;
Where there is despair, hope;
Where there is darkness, light;
And where there is sadness, joy.
Grant that I may not so much seek
to be consoled as to console;
To be understood as to understand;
To be loved as to love;
For it is in giving that we receive;
It is in pardoning that we are pardoned;
And it is in dying that we are born to eternal life.

All scripture quotations,
unless otherwise indicated,
are taken from the *New King James Version*.
Copyright © 1982 by Thomas Nelson, Inc.
Used by permission. All rights reserved.

Scripture quotations marked "NRSV" herein
are from the *New Revised Standard Version Bible*,
Copyright © 1989 by the Division of Christian Education
of the National Council of the Churches of Christ in the U.S.A.
Used by permission. All rights reserved.

Contents

I. FOREWORD 10
II. PREFACE 14
III. INTRODUCTION 17

SECTION 1: MONOTHEISM 23
    (1.A) Judaism 25
    (1.B) Christianity 27
    (1.C1) Islam [Part I] 35
    (1.C2) Islam [Part II] 43

SECTION 2: GOD 55
    (2.A) Understanding and Approaching God 57

        (2.A1) God's Name 57
        (2.A2) God's Name and the Royal Plural 65
        (2.A3) Understanding of God 68

    (2.B) Doctrinal Differences 73

        (2.B1)   Christ Jesus 83
        (2.B2)   Word of God 87
        (2.B3)   Messiah (Christ) 91
        (2.B4)   Immaculate Conception 97
        (2.B5)   Jesus Begotten? 99
        (2.B6)   Christ Jesus, Son of God? 107
        (2.B7)   The Trinity 133
        (2.B8)   Divinity of Jesus? 155
        (2.B9)   Holy Spirit 192
        (2.B10) Crucifixion 203
        (2.B11) Lamb of God 223
        (2.B12) Original Sin 227
        (2.B13) Atonement 231
        (2.B14) Return of Jesus 240

SECTION 3: BOOKS OF SCRIPTURE 245

   (3.A) The Old Testament 255

   (3.B) The New Testament 270

   (3.C) The Holy Qur'an 311

      (3.C1) Brief History of the Qur'an   311
      (3.C2) Evidences: Introduction   327
      (3.C3) Evidence 1: Innate Appeal   330
      (3.C4) Evidence 2: Language of The Qur'an   339
      (3.C5) Evidence 3: Relation of Revelation to Preceding Events   360
      (3.C6) Evidence 4: Relation of Revelation to Contemporaneous Events   379
      (3.C7) Evidence 5: Relation of Revelation to Subsequent Events   386
      (3.C8) Evidence 6: Revelation of the Unknown (ie., that which was beyond the experience of the Prophet)   406
      (3.C9) Evidences: Summary   446

SECTION 4: MESSENGERS 451

   (4.A) Adam to Moses 456

   (4.B) Moses 459

   (4.C) Christ Jesus 472

   (4.D) Muhammad 479

      (4.D1) Predictions in Previous Scripture   490
      (4.D2) Miraculous Signs   491
      (4.D3) Miracles Performed   498
      (4.D4) Character   504
      (4.D5) Persistence   521
      (4.D6) Steadfastness   523
      (4.D7) Lack of Disqualifiers   533
      (4.D8) Maintenance of The Message   541

SECTION 5: THE UNSEEN 551
    (5.A) Angels 553
    (5.B) Day of Judgement 557
    (5.C) Divine Decree 561

SECTION 6: CONCLUSIONS 571
    (6.A) The Deviant Religion 573
    (6.B) Surrender 576
    (6.C) Consequences of Logic 585

APPENDIX: RECOMMENDED READING 589
BIBLIOGRAPHY 593
GLOSSARY OF TERMS 605

(I) Foreword

Biblical quotes in the following work, unless otherwise noted, are taken from the *New King James Version* of the Bible. The reason for selecting this reference does not relate to the degree of scriptural faithfulness, which is debatable, but rather to the well-known popularity of the text. Within the borders of English-speaking Western nations, the 1611 edition of the *King James Version* remains the most popular and widely read version of the Bible. The *New King James Version* grew from an effort to "keep abreast of changes in English speech."[2] Hence, the *New King James Version* represents an effort to render the 1611 *King James Version* into more contemporary, more readable, more 'audience friendly' text. However, disappointingly little, if any, effort has been made to reconcile differences between the 1611 *King James Version* and the highly authoritative Sinaitic and Vatican manuscripts, discovered in the late nineteenth and twentieth centuries. As a result, the *New King James Version*, regardless of popularity, is open to criticism on the basis of retaining questionable passages in conflict with the most ancient and respected New Testament manuscripts known to the present day. Therefore, while this current work predominantly cites the *New King James Version*

---

2. *The Holy Bible, New King James Version*. 1982. Thomas Nelson Publishers, preface, p. iv.

(I) Foreword

of the Bible in the interest of satisfying the Protestant majority of Western Christianity, a complementary version of the Bible is required where greater faithfulness to scriptural authority is desired.

The *New Revised Standard Version* (NRSV) of the Bible is quoted in relation to those subjects where greater accuracy or objectivity is required. The *New Revised Standard Version*, representing the compiled effort and approval of an ecumenical body of scholars spanning the various Protestant denominations, the Roman Catholic Church, and the Eastern Orthodox Church, and containing at least one Jewish member for accuracy of Old Testament translation, appears to enjoy the most universal acceptance amongst Christian scholars. The *New Revised Standard Version* replaces the *Revised Standard Version*, which had such wide acceptance as to have been "officially authorized for use by all major Christian churches: Protestant, Anglican, Roman Catholic, and Eastern Orthodox."[3] Given the myriad of Modern English versions of the Bible, there is unlikely to be any version as objectively derived and widely accepted by the Christian community as a whole as either the *Revised Standard Version* or the *New Revised Standard Version*.

Quotations from the English Translation of the Meaning of the Holy Qur'an (hereafter denoted 'TMQ'), unless otherwise noted, are taken from the Abdullah Yusuf Ali translation. Where specific passages benefit from complementary translation, that of Saheeh International or of the co-translators Muhammad Al-Hilali and Muhammad Khan, is cited.

The reader should appreciate that Arabic-speaking Muslims and non-Muslims alike do not regard any translation of the Holy Qur'an as wholly adequate, as the Holy Qur'an is held to be inimitable, defying translation in anything but meaning. Appreciation of the

---

3. *The Holy Bible, New Revised Standard Version*. Grand Rapids, MI: Zondervan Publishing House. Foreword, p. vii.

unique beauty of the native Arabic language, the depth of emotions evoked in company with comprehension, and the spiritually soothing character of the scripture can only be approached with knowledge of the Arabic in which the Holy Qur'an was revealed. Furthermore, no language, especially one as complex as Arabic, can be translated with complete accuracy into a foreign tongue. Hence, the comment of Professor A. Guillaume,

> "The Qur'an is one of the world's classics which cannot be translated without grave loss."[4]

Such opinions are strongly reinforced by those who actually attempted the task of translation, including both the British Muslim translator, Marmaduke Pickthall, and the British non-Muslim translator, Professor A. J. Arberry. Having faced the challenges involved, Professor Arberry commented,

> "In choosing to call the present work *The Koran Interpreted* I have conceded the relevancy of the orthodox Muslim view, of which Pickthall, for one, was so conscious, that the Koran is untranslatable."[5]

Furthermore, once translated, the sanctity of the text of the Holy Qur'an is violated and the work can no longer be regarded as presenting the perfection of the original. Should the revealed scripture represent the literal word of God, any translation not qualified as a 'translation of meaning' risks falling into the realm of the blasphemous, for the translated word of a human being can never rival the chosen language and words of God.

---

4. Guillaume, Alfred. 1990. *Islam*. Penguin Books. pp. 73-74.
5. Arberry, A. J. 1996. *The Koran Interpreted*. A Touchstone book: Simon & Schuster. Preface, p. 24.

(I) Foreword

Just such sentiments resulted in the first English translations of the Bible witnessing bitter opposition over issues relating to the sanctity of scripture. As a result, both John Wycliffe's and William Tyndale's versions were publicly burned, with the authors faring little better. William Tyndale was burned at the stake in October 1536, whereas Wycliffe's bones were posthumously exhumed and publicly burned. How much greater caution would be observed in translating Biblical texts, were the original scripture of Jesus available, is impossible to guess. Were the original scripture of Jesus extant, pure and unadulterated, significant resistance would be expected, amongst the faithful, to any translation other than one qualified as a 'translation of meaning.' For no doubt the flow of the language, beauty of the revealed words, and soothing bliss of the original could never be adequately conveyed in translation to any language other than that chosen by design of The Creator Himself.

(II) Preface

"Where shall I begin, please your Majesty?" he asked.
"Begin at the beginning," the King said, gravely,
"and go on till you come to the end: then stop."
– Lewis Carroll, *Alice's Adventures in Wonderland*

Recent decades have witnessed a society-wide shift with regard to the values by which truth and quality are measured. The present generation's forefathers spent much of their free time in discussion of topics which rarely breach the lips of men today. Subjects of depth and importance, such as political ethics, societal morals, methodology of reason, etc. were freely debated from the home and workplace to the local community center and town hall. In contrast, average conversations in the modern Western workplace and home center on alcohol, relationships, money, sports and entertainment. Whereas previous generations may have spent evenings in forums of discourse, analysis and intellectual exchange, the average citizen in the modern and developed West spends vacuous hours absorbing cathode rays and media brainwashing from that master of hypnosis, the television.

Consequently, modern salesmanship has, in congruity with the profile of contemporary man, come to be based less on factual analysis than on stylized presentation. Political offices are no longer won and lost on the basis of leadership qualities, social consciousness

(II) Preface

and moral example, but on showmanship. Trial judgements concerning issues of national impact frequently overlook conclusive evidence in consideration of social and political agendas. Deviant sexual groups, which for centuries were summarily hacked up and spat from the mouth of society are currently not only accepted but actually encouraged out of complacent liberalism, political correctness, and moral flaccidity.

Within recent generations the general public has grown to become less analytical of the nature of truth and more drawn to socially accepted fads and emotional, though unfounded, influences of media. Nowhere is this more evident than in the field of religion, where the beliefs of billions have been swayed more by media than by their own scripture and scholars. Consequently, the image of Moses portrayed in the animated film, *The Prince of Egypt,* replaces previous generations' mental association between Moses and the Charlton Heston figure in Cecil B. DeMille's *The Ten Commandments.* Yet both movies glorify the appearance of Moses far beyond the Old Testament description of a man disfigured by "uncircumcised lips" (Exodus 6:12 and 6:30). Recent movies and characterizations of Jesus have similarly corrupted the imaginations of the average mind, creating media imagery spanning a broad spectrum from the portrait sketched by the rock-and-roll opera of *Jesus Christ, Superstar* to blasphemous accounts of this great messenger of God indulging in illicit sex with Mary Magdalene.

Spinning off from the swirl of stylish presidents, trendy fashion lines, and illegitimate media-engineered convictions, many religions have emerged with a new focus—that of style and emotional appeal. Rational analysis and theological discussion have been largely buried beneath an avalanche of psychological ploys, including popularized slogans, staged presentation and designer dogma. Hearts and souls are being seduced more by salesmanship than by truth.

But that is not what this book is about.

Throughout time there have always been honorable individuals who refused to base religious beliefs upon such frail foundations as the whims of others, the fads of peers, the traditions of family, or even the convictions of seemingly sincere and pious clergy. These individuals cross the currents of cultural convention, demanding answers to well-conceived questions and satisfactory explanation of the history of revelation and man. And *that* is what this book is about—the questions, the history, the revelation, and most of all, the answers.

(III) Introduction

"They decided that all liars should be whipped. And a man came along and told them the truth. And they hanged him."
— T.W.H. Crosland, *Little Stories*

While most religious gatherings, seminars and services congregate like-thinking individuals for the purpose of reinforcement—everybody discussing why they all believe the same things—this present work is devoted to the objective analysis of religious evidences. Some of the resulting conclusions may be poorly received by those who side with Benjamin Franklin's comment, "The way to see by Faith is to shut the Eye of Reason," but this book was not written for them. Rather, this book was written for those who respect William Adams sentiment, "Faith is the continuation of reason." Such individuals propose correctness of religious choice to be conceived through the union of common sense, objective scriptural analysis, and innate understanding of The Creator, and such is the mindset of this author.

The intent of this book, then, is to search the three Abrahamic faiths of Judaism, Christianity and Islam for truth in revelation. The primary concern being one of identifying the framework of rules to which God commands His creation, the attempt is made herein to trace the chain of revelation to its conclusion.

With regard to methodology, there is simply no substitute for shaking the trees from which different faiths claim to harvest fruits of sacred knowledge, and seeing what falls out. Examination of the foundation of specific Christian doctrines, in particular, frequently brings to light the fact that such doctrines were conceived from extra-Bibllical sources, sometimes even in open conflict with the clear teachings of Christ Jesus himself. This finding is of considerable interest, for the persuasive scriptural teachings found to be common to all three Abrahamic faiths support a theory of continuity in revelation, whereas scriptural differences might be held to suggest otherwise, were such differences real. The fact that many are not proves problematic for the Christian, but highly supportive of the Islamic claim to continuity of revelation.

The analysis, then, focuses upon scriptural evidence. Where conflict is suggested, the evidence is first evaluated to determine whether the proposed conflict is real or not. Should scriptural conflict exist, an attempt is made to establish scriptural authority where it is due. Where agreement exists the consequence of the consistency deserves to be stressed.

The results of this analysis prove provocative, and suggest a need to reset established religious thought in the West. Astonishing though it may be, a pattern suggestive of continuity between the three Abrahamic faiths may be seen to emerge once the truth is teased from beneath layers of popularized, though poorly substantiated, Christian canon.

Robert W. Funk, the author of the book *Honest to Jesus,* lays out certain ground rules for those who are upon a religious quest. Rule number four conveys the requirement to take knowledge from scholars. The same author, however, bemoans the corruption, closed-mindedness and sectarian doctrinal entrenchment of many, if not most, of those who are regarded as scholars by the religious world.

(III) INTRODUCTION

Perhaps for this reason, Mr. Funk narrows his definition by outlining those characteristics and qualifications which he holds to be representative of true scholarship. His definition is compelling, and although *this* author certainly does not endorse many of Mr. Funk's religious conclusions, his book is a valuable read for the reason that most of his research and much of his argument are worthy of respect. Respect, all the same, is a meal to be taken with the relish of personal analysis. For example, like the child who announces the conspicuous absence of the Emperor's clothes, the herald of truth is often an open-minded, clear-sighted individual regarded by others as possessing scholastic immaturity and incautious opinion. The effect of such a person's outburst may ripple through the still waters of an entire society. Yet, in fact, the simple-minded statement of truth is nothing more than a voice of the obvious, which serves to jog the minds of those present to cast aside whatever cloak of prejudice or denial hoods recognition of a clear, and in the case of the emperor, naked reality.

The author of this work, therefore, offers neither the pretension of scholarship nor apology for simplicity of thought, for neither measure is relevant regarding validation of a proposal. Truth is absolute, and stands firm regardless of argument or opinion. Those truths which can be held in hand, seen with eye, or tasted on tongue leave little room for dissenting opinion. Child and scholar alike can testify to the fact that sugar is sweet. Tangible truths afford the comfort of proof through demonstration while religious truths, though equally concrete, lack the reassurance of confirmation by material senses. Rather, religious truths are evaluated as much by the heart as by the mind. Hence, this author proposes that truth is not the moving target described by Robert Funk in the first chapter of his aforementioned book, but rather a stable and concrete reality exposed as a guiding light within the hearts and minds of those God chooses to illuminate.

The First And Final Commandment

The problem is, those upon true guidance and those living in the shadows of religious deception outwardly present similar profiles of certainty and conviction. The persecuted have died testifying to their faith, whether correct or deviant, for most of the history of mankind. Therefore, strength of personal commitment bears zero weight as evidence of correctness. The facts, and just the facts, have relevance.

St Anselm of Canterbury was once quoted as having presented an opposing order of priorities with his statement, "For I do not seek to understand that I may believe, but I believe in order to understand."[6] The proposal of *this* author is that such a thought sequence makes about as much sense as saying, "I had to taste the sandwich before I could pick it up." The true order of priorities, in the minds of most people, appears to be the exact opposite of that expressed by St Anselm. In other words, belief logically follows understanding – not the other way around. Most people demand sufficient explanation to nurse the embryo of a proposal to a formed and rational conclusion before embracing it. The proposal of *this* author, then, is that the truth of God is available to each and every person. The barriers which separate disbelief from belief are two. The first is the simple fact that air cannot enter a sealed room without an opening. The windows to many hearts are not only nailed shut, but the curtains are closed, the blinds drawn, the shutters sealed. A person does not have to go far to find such individuals; they are characterized by the awkward combination of an unwillingness to examine evidences, and obstinate conviction resting on a foundation of popularized opinion. Such individuals frequently fire off parroted teachings with an eagerness which overrides caution and, all too commonly, correctness. The fact that the proposed conclusions are frequently unbalanced and devoid of scriptural foundation often goes unrecognized by the individuals concerned – all the more so amongst those who have been trained to

---

6. Tugwell, Simon OP. 1989. *The Apostolic Fathers*. Harrisburg, Pennsylvania: Morehouse Publishing. Editorial Foreword, p. vi.

(III) Introduction

believe that, by nature of being 'filled with the holy spirit,' they are justified in anything they think or say.

The history of monotheism teaches nothing if not that prophets were sent to correct those astray from prior revelation. Those whose hearts and minds were closed suffered the consequences of denying the messengers of God, whereas those receptive of God's messengers found their openness rewarded with guidance. The fact that both Judaism and Christianity teach of a final messenger to follow should caution adherents to these faiths to be openhearted and on the lookout. Should that final messenger become evident, as predicted, lack of hospitality will someday bring regret.

The first barrier to belief, then, is simply unreceptiveness. Each person has the freedom to believe as he or she feels directed, but until a door is left open, nothing more can enter to either substantiate an unexpected truth or refute an accepted falsehood.

The second barrier to the acceptance of religious truth is the ages-old factor of whatever worldly considerations a person must compromise in order to embrace faith. Those of humility and sincerity can be expected to be open to discussion, and to objectively assign priorities based upon the information received. If, after hearing a convincing message, an individual rejects faith due to assigning higher priority to worldly interests, he or she will get the pleasure of that which is chosen. And lose the pleasure of He Who is denied. On the other hand, those who accept the truth of God and compromise for His pleasure that which He bestows upon them in the first place (i.e., the worldly concerns with which He tests them), have reason to expect God to provide for His servants, both in this life and in the next.

Having written the above, a request of the reader may be fairly in order. The attempt is made herein to render sense from the continuity of revelation of the three aforementioned Abrahamic faiths. The result that some doctrines can be shown to stand firmly on a foundation of tangible evidence, whereas others are exposed to lack the slightest scriptural support whatsoever, should be of little surprise. Yet, should the reader take affront to offered evidences and conclusions, a moment of contemplation may be appropriate. Do the presented issues represent slanderous falsehoods, blatant blasphemies, or previously unrealized, painful realities? The old adage, 'truth hurts,' is undeniable – no doubt truth hurts in direct proportion to the degree of conflict with previous, though unfounded, convictions. So prior to disapproval and rejection, the reader may wish to first confirm the referenced sources, which should be noted to represent many of the most academically respected works in the field. Familiar references such as popular encyclopedias and religious dictionaries are also frequently quoted, for the reason that while such sources lack the sophisticated appeal of more esoteric works of acclaimed academics, such references testify to the fact that, at least in certain circles, much of the presented information is common knowledge. Why many of the quoted items lack exposure in public discussion and religious discourse is a question left to the conclusions of the readers.

And may God guide all those who turn to Him in sincerity, seeking His pleasure.

Section 1
Monotheism

*"Men despise religion.
They hate it and are afraid
it may be true."*

– Blaise Pascal, *Pensées*

(SECTION 1) MONOTHEISM

Judaism, Christianity, and Islam constitute the three Abrahamic faiths, and as such deserve definition prior to further discussion. While Judaism is not particularly easily defined, the words 'Christian' and 'Christianity' prove even more problematic. Islam, being the least understood and the most maligned of the Abrahamic faiths in Western civilization, deserves more extensive discussion for the purpose of clarification.

(1.A)
Judaism

"The Foundation of all foundations, the pillar supporting all wisdoms, is the recognition of the reality of God."

– Moses Maimonides

The term 'Jew' originated as an ethnic definition of the descendents of the tribe of Judah, with Judaism being an extraction from 'Judah-ism.' Orthodox Judaism defines a Jew as one born of a Jewish mother or one, independent of bloodline, converted to the Judaic faith.[7] More liberal (Reform) movements deny the necessity of the maternal bloodline, and propose that a child born of a Jewish father is equally considered a Jew, if raised Jewish. Although definitions in the modern day are seen to vary, most include, either implicitly or explicitly, adherence to Mosaic law as expressed in the Torah and Talmud. Historically, however, even this was not agreed upon, for the Sadducees believed only the written law and prophets to be binding, and rejected the Talmud.

Ideological differences divide Orthodox from Conservative, Reform, and Reconstructionist movements (all of which possess

---

7. Werblowsky, R. J. Zwi and Geoffrey Wigoder (editors in chief). 1997. *The Oxford Dictionary of the Jewish Religion.* Oxford University Press. p. 369.

(SECTION 1) MONOTHEISM

smaller sectarian subdivisions); geographic origins distinguish the Sephardim (from Spain) from the Ashkenazi (from Central and Eastern Europe); religious/political differences cleave Zionists from non-Zionists (such as the *Neturei Karta Jews*); and Hasidic Jews are dissociated from non-Hasidic (also known as *Misnagdim*, or "opponents") on the basis of their practices, extreme religious zeal, and devotion to a dynastic leader (known as a '*Rebbe*').

Although considering themselves a nation, present day Jews are not united upon culture or ethnicity, are not a race in the genetic sense of the term, and do not unanimously agree upon a creed. In fact, there are even Jews who claim atheism (i.e., Atheist Jews) or supremacy of secular over Mosaic law (i.e., Secular Jews). Nonetheless, one of the most widely accepted lists of tenets of Jewish faith is that defined by the twelfth century rabbi, Moshe ben Maimon (Maimonides), and is known as 'Rambam's Thirteen Principles of Jewish Faith':

1. God is the Creator and Ruler of all things
2. God is One and unique
3. God is incorporeal, and there is nothing like unto Him
4. God is eternal
5. Prayer is to be directed to God alone
6. The words of the prophets are true
7. Moses was the greatest of the prophets
8. The Written Torah (i.e., Pentateuch – the first five books of the Old Testament) and Oral Torah (teachings now codified in the Mishna and Talmud) were given to Moses
9. The Torah will never be changed, and there will never be another given by God
10. God knows the thoughts and deeds of men
11. God will reward the good and punish the wicked
12. The Messiah will come
13. The dead will be resurrected

(1.B)
Christianity

"Even if you're on the right track, you'll get run over if you just sit there."

--Will Rogers

The term 'Christian' is considerably more difficult to define. One stumbling block is simply the lack of division between Judaism and 'Christianity' in the minds of the early 'Christians,' as acknowledged in the following: "The Christians did not initially think of themselves as separate from the Jewish people, though Jesus had had severe things to say about Pharisees. (But then, so has the Talmud.)"[8] A person may wonder why the early followers of Jesus regarded what has grown to be a vast, gaping chasm separating the shores of Judaism and Christianity to have been nonexistent in the apostolic age, or narrow at most. There is no doubt that the steady, persistent trickle of two thousand years of doctrinal evolution has eroded a giant crevasse between the Judaic and 'Christian' religions. There is also little historical doubt that the appearance of Christ Jesus forced an immediate split between the Jews who accepted him as a prophet and teacher, and

---

8. McManners, John (Editor). 1990. *The Oxford Illustrated History of Christianity*. Oxford University Press. p. 22.

(SECTION 1) MONOTHEISM

those who stood in denial thereof. Yet both groups considered themselves 'Jews.' Only later was the term 'Christian' conceived.

Colloquially, the term 'Christian' has come to refer to the followers of Christ Jesus. However, there are problems with this definition. The first difficulty is that the word 'Christian' is only encountered three times in the New Testament (Acts 11:26, Acts 26:28, Peter 4:16), and all three mentions occurred long after the ministry of Jesus. None of these three verses utilize the label 'Christian' in a context which bears the authority of Jesus or of God.[9] In other words, Jesus never identified himself as a Christian and never proclaimed himself to have established Christianity on Earth. In fact, while the word 'Christian' is encountered only three times in the Bible, the term 'Christianity' is nowhere to be found.

Most significantly, the term 'Christian' does not exist in any of the four Gospels, so there is no record of this word ever issuing from the lips of Jesus. A person finds in Acts 11:26 that "...the disciples were called Christians first in Antioch," which means the term 'Christian' was first applied to the disciples by non-believers around 43 CE ('CE,' meaning either 'Common Era' or 'Christian Era,' is adopted herein in preference to 'AD,' or *Anno Domini*, meaning 'the year of the Lord,' in concession to the fact that Jews, Muslims, and many Unitarian* Christians deny the 'Lordship' of Jesus). Contrary to popular belief, conception of the term 'Christian,' long after God raised Jesus from

---

9. Achtemeier, Paul J. (General Editor). *Harper's Bible Dictionary*. 1985. New York: Harper and Row. p. 163.

* Since the middle to late 19th century, Unitarianism, in some circles, has come to be regarded as synonymous with Universalism, despite the fact that the two are in fact entirely separate and distinct theologies. The union of the Universalist Church of America with the American Unitarian Association in 1961, to form the Unitarian Universalist Association, has done little to alleviate this misunderstanding. However, while most Universalists may be Unitarians, the opposite is certainly not the case, for the Universalist concept of salvation of all souls is in fact contrary to the creed of Unitarian Christianity, which teaches salvation conditional upon

(contd. on page 29)

(1.B) CHRISTIANITY

this Earth, is historically recognized to most likely represent a derogatory label for the followers of Christ. And yet, that very label is now worn with pride, despite the fact that, "It is not the usual designation of the NT, which more commonly uses such terms as brethren (Acts 1.16), believers (Acts 2.44), saints (Acts 9.32), and disciples (Acts 11.26)."[10] Furthermore, with regard to the term 'Christian,' "It appears to have been more widely used by pagans, and according to Tacitus it was in common use by the time of the Neronian persecution (Annals, 15.44)"[11] – a comment which reminds a person of the derogatory nature of a term conceived in contempt by those who hunted down those whom they so labeled. So the first major problem with the terms 'Christian' and 'Christianity' is that they do not bear the validation of God or of Jesus, while the descriptors 'brethren, disciples, or believers' have more Biblical authority.

The second difficulty with the word 'Christian' is one of definition. Should the term 'Christian' be employed to identify all

---

(contd. from page 28)

correct belief and practice, according to the revelation as conveyed through the person of Christ Jesus. Perhaps for this reason, as well as that of the tremendous diversity of Universalist beliefs and philosophies, the Universalist church, to this day, has been unsuccessful in formulating a statement of creed which is accepted by all affiliates. Furthermore, Universalism is not only a religion of relatively modern construction, but it is a theology more heavily based upon philosophy than upon scripture, which no doubt explains the disunity in conceptualization of creed. Therefore, for the purposes of this work, 'Unitarian Christianity' refers to the classic Unitarian Christian theology which has been honored by 2,000 years of history, founded upon scriptural interpretation, and united upon the creed of affirming divine unity and the human nature of Christ Jesus, in denial of the Trinity, Divine sonship, and proposed divinity of Christ Jesus. Universalism is by no means to be inferred in the mention of Unitarianism herein, and will not be discussed any further in this work.

10. Meagher, Paul Kevin OP, S.T.M., Thomas C. O'Brien, Sister Consuelo Maria Aherne, SSJ (editors). 1979. *Encyclopedic Dictionary of Religion*. Vol 1. Philadelphia: Corpus Publications. p. 741.

11. Meagher, Paul Kevin et al. Vol 1, p. 741.

(SECTION 1) MONOTHEISM

who affirm the prophethood of Christ Jesus, then Muslims fulfill this requirement as well, for the Islamic religion requires belief in Christ Jesus as an article of faith. Granted, the Islamic understanding of Jesus differs from that of the Trinitarian majority of those who would identify themselves as 'Christians.' However, many Islamic beliefs are remarkably consistent with those of classic Unitarian 'Christianity.'

Perhaps the label 'Christian' should be applied to those who follow the teachings of Jesus. Herein lies yet another problem – Muslims consider themselves to follow the teachings of Christ Jesus more faithfully than do those who call themselves 'Christian.' That claim hurls a hefty gauntlet in the face of those who identify with the label of 'Christian;' yet this assertion is made with sincerity and commitment by the followers of Islam, and deserves examination.

Should the label of 'Christianity' be associated with the doctrines of Original Sin, Divine son-ship, the Trinity, Crucifixion, and Atonement? Herein lie defining differences in creed between Trinitarian 'Christianity' and Islam, no doubt. Herein also lie defining differences between various sects of 'Christianity.' Not all 'Christians' accept the Trinity, and many deny the concept of Jesus being divine. Even the doctrines of Original Sin, Crucifixion, and Atonement do not achieve universal acceptance within the fractured sphere of the world known as 'Christianity.' Subgroups of 'Christianity' have, at different points in time, canonized specific belief systems upon which classification can be based – but no one definition has ever met with unanimous acceptance. No single canonized creed has ever universally encompassed all those who identify themselves as 'Christian.'

The world of 'Christianity' has been divided into various disparate sects since the time of Jesus. A brief history of 'Christianity' chronicles an initial two hundred years, during which the strictly

(1.B) CHRISTIANITY

monotheistic disciples and their followers experienced an early split from Paul (previously known as Saul of Tarsus – a zealous Pharisee who initially persecuted the disciples and the new Church, eventually claimed conversion, and subsequently turned his efforts to 'reforming' Christian thought) and his divergent theology. This early period is crucial to an understanding of Christianity, for a person can reasonably expect the purity of Christology (doctrines of Christ) and Christian creed to have been best represented amongst those closest to the teachings of the rabbi Jesus. However, knowledge of this period is vague, at best, with disappointingly little verifiable and unambiguous information surviving to the present day. How the disciples and their immediate followers understood the relevant issues remains unclear. Hence, although the Early Christians were divided as regards their concept of how God manifested His message on earth (inspiration, as suggested by the Synoptic gospels, versus incarnation, as suggested by the gospel of 'John'), of how understanding of that message was conveyed (direct transmission and interpretation by the prophet himself, as received by the disciples, versus mystical spiritual enlightenment, as claimed by Paul), of the Law of God upon His subjects (the Old Testament Law of the Christian-Jews versus the 'Justification by Faith' proposed by Paul), and of how God's revealed Law was to be interpreted (literally, as with the disciples, versus allegorically, as with Paul), the resultant creed which formed in the minds of the apostles is poorly documented. What is commonly known as the "Apostles' Creed" is *not*, in fact, known with certainty to have been the creed of the apostles. Rather, the "Apostle's Creed" is a baptismal formula which evolved over an indefinite period. As per a well-respected and relatively objective source (i.e. the *Encyclopaedia Britannica*),

> "To comprehend the faith of the early church regarding Christ, we must turn to the writings of the New Testament, where that faith found embodiment. It was also embodied in

(SECTION 1) MONOTHEISM

brief confessions or creeds, but these have not been preserved for us complete in their original form. What we have are fragments of those confessions or creeds in various books of the New Testament, snatches from them in other early Christian documents, and later forms of them in Christian theology and liturgy. The so-called Apostles' Creed is one such later form. It did not achieve its present form until quite late; just how late is a matter of controversy."[12]

The final form of the "Apostle's Creed" was not obtained until relatively late in the overall scheme of the historical foundation of Christianity. Similarly, just as the different understandings of Christology evolved over a period of centuries, first coming to critical debate between the schools of Antioch and Alexandria in the 4th century, so too has the fundamental creed of Christianity remained in debate to the present day. As regards the above quote that "...we must turn to the writings of the New Testament...", such a proposal demands confidence in the integrity of the New Testament in the first place – a conviction which is not universally shared, and which itself demands discussion (which, for the purposes of this book, is deferred to later chapters, in particular Sections 3.A. and 3.B.).

From these murky origins, the second and third centuries saw the Unitarian understanding of Christology develop along the lines of Monarchianism, which itself was divided into Dynamic (Adoptionist) and Modalistic (Sabellian) subcategories. Monarchianism affirmed divine unity, declared Christ Jesus as Redeemer, but refused to admit Jesus to the Godhead given the conviction of strict and indivisible unity of The Creator. The Dynamic form of Monarchianism declared Christ Jesus a man conceived by immaculate conception, but elevated in status to 'Son of God' *in a colloquial sense* only, due to

---

12. *Encyclopaedia Britannica*. 1994-1998. CD-ROM.

his endowment with wisdom and miracles. The Modalistic version of Monarchianism held God to have been One in Unity, but manifest as the Father when transcendentally above His creation, and as the Son when reduced to human form – One God known by different designations dependant upon His station in relation to man. These two somewhat disparate forms of Monarchianism form the divergent stalks from which the main two bodies of Unitarian Christianity have branched into the present day.

Unitarian and Trinitarian schools of thought having been pitted against one another since the inception of the Trinitarian formula in the 3rd century, the conflict came to a head when Emperor Constantine sought to unify his empire under one 'Christian' theology. A series of eight ecumenical councils were ultimately convened in order to address the relevant religious issues, beginning with the Council of Nicaea in 325, imperially summoned by Emperor Constantine to address the Unitarian theology of Arius, the famous Unitarian Christian priest of Alexandria. Seven ecumenical councils (the first council of Constantinople in 381, the council of Ephesus in 431, the council of Chalcedon in 451, the second council of Constantinople in 553, the third council of Constantinople in 680-681, the second council of Nicaea in 787, and the fourth council of Constantinople in 869-870) followed in well-spaced sequence remarkable for the degree of canonical concordance and theological reinforcement. Thirteen subsequent councils, making a grand total of 21, are considered ecumenical by the Roman Catholic Church (with the most recent being the second Vatican council of 1962-65). However, the Orthodox Churches only recognize the first eight (and in some cases, only the first seven) councils as having been truly ecumenical, for the others lacked comprehensive representation of all Christian sects.

Trinitarian theology, initially endorsed (and brutally enforced) by

(SECTION 1) MONOTHEISM

the powerful Roman empire, subsequently by that of the Byzantines, and eventually by the courts and governments of Western Europe, remained in conflict with a strong and persistent undercurrent of Unitarian theology throughout the history of 'Christianity.' Likewise, Trinitarianism faced frequent strife within its *own* theology, the most notable being the virtually continuous contest against the inroads of gnostic theosophy, the early split between the Eastern Orthodox and Roman Catholic Churches, and the later eruption of the Protestant reform movement of the 16th century. From the metaphysical seeds planted by Martin Luther, John Calvin, the Anabaptists and the Anglican reformers into the imaginations of the masses, a myriad theologies grew, persisting to the present day in such a plethora of sects as to require religious encyclopedias to catalog the variants.

With such huge diversity amongst those who claim to follow the teachings of Christ Jesus, how, then, should the terms 'Christian' and 'Christianity' be defined? If defined as identifying those who claim to follow Jesus, Muslims demand inclusion in the definition. If defined by *any* canonical system of beliefs, in order to ideologically separate Christianity from Islam, these same defining doctrines divide the world of 'Christianity' itself.

Hence, any attempt to define a term of such uncertain origin and meaning, and one which has defied definition by billions spanning two thousand years of contemplation and argument, would seem futile at this point in history. Consequently, for the purposes of this present work the term 'Christian' will be applied in the colloquial sense of the word, referring to all who identify with the label, whatever the beliefs of their particular 'Christian' sect may be.

(1.C1)
Islam [Part-I]

"Man's mind, once stretched by a new idea,
never regains its original dimension."
— Oliver Wendell Holmes

The term 'Islam' is the infinitive of the Arabic verb *'aslama'*, and is translated, "to submit totally to God."[13] Furthermore, "The participle of this verb is *muslim* (i.e. the one who submits completely to God) by which the followers of Islam are called."[14] The word Islam also connotes peace (being from the same root as the Arabic word 'salaam'), with the understanding that peace comes through submission to God. Unlike the terms 'Judaism' and 'Christianity,' both of which lack mention in their own Bibles, 'Islam' and 'Muslim' are mentioned numerous times throughout the Holy Qur'an. Hence, those who take the Holy Qur'an to be the revealed word of God find Divine authority for the terminology 'Islam' and 'Muslim' within their own scripture.

---

13. Meagher, Paul Kevin et al. Vol 2, p. 1842.
14. Meagher, Paul Kevin et al. Vol 2, p. 1842.

(Section 1) Monotheism

The above is the lexical definition of 'Muslim' – a person who submits to the will of God. What, then, is the juristic, or legal, definition in accordance with Islamic ideology? The Islamic understanding is that true believers, since the creation of mankind, have always accepted belief in God as one God and belief in the teachings of the messenger of their time. For example, Muslims during the time of Moses would have borne witness that there is no God but Allah, and Moses is the messenger of Allah. Muslims during the time of Jesus would have testified that there is no God but Allah, and Jesus is the prophet of Allah. For the last 1,400 years, Muslims have acknowledged Muhammad Ibn (i.e., son of) Abdullah to be the last and final messenger of God, so a person of this present age enters Islam and becomes Muslim, by ideological definition, with the testimony (transliterated from Arabic), "*Ash-hadu an la ilaha illa Llah(u), wa ash-hadu anna Muhammadan Rasulu Llah,*" which bears the translation, "I testify that there is no god but Allah and I testify that Muhammad is the Messenger of Allah."

The Islamic religion acknowledges the above testimony of faith to be legally valid only if made by a sane adult who understands the full meaning and implications of what he or she is saying, and who offers testimony voluntarily and of free will. Disturbing though it may be to those raised upon the myth of Islam having been spread by coercion, the Islamic religion forbids forced conversion, as per the commandment, "Let there be no compulsion in religion…" (TMQ 2:256). Furthermore, an entire chapter or the Holy Qur'an (chapter 109) teaches the following:

> "In the name of Allah, Most Gracious, Most Merciful,
> Say: O you that reject faith!
> I worship not that which you worship,
> Nor will you worship that which I worship.

(1.C1) Islam – Part I

And I will not worship that which
you have been wont to worship,
Nor will you worship that which I worship.
To you be your way, and to me mine." (TMQ 109)

John Locke, though ranked in history as a Unitarian Christian, provided a most beautifully conceived comment, which might serve the purpose of all (Muslims included) who seek to explain the futility of coercion as regards religious belief:

> "No way whatsoever that I shall walk in against the dictates of my conscience, will ever bring me to the mansions of the blessed. I may grow rich by art that I take not delight in; I may be cured of some disease by remedies that I have not faith in; but I cannot be saved by a religion that I distrust, and by a worship that I abhor....Faith only, and inward sincerity, are the things that procure acceptance with God....In vain therefore do princes compel their subjects to come into their church-communion, under pretence of saving their souls. If they believe, they will come of their own accord; if they believe not, their coming will nothing avail them…"[15]

The mandate that acceptance of Islam is invalid unless made of an individual's own free will is in clear conflict with the popular Western myth of Islam having been spread 'by the sword' – a slander largely perpetuated by religious institutions which are themselves notorious for nearly two millennia of conversion by means of virtually every inhumanity conceived by the sadistic mind of overzealous man. Clearly, testimony of faith cannot be coerced when a religion requires sincerity in the first place. Nearly 300 years ago, the following comment was offered by George Sale, one of the first to translate the

---

15. Parke, David B. 1957. *The Epic of Unitarianism*. Boston: Starr King Press. p. 35.

(SECTION 1) MONOTHEISM

Koran into the English language, a self-professed antagonist of the man, Muhammad, and a hater of the Islamic religion:

> "I shall not here enquire into the reasons why the law of Mohammed has met with so unexampled a reception in the world, (for they are greatly deceived who imagine it to have been propagated by the sword alone), or by what means it came to be embraced by nations which never felt the force of the Mohammedan arms, and even by those which stripped the Arabians of their conquests, and put an end to the sovereignty and very being of their Khalifs: yet it seems as if there was something more than what is vulgarly imagined, in a religion which has made so surprising a progress."[16]

Just such observations and sentiments have prompted modern scholars to cast aside the popularized claims of coercion. For how can such a claim be made when the country with the largest Muslim population in the world, that is to say Indonesia,[17] "...never felt the force of the Mohammedan arms," having assimilated the Islamic religion from nothing more than the teachings and example of a few merchants from Yemen? Such forces of Islamic progress are witnessed to this day, with the Islamic religion having grown within the borders of countries and cultures which were not the conquered, but rather the conquerors of many of the Muslim lands. In addition, Islam continues to grow and prosper within populations which stand in expressed contempt of the religion in the modern day. No difficulty should be encountered, then, in accepting the following comment:

> "No other religion in history spread so rapidly as Islam. By the time of Muhammad's death (632 A.D.) Islam controlled a

---

16. Sale, George. 1734. *The Koran*. London: C. Ackers. Preface, A2.
17. *Guinness Book of Knowledge*. 1997. Guinness Publishing. p.194.

(1.C1) Islam – Part I

great part of Arabia. Soon it triumphed in Syria, Persia, Egypt, the lower borders of present Russia and across North Africa to the gates of Spain. In the next century its progress was even more spectacular.

The West has widely believed that this surge of religion was made possible by the sword. But no modern scholar accepts that idea, and the Koran is explicit in support of freedom of conscience. The evidence is strong that Islam welcomed the peoples of many diverse religions, so long as they behaved themselves and paid extra taxes.* Muhammad constantly taught that Muslims should cooperate with the 'people of the Book' (Jews and Christians)."[18]

Of interesting note is the fact that the Islamic religion does not differentiate between believers of different time periods. The Islamic belief is that all messengers since Adam brought God's truth to mankind. The faithful submitted and followed, the unfaithful didn't. Therefore, since the time of the sons of Adam, mankind has been divided between the faithful and the transgressors, between good and evil.

The Islamic religion teaches consistency in creed, asserting that the tenets of faith declared at each and every stage in the chain of revelation were the same – without change, without evolution or

---

* The *jizya* is a tax levied on non-Muslim residents in an Islamic state to offset:

    1. The fact that non-Muslims are not obligated to pay the *zakat*, or poor-due, which is incumbent on Muslims on an annual basis;

    2. To compensate for the state services afforded to all citizens, Muslim and non-Muslim alike;

    3. And to compensate for the fact that non-Muslims receive the protection of the state military, but do not serve within the military themselves.

18. Michener, James A. May, 1955. 'Islam: The Misunderstood Religion,' in *Reader's Digest* [American Edition]. p. 73.

(SECTION 1) MONOTHEISM

alteration. As the reality of The Creator has remained unchanged throughout time, so has His creed. Modern Christian claims, to the effect that the tenets of faith and mode of salvation underwent transformation between the period of revelation of Old and New Testaments, are not honored by the Islamic religion. Nothing changes but that it transitions from better to worse, or vice-versa. Alteration of anything of perfection introduces flaws. Even a transition from good to better implies imperfection in the initial stage, for if perfect in the primary phase, what need for change? To claim that God changed is to suggest that He was imperfect in the first place, necessitating alteration to a higher, more faultless state. Such views are unacceptable to those who conceive God to have been without imperfection from the outset. Hence, the Islamic religion does not honor the Christian claim of transition from a wrathful God of the Old Testament to a loving and benevolent God of the New Testament, for to do so is to admit imperfection of The Creator at one of the two stages. Likewise, the assertion that God's substance and the spiritual realities which surround Him altered with the suffering and alleged sacrifice of Christ Jesus is held to be incompatible with His perpetual perfection and permanent reality.

Since the Islamic religion professes a consistent creed from the time of Adam, there is no uncertainty concerning the fate of early man. Whereas both Judaism and Christianity claim historical cut-offs regarding the method of achieving God's saving grace, the Islamic religion makes no such claim. Whereas Christianity asserts that all who lived and died prior to the time of Christ Jesus were deprived of his atoning sacrifice, the Islamic religion claims the salvation of each and every element of humanity, from the time of Adam onwards, to have depended upon acceptance of the same eternal creed – that of recognizing Allah as one God and accepting the teachings of His prophets. Along this line of thought, a person might question how

(1.C1) Islam – Part I

different religions view the fate of Abraham, as well as that of other early prophets. Was Abraham subject to the laws of Judaism? Apparently not. Judaism, as defined above, refers to the descendants of Judah, of whom Abraham (being the great-grandfather of Judah) was most certainly not a descendant. Genesis 11:31 defines Abraham as being from "Ur of Chaldees," better known as an area in Lower Mesopotamia, now a section of Iraq. Geographically, Abraham was (applying the terminology of the present age) an Arab. Genesis 12: 4-5 describes Abraham's move to Canaan (i.e., Palestine) at the age of 75, and Genesis 17:8 confirms that he was a stranger in that land. Genesis 14:13 identifies the man as "Abraham the Hebrew"–'Hebrew' meaning:

> "Any member of an ancient northern Semitic people that were the ancestors of the Jews. Historians use the term Hebrews to designate the descendants of the patriarchs of the Old Testament (i.e., Abraham, Isaac, and so on) from that period until their conquest of Canaan (Palestine) in the late 2nd millennium BC. Thenceforth these people are referred to as Israelites until their return from the Babylonian Exile in the late 6th century BC, from which time on they became known as Jews."[19]

So Abraham was a Hebrew, in a time when the term 'Jew' did not even exist. The descendants of Jacob were the twelve tribes of the Israelites, and only Judah and his line came to be known as Jews. Even Moses, despite popular opinion, was not a Jew. Exodus 6:16-20 defines Moses as a descendant of Levi and not of Judah, and therefore a Levite. He was a lawgiver to the Jews, certainly, but not a Jew by the operational definition of that date and time in history. Not to take away from who he was and what he did, certainly, but just to state the case for the record.

---
19. *Encyclopaedia Britannica*, CD-ROM.

(SECTION 1) MONOTHEISM

So if Abraham was not a Jew, and most certainly not a Christian, what laws of salvation was he subject to? And what about the rest of the prophets preceding Moses? While the clergy of Judaism and Christianity struggle over this point, the Islamic religion teaches that, "Abraham was not a Jew nor yet a Christian; but he was true in Faith, and bowed his will to Allah's, (which is Islam), and he did not join gods with Allah (God)" (TMQ 3:67). In addition to stating the fact that the religion of Abraham, as of all the prophets, was that of 'submission to God' (i.e., Islam), this passage of the Holy Qur'an teaches that an individual's faith and submission is more important than the label by which that person is known.

(1.C2)
Islam (Part-II)

"Knowledge is the only instrument of production
that is not subject to diminishing returns."
— J. M. Clark, *Journal of Political Economy*, Oct., 1927

The above definitions clarify the fact that, according to Islamic theology, many people are Agnostic, Jewish and Christian by ideology, but 'Muslim' by lexical definition, for they are living in submission to the will of The Creator in the best way they know how. These individuals willingly submit themselves to the evident truths of God, whether to their liking or not, and live by God's decree as they know it. By so doing they assign priority to God over all other considerations.

Ironically, the historical archetype of a Muslim by definition, but not necessarily by ideology, may very well be Thomas H. Huxley, the father of Agnosticism. Huxley penned one of the most simple, fluently beautiful statements of willingness, nay, desire, to submit his will totally and completely to that of The Creator, as follows:

"I protest that if some great Power would agree to make me always think what is true and do what is right, on condition of being turned into a sort of clock and wound up every morning before I got out of bed, I should instantly close with the offer."[20]

Whether Huxley accepted the religious truths to which he was exposed during his lifetime remains a mystery which died with the man. Surrounded as he was by proponents of a wide variety of belief systems which he found untenable, he may have had insufficient exposure to the purity of religious truths which can be gleaned from scriptural analysis in the present day. His intention, as voiced in the above quote, appears to have been pure. Whether or not he made good on his design is a separate issue.

Many may profess similar desire to live in submission to God, but the ultimate test of such intention is the actual act of embracing divine truths when evident. To leap backwards from T. H. Huxley to the Bible, Muslims and Christians alike cite the story of Lazarus (John 11:1-44) by way of example. Jesus is reported to have raised Lazarus from the dead by the power of God as proof of his having been sent from God, or as he is reported as having said, "that they may believe that You sent me" (John 11:42). Many Jews subsequently believed in him, yet many did not. Those who stood in denial chose to report Jesus to the Pharisees, who sided with the High Priest Caiaphas's peculiar advice to satisfy the Romans more than God. The "Thou shalt not kill" clause seems to have lacked relevant qualifiers for the referenced circumstance, but Caiaphas claimed a convenient and politically expedient prophecy that Jesus must die for the nation. Everyone knows what events are related as having followed.

The main lesson to be learned from the above story, with regard to the Islamic viewpoint, is that when presented with clear evidence of prophethood the sincere (Muslim by definition) will follow (becoming Muslim by ideology). Meanwhile, the insincere will refuse the direction of God in favor of worldly considerations.

---

20. Huxley, Thomas H. 1870. *Discourse Touching The Method of Using One's Reason Rightly and of Seeking Scientific Truth.*

(1.C2) Islam – Part II

But the story doesn't end there. There is a moral to the story of Lazarus with regard to the purpose behind revelation. A person may question why God would send messengers if not to guide mankind back from lost wanderings in ignorance to the straight path of His design. Who will reap the rewards of following God's directions if not those who submit to His evidences? And who is more deserving of punishment than those who deny the truth when made clear?

Muslims assert that all messengers and prophets were presented to correct the deviancies of their target populations. After all, what would be the purpose of God sending a prophet to a people who were doing everything right? Muslims assert that just as Jesus was sent to an astray group of people (i.e., the 'lost sheep of the house of Israel' [Matthew 15:24]) with divine evidences of prophethood and a corrective revelation, so Muhammad was presented to all people, from his time to the Day of Judgement, with evidences of messengership and a final revelation. This final revelation was revealed to redress the deviancies which had crept into the various world religions, Judaism and Christianity included. Muslims assert that those who live in submission to God and His evidences will recognize and accept Muhammad as the messenger of Islam, just as the pious Jews recognized and accepted Jesus. Conversely, those who live in submission to anything other than God – be it money, power, worldly enjoyment, cultural or family tradition, unfounded personal prejudices, or any religion which is more self than God-centered – would be expected to reject Muhammad, just as the impious Jews rejected Jesus.

An interesting point to ponder is that Islam demands submission to God, with the expectation that God guides those who submit to Him. Correctness of doctrine is expected to follow, not through any special ability of man to recognize truth, but through the guidance which God grants to those who seek His direction. This concept is diametrically opposed to that of the remaining Abrahamic religions,

(Section 1) Monotheism

which first and foremost demand submission to ecclesiastical doctrine. Implied is the expectation that God will come to be known through acceptance of what are assumed to be correct doctrinal teachings. Speculation peeks around the cornerstone of any religion constructed on such a foundation, surreptitiously whispering concern over the end result should the enforced doctrinal teachings be wrong to begin with.

The Islamic concept trusts God to guide, placing faith in One Who is supremely trustworthy. The Muslim presents the suggestion that God-given evidence, when in conflict with tradition, custom, or man-given canon, should have priority in the acceptance of creation. In contrast, Muslims accuse Judeo-Christian institutions of demanding faith in man-made doctrines, commanding trust in the conclusions of institutions more than in the evidences and commands of The Creator.

A person can argue that Muslims similarly embrace the ideology of the Islamic religion, and this is true. Muslims, however, respond by pointing out that, first and foremost, the ideology of the Islamic religion is nothing more than complete and uncompromising submission to God. According to Islamic thought, should a person choose to commit to God, God then opens doors of understanding and the importance of religious rites and rituals becomes recognized.

Interestingly, there is no clergy in Islam to define an ecclesiastical body. To quote the *Encyclopedic Dictionary of Religion*,

> "There is no centrally organized religious authority or magisterium in Islam and for this reason its character varies sometimes widely from traditional norms, esp. in areas of Africa and the Far East where it has only recently taken root and mixtures of pagan and Islamic practice still mingle."[21]

---

21. Meagher, Paul Kevin et al. Vol 2, p. 1843.

(1.C2) Islam – Part II

H. G. Wells,

> "Islam to this day has learned doctors, teachers, and preachers; but it has no priests."[22]

and the *New Catholic Encyclopedia*,

> "Islam has no church, no priesthood, no sacramental system, and almost no liturgy."[23]

There is no papal equivalent. There are no intercessors between man and God. There *are* men and women occupying different levels on the steep slope of religious knowledge, at the peak of which are scholars who serve to define answers to religiously challenging issues. However, scholarship does not necessarily imply any greater closeness to God than that of a simple and pious, though uneducated, Muslim. Congregational prayer is led by an *Imam*, but this word means nothing more than 'somebody who goes out in front' – in other words, a leader of the prayer. The *Imam* is not ordained and does not administer sacraments. His function is nothing more than to synchronize prayer by providing leadership in the recitation and rituals. This is a position which does not require any particular office or appointment, and which can be fulfilled by any adult member of the congregation.

Much to the frustration of others, Muslims frequently challenge missionaries of other religions with the above perspectives. A common Islamic challenge is that if anybody can prove the reality of God to differ from that taught in the Qur'an and teachings (*hadith*) of Muhammad, then the Muslim world will accept and submit.

---

22. Wells, H. G. 1922. *The Outline of History.* Fourth Edition. Volume 2. Section XXXI – "Muhammad and Islam" New York: The Review of Reviews Company. p. 687.

23. *New Catholic Encyclopedia.* 1967. Vol 7. Washington, D.C.: The Catholic University of America. p. 680.

(SECTION 1) MONOTHEISM

Despite nearly 1400 years since the revelation of the Holy Qur'an, it hasn't happened yet. Certainly, rare Muslims have converted to religions other than Islam, but nobody has ever proven the reality of God to be other than the Islamic understanding. Had they done so the entire Islamic world, being committed to God in primacy over doctrine, should have converted. What *has* happened, much to the consternation of many congregations, is that many sincere nuns, priests, ministers and rabbis (i.e. the educated clergy who know their respective religions best) have embraced Islam.

Bahira, a Christian monk of Syria stated recognition of Muhammad as the final prophet of God when he was still a small boy, decades prior to his first revelation.[24] Waraqah Ibn Nawfal, the old, blind Christian cousin of Khadijah (Muhammad's first wife) swore,

> "By Him in whose hand is the soul of Waraqah, you (Muhammad) are the prophet of this nation and the great *Namus* (angel of revelation – i.e., angel Gabriel) has come to you – the one who came to Moses. And you will be denied (by your people) and they will harm you, and they will expel you and they will fight you and if I were to live to see that day I would help Allah's religion with a great effort."[25]

In the early days of Islam, when the Muslims were a weak and oppressed people, the religion was embraced by such seekers of truth as Salman Farsi, a Persian Christian who had been directed by his mentor – a Christian monk – to seek the arrival of the final prophet in the "country of the date-palms."[26] The Negus, the Christian ruler of Abyssinia, accepted Islam without ever having met

---

24. Ibn Hisham. *As-Seerah An-Nabiwwiyyah.*
25. Ibn Hisham. *As-Seerah An-Nabiwwiyyah.*
26. *Musnad Ahmad*

(1.C2) Islam – Part II

Muhammad, and while the Muslims were still a small group, widely held in contempt and running for their lives.[27]

A person wonders, if high Christian scholars and Christians of prominent position accepted Islam during a time when the Muslims were a weak and persecuted minority lacking wealth, strength, and political position by which to attract, much less protect, new Muslims, what drew these Christians to Islam if not sincere belief? History records that even Heraclius, the Christian emperor of Rome, is recorded as having entertained the thought of accepting Islam, only to renounce his resolve when he saw that conversion would cost him the support of his people and hence his empire.[28]

One of the most striking early conversions was that of Abdallah Ibn Salam, the rabbi whom the Jews of Medina were quoted as having appraised, "He (Abdallah) is our master and the son of our master."[29] *Encyclopedia Judaica* explains that when his co-religionists were invited to accept Islam as well, "The Jews refused, and only his immediate family, notably his aunt Khalida, embraced Islam. According to other versions, Abdallah's conversion occurred because of the strength of Muhammad's answers to his questions."[30]

So the conversions started, and so they have continued to the present day, leaving not-so-casual observers wondering what these religious scholars find which leads them to embrace such an abrupt change. Contrary to what their co-religionists might imagine, these Islamic converts typically do not perceive their conversion to be a reversal or even a change of ideology. Rather, when questioned, they frequently express the belief that conversion to Islam is consistent

---

27. Ibn Hisham. *As-Seerah An-Nabiwwiyyah.*
28. *Sahih Al-Bukhari*
29. *Encyclopaedia Judaica.* 1971. Vol 2. Jerusalem: Keter Publishing House Ltd. p. 54.
30. *Encyclopaedia Judaica.* Vol 2, p. 54.

(SECTION 1) MONOTHEISM

with, if not dictated by, their own scripture. In other words, they present the challenging and disconcerting assertion that Islam is the fulfillment of, rather than in conflict with, teachings of the Old and New Testaments. This assertion demands examination, for the claim that it is the adherent to Judaism or Christianity, in the face of the revelation of the Holy Qur'an, who is in defiance to God and His chain of revelation cuts at the very roots of the theological debate. The Muslim claim is that, as was the case of those who denied Christ Jesus in the face of his accompanying signs of prophethood, those who rebel against the prophethood of Muhammad may continue to be accepted by their people and regarded highly amongst men, but at the cost of losing favor with God. If true, the claim of these Muslim converts deserves to be heard. If not, the error of their convictions demands exposure. In either case, there is no substitute for an examination of the evidence.

One noteworthy evidence, which is again disturbing to the Judeo-Christian community, is the fact that a similar countercurrent of educated and practicing Muslims embracing Judaism or Christianity has never been seen at any time in history. There are infrequent cases of lay 'Muslims' converting to different religions, but this is hardly surprising. With regard to the many deviant sects of Islam, the 'pull' of the worldly permissiveness of other religions combines with the 'push' of unacceptable teachings common to deviant sects, overwhelming those ignorant of the true teachings of the Islamic religion. Examples include the Baha'i, the Nation of Islam, the Ahmadiyyah or Qadianis, the Ansar, extreme Sufi orders and many, if not most, of the Shi'ite sects. These deviant groups may identify with the label of Islam, but like a man who calls himself a tree, lack sufficient roots in the religion to substantiate the claim. More importantly, the deviant doctrines of the astray sects serve as wedges between themselves and orthodox (Sunni) Islam. The deeper these doctrinal wedges are

(1.C2) Islam – Part II

driven into the heart of an astray sect's creed, the greater the gap between the aberrant and the orthodox, to the point where separation becomes complete. Once cleaved from the framework of true Islam, the deviant ideology demands rejection by all Muslims. Apostatizing from such deviancy is the duty of all true Muslims, and therefore such groups fail to reflect upon the state of true, orthodox (Sunni) Islam.

With regard to those born Muslim and raised in ignorance of the religion, conversion can be viewed to be less a matter of turning away from Islam (since the individual's understanding thereof is lacking) and more a matter of pursuing faith in the religion of a person's exposure. Those born or raised Muslim, but weak of faith, may find religious conviction overridden by worldly priorities. And in the end not every person born into a religion is an example of piety.

Many doctrinally-defined Christians seek to catalogue converts from Islam in support of what they conceive to be superiority of their own faith. However, these men and women of doctrine may be shaken to find that examination of apostates from Islam typically reveals profiles which neatly slip into the above-described pigeon-holes. Such apostates are few to begin with, and are typically found to be ignorant of the Islamic religion, abandoning a deviant sect unacceptable to any person of piety and God-fear, a person of impiety themselves, or simply one of many who cast religion aside for the sake of worldly considerations. The religious choice of such individuals simply does not carry weight sufficient to counterbalance 1,400 years of Jewish and Christian clergy converting in the opposite direction. Conspicuously absent from the equation is the conversion of sincere and committed, educated and practicing orthodox (Sunni) Muslims, much less scholars (the Islamic equivalent of the convert rabbis and priests).

The question pops into the average Western mind, "Why *do* some scholars of Christianity and Judaism embrace orthodox (Sunni) Islam?" There is no pressure upon them to do so, and a world of fleshy

(SECTION 1) MONOTHEISM

reasons not to -- things like losing their congregation, position, status, friends, family, job, retirement pension, etc. And why don't Islamic scholars turn to something else? Other religions are much more permissive of worldly desires, and there is no enforcement of a law against apostatizing from Islam in Western lands.

So why have many Jewish and Christian scholars embraced Islam, while educated Muslims remain firm in their faith? Muslims suggest that the answer returns once again to the definition of Islam. The person who submits to God and not to a particular ecclesiastical belief will recognize a divine sense to revelation. The Muslim presents a continuum between Judaism, Christianity and Islam which, once recognized, sweeps the sincere seeker down the smooth flow of revelation. The claim is that once a person sees past Western prejudices and propaganda, doors of understanding open.

The Islamic viewpoint is that, during the time of and following Jesus, but before Muhammad, the Jews who recognized the common source of revelation, and Jesus as the fulfillment of specific Old Testament prophesies, became Muslims. Muslims remind us that Jesus could not have called to things which did not exist in the period of his ministry, such as the label of 'Christianity' (discussed in Section 1.B. above) and Trinitarian doctrine (which was to evolve over the first few centuries in the post-apostolic age, as discussed in Section 2.B.7. below). Neither the label nor the doctrine were known to Christ Jesus. However, what *was* known to Christ Jesus, and what he most certainly did call his followers to recognize and bear witness to was the simple truth of God being One, and of God having sent himself as a messenger. For example, "...And this is eternal life, that they may know You, the only true God, and Jesus Christ whom You have sent" (John 17:3), and "let not your heart be troubled; you believe in God, believe also in me" (John 14:1). Hence, the Islamic viewpoint is that whatever this group of early followers called them-

(1.C2) Islam – Part II

selves for the forty years following Jesus, but before the word 'Christian' was even invented, they lived in submission to the truth of God as conveyed in the teachings of Jesus. The argument is that whatever label they identified with back then, in the present day their character would be defined by a word attributed to those who live in submission to God via the message conveyed by His prophets – i.e., 'Muslim'.

Similarly, during and following the prophethood of Muhammad, many Jewish and Christian scholars apparently recognized what they felt to be the fulfillment of Old and New Testament prophecies in the life of Muhammad. Many readers would object on the basis of having read the Bible, and never having found the name 'Muhammad.' The standard Muslim response is to question how many times the name 'Jesus' can be found in reference to the predicted messiah in the Old Testament. The answer is "None." Consequently, the open-minded reader has reason to pause and reflect, for the Old Testament contains numerous predictions of prophets to come – some thought to describe Jesus, some relating to John the Baptist, and others which appear to be unsatisfied by any Biblical personage. Hence the reason why all Jews and many Christians are waiting for a final prophet, as predicted by their own scripture.

The Muslim perspective, of course, is that the final prophet has already come, and his name was Muhammad. Through him the Holy Qur'an was revealed by Almighty God (i.e., Allah). Those who adhere to the Holy Qur'an as the revealed word of Allah, and to the teachings of the last and final prophet, Muhammad Ibn Abdullah, are regarded to be Muslims both by lexical definition *and* by ideology.

Section 2
God

"We are all bound to the throne of the Supreme Being by a flexible chain which restrains without enslaving us. The most wonderful aspect of the universal scheme of things is the action of free beings under divine guidance."

– Joseph de Maistre, *Considerations on France*, chapter 1

(SECTION 2) GOD

While adherents to monotheistic faiths share a fundamental belief in one God, understanding of His attributes differs. Many of these differences, like individual strands of a spider's web, may appear to be separate and divergent when viewed too closely. Strikingly, however, individual threads knit together a larger design, the full significance of which is recognized only when viewed in the context of the whole. Only from a distanced and objective perspective does the complexity of design become known, and the fact that each strand points to a central reality becomes recognized.

(2.A) Understanding and Approaching God

(2.A1) God's Name

> "The difference between the *almost*-right word and the *right* word is really a large matter – it's the difference between the lightning bug and the lightning."
>
> – Mark Twain, *Letter to George Bainton*

A simple example of how several suggestive strands weave together a logical conclusion relates to the name of God. Evidences taken from Judaism, Christianity, and Islam tie together to support a conclusion which should be acceptable to adherents of all three religions. For example, recognition of God as 'The Creator' is universal. Ditto identification as 'The All-Powerful' and 'All-Knowing.' And perhaps a person need look no deeper into the issue than this, for God is unanimously recognized by many beautiful names and glorious attributes. When a person calls upon The Creator by any of His many beautiful names or perfect attributes, He is certain to perceive the call. In the end, for those who seek the solace of communion with their Creator, the bounties of His generosity and the succor which only He can provide, establishing contact in a manner befitting His majesty is the primary issue of importance. What more is needed?

(SECTION 2) GOD

Well, for some people, a name. A definitive name is needed.

So what is His name? That the name of God in Islam is 'Allah' should be of no surprise to anybody. That a person might suggest that the name of God in Christianity is also 'Allah' risks provoking consternation, if not violent protest, from the entrenched community of Western Christianity. But lest a person rebound too violently from the above assertion, one needs go no further than the *Encyclopaedia Britannica* to learn the truth of this statement.

A trip to Palestine is even more convincing, for a visitor to the Holy Land quickly comes to appreciate that 'Allah' is the name by which God is known to all Arabs, Christians and Muslims alike. The Arab Christians have a heritage which goes back to the days of revelation, and they identify The Creator as 'Allah.' Their distant ancestors walked the same land as the prophet Jesus, and they identify The Creator as 'Allah.' Their lineage prospered for 2,000 years in an area of the world historically renown for religious tolerance up until the creation of the Jewish state of Israel (a little known fact, and one hugely disfigured by the prejudiced slanders of Western media), freely practicing their beliefs up until the present day. And they identify The Creator as 'Allah.' A person wonders what happened between the Old World of the original 'Christians' and the New World of the many Western sects of modern popularity.

The *New International Dictionary of the Christian Church*, a tome comprising contributions of over 180 scholars, many of them of international repute, comments under the entry 'Allah' as follows: "The name is used also by modern Arab Christians who say concerning future contingencies: *'In sha' Allah.'*"[31] This phrase *'In sha' Allah'* bears the translation, 'Allah willing' or 'If Allah wills.' The *Encyclopaedia Britannica* confirms the common Arabic usage of the name 'Allah' as follows: "Allah is the standard Arabic word for "God"

---

31. Douglas, J. D. (general editor). *The New International Dictionary of the Christian Church.* 1978. Grand Rapids, MI: Zondervan Publishing House. p. 27.

(2.A1) Understanding and Approaching God / God's Name

and is used by Arab Christians as well as by Muslims."[32]

In fact, from the Orthodox Christians of the Iraq that was birthplace to Abraham, to the Coptic Christians of the Egypt of Moses, to the Palestinian Christians of the Holy Land trod by Christ Jesus, to the entire Middle Eastern complex that was the epicenter from which the shockwaves of revelation radiated out to the remainder of the world, 'Allah' is recognized as the proper name for what Western religions call 'God.' The Christian Arabs are known to call Jesus '*Ibn* Allah,' '*Ibn*' meaning son. Pick up any copy of an Arabic Bible and a person will find The Creator identified as 'Allah.' So 'Allah' is recognized as the name of God in the land of revelation of the Old and New Testaments, as well as of the Qur'an.

What is *not* recognized by Christian and Muslim purists in the 'Holy Land' is the generic Westernized name, 'God.' The word 'God' is completely and absolutely foreign to the untranslated, foundational scriptures of the Old and New Testaments, as well as the Qur'an – it simply does not exist in the foundational manuscripts of *any* of the three Abrahamic religions. Not even a single word can be found which can be transliterated to 'God.'

So while the concept of God is readily recognized, research in books of etymology reveals that the word 'God' has uncertain origin. It may have arisen from the Indo-European '*ghut-*,' may have the underlying meaning of 'that which is invoked,' and may bear the prehistoric Germanic '*guth-*' as a distant ancestor (from which the modern German '*gott*,' the Dutch '*god*,' and the Swedish and Danish '*gud*' are derived).[33] Lots of 'maybes.' No matter how the origin of the word is traced, the name 'God' is of Western and extra-Biblical construction, and the historical origin and meaning are uncertain.

---

32. *Encyclopaedia Britannica*. CD-ROM.

33. Ayto, John. *Dictionary of Word Origins*. 1991. New York: Arcade Publishing, Inc. p. 258.

(SECTION 2) GOD

The fact that all Middle Eastern Christians recognize 'God' as 'Allah' is an affront to the opinions of those who associate 'Allah' with heathens. Be that as it may. The relevant question is not if or how much an assertion hurts, but whether it can be substantiated as truth. Most people would like to be assured that religious beliefs and practices have a basis in scripture and not just local custom, so a person may well question whether the Old and New Testaments support use of the name 'Allah' in Judaism and/or Christendom.

In Judaic texts a person finds 'Yahweh,' 'Elohim,' 'Eloah,' and 'El' in reference to God. In Christian texts the terminology is little different, for the Greek 'theos' is nothing more than the translation of 'Elohim.' 'Eloi' and 'Eli' are also encountered.

In the Old Testament, 'Yahweh' was used more than 6,000 times as God's personal name, and 'Elohim' is found in excess of 2,500 entries as a generic name for God; 'Eloah' is encountered 57 times and 'El' more that two hundred times as additional generic names for God in the Old Testament.[34, 35] How do these Old Testament names tie in with the name 'Allah?' Simple; 'Elohim' is the royal plural (a plural of majesty, not numbers – to be discussed below) of 'Eloah.'[36] The *Encyclopedia of Religion and Ethics* states confirmation that the Arabic word 'ilah' (the generic Arabic word for 'god') is "…identical with the eloah of Job."[37] The linguistic explanation of the origin of the name 'Allah' is that contraction of the Arabic definite article 'Al' (the) and 'ilah' (god), according to the rules of Arabic grammar, becomes 'Allah' (The God). Consequently, the 2,500+ entries of 'Elohim' and the 57 entries of 'Eloah' in the Old Testament bear direct relation to the

---

34. Achtemeier, Paul J. pp. 684-686.
35. Werblowsky, R. J. Zwi and Geoffrey Wigoder. p. 277.
36. *Encyclopaedia Britannica*. CD-ROM. (Under "Elohim").
37. Hastings, James (editor). 1913. *The Encyclopedia of Religion and Ethics*. Vol. VI. Charles Scribner's & Sons. p. 248.

name of God as 'Allah,' for 'Elohim' is the plural of 'Eloah,' which itself is identical with the Arabic 'ilah,' from which 'Allah' appears to be linguistically derived.

Muslim scholars offer yet another tantalizing thought, for when calling upon their Creator Muslims beseech Allah by the appellation of 'Allahuma,' which means 'Oh, Allah.' The Siamese twin similarity of the Semitic cousins of 'Allahuma' and 'Elohim' simply cannot escape easy recognition.

The above evidences are well recognized but obstinately concealed by those who approach scriptural analysis more as religious turf wars than as an objective search for truth. When made known the above, and much of that which follows, has historically been aggressively suppressed. An example of the extreme sensitivity of such reactionary editing concerns the *Scofield Reference Bible*, a respected British version produced by Rev. C. I. Scofield, D.D. in consultation with a team of editors (all of whom are also Doctorates of Divinity), which appears to have excited Christian censuring interest when it published a Bible edition with the name 'Alah.' Specifically, a footnote to Genesis 1:1 explained that the name 'Elohim' is derived from the contraction of 'El' and 'Alah.' The fact that this explanation closely matches the aforementioned linguistic explanation that the origin of the name 'Allah' may derive from the contraction of the Arabic definite article 'Al' (the) and 'ilah' (god) to 'Allah' (The God) did not escape the notice of certain Muslim apologists, the well-known Mr. Ahmed Deedat, of South Africa, in particular. However, the conclusions which can be drawn from the circumstance are speculative, for the *Scofield Reference Bible* did not identify 'Alah' as the proper name of The Creator, but rather offered the definition: "El – strength, or the strong one, and Alah, to swear, to bind oneself by an oath, so implying faithfulness." Certainly the claim that the authors of the *Scofield Reference Bible* in any way implied that the proper name of The Creator is 'Allah' would be an inappropriate extraction from

(SECTION 2) GOD

that which the authors actually proposed. However, the comment of the footnote has relevance within the sphere of what the authors meant to convey, and this comment does not seem in any way improper, incorrect, or inflammatory. Yet compromise of the convictions of the Bible translators was forced, for the least suggestion that the name of God in the Old Testament matches that of the Holy Qur'an excites a tender nerve in the ganglion of Christian hypersensitivities. As consequence, the explanation under discussion was edited from all subsequent editions.

To move from Old to New Testaments, the Christian audience can fairly ask, "How does the New Testament fit into the above-described scheme?" Once again the answer is fairly simple, boiling down to a few concrete points. The first is that the most frequently used word for God (1,344 of the 1,356 entries) in the Greek transcripts of the New Testament is *'theos.'*[38] This word *'theos'* is found in the Septuagint (LXX) *primarily as the translation of 'Elohim,'* the Hebrew nomenclature for God.[39] On authority of the 72 (six from each of the twelve tribes of Israel) Jewish scholars entrusted to translate the Septuagint, all of whom, according to tradition, chose to translate 'Elohim' to 'theos,' a person finds that the most frequently encountered name for God in the New Testament takes origin from 'Elohim.'

Recognizing that the basis of the *'theos'* of the New Testament is the 'Elohim' of the Old Testament, a person is led back to the above-described link between 'Elohim' and 'Allah.'

And truly a person should not be surprised. The 'Eli' and 'Eloi' allegedly found on the lips of Jesus in the New Testament (Mathew 27:46 and Mark 15:34) are immeasurably closer to 'Allah' than to the word 'God.' As is the case with 'Elohim' and 'Eloah,' 'Eloi' and 'Eli'

---

38. Achtemeier, Paul J. p. 684.
39. Achtemeier, Paul J. p. 684.

(2.A1) Understanding and Approaching God / God's Name

sound like 'Allah' and linguistically match 'Allah' in form and meaning. All four of these Biblical names are Hebrew, a sister language to Arabic and Aramaic. The languages commonly acknowledged by scholars to have been spoken by Jesus are Hebrew and Aramaic. For example, in the phrase "Eloi, Eloi, lama sabachthani" (Mark 15:34) the words 'Eloi' and 'lama' are transliterated from Hebrew, while 'sabachthani' is transliterated from Aramaic. Hence, being sister languages, Hebrew, Aramaic and Arabic words having similar or the same meaning would be expected to sound like phonetic cousins. All three are Semitic languages, with slight pronunciation differences for words of the same meaning, like the Hebrew greeting 'shalom' and the Arabic greeting 'salaam,' both meaning peace. Suspicion that the Hebrew 'Elohim,' 'Eloah,' 'Eloi,' and 'Eli' equate to the Arabic 'Allah' in the same way that the Hebrew 'shalom' equates to the Arabic 'salaam' seems relatively solidly founded.

Despite the above, there are still those who have been conditioned to propose that 'Allah' is the name of a pagan god. Of note is that pagans generically use the word 'God,' spelled 'G-o-d,' in the same way that Christians, Jews, and Muslims use it, and it does not change the fact that there is only one God. For example, the word 'Elohim' was used in the Septuagint to refer to pagan gods, as well as to the Greek and Roman gods, in addition to the one true God of the Old and New Testaments.[40] *Encyclopaedia Judaica* clarifies this opinion of *Harper's Bible Dictionary* with the comment, "The plural form 'elohim' is used not only of pagan "gods" (e.g., Ex. 12:12; 18:11; 20:3) but also of an individual pagan "god" (Judg. 11:24; II Kings 1:2ff.) and even of a "goddess" (I Kings 11:5). In reference to Israel's "God" it is used extremely often—more than 2,000 times..."[41] Remembering that 'Elohim' is the word from which the New

---

40. Achtemeier, Paul J. p. 684.
41. *Encyclopaedia Judaica.* Vol 7, p. 679.

Testament 'theos' is primarily derived, a person finds that use of this Biblical word for God flowed from the lips and pens of the pagans, as well as from those of the Jews and Christians. Does this mean that 'Elohim' is a pagan god, or even an exclusively Jewish or Christian God? Quite obviously, the fact that different religions, pagan religions included, have utilized 'God,' 'Elohim,' and 'Allah' to identify their concept of the Supreme Being reflects nothing more than their adoption of a commonly recognized name for God.

"Commonly recognized? Sounds strange to me," some will say. Such is also likely to be the case with the names Shim'own Kipha, Yehowchanan, Iakobos, and Matthaios – but how strange are these names really? Not very. Unknown to some, maybe. But strange? No. These are transliterations of the Hebrew and Greek from which the Biblical names Simon Peter, John, James, and Matthew are translated into English.

So which is really more strange, to invent and popularize new names to those identified in scripture, or to remain faithful to what are held to be holy texts? To identify The Creator by the 'God' label hatched from human creativity and incubated in Western culture, or by the name specified by The All-Mighty, as He declares His own appellation in scripture?

Undeniably, one who speaks of 'Yehowchanan,' 'Iakobos,' and 'Allah' will be greeted with a certain reserve in the West, but the concern of true believers has never been one of popularity of presentation to fellow man, but rather truth of testimony in front of The Creator.

(2.A) UNDERSTANDING AND APPROACHING GOD
(2.A2)
God's Name and The Royal Plural

"You see things; and you say 'Why?'
But I dream things that never were; and I say 'Why not?'"
— George Bernard Shaw, *Back to Methuselah*

An equally common concern is frequently voiced in the question, "Why is God referred to in the plural, translated as 'We' or 'Us" in certain passages of both the Bible and the Qur'an – doesn't this imply polytheism?" Examples include Genesis 1:26 and 11:7, which record God as having said, "Let Us make man..." and "Come, let Us go down..." Of initial note is that the name 'Allah,' unlike the Biblical 'Elohim,' is singular and cannot be made plural.[42] Some Arabic terms (for example, pronouns and verbal pronoun suffixes) do describe Allah in the plural, but in what is known as the royal plural – a plural not of numbers, but rather a literary device of Oriental and Semitic languages denoting majesty. Comparison with the 'Elohim' common to both Old and New Testaments reveals that 'Elohim' is plural; 'Eloah' (the closest name to 'Allah' in transliteration, meaning,

---

42. Douglas, J. D. p. 27.

(SECTION 2) GOD

and lack of plurality) is singular.[43] In the same way that the royal plural in the Qur'an denotes the majesty of God (Allah), so 'Elohim' in the Old and New Testaments bore the plural of respect consistent with the majesty of God.[44, 45] The *Theological Dictionary of the New Testament* comments, "elohim is clearly a numerical plural only in a very few instances (cf. Ex. 15:11). Even a single pagan god can be meant by the word (e.g., 1 Kgs. 11:5). In the main, then, we have a plural of majesty."[46]

The concept of the 'royal plural' or the 'plural of majesty' is foreign to most of the modern Western world. However, the royal plural was preserved in the English language as recently as the seventeenth century. The word 'thou' used to be applied to commoners while the word 'you,' the Old English plural of respect, was reserved for royalty and members of the social elite. Hence 'your Highness,' and 'your Lordship,' rather than 'thou Highness' or 'thou Lordship.' Hence also Queen Victoria's "*We* are not amused" and Margaret Thatcher's "*We* are a grandmother."

People may lob opinions on this subject back and forth from the respectful distance of their individual faiths, but it is interesting to note the conclusion of at least one scholar who spent time on both sides of the theological fence. Reverend David Benjamin Keldani, B.D., served as a Roman Catholic priest for nineteen years and as the Bishop of Uramiah before converting to Islam at the beginning of the twentieth century. Known by the Islamic name of Professor Abdul-Ahad Dawud, he authored one of the earliest scholarly works

---

43. *Encyclopaedia Britannica*. CD-ROM. (under "Elohim").
44. Achtemeier, Paul J. p. 686.
45. Meagher, Paul Kevin et al. Vol 1, p. 1187.
46. Kittel, Gerhard and Gerhard Friedrich (editors). 1985. *Theological Dictionary of the New Testament*. Translated by Geoffrey W. Bromiley. William B. Eerdmans Publishing Co., Paternoster Press Ltd. p. 325.

(2.A2) Understanding & Approaching God / God's Name & Royal Plural

in the English language on the subject of Biblical correlates with the prophet of Islam, Muhammad. In this work, he wrote,

> "It would be a mere waste of time here to refute those who ignorantly or maliciously suppose the Allah of Islam to be different from the true God and only a fictitious deity of Muhammad's own creation. If the Christian priests and theologians knew their Scriptures in the original Hebrew instead of in translations as the Muslims read their Qur'an in its Arabic text, they would clearly see that Allah is the same ancient Semitic name of the Supreme Being who revealed and spoke to Adam and all the prophets."[47]

A person may trust the opinion of a former Bishop, or perhaps judge the presented evidence convincing. Either way, coming to understand the name of God to be 'Allah' and the significance of the royal plural is all very fine and good, but faith need not pivot on such issues. The mind might be broadened a little, but just as Arab Christians identify God as 'Allah,' and just as the Bible employs the royal plural both in pronouns and in the proper name 'Elohim,' Western Christians can adopt the same practice without compromise to their creed. Hence, a more relevant question might be, "Regardless of His name, how does God command humankind to understand Him?"

---

47. Dawud, Abdul-Ahad (Formerly known as Reverend David Benjamin Keldani, Bishop of Uramiah). 1992. *Muhammad in the Bible*. Jeddah: Abul-Qasim Publishing House. p. 14.

(2.A) Understanding and Approaching God
(2.A3) Understanding of God

"Those who agree with us may not be right,
but we admire their astuteness."
– Cullen Hightower

The Jewish understanding of God is relatively concrete, although some may suggest that the strict definitions of Orthodox Judaism gave way to a certain degree of mysticism in the transition to Reform Judaism. Having said that, the One-ness of God remains the primary attribute, followed by many others, to include Justice, Love, Mercy, Omniscience, Omnipresence, Omnipotence, Sovereignty, Truth, Wisdom, Self-Existence, Goodness, Holiness, and Infinity. Furthermore, Jews consider God to be incomprehensible, for there is nothing like unto Him in the frame of reference of His creation.

The Jewish attributes of God carry over into Christian definitions as well, although the primary attribute of God, being His One-ness, suffered in the transformation from the strict monotheism of the apostolic age to the mysticisms of the Trinity. Coming out of one corner is the Trinitarian understanding of a synthesis of three in one –

(2.A3) Understanding & Approaching God / Understanding of God

a concept bounced off the ropes and bodyslammed by Unitarian challenges regarding how two substances with opposite properties (i.e., mortality/immortality; with beginning/without beginning; mutable/immutable, etc.) could possibly exist in one entity, why Christ Jesus ascribed all his miraculous works exclusively to God and not to any divinity of his own if he was in fact a partner in divinity, and why Christ Jesus testified to receiving his gifts from God and not to such gifts being integral with his own being if he and The Creator are coequal (see John 3:35, 5:19-23, 5:26-27, 10:25, 13:3, 14:10, Acts 2:33, 2 Peter 1:17, Rev 2:26-27).

The doctrine of God being Three, but One, that is to say Three in One, lives up to its label of a religious mystery, for explanation thereof remains elusive, leaving the critic mystified. The struggle to explain how 'the created' can possibly be considered equivalent to The Creator is ages-old, as are discussions regarding the religious mysteries of the proposed resurrection and atoning sacrifice. Cutting across such issues, the most common Christian image of God is the 'big man in the sky' concept, along the lines of Michelangelo's aged, white-bearded representation preserved in the flowing-robed fresco of the Sistine chapel. Being an image not even the slightest bit dissimilar to the ancient Greek representation of Zeus, the harmony has not gone unnoticed by religious historians. Yet many find such a concept unacceptable. After all, does the Biblical statement that God created man "in His own image" mean that God created man in *God's* own image, or in *man's* own image – separate and distinct from the rest of creation? The Greek word translated to 'His' with a 'let's-make-it-look-like-God' capital 'H' is *not* capitalized in the foundational manuscripts. There is no clue as to whether the word 'his' should properly be capitalized or not. The verse is structured in such a manner as to support orthodox thought, yet greater transgressions with regard to scriptural manipulation have been made within both Old and New

(SECTION 2) GOD

Testaments, as discussed in the relevant chapters to follow. As a result, like many elements of the Bible, no certain conclusion can be drawn, no concrete understanding can be recognized which unanimously satisfies the world of Christianity.

Such is also the case with the common Christian claim that the God of the Old Testament repented and changed from a harsh and wrathful God to the loving and forgiving God of the New Testament. Such an opinion is not universally accepted, and in fact is held by many to be contradicted both by scripture ("God is not a man, that He should lie, nor a son of man, that He should repent. Has He said, and will He not do? Or has He spoken, and will He not make it good? – Numbers 23:19) and by common sense.

The Islamic understanding of God enjoys more consistent approval amongst those who identify themselves as Muslims, with a simplicity and clarity which is reminiscent of the Jewish understanding in many respects. The critical elements upon which Islamic faith rests are described by the word, *'tawheed,'* – a concept which defines the Oneness of Allah in His existence, affirms His many unique names and attributes, and focuses a person's words and actions upon the pleasure of Allah.

According to the Islamic religion Allah's attributes include His being One in essence, eternal and absolute. He is living, self-subsisting, all-knowing, all-powerful. He is in need of none, but all are in need of Him. He does not beget, and is not begotten. He is "the First," without beginning, "the Last," without end, and He has no partners or co-sharers in divinity.

Allah is "the Predominant," above Whom there is none, and "the Internal," closer to Whom there is none. His attributes are eternal, and there is nothing comparable to Him. He does not indwell in his creatures, nor they in Him. He is "the Omniscient," perfect in knowledge, comprehending all things large and small, open and concealed, and "All-Wise," free from the smallest error in judgement. He is "the Compassionate," "the Merciful," whose mercy encompasses all creation. However, while Allah loves and rewards belief and piety, He hates disbelief, angers, and promises punishment to the disbelievers who rebel against the truth of Him and against His commandments. Being "the Omnipotent," His power is absolute, and none can frustrate His smallest decree.

Many other characteristics of Allah are described in the Holy Qur'an, such as Allah being the Lord and Master of creation – humankind having been created through His will, and living, dying, and returning to Him on The Day of Judgement according to His decree. Muslims further recognize that Allah is beyond complete human understanding, as there is nothing comparable to Him. Perhaps in the afterlife humans will be gifted greater understanding of their Lord and Creator, but in this worldly life knowledge is confined within the boundaries of revelation.

Similar to Judaism, but unlike Christianity, there are no representations of Allah in Islam. Consequently, the minds of the believers are not befuddled with the blasphemous 'big man in the sky' imagery which springs from the anthropomorphic mind of man. Furthermore, the Islamic religion does not even assign gender to Allah, Allah being understood to be transcendentally above all such characteristics of His creation, with the attribution of sexual traits considered especially offensive – blasphemous even. While referred to by the male pronoun in the revelation of the Qur'an, this is nothing more than a literary device employed out of necessity, for there is no pronoun of neutral gender in the Arabic language. Lord, God, Creator and Master, nowhere is Allah referred to as 'Father' in the Islamic religion.

The Islamic understanding of God meets a few objections in the predominantly Christian West. The first is that Islam recognizes Jesus

(SECTION 2) GOD

as a prophet but not as a 'son of God,' and especially not in a 'begotten, not made' sense. The second is that Islam teaches the oneness of God and condemns the Trinity. The third is that Muslims do not believe the concept of original sin to be compatible with God's justice and mercy. The last is that Muslims believe Jesus to have been raised up and saved from crucifixion, hence rendering the doctrine of atonement invalid, and of human construction.

The above differences in creed constitute the major fault-lines where the continental shelves of Christianity and Islam collide.

(2.B)
Doctrinal Differences

"The trouble with people is not that they don't know,
but that they know so much that ain't so."
— Josh Billings, *Josh Billings' Encyclopedia of Wit and Wisdom*

The differences between Judaism, Christianity, and Islam can be addressed on a number of levels, the most basic of which is that of innate common sense. Plain 'Alice in Wonderland' kind of sense, exemplified by such simple and sensible exchanges as:

> "'That's not a regular rule: you invented it just now.'
> 'It's the oldest rule in the book,' said the King.
> 'Then it ought to be Number one,' said Alice."[48]

This inborn and irrefutable form of logic is so conclusive as to obviate any need for further discussion. The resolution of many doctrinal differences falls into this category. However, a complementary avenue of discussion is to present Biblical and Qur'anic lessons, contrasting Judaic, Christian, and Islamic teachings, and leaving the readers to weigh the respective evidences against their own beliefs and/or preconceptions.

---

48. Carroll, Lewis. *Alice's Adventures in Wonderland*. Ch. 12.

(SECTION 2) GOD

Perhaps most interesting is the examination of Unitarian thought in consideration of Trinitarian doctrine. Herein a person finds many foundational elements of Trinitarian faith – teachings which are held to be the 'oldest rules in the book' – to be derived from extra-Biblical sources. Rather than being 'rule number one,' as a person might logically expect given the primacy of these teachings within Trinitarian doctrine, the foundation of many of these elements is not to be found in the Bible at all. Alice would object.

And, in fact, many great thinkers already have – people like Bishop Pothinus of Lyons (murdered in the late second century along with *all* the dissenting Christians who petitioned Pope Elutherus for an end to persecution), Iranaeus (murdered in 200 CE for defending Christians who did not follow the Pope), Leonidas (a follower of Apostolic Christianity and expositor of Pauline innovations, murdered in 208 CE), Origen (who died in prison in 254 CE after prolonged torture for preaching the Unity of God and rejection of the Trinity), Diodorus, Pamphilus (tortured and murdered, 309 CE), Lucian (tortured for his views and killed in 312 CE), Donatus (chosen to be Bishop of Carthage in 313 CE, and subsequently the leader and inspiration of a Unitarian movement which grew to be the dominant Christian sect of North Africa right up until Emperor Constantine ordered their massacre and the destruction of their literature – so complete was their obliteration that little of the sacred writings of this once-upon-a-time huge sect remains), Arius (the presbyter of Alexandria, whose motto was "follow Jesus as he preached" – killed by poisoning in 336 CE), Eusebius of Nicomedia (not to be confused with Eusebius of Caesaria), and not to mention the million (and some) Christians killed for refusing acceptance of official Catholic doctrine in the immediate period following the council of Nicaea

Later examples include Lewis Hetzer (decapitated February 4, 1529), Michael Servetus (burned at the stake October 27, 1553, using green branches still in leaf to produce an agonizingly slow, smoldering

(2.B) Doctrinal Differences

fire which tortured Servetus to a lingering death stretched over a period of more than two hours),* Francis Davidis (died in prison in 1579), Faustus Socinus (died in 1604), John Biddle (who suffered banishment to Sicily, followed by multiple imprisonments, during the last term of which he contracted a fatal disease from the foul prison conditions, ushering in death September 22, 1662). Biddle, who considered the terminology employed by Trinitarians "fitter for conjurers than Christians,"[49] established a breastwork of arguments against the assault of Trinitarian theology of such effectiveness that, at least on one occasion, debate opponents arranged his arrest in order to avoid facing him in public forum.[50] He left a legacy of free-thinkers affirming Divine Unity, not to mention some of the leading intellectuals of the age, to include Sir Isaac Newton, John Locke, and John Milton. Biddle's days in banishment also gave rise to one of the most touching comments on religious persecution, penned by a sympathetic correspondent of *The Gospel Advocate*:

"The conclave met, the judge was set,
   Man mounted on God's throne;
And they did judge a matter there,
   That rests with Him alone;
A brother's faith they made a crime,
And crushed thought's native right sublime."[51]

---

* Those who associate the burning of heretics with the punitive arm of the Roman Catholic church may be interested to note that the practice was not unknown to the Protestant church as well. For example, Michael Servetus was condemned to his horrific fate by none other than John Calvin, one of the founders of Protestantism. Despite the fact that Servetus, a Spaniard, possessed a letter of safe conduct, he was executed in Geneva for the alleged crime of being an Anabaptist and a Unitarian.

49. Wallace, Robert, F.G.S. 1850. *Antitrinitarian Biography.* Vol. III. London: E.T. Whitfield. p. 180.
50. Wallace, Robert, F.G.S. Vol. III, p. 190.
51. Wallace, Robert, F.G.S. Vol. III, p. 191.

(SECTION 2) GOD

Whereas Parliament had attempted to kill – literally, that is – Biddle's movement during his lifetime by voting the death penalty to deniers of the Trinity into law May 2, 1648, Parliament went on to pass the British 'Act of Uniformity' in the year of Biddle's death, outlawing all non-Episcopal worship and clergy.[52] Under this latter act, 2,257 priests were ejected from the clergy and over 8,000 people died in prison out of refusal to accept the doctrine of the Trinity.

And then there are Thomas Emlyn, Theophilus Lindsey, Joseph Priestley (who suffered tremendous persecution and lawless violence while contending that "Absurdity supported by power will never be able to stand its ground against the efforts of reason."[53]), Charles Chauncy, Thomas Jefferson, James Freeman, William Ellery Channing, Benjamin Franklin and many others.

The individuals mentioned above were associated with movements, but there is at least one case where, in the selective wisdom of the Church, the population of an entire country was condemned:

> "Early in the year, the most sublime sentence of death was promulgated which has ever been pronounced since the creation of the world. The Roman tyrant wished that his enemies' heads were all upon a single neck, that he might strike them off at a blow; the inquisition assisted Philip to place the heads of all his Netherlands subjects upon a single neck for the same fell purpose. Upon the 16th February 1568, a sentence of the Holy Office condemned all the inhabitants of the Netherlands to death as heretics. From this universal doom only a few persons, especially named, were excepted. A proclamation of the King, dated ten days later, confirmed this decree of the Inquisition, and ordered it to be carried into instant

---

52. Parke, David B. pp. 31, 33.
53. Parke, David B. p. 48.

(2.B) Doctrinal Differences

execution, without regard to age, sex, or condition. This is probably the most concise death-warrant that was ever framed. Three millions of people, men, women, and children, were sentenced to the scaffold in three lines; and, as it was well known that these were not harmless thunders, like some bulls of the Vatican, but serious and practical measures, which were to be enforced, the horror which they produced may be easily imagined. It was hardly the purpose of government to compel the absolute completion of the wholesale plan in all its length and breadth, yet in the horrible times upon which they had fallen, the Netherlanders might be excused for believing that no measure was too monstrous to be fulfilled. At any rate, it was certain that when *all* were condemned, *any* might at a moment's warning be carried to the scaffold, and this was precisely the course adopted by the authorities. Under this universal decree the industry of the Blood-Council might now seem superfluous. Why should not these mock prosecutions be dispensed with against individuals, now that a common sentence had swallowed the whole population in one vast grave? Yet it may be supposed that if the exertions of the commissioners and councilors served no other purpose, they at least furnished the government with valuable evidence as to the relative wealth and other circumstances of the individual victims. The leading thought of the government being, that persecution, judiciously managed, might fructify into a golden harvest, it was still desirable to persevere in the cause in which already such bloody progress had been made.

And under this new decree, the executions certainly did not slacken. Men in the highest and the humblest positions were daily and hourly dragged to the stake. Alva, in a single letter to Phillip, coolly estimated the number of executions which

(SECTION 2) GOD

were to take place immediately after the expiration of holy week, at "eight hundred heads." Many a citizen, convicted of a hundred thousand florins and of no other crime, saw himself suddenly tied to a horse's tail, with his hands fastened behind him, and so dragged to the gallows. But although wealth was an unpardonable sin, poverty proved rarely a protection. Reasons sufficient could always be found for dooming the starveling labourer as well as the opulent burgher. To avoid the disturbances created in the streets by the frequent harangues or exhortations addressed to the bystanders by the victims on the way to the scaffold, a new gag was invented. The tongue of each prisoner was screwed into an iron ring, and then seared with a hot iron. The swelling and inflammation which were the immediate result, prevented the tongue from slipping through the ring, and of course effectually precluded all possibility of speech."[54]

The above list catalogs individuals who are, at one and the same time, regarded by the Catholic church as the most notorious of heretics and by Unitarian Christians as the greatest of martyrs to the cause of religious free-thought and revival of the pure teachings of the prophets – Christ Jesus in particular. Some of the Unitarians mentioned above were associated with movements of such significance as to have swept countries or influenced significant portions of entire continents, but in all cases the Trinitarian Christians eventually dominated through the combination of superior force, inferior tolerance, and willingness to sacrifice fellow man to the cause of religious purification. Of note is that the standards by which these two groups measure correctness differ. The Catholic Church and Trinitarian Christian sects condemn that which conflicts with derived doctrine,

---

54. Motley, John Lothrop. 1884. *The Rise of the Dutch Republic: A History.* Volume II. London: Bickers & Son. pp. 155-156.

(2.B) DOCTRINAL DIFFERENCES

whereas Unitarian Christianity condemns that which conflicts with scriptural evidence. That these two standards are in conflict lies at the heart of the Christian debate. The Catholic Church succeeded in killing off many dissenting individuals, but failed to suppress the challenging thoughts they expressed. Far greater success would have been achieved had the Church provided rational and conclusive rebuttal to the challenges of these above-mentioned individuals, and allowed them to live with the humiliation of intellectual defeat. However, Church history documents nearly two millennia of failure to overthrow the rational arguments of the Unitarians, much to the discredit of the Trinitarian institutions.

Examples can be taken from the life of Arius, but with the caution to the reader that almost all of the books devoted to an examination of the life and teachings of Arius in existence today are written by his enemies. Given such a scenario, examination of different authors' opinions would no doubt betray an unkind prejudice, and the only reasonable course is to consider some examples of the pure teachings of Arius.

Perhaps one of the earliest of Arian arguments was that if Jesus was the 'son of God,' then there must have been a time when Jesus did not exist. If Jesus was created of the Father, then there must have been a time when the Eternal Father pre-existed the later-created Jesus. Since God is Eternal, Jesus cannot be considered to be partners in God-head if he was in fact created. The Creator and His creation are not the same, and so can not be partners in Divinity.

Arius held that if Jesus truly did say, "...My Father is greater than I" (John 14:28), then equating Jesus with God is to deny the Bible. Arius suggested that if there is anything evident from the teachings of Jesus, it is that he affirmed Divine Unity.

When the Trinitarian clergy claimed Jesus to be 'of the essence of God,' objections were raised by Arian and Trinitarian Christians alike,

79

(SECTION 2) GOD

on the bases that 'from the essence' and 'of one essence' are materialist expressions, are Sabellian* in origin, are words not to be found in the foundational scriptures themselves, and are contrary to church authority, as evidenced by the fact that the expression first materialized at a council at Antioch convened against Paul of Samosata in 269 CE.[55] When the Catholic church subsequently asserted that Jesus was 'of God,' the Arians responded that the Bible describes all people as being 'of God' in the verse, "Now all things *are* of God..." (II Corinthians 5:18 -- see also I Corinthians 8:6).[56] Forced to correct the exclusivity of the assertion, the Catholics then asserted that Christ Jesus "...is not a creature, but the power and eternal image of the Father and true God."[57] The Arian response that the Bible describes *all* men as "...the image and glory of God" (I Corinthians 11:7) left the Church confounded.[58] In the words of Prof. Gwatkin, "The longer the debate went on, the clearer it became that the meaning of Scripture could not be defined without going outside Scripture for words to define it."[59] To adopt such a methodology is to propose that mankind can explain revelation better than The One Who not only revealed the scripture, but Who gave mankind the facility of language to begin with. The proposal boils down to approaching God with the compliment of reverence admixed with the insult of claiming better ability to explain revelation than The Source of revelation Himself.

---

* Sabellianism was an early Christian heresy which conceived God in unity, but triune operationally, being manifest as Creator in the Father, Redeemer in the Son, and Sanctifier in the Holy Spirit. Sabellianism was denounced by Arius and the Trinitarian church alike.

55. Gwatkin, H.M. 1898. *The Arian Controversy.* London: Longmans, Green, and Co. pp. 32-33.

56. Gwatkin, H.M. p. 34.

57. Gwatkin, H.M. p. 35.

58. Gwatkin, H.M. p. 35.

59. Gwatkin, H.M. p. 35.

(2.B) Doctrinal Differences

So the arguments started and so they have continued to the present day. Lacking the ability to win through rational argument, the Trinitarian Church has violently suppressed dissention to the point where entire populations have been terrorized into unthinking acceptance. In the process the Church has failed to address the issues. As Castillo, one of the followers of Servetus, was prompted to comment, "To burn a man is not to prove a doctrine." The Church can reduce a man to ashes but cannot disintegrate his thoughts without providing intelligent rebuttal. Typical of those who lack the ability to substantiate their beliefs but who possess the power of oppression, violent response has been the historical reflex against those who challenged Trinitarian creed. That this violence existed in the vacuum of intelligent justification signals a lack of foundation of the institution. As John Toland commented,

> "This conduct, on the contrary, will make them suspect all to be a cheat and imposture, because men will naturally cry out when they are touched in a tender part…no man will be angry at a question who's able to answer it…"[60]

Pythagoras further summed up the risk of speaking one's mind with the words, "To tell of God among men of prejudicial opinion is not safe." Unitarians throughout history would no doubt note that Jesus himself predicted:

> "They will put you out of the synagogues; yes, the time is coming that whoever kills you will think that he offers God service. And these things they will do to you because they have not known the Father nor Me." (John 16:2-3)

---

60. Toland, John. 1718. *Tetradymus; bound with, Nazarenus: or, Jewish, Gentile and Mahometan Christianity.* London. pp. 75-76.

(Section 2) God

Such efforts to establish Trinitarian doctrine with fire and sword rarely threaten personal freedom in the present day, having been displaced by a variety of emotionally provocative justifications coupled with a systematic avoidance of relevant issues. Given the absence of Roman Catholic authority to continue a program of religious enforcement, much of the modern Christian world follows the example of Myser of Nicholas – a bishop at the Council of Nicaea who bore the ignoble reputation of boxing his own ears whenever Arius spoke. The present day response of clergy to such challenges to Trinitarian creed has changed very little, largely consisting of various tactics of issue avoidance, usually cloaked in a mantle of emotionally charged, psychologically manipulative oratory, embroidered with the impressive glitter of self-righteousness.

Some allow themselves to be swayed by the sanctimonious presentation and sectarian party lines parroted by clergy, others don't. More than a few people of God view such devices as distracters from the higher priority of confronting and resolving the relevant issues, and hope for a world which will courteously eject the unfounded tenets of the past and usher in a fresh new age of open-minded analysis.

(2.B) Doctrinal Differences
(2.B1)
Christ Jesus

"But why do you call me 'Lord, Lord,' and not do the things which I say? Whoever comes to me, and hears my sayings and does them, I will show you whom he is like: He is like a man building a house, who dug deep and laid the foundation on the rock. And when the flood arose, the stream beat vehemently against that house, and could not shake it, for it was founded on the rock. But he who heard and did nothing is like a man who built a house on the earth without a foundation, against which the stream beat vehemently; and immediately it fell. And the ruin of that house was great."

– Christ Jesus (Luke 6:46-49)

Who was the historical Jesus? That question has assaulted the minds of all who wished to form a mental construct in the period following his ministry on earth. Jews have one concept, Unitarian Christians another, Trinitarians yet one more; and these viewpoints are well known. What is not so widely understood is the Islamic perspective.

Most Christians are pleasantly surprised to learn that Muslims recognize Jesus as Messiah and the Word of God. Most Jews are…well…not so positively impressed.

(SECTION 2) GOD

Translation of the meaning of the Holy Qur'an, *surah* (chapter) 3, *ayat* (verses) 45-47, reads,

> "Behold! The angels said: "O Mary! Allah gives you glad tidings of a Word from Him: his name will be Christ Jesus, the son of Mary, held in honor in this world and the Hereafter and of (the company of) those nearest to Allah;
>
> He shall speak to the people in childhood and in maturity. And he shall be (of the company) of the righteous."
>
> She said, "O my Lord! How shall I have a son when no man has touched me?"
>
> He said: "Even so: Allah creates what He wills: when He has decreed a Plan, He says to it, 'Be,' and it is!"

In a theological nutshell, Muslims believe Jesus to be a Word of Allah, a Messiah, born by immaculate conception to the chaste virgin Mary (Maryam) and strengthened with the Holy Spirit. Muslims believe he performed miracles by the will of God from the cradle, grew to convey the revelation of Allah to mankind in fulfillment of previous scripture, healed lepers, cured the blind, and raised the dead by the will of God, and at the end of his ministry was raised up to be spared the persecution of the people. Muslims believe a time will come when there will be an anti-Christ on Earth, and during that time Jesus will be sent back to vanquish the anti-Christ. He will then eradicate deviant beliefs and practices in all religions, which will include correcting those who consider themselves to be following his teachings as Christians, but who in fact are astray. Jesus will then establish submission to God's will (Islam) throughout the world, live an exemplary life, die, and shortly thereafter the Day of Judgement will follow.

(2.B1) Doctrinal Differences / Christ Jesus

Given the complexity of the issues, discussion of the individual elements of the above points of view would seem appropriate. The reader, no doubt, hopes to find that once the personality map of the scriptural Jesus is exploded into fine detail, reconstruction following bitmap analysis will yield a profile consistent with expectations. However, to be objective and fair, a person must be prepared to find a likeness which will discard the iron mask of 2,000 years of canonical corruption and walk twenty paces, turn and fire upon the popularized notions which have hitherto unjustly imprisoned the real Jesus under the false charge of being an imposter. A person must be prepared to find the real Jesus in conflict with personal preconceptions, media profiles, and, more than anything else, modern Christian teaching. A person must accept the possibility of a Jesus so contrary to instilled notions, a Jesus so foreign to experience and expectations, a Jesus so at variance with personal and societal constructs that he will openly oppose the churches constructed around his existence. Popes and priests, parsons and pastors, bishops and cardinals, evangelists and monks, ministers and messianic pretenders all may find themselves suffering the same condemnation as did the Pharisees in the time and homeland of Christ Jesus. In other words, a Jesus may surface who will disown those who claim to follow in his name, *just like he said he would,* as recorded in Matthew 7:21-23:

> "Not everyone who says to me, 'Lord, Lord,' shall enter the kingdom of heaven, but he who does the will of my Father in heaven. *Many* will say to me in that day, 'Lord, Lord, have we not prophesied in your name, cast out demons in your name, and done many wonders in your name?' And then I will declare to them, 'I never knew you; depart from me, you who practice lawlessness!'"

(Section 2) God

This passage clearly predicts a time when seemingly pious 'followers,' despite the impressive performance of prophecies, wonders, and exorcisms sufficient to mislead the masses, will be disowned as deceivers. Just as the Christian audience is warned by their own scripture that all may not be as they have been told by congregation and clergy, the evidence presented herein warns against having a closed mind on the main issue of concern -- namely the nature of God and the reality of Jesus. True believers will acknowledge Jesus in whatever form he emerges, whether a model of the desires or a Jesus who will oppose the churches of present day as he opposed the Pharisees during his ministry in Palestine. Those who do not accept the Jesus of scripture cannot be counted amongst the faithful who follow in the path of Jesus, for such are those who appoint their desires and preconceptions as master of their direction. And there is only room for one master to man.

(2.B) Doctrinal Differences
(2.B2)
Word of God

"It was then that I began to look into the seams of your doctrine. I wanted only to pick at a single knot; but when I had got that undone, the whole thing raveled out. And then I understood that it was all machine-sewn."

– Henrik Ibsen, *Ghosts*, act 2.

Jesus is identified in the Holy Qur'an as a 'Word' from Allah. *Surah* 3:45 reads,

> "Behold! the angels said:
> "O Mary! Allah gives you glad tidings of a Word from Him: his name will be the Messiah, the son of Mary, held in honor in this world and the Hereafter and of (the company of) those nearest to Allah" (TMQ 3:45).

In Biblical contrast, John 1:1 reads: "In the beginning was the Word, and the Word was with God, and the Word was God." This Biblical language is cryptic enough to lend itself to diverse interpretations. Almost any doctrine can be constructed on the basis of this verse, as in fact several have. A person might wish to question, "What is 'the Word?'" Could it be the message of God (i.e., the revelation)?

(SECTION 2) GOD

If the Christian explanation of Jesus being 'the word' is to be grasped, a person is beholden not to delve too deeply into the doctrine. The foundation of Christian exegesis on this point rests on, well, nothing – nothing concrete, that is. The standard answer that Jesus is the Word of God, and that means the '*logos*,' reads along the lines of Jesus being the Word of God, and that means 'Word.' For '*logos*' is nothing more than Greek for 'word,' or 'saying.' This redundant mode of circular thought is only satisfying to those who do not wish to delve into the issue to any significant depth. A person may well ask, "What does it mean that Jesus is 'the Word?'" only to be told, "It means he is the '*logos*.'" Those who reflect upon the issue, however, recognize that the answer does nothing more than repeat the assertion, failing to resolve the question, "What is the *meaning*?"

The point is that the factual nature of a statement must necessarily rest upon a foundation of self-evident truths. Such axioms establish a clear material base from which knowledge is derived. Should conclusions be drawn which violate foundational axioms, these same conclusions can be demonstrated to fall outside the bounds of reason. In the case of mathematics a simple axiom is that one plus one equals two. Anyone in the world can place an apple next to an apple and see that, by definition, there are now two apples. Add one more and there are three. Should a scientist later derive some new and revolutionary concept, and yet one of the equations by which the theory is derived violates the axiom that one plus one equals two, the whole theory is rendered invalid. In the case of the Christian concept of Jesus being 'the Word,' the doctrine unravels, for the simple reason that there *are* no axioms. There are no self-evident truths at the foundation of the Christian teachings of this point. All that exists is a reshuffling of words.

On the other hand, the Islamic understanding is relatively concrete, proposing the 'Word of God' to be Allah's word of creation.

(2.B2) Doctrinal Differences / Word of God

This word, in Arabic, is roughly pronounced '*Kun*,' and means 'Be.' The foundational axiom in this regard is one which every human already knows -- namely that God creates through willing things into existence, and just as He willed into existence every big, every little, every *thing*, He created Jesus through His divine command, "Be." *Surah* 3:47 points out: "...Allah creates what He wills: when He has decreed a Plan, He but says to it, 'Be,' and it is!"

Reading the Bible with the above understanding provides alternative insights. A person doesn't have to go far to find the first example of the 'Word of God,' Islamically speaking. If a person starts with Genesis, the creation of the world is discussed. As early as Genesis 1:3, when God said "Let there *be*...," it was! As another practical example, *surah* 3:59 (TMQ) reads, "The similitude of Jesus before God is as that of Adam; He created him from dust, then said to him: 'Be': and he was."

For those who claim the 'Word' of John 1:1 ("In the beginning was the Word, and the Word was with God, and the Word was God") not only refers to Jesus but also implies equality between Jesus and God, I Corinthians 3:23 appears to muddy the doctrinal waters. This verse states,"And ye are Christ's; and Christ is God's." A person might reasonably question "In what way are ye Christ's? A follower of his teachings? Then in what way is Christ God's? An element of His creation, to be sure, but also a follower of His divine law, if the analogy is to be respected. And if Jesus were God, why doesn't the passage read 'Christ *is* God' rather that 'Christ is God's?'"

I Corinthians 3:23 appears to emphasize the fact that just as the disciples were subordinate to the prophet Jesus, so too was Jesus subordinate to God. Surely this distinction comes as no surprise to those who respect the authority of Isaiah 45:22 ("For I am God, and there is no other"), Isaiah 44:6 ("Thus says the Lord...'I am the First and I am the Last; Besides Me there is no God.'"), Deuteronomy 4:39

(Section 2) God

(...the Lord Himself is God in heaven above and on the earth beneath; these is no other."), and Deuteronomy 6:4 ("Hear, O Israel: The Lord our God, the Lord is one!"). Given the above, claiming the wording of John 1:1 to equate Jesus to God certainly could be understood by some to be selective reasoning at best – which leaves a person to wonder what really is wrong with the Islamic viewpoint on this issue, whether understood in the framework of either Unitarian Christianity or Islam.

(2.B) Doctrinal Differences
(2.B3)
Messiah [Christ]

"The Old Testament teems with prophecies of the Messiah, but nowhere is it intimated that that Messiah is to stand as a God to be worshipped. He is to bring peace on earth, to build up the waste places, to comfort the broken-hearted, but nowhere is he spoken of as a deity."
— Olympia Brown, first woman minister ordained in the U.S., Sermon of 13 January 1895.

The concept of Jesus being the predicted messiah is so well known to the world of Christianity as to obviate need for discussion. But Jesus a messiah, in Islam? The fact that Muslims recognize Jesus as a messiah has long confused Christian evangelists, who propose that some conclusion in support of Trinitarian dogma should be drawn based upon this belief. The Christian evangelist questions, "Was Jesus the Messiah?" (Muslims answer, "Yes"), and "Was Muhammad the messiah?" (Muslims answer, "No"). In the mind of the evangelist, the conclusion based upon the answers to these questions is twofold: first that Muhammad was not a messiah, and therefore not a prophet, and second that Jesus, being the predicted messiah, occupies an exclusive

(SECTION 2) GOD

position at some locus in partnership with divinity. Muslims point out, however, that a few additional questions demand consideration before a valid conclusion can be made. For example:

> 1. Are there other Biblical messiahs? Answer: Yes, lots of them -- no less than 38.[61] (for specifics, see below)
> 2. Were all Biblical messiahs, such as the Davidic kings and high priests of ancient Palestine (now called Israel), prophets? Answer: No.
> 3. Conversely, were all Biblical prophets, such as Abraham, Noah, Moses, etc., messiahs? Answer: No.
> 4. Therefore, if not all Biblical prophets were messiahs, how can a person disqualify any man's claim to prophethood on the basis of not being a messiah? For in that case, Abraham, Noah, Moses, and many other true Biblical prophets would also have to be disqualified by the same standard.
> 5. And lastly, if there were Biblical messiahs who were not even prophets, how can being a messiah equate to divinity when the label doesn't even equate to piety?

The fact is that the word 'messiah' simply means 'anointed one,' and bears no connotation of divinity or partnership in Godhead. So there is no difficulty with both Unitarian Christians and Muslims alike recognizing Jesus as Messiah, or in the language of the English translations, Jesus as Christ, but without transgressing into the error of apotheosis (equating with divinity, i.e., deification). A person may well wonder, then, where the label 'messiah' and the name 'Christ' come from in the first place.

The name 'Christ' is derived from '*christos*,' which is the Greek translation of the Hebrew 'messiah.' The word '*christos*' was subsequently latinised to the title of 'Christ.' The *Theological Dictionary of*

---

61. Kittel, Gerhard and Gerhard Friedrich. p. 1323.

(2.B3) Doctrinal Differences / Messiah (Christ)

the New Testament clearly defines *'christos'* as "Christ, Messiah, Anointed One."[62] A second opinion is as follows: "The word Messiah (sometimes Messias, following the Hellenized transcription) represents the Hebrew *mashiah*, or *mashuah* 'anointed,' from the verb *mashah* 'anoint.' It is exactly rendered by the Greek *christos* 'anointed.'"[63] Translated into plain English, if people read the Old Testament in ancient Hebrew they will find *'mashiah,' 'mashuah,'* and *'mashah.'* Read it in ancient Greek, and the above three are found "exactly rendered" as *'christos.'* The subject becomes interesting at this point because the Aramaic, Hebrew, and ancient Greek languages do not have capital letters, so how Bible translators got 'Christ' with a capital 'C' from *'christos'* with a small 'c' is a mystery known only to them.

A person may claim that context implies uniqueness or dictates emphasis, mandating capitalization in the case of Christ Jesus. This justification, however, simply doesn't work, for the reason that the word *'christos'* is applied to a wide variety of subjects throughout the Bible. The verb *'chrio,'* meaning 'to anoint,' is found 69 times in the Old Testament in reference to Saul, David, Solomon, Joash, and Jehoahaz, among others. The noun *'christos'* (the same *'christos'* translated to 'Christ' in the case of Jesus) is found 38 times – 30 times in reference to kings, 6 times in reference to the high priest, twice in reference to the fathers.[64]

According to the *New Catholic Encyclopedia* (hereafter abbreviated NCE),

> "The king was called 'the anointed of Yahweh' (1 Sm 24.7, 11; 26.9, 11, 16, 23; 2 Sm 1.14, 16; 19.22; Lam 4.20), or simply 'His anointed,' in a context that clearly shows that he was

---
62. Kittel, Gerhard and Gerhard Friedrich. p. 1322.
63. Hastings, James (editor); Revised edition by Frederick C. Grant and H. H. Rowley. 1963. *Dictionary of The Bible*. Second Edition. Charles Scribner's Sons. p. 646.
64. Kittel, Gerhard and Gerhard Friedrich. p. 1323.

(SECTION 2) GOD

Yahweh's anointed [1 Sm 2.10; 12.3, 5; 16.6; 2 Sm 22.51; Ps 2.2; 19 (20).7; 27 (28).8]. Again, Yahweh spoke to the king as 'my anointed one' [1 Sm 23.5; Ps 131 (132).17; cf. Also 'your anointed,' said to Yahweh in Ps 83 (84).10; 'the anointed of the God of Jacob' in 2 Sm 23.1]."[65]

The argument can be made that Christ with a capital 'C' was the anointed of God in some special sense, different from all others described in the Bible with the exact same terminology. Either the difference deserves to be defined or the argument abandoned. To quote, "Saul is most commonly called 'the Lord's anointed.' Apart from Saul, only Davidic kings bear the title (except in Is. 45:1)"[66] In reading this quote, few people are likely to take notice of the inconspicuous exception bracketed by parentheses – a literary cloaking device. The few readers who stop and overturn that little exception will find that what crawls out of Isaiah 45:1 is Cyrus the Persian – Cyrus the king of the fire-worshipping Zoroastrians, that is.

Graham Stanton effectively summarizes the above information as follows:

"The Hebrew word 'messiah' means an anointed person or thing. It is thanslated by 'christos' (hence Christ) in the Greek translation of the Old Testament, the Septuagint (LXX). In numerous passages in the Old Testament 'anointed one' is applied to the divinely appointed King. (See, for example, I Sam. 12:3 (Saul) and 2 Sam. 19:22 (David)). In a few passages 'anointed one' is used of prophets (most notably in Isa. 61:1) and of priests (Lev. 4:3,5,16), but without further designation the term normally refers to the king of Israel."[67]

---

65. *New Catholic Encyclopedia.* Vol 9, p.714.
66. Kittel, Gerhard and Gerhard Friedrich. p. 1323.
67. Stanton, Graham N. 1989. *The Gospels and Jesus.* Oxford University Press.p. 221.

(2.B3) Doctrinal Differences / Messiah (Christ)

Consequently, the 'Lord's Christ' (i.e. the 'Lord's *christos*' – the 'Lord's anointed,' or the 'Lord's messiah') list includes Saul the Christ, Cyrus the Christ, and the many Davidic kings – all 'Christs.' Or, at least, that is how the Bible would read if the translators were unbiased in their translation.

The fact of the matter, however, is that in the selective wisdom of the Bible translators, '*christos*' is translated 'anointed' in every case but that of Christ Jesus. When the word 'anointed' is found in any English translation of the Bible, a person can safely assume that the underlying Greek is the same '*christos*' from which Jesus gets his unique label of 'Christ.' This exclusive title of 'Christ' with a capital 'C,' and 'Messiah' with a capital 'M,' is singularly impressive. In fact, it makes a person believe that the term implies some unique spiritual link, distinctly separate from the flock of lay 'messiahs' with small 'm's' and no 'c' at all – the '*christos*' hidden in the alternative translation of 'anointed.'

The above information represents a point of embarrassment to the educated Christian community, for it suggests the questionable ethic of doctrinally-driven Bible translation. Should a person recognize the validity of the concern, one might also recognize that yet another fundamental difference between Unitarian/Islamic and Trinitarian beliefs exists in a vacuum of Biblical support for the Trinitarian viewpoint.

Contrary to popular opinion, the weight of the Biblical evidence appears to support the Islamic and Unitarian Christian viewpoints more than that of the Trinitarian Christian majority. The Islamic religion confirms that Jesus was *an* 'anointed' one of God, but does not strain to elevate him beyond the station of a prophet, or to appear more unique than others bearing similar title or prophetic office. The most ancient of Biblical scriptures, as discussed above, supports the Islamic belief that just as all prophets and Davidic kings were '*christos*,' so was Jesus. The conclusion that no particular king or prophet should bear unique labeling, different from all others bearing similar title, is not unreasonable.

One intriguing directive of the Islamic religion is for mankind to be truthful and to avoid going to extremes. In this instance, unjustified literary license with translation is to be shunned. Honest and unbiased translation should absolutely avoid the tainting influence of doctrinal prejudice. A document perceived to be revelation from God should not be adjusted to suit personal or sectarian desires. Such a document should be held in due respect and reverence, and translated with faithfulness. And the challenge to mankind has always been just this – for the faithful to mold their lives to fit the truth, adjusting beliefs and actions in synchrony with revelation, rather than the other way around. This concept, encompassing the recognition of Jesus and cautioning against extremes in religion, is succinctly expressed in *surah* 4:171 of the Holy Qur'an:

> "O People of the Book! Commit no excesses in your religion: nor say of Allah anything but the truth. Christ Jesus the son of Mary was (no more than) a Messenger of Allah, and His Word, which He bestowed on Mary, and a Spirit proceeding from Him: so believe in Allah and His messengers." (TMQ 4:171)

Once again, a person may find difficulty in the face of the evidence not to value the Islamic perspective, whether as a Christian or as a Muslim.

(2.B) DOCTRINAL DIFFERENCES
(2.B4)
Immaculate Conception

"A baby is God's opinion that life should go on."
— Carl Sandburg, *Remembrance Rock*

And in the case of Jesus, a baby was God's determination that revelation should go on.

A few 'progressive' churches are coming to deny this traditional element of 'Christian' belief. They shouldn't. It happened. At least, that is the traditional teaching of both Christianity and Islam.

The Christian viewpoint is well known, although the lack of Biblical detail is dissatisfying to some. The Islamic teaching is that just as God created Adam from nothing more than clay, He created Jesus without biological father as a sign to the people -- a miraculous origin portending prophetic office. *Surah* 19:17-22 (TMQ) describes Mary receiving the good news of her son as follows:

> "She placed a screen (to screen herself) from them; then We sent to her Our angel, and he appeared before her as a man in all respects.
>
> She said: "I seek refuge from you to (Allah) Most Gracious: (come not near) if you fear Allah."

(Section 2) God

He said: "Nay, I am only a messenger from your Lord, (to announce) to you the gift of a holy son."

She said: "How shall I have a son, seeing that no man has touched me, and I am not unchaste?"

He said: "So (it will be): your Lord says, 'That is easy for Me: and (We wish) to appoint him as a Sign to men and a Mercy from Us': it is a matter (so) decreed."

So she conceived him, and she retired with him to a remote place."

Muslims hold that through the miraculous birth of Jesus Allah demonstrates the completeness of His creative powers with regard to humankind, having created Adam without mother or father, Eve from man without mother, and Jesus from woman without father.

(2.B) Doctrinal Differences

(2.B5)
Jesus Begotten?

"To create is divine, to reproduce is human."
— Man Ray, *Originals Graphic Multiples*

The doctrines of Jesus being 'begotten, not made' and of Divine sonship have been unquestioningly accepted for so many centuries as to have largely fallen from scrutiny in the minds of Christian laity. Historically, dissenting views have been reflexively labeled 'heresy' and suppressed by such horrific means as to drive intellectual challenges underground. Only in recent times have laity been freed from the oppressive arm of a punitive and politically dominant church, allowing free expression of religious thought. Within the Christian world public critique of these doctrines has become survivable only in the last two to three centuries. Within the Islamic world, these same Christian doctrines are viewed to be unjustified extremes and misunderstandings of God's message to mankind. The Christian doctrines of Jesus being 'begotten, not made' and of Divine sonship have been freely opposed in Muslim lands since the revelation of the Holy Qur'an, 1,400 years ago.

The Islamic understanding is that the act of 'begetting,' which is defined in *Merriam Webster's Collegiate Dictionary* as "to procreate as the father," is a physical act implying the lower carnal element of

(SECTION 2) GOD

sex – an animal trait light-years below the majesty of The Creator. A person may rightfully question, "What does 'begotten, not made' mean, anyway?" Many religious analysts seem to conclude that nearly 1,700 years of exegesis (from the time of the Nicene Council in 325 CE to the present day) have failed to provide a sensible explanation. Digging for understanding in a barren mine, devoid of the veins of rational explanation, a person is forced to examine the source of this doctrine as expressed in the Nicene Creed:

> "...We believe in one Lord, Jesus Christ, the only Son of God, eternally begotten of the Father, God from God, Light from Light, true God from true God, begotten, not made, one in Being with the Father..."

The question has been raised before, "What language is this?" If somebody can make sense of the above and explain it in rational terms which an average child can understand, and not just be forced to blindly accept in the process of religious indoctrination, then they have succeeded where 1,700 years of exegesis have failed. The oft-recited Athanasian Creed, which was composed roughly a hundred years following the Nicene Creed, bears such strikingly similar convolutions of conceptualization as to have prompted the following response:

> "Gennadius, patriarch of Constantinople, was so much amazed by this extraordinary composition, that he frankly pronounced it to be the work of a drunken man."[68]

More direct challenges arise. If Jesus is the "only begotten Son of God," who is David? Answer: Psalms 2:7 – "The LORD has said to me, 'You are My Son, Today I have begotten you." Jesus the "only begotten son of God," with David 'begotten' just a scant 40 generations earlier? The label of 'religious mystery' may not satisfy all

---

68. Gibbon, Edward, Esq. 1854. *The History of the Decline and Fall of the Roman Empire.* Vol. 4. London: Henry G. Bohn. Chapter XXXVII, p. 146.

(2.B5) Doctrinal Differences / Jesus Begotten?

free-thinkers. One wonders why an acceptable explanation is lacking, especially if a person considers that the message of God should be clear and easily understandable to even the least intellectual of humankind. However, if the label of 'religious mystery' means that a person has to believe despite evidence to the contrary, then this doctrine appears to qualify for the title. Nonetheless, the problems inherent to this doctrine demand recognition, and an official church policy of "believe what I say, not what you see with your own two eyes" may satisfy those who are subjects of mental alienation, but for the cognitive majority serves only to cloak such difficulties in denial.

In the face of such conflicts between scripture and doctrine, a reasonable person might question whether God is unreliable (an impossibility), whether the Bible contains errors (a serious possibility, and if so, how does a person know which elements are true and which false), or whether or not an incorrect creed has been constructed around a nucleus of colloquialism found in the Bible.

One very disconcerting challenge revolves around the word, *'monogenes.'* The word *'monogenes'* is the *only* word in the ancient Greek Biblical texts which bears the translation 'only begotten.'[69] This term is found a total of nine times in the New Testament Greek manuscripts, and the translation of this term in the gospel known as 'John' and the 'First Epistle of John' form the foundation of this 'Christian' doctrine. Of the nine occurrences of this term, *'monogenes'* is found three times in Luke (7:12, 8:42, and 9:38), but only in reference to individuals other than Jesus, and in *none* of these cases is it translated 'only begotten.' That fact alone is curious. A person would rationally expect an honest and unbiased translation to render the same Greek word into equivalent English in all instances. Clearly that is not the case, despite reasonable expectations.

Only John uses the term *'monogenes'* in reference to Jesus.[70] The

---

69. Kittel, Gerhard and Gerhard Friedrich. p. 607.
70. Kittel, Gerhard and Gerhard Friedrich. p. 607.

(SECTION 2) GOD

term is found in five of the six remaining New Testament occurrences of the term, namely John 1:14, 1:18, 3:16, 3:18, and First Epistle of John 4:9. John 3:16 reads, "For God so loved the world that He gave His only begotten son…" Such a crucial element of church doctrine, and the other three gospel authors neglected to record it? The doctrine does not exactly exorcise the ghost of doubt which suggests that, viewed objectively, the vote appears to be three gospel writers to one that this exclusive label doesn't apply. By way of comparison, all four gospel authors agree that Jesus rode the donkey (Matthew 21:7, Mark 11:7, Luke 19:35, and John 12:14), which is relatively low on the list of significant details. But three of the gospel authors fail to support the critical "begotten, not made" element of creed? Hardly a sensible balance of priorities, one would think. Should the doctrine be true, that is.

So three of the nine New Testament occurrences of the term *'monogenes'* are in the gospel known as 'Luke,' and refer to other than Jesus. Of the remaining six occurrences, the four found in the gospel known as 'John' and the one found in the First Epistle of John are held to describe Jesus. The ninth occurrence of the term *'monogenes'* unroofs a hornet's nest of difficulties, for "Isaac is *monogenes* in Heb. 11:7."[71] One is led to question Biblical accuracy at this point, for Isaac was never the only begotten son of Abraham. How could he have been, when Ishmael was born 14 years prior to the birth of Isaac? Comparison of Genesis 16:16 "Abram was eighty-six years old when Hagar bore him Ishmael." with Genesis 21:5 "Abraham was a hundred years old when his son Isaac was born to him" reveals the age difference. Noting that in Genesis 17:25 Ishmael was circumcised at the age of thirteen, one year prior to the birth of Isaac, confirms. Furthermore, Ishmael and Isaac both outlived their father, Abraham, as documented in Genesis 25:8-9. So how could Isaac ever, at any moment in time, have been Abraham's 'only begotten son?'

---

71. Kittel, Gerhard and Gerhard Friedrich. p. 607.

(2.B5) Doctrinal Differences / Jesus Begotten?

A frequently encountered reflex defense is the assertion that Ishmael was born out of illicit union between Abraham and Hagar, Sarah's maidservant. Therefore, some people assert that Ishmael was illegitimate – a bastard child – and so he doesn't count. This sounds like an argument worthy of consideration, but does it hold holy water? A common sense observation is that Ishmael was Abraham's begotten son regardless of the nature of the parental relationship. More concrete validation of the rank of Ishmael as Abraham's legitimate son is simply that *God* recognized him as such, as found in many passages of the Bible, including Genesis 16:11, 16:15, 17:7, 17:23, 17:25, 21:11. If God recognized Ishmael as Abraham's son, who of mankind dares to differ?

But man is inclined to argument, so looking at all angles a person should recognize that polygamy was an accepted practice according to the laws of the Old Testament.[72] Examples include Rachel, Leah, and their handmaids (Gen ch. 29 and 30), Lamech (Gen 4:19), Gideon (Judges 8:30), David (II Samuel 5:13), and the archetype of marital plurality, Solomon (1 Kings 11:3). *The Oxford Dictionary of the Jewish Religion* notes that polygamy was permitted in the laws of the Old Testament, and was recognized as legally valid by the rabbis.[73] *Encyclopedia Judaica* further acknowledges the common nature of polygamy amongst the upper classes in Biblical times.[74] Polygamy persisted up until the tenth century, at which time it was officially banned amongst the Ashkenazi Jews by Rabbenu Gershom; the practice, however, persisted amongst the Sephardi Jews.[75,76] To give an idea of the acceptability of polygamy even in modern Judaic law (not

---

72. Meagher, Paul Kevin et al. Vol 3, p. 2821.

73. Werblowsky, R. J. Zwi and Geoffrey Wigoder. p. 540.

74. *Encyclopaedia Judaica*. Vol 11, p.1026.

75. Werblowsky, R. J. Zwi and Geoffrey Wigoder. p. 540.

76. Roth, Cecil B. Litt., M.A., D. Phil. and Geoffrey Wigoder, D. Phil. (editors-in-chief). 1975. *The New Standard Jewish Encyclopedia*. W. H. Allen. p. 1550.

to mention an indication of the religiously overriding influence of politics), the chief rabbis of Israel officially banned the practice only as recently as 1950.[77]

For all of the above reasons, it would seem reasonable for a person to accept that when the Bible describes Hagar as Abraham's second wife (Genesis 16:3, "...Sarai, Abram's wife, took Hagar the Egyptian, her slave-girl, and gave her to her husband Abram as a *wife*." [emphasis mine]), it means precisely what it says. The idea of polygamy being permissible may offend a lot of modern Western sensitivities. Be that as it may. Whether a person likes it or not, the point is that Abraham was acting within the laws of his time, and Ishmael was therefore a legitimate child.

Nonetheless, there are still those who assert that Hagar was Abraham's concubine, despite scripture to the contrary. Even that claim has an answer. According to Old Testament law, concubines (as well as multiple wives) were legally permitted, and the offspring of a man's concubines and wives had equal rights. To quote Hasting's *Dictionary of the Bible*, "...there does not seem to have been any inferiority in the position of the concubine as compared with that of the wife, nor was any idea of illegitimacy, in our sense of the word, connected with her children."[78] Jacob M. Myers, professor at the Lutheran Theological Seminary, contributor to the *Interpreter's Dictionary of the Bible,* and acknowledged Old Testament scholar, comments in his *Invitation to The Old Testament*:

> "Archaeological discoveries help us to fill in the details of the Biblical narrative and to explain many of the otherwise obscure references and strange customs that were commonplace in Abraham's world and time. For instance, the whole series of practices relating to the birth of Ishmael and the

---

77. Werblowsky, R. J. Zwi and Geoffrey Wigoder. p. 540.
78. Hastings, James. *Dictionary of The Bible*. p. 292

(2.B5) Doctrinal Differences / Jesus Begotten?

subsequent treatment of Hagar, his mother...all are now known to have been normal everyday occurrences regulated by law.

A Nuzi marriage contract provides that a childless wife may take a woman of the country and marry her to her husband to obtain progeny. But she may not drive out the offspring even if she later has children of her own. The child born of the handmaid has the same status as the one born to the wife."[79]

Returning to the '*Alice in Wonderland*' perspective on reality, what makes more sense, anyway? Would God design a prophet to set less than an ideal example, by violating the exact same commandments which he bears from The Creator? Would God send a prophet with a 'do as I say, not as I do' message? Alice might find much more comfort in the assumption that God created prophets to embody the message of revelation in their actions as well as their words.

So could Hellenized Western opinions be wrong? Does it not make more sense for Abraham to have acted, as would be expected of a prophet, within the laws of his time by engaging Hagar in a lawful relationship?

Given the above evidences, no matter how a person cuts the cake of Ishmael's conception, the union between his parents was legal according to Old Testament law, God Himself endorsed Ishmael as Abraham's son, and the chronology in the Old Testament reveals that Ishmael was without a doubt the first begotten son of Abraham. Look up 'Ismael' in the *New Catholic Encyclopedia* (the reference of those who would be most likely to oppose, on ideological grounds, the piecing together of this puzzle), and a person finds the following agreement: "Ismael (Ishmael), son of Abraham, Abraham's firstborn..."[80]

---

79. Myers, Jacob M. 1966. *Invitation to the Old Testament.* New York: Doubleday & Company. p. 26.

80. *New Catholic Encyclopedia.* Vol 7, p. 690.

(SECTION 2) GOD

A person might reasonably question why Trinitarian Christianity would wish to conceal this truth. The answer, though distasteful to those who do not accept any reality contrary to their own opinion, is that Biblical use of the term *'monogenes'* to describe Isaac as the only begotten son of Abraham is clearly either metaphorical, a mistranslation, or inaccurate. If a person accepts the term to be metaphorical, then literal understanding of *'monogenes'* as it relates to Jesus in the five passages of 'John' is indefensible. The doctrine of Jesus actually being 'begotten' of God is readily recognized as unacceptable, especially when the aforementioned Biblical reference to David as a previously 'begotten son of God' (Psalms 2:7) is factored into the equation.

Should the error be understood to fall into the realm of mistranslation, then both the mistranslation and the doctrine deserve correction.

On the other hand, should the term *'monogenes'* be considered a Biblical inaccuracy a greater challenge surfaces – that of reconciling a Biblical error with the infallibility of God.

Understandably, the most modern and faithful translations of the Bible are quietly discarding the word 'begotten.' The *Revised Standard Version*, the *New Revised Standard Version*, *The Good News Bible*, *The New English Bible*, *The Jerusalem Bible*, the *New International Version*, and many others have unceremoniously expunged the word 'begotten' as an interpolation. By so doing, they are narrowing the gap between Christian and Islamic theology, for as stated in the Holy Qur'an, "...it is not consonant with the majesty of (Allah) Most Gracious that He should beget a son" (TMQ 19:92), and, "He (Allah) begets not, nor is He begotten" (TMQ 112:3).

(2.B) DOCTRINAL DIFFERENCES
(2.B6)
Christ Jesus, Son of God?

> "One of the most striking differences between
> a cat and a lie is that a cat has only nine lives."
> – Mark Twain, *"Pudd'nhead Wilson's Calendar,"* ch. 7

Son of God, son of David, or son of man? Jesus is identified as 'son of David' 14 times in the New Testament, starting with the very first verse – Matthew 1:1. Luke 3:23-31 documents that Jesus is 41 generations removed from being a true son to David, while Matthew 1:1-16 lists 26 generations of separation between Jesus and the literal title of 'son of David.' Jesus, a distant descendant of David and a prophet in his lineage, can only wear the title metaphorically. But how, then, should a person understand the title 'son of God?'

The 'Trilemma' is a common proposal of Christian missionaries, stating that "Jesus was either a lunatic, a liar, or the Son of God, as he claimed to be." The problem with this statement is that a person's choices are limited to the offered options, two of which are selectively implausible. Catchy though the proposal may be, it neglects to mention the one other most likely option. There should be no doubt that Jesus was not a lunatic, neither was he a liar. There should also

(SECTION 2) GOD

be no doubt that Jesus was *precisely* what he claimed to be – but what, exactly, was that? Jesus called himself 'Son of Man' frequently, consistently, perhaps even emphatically, but where did he elevate himself above the status of human prophethood? Bluntly put, where in the Bible did Jesus claim the title of 'Son of God?'

Discussion of this issue necessarily begins with consideration of what the phrase 'Son of God' means in the first place. A person can safely assume that no popular religion suggests that God took a wife and had a child. Even safer is the assumption that no popular religion conceives God to have fathered a child through a human mother *outside* of marriage. Furthermore, any suggestion of God having physically mated with an element of His creation is so far beyond the limits of religious tolerance as to plummet down the sheer cliff of blasphemy, chasing the mythology of the Greeks.

With no rational resolution available within the tenets of Christian doctrine, the only avenue for closure on this issue is to claim yet another doctrinal mystery. Here is where the Muslim recalls the common sense question posed in the Qur'an, "How can He have a son when He has no consort?" (TMQ 6:101), while others throw the line, "But God can do anything" into the arena of discussion. The Islamic challenge, however, is that Allah does not do inappropriate things – Allah (God) does Godly things. In the Islamic viewpoint God's character is integral with His being and consistent with His Majesty.

Regardless of a person's viewpoint, both Christians and Muslims should question whether Biblical teachings support the theory of Jesus being the 'son of God.' For Christians, the answer to this query will either confirm or destroy a critical tenet of Trinitarian faith. The issue likewise has significance for Muslims, who are bidden by their own book to assign priority to truth over doctrine. No matter how strongly a Muslim believes any specific doctrine, Muslims are

(2.B6) Doctrinal Differences / Christ Jesus, Son of God?

commanded to give priority to the truth of God over personal preconceptions and institutionalized beliefs. Thus, although Islam teaches that God is One and Eternal, alone and without partner, not begotten and not begetting (i.e., without a son), all Muslims are commanded to put the truth of God above doctrine – even their own. The ritualized Muslim prayer contains the first *surah* (Al-Fatiha) as an integral element, repeated no less that 17 times in the day, and this *surah* does *not* give thanks to being Muslim or guided to Islam. Rather, God is glorified and guidance is sought to 'the straight way' – whatever that may be – even if it differs from a person's preconceptions and desires. In regard to the present topic, the Qur'an bears the following message:

"Say: 'If (Allah) Most Gracious had a son, I would be the first to worship.'" (TMQ 43:81)

Islam, then, commands something foreign to the framework of other 'accept or be ostracized' religions, and that is a willingness, nay, a *commandment* to prove all things and live by that proof. The significance for Muslims, then, is to accept the challenge of defending their doctrinal viewpoint, for they are religiously bound to the truth of the situation.

With regard to the alleged sonship of Jesus, a person could reasonably begin by questioning why, if Jesus is the 'Son of God,' Israel (also referred to as Ephraim) is described in Jeremiah 31:9 as, "...for I (God) am a father to Israel, and Ephraim (i.e., Israel) is my firstborn" and in Exodus 4:22 as, "...Israel is My son, even my firstborn." Unless a person conceives God to have lost count, selective application of the phrase 'son of God' to support the doctrine of divine sonship of Jesus may begin to look suspect. Many suggest it is more sensible to resolve this issue by interpreting the above in the context of Romans 8:14, which reads, "For as many as are led by the Spirit of God, they are the sons of God."

(SECTION 2) GOD

The conclusion that the Biblical translation 'Son of God' is metaphorical and, as is the case with the term *'christos,'* not intended to imply exclusivity is a matter of course in the minds of many. After all, *The Oxford Dictionary of the Jewish Religion* states in no uncertain terms that in Jewish idiom the Hebrew which is translated to 'Son of God' is clearly metaphorical. To quote, "Son of God, term occasionally found in Jewish literature, Biblical and post-Biblical, but nowhere implying physical descent from the Godhead."[81] The world knows where the Jews stand on the issue of Jesus, but this comment is not in reference to Jesus but to the usage of the Hebraic term which is translated "Son of God" in the Old and New Testaments. The teaching of the above reference coincides with the conclusion that the expression 'Son of God' is nothing more than a metaphor for a righteous individual. Hasting's *Bible Dictionary* comments:

> "In Semitic usage 'sonship' is a conception somewhat loosely employed to denote moral rather than physical or metaphysical relationship. Thus 'sons of Belial' (Jg 19:22 etc.) are wicked men, not descendants of Belial; and in the NT the 'children of the bridechamber' are wedding guests. So a 'son of God' is a man, or even a people, who reflect the character of God. There is little evidence that the title was used in Jewish circles of the Messiah, and a sonship which implied more than a moral relationship would be contrary to Jewish monotheism."[82]

And in any case, one would think that if anyone should be considered a 'son of God,' the first candidate according to the Bible should be Adam, as stated in Luke 3:38: "...Adam, which was the son of God."

---

81. Werblowsky, R. J. Zwi and Geoffrey Wigoder. p. 653.
82. Hastings, James. *Dictionary of The Bible*. p. 143.

(2.B6) DOCTRINAL DIFFERENCES / CHRIST JESUS, SON OF GOD?

Those who rebut by quoting Matthew 3:17 ("And suddenly a voice came from heaven, saying, 'This is My beloved son, in whom I am well pleased'") have overlooked the point that the Bible describes many people (Israel and Adam included) as 'sons of God.' Both II Samuel 7:13-14 and I Chronicles 22:10 read, "He (Solomon) shall build a house for My name, and I will establish the throne of his kingdom forever. I will be his Father, and he shall be My son." What follows is a clear reference to the humanity of this 'son of God,' for the very next verse points out that not even a 'son of God' is exempt from iniquity and error, and if so deserving, will be punished.

Entire nations are referenced as sons, or children of God. Examples include:

Genesis 6:2, "That the *sons of God* saw the daughters of men..."

Genesis 6:4, "There were giants on the earth in those days, and also afterward, when the *sons of God* came in to the daughters of men..."

Deuteronomy 14:1, "Ye are the *children* of the Lord your God."

Job 1:6, "Now there was a day when the *sons of God* came to present themselves before the LORD..."

Job 2:1, "Again there was a day when the *sons of God* came to present themselves before the LORD..."

Job 38:7, "When the morning stars sang together, and all the *sons of God* shouted for joy?"

Philippians 2:15, "that you may become blameless and harmless, *children of God* without fault in the midst of a crooked and perverse generation..."

(SECTION 2) GOD

1 John 3:1-2, "Behold what manner of love the Father has bestowed on us, that we should be called *children of God!*...Beloved, now we are *children of God*...

Jesus, himself, is recorded as having declared, "Blessed are the peacemakers, for they shall be called *sons of God*" (Matthew 5:9). In Matthew 5:45, Jesus is recorded as having prescribed to his followers the attainment of noble attributes, "that you may be sons of your Father in heaven." Not exclusively *his* Father, but *their* Father. Furthermore, John 1:12 reads, "But as many as received Him, to them He gave the right to become *children of God*...". If the scripture of the Bible and the words of Jesus were respected, it would appear that the office of 'child of God' could be aspired to by any person of piety, and not just an imaginary birthright of one particular prophet.

Graham Stanton comments,

"In the Graeco-Roman world heroes, rulers, and philosophers were called sons of God. In the Old Testament 'son of God' is used of angels or heavenly beings (e.g. Gen. 6:2, 4; Deut. 32:8; Job 1:6-12), Israel or Israelites (e.g. Ex. 4:22; Hosea 11:1), and also of the king (notably in 2 Sam. 7:14 and Psalm 2:7)."[83]

And Joel Carmichael elaborates,

"The title "son of God" was of course entirely familiar to Jews in Jesus' lifetime and indeed for centuries before: *all* Jews were sons of God; this was in fact what distinguished them from other people....

---

83. Stanton, Graham N. Pp. 224-225.

(2.B6) Doctrinal Differences / Christ Jesus, Son of God?

During the postexilic period in Jewish history the word was further applied to any particular pious man; ultimately it became common in reference to the Righteous Man and the Prince.

In all these cases of Jewish usage, the phrase was plainly a mere metaphor to emphasize a particularly close connection between individual virtue and divine authority."[84]

So if the phrase *'son of God'* was "plainly a mere metaphor," why does modern Christianity elevate Christ Jesus to 'son of God' in the literal sense of the phrase? The question echoes down the corridors of the establishment, "So where does the concept of an exclusive, unique Jesus as 'Son of God' come from?"

If a person were not confused before, they almost certainly would become so upon reading Hebrews 7:3, where Melchizedek, king of Salem, is described as, "without father, without mother, without genealogy, having neither beginning of days nor end of life, but made like the Son of God, remains a priest continually." An immortal, preexisting without origin and without parents? Fanciful thinking, or does Jesus have scriptural competition?

Harper's Bible Dictionary, under the heading 'Son of man,' points out that, "With one exception (Acts 7:56)...the term (Son of man) is used exclusively by the earthly Jesus in reference to himself."[85] Furthermore, "Jesus must have used 'Son of man' as a simple self-designation, perhaps as a self-effacing way of referring to himself simply as a human being."[86] The *New Catholic Encyclopedia*, under the heading of 'Son of man,' complements this view by stating,

---

84. Carmichael, Joel, M.A. 1962. *The Death of Jesus*. New York: The Macmillan Company. pp. 253-4.

85. Achtemeier, Paul J. p. 981.

86. Achtemeier, Paul J. p. 981.

(Section 2) God

"This title is of special interest because it was the one employed by Jesus by preference to designate Himself and His mission."*[87]

As a matter of detail, a concordance search should confirm that whereas Christ Jesus described himself as 'son of man' a total of 88 times in the New Testament, it is doubtful that he ever called himself 'son of God.' The term 'son of God' is encountered 47 times in the New Testament, but always on the lips of others, and most likely never from the mouth of Jesus himself. As per *Harper's Bible Dictionary*,

> "Although the synoptic tradition contains two sayings in which Jesus refers to himself as "son" in relation to God as his Father (Mark 13:32; Matt. 11:27 [Q]), the authenticity of these sayings is widely questioned, and it remains uncertain whether Jesus actually called himself "son" in relation to God as Father."[88]

---

87. *New Catholic Encyclopedia*. Vol 13, p. 431.

* Please note that the Aramaic, ancient Hebrew, and not-so-original 'original Greek' from which the Bible is translated all lack capitalization as a literary device. Capitalization in the translation is more a result of religious conviction than scholastic accuracy, conceived more out of doctrine than out of faithfulness to Biblical narratives. For a blatant example of such textual manipulation, a person can compare Matthew 21:9 with Psalm 118:26. Matthew 21:9 quotes Psalm 118:26, but conveniently capitalizes 'he' in an effort to support, by less than accurate or honest means, the alleged divinity of Jesus. Lest a person make excuses, this is not a typographical error – Matthew 23:39 duplicates the exaggeration. The problem is, this textual manipulation is blatant. Genetic analysis of the stains on the fabric of religious history is simply not necessary, for the verdict is obvious – someone has defiled the text. And lest a person defend the Bible on the basis of this being a very small inaccuracy, any group who takes the Bible for a book of guidance finds themselves painted into a corner by the Biblical caution that, "He who is faithful in what is least is faithful also in much; and he who is unjust in what is least is unjust also in much" (Luke 16:10). How, then, does this quote apply to the Bible scribes and translators themselves? For if unjust in what is least are they not, according to their own scripture, to be judged unjust in what is much (i.e., the rest of their work)?

88. Achtemeier, Paul J. p. 979.

(2.B6) Doctrinal Differences / Christ Jesus, Son of God?

Add to that,

> "It is noteworthy, however, that Jesus never claims for himself the title 'Son of God.' While he is represented as accepting it in Mark 14:61-62, both Matthew (27:64) and Luke (22:67) are at pains to tone down Jesus' acceptance of the title as though what he says to the High Priest is, "It – like the title 'messiah' – is your word, not mine."[89]

One more opinion on the use of the term "son of God" is, "Whether Jesus used it of himself is doubtful…"[90]

So might the phrase 'son of man' imply uniqueness? Apparently not -- the book of Ezekiel contains 93 references to Ezekiel as 'son of man.'

In brief, the four gospels are unanimous that Jesus referred to himself as 'son of man.' 88 times. Yet there is no verifiable passage in any single one of the gospels where Jesus unambiguously identifies himself as 'Son of God.' Not one. Anywhere.

All of which leaves an objective researcher with the following notes:

1. Jesus is assumed to be exactly what he called himself.
2. Jesus called himself "son of man."
3. Nowhere in the Bible did Jesus ever lay claim to the literal title of "son of God."
4. And in any case, in Jewish idiom the term "son of God" was either metaphorical or contrary to monotheism.

Christian clergy openly recognize the above points, but claim that although Christ Jesus never called himself 'son of God,' others did. This too has an answer.

---

89. Achtemeier, Paul J. p. 980.
90. Hastings, James. *Dictionary of The Bible*. p. 143.

(SECTION 2) GOD

Investigating the foundational manuscripts upon which the New Testament is based, a person finds that the alleged 'sonship' of Jesus is based upon the mistranslation of two Greek words -- '*pais*' and '*huios*,' both of which are taken to mean 'son.' However, such a translation appears disingenuous. The Greek word '*pais*' comes from the Hebrew '*ebed*,' which bears the primary meaning of servant, or slave. Hence, the primary translation of the phrase '*pais theou*' is 'servant of God,' with 'child' or 'son of God' being an extravagant embellishment. To quote the authority, "The Hebrew original of *pais* in the phrase *pais theou*, i.e., '*ebed*,' carries a stress on personal relationship and has first the sense of 'slave.'"[91] Interesting. More interesting because the understanding that Jesus was a prophet in the servitude of God dovetails perfectly with the fulfillment of the prophecy of Isaiah 42:1, upheld in Matthew 12:18; "Behold, My **servant** (i.e., from the Greek '*pais*') whom I have chosen, My beloved in whom my soul is well pleased..." (emphasis mine). Whether a person reads the *King James Version,* the *New King James Version*, the *New Revised Standard Version*, or the *New International Version*, the word is 'servant' in all. Considering that the purpose of revelation is to make the truth of God clear, one might think this passage to be an odd and ugly mole on the face of the doctrine of Divine sonship. After all, what better place for God to have made the doctrine clear, to have smoothed over the turbulent waters of religious difference, and to have declared Jesus to be His son along unambiguous lines such as, "Behold, My son whom I have begotten..." But He doesn't say that. For that matter, the doctrine lacks Biblical support in the recorded words of both Jesus and God, and all followers of Jesus and all men and women of God might wonder why. Unless, that is, Jesus was nothing more than the servant of God this passage seems to clearly describe.

---

91. Kittel, Gerhard and Gerhard Friedrich. p. 763.

(2.B6) Doctrinal Differences / Christ Jesus, Son of God?

Regarding the religious use of the word '*ebed*,' "The term serves as an expression of humility used by the righteous before God."[92] Furthermore, "After 100 B.C. *pais theou* more often means 'servant of God,' e.g., when applied to Moses, the prophets, or the three children (Bar. 1:20; 2:20; Dan. 9:35)."[93] A person gets into doctrinal quicksand when encountering, "Of eight instances of this phrase, one refers to Israel (Lk. 1:54), two refer to David (Lk 1:69; Acts 4:25), and the other five to Jesus (Mt. 12:18; Acts 3:13, 26; 4:27, 30)....In the few instances in which Jesus is called *pais theou* we obviously have early tradition." So Jesus did not have an exclusive on this term, and where employed the term stemmed from "early tradition."[94] Furthermore the translation, if impartial, should identify all individuals to whom the phrase was applied in similar manner. Such, however, has not been the case. Whereas *pais* has been translated 'servant' in reference to David (Acts 4:25 and Luke 1:69) and Israel (Luke 1:54), it is translated 'Son' or 'holy child' in reference to Jesus (Acts 3:13; 3:26; 4:27; 4:30). Such preferential treatment is canonically consistent, but logically flawed.

Lastly, an interesting, if not key, religious parallel is uncovered, for,

> "Thus the Greek phrase *pais tou theou*, 'servant of God,' has exactly the same connotation as the Muslim name Abdallah -- the 'servant of Allah.'"[95]

The symmetry is all the more shocking, for The Qur'an relates Jesus as having identified himself as just this – Abdallah ('abd' being Arabic for slave, or servant, Abdallah [Abd-Allah] means slave or servant of Allah). According to the story, when Mary returned to her

---

92. Kittel, Gerhard and Gerhard Friedrich. p. 763.
93. Kittel, Gerhard and Gerhard Friedrich. p. 765.
94. Kittel, Gerhard and Gerhard Friedrich. p. 767.
95. Carmichael, Joel. pp. 255-6.

(SECTION 2) GOD

family with the newly born baby, she was accused of having been unchaste. Speaking from the cradle in a miracle which gave credence to his claims, the baby, Christ Jesus, began his defense of his mother's virtue with the words, "*Inni Abdullah...*" which means, "I am indeed Abdullah (i.e., a servant of Allah)..." (TMQ 19:30).

Translation of the New Testament Greek, '*huios*', to 'son' (in the literal meaning of the word) is similarly flawed. On page 1210 of Kittel and Friedrich's *Theological Dictionary of the New Testament*, the New Testament usage of *huios* is shown to journey from literal meaning (Jesus as the son of Mary), to metaphorical (believers as sons to the king as in Matt. 17:25-26), to more metaphorical (The believers as God's sons, as in Matt. 7:9 and Heb 12:5), to understandably metaphorical (as God's elect being sons of Abraham [Luke 19:9]), to extremely metaphorical (with students being identified as sons of the Pharisees [Matt. 12:27, Acts 23:6]), to biologically metaphorical (as in John 19:26, where Jesus describes his favorite disciple to Mary as 'her son'), to blindingly metaphorical as "sons of the kingdom," (Matt. 8:12), "of peace" (Luke. 10:6), "of light" (Luke. 16:8), and of everything from "this aeon" (Luke 16:8) to "of thunder" (Mark 3:17). The predominant relationship 'metaphor' reverberates in harmonic oscillation down the receptors of reason, settling with satisfaction on the words of Stanton:

"Most scholars agree that the Aramaic or Hebrew word behind 'son' is 'servant.' So as the Spirit descends on Jesus at his baptism, Jesus is addressed by the voice from heaven in terms of Isaiah 42:1: 'Behold my servant...my chosen...I have put my Spirit upon him.' So although Mark 1:11 and 9:7 affirm that Jesus is called by God to a special messianic task, the emphasis is on Jesus' role as the anointed servant, rather than as Son of God."[96]

---

96. Stanton, Graham N. p. 225.

(2.B6) Doctrinal Differences / Christ Jesus, Son of God?

The objective researcher now needs to expand the list of notes as follows:
1. Jesus is assumed to be exactly what he called himself.
2. Jesus called himself "son of man."
3. Nowhere in the Bible did Jesus ever lay claim to the literal title of "son of God."
4. And in any case, in Jewish idiom the term "son of God" was either metaphorical or contrary to monotheism.
5. The primary translation of the phrase '*pais theou*' is 'servant of God,' and not 'son of God.'
6. '*huios*,' which is translated from New Testament Greek to the word 'son,' is used metaphorically with such frequency as to make literal translation indefensible.
7. Hence, when others spoke of Jesus as 'son of God,' the metaphorical sense can be assumed given Jewish idiom, in combination with the fact that identifying Christ Jesus as a literal 'son of God' would have provoked stoning on the basis of blasphemy, given the strictness of Jewish monotheism.

So, having ruled out what Jesus calls himself, as well as what others called him, a person returns to the question of how the Church justifies the claim of divine sonship of Jesus.

Some assert that Jesus was the 'son of God' in a unique and literal sense because he called God, 'Father.' ...But what do other people call God? For that matter, what is Jesus recorded as having taught in the Bible, if not, "In this manner, therefore, pray: Our Father..." (Matthew 6:9)? So not only did Jesus teach that any person can attain the title of 'son of God,' but he taught mankind to identify God as 'Father.'

Some skirt the issue by asserting that Jesus was human during life but became partner in divinity following crucifixion. But in Mark

(SECTION 2) GOD

14:62, Jesus alludes to the Day of Judgement, in which he states that people will see him as, "the Son of Man sitting at the right hand of the Power, and coming with the clouds of heaven." So if Jesus is the 'Son of Man' come the Day of Judgement, what is he between now and then? And if he was mistaken in his statement, was he receiving divinely inerrant revelation or was he speaking from his own mind and making mistakes in so doing? For if his words were revelation then he could be no other than the 'Son of Man' as claimed, but if his words were in error, what part of his teachings *can* a person trust?

The question repeats itself, "Where did the concept of exclusive divine son-ship come from?"

The scholars of the Church in which the doctrine was established can answer that question, as follows:

> "It was, however, at the Council of Nicaea that the Church was constrained by circumstances to introduce non-Biblical categories into its authentic description of the Son's relation to the Father. The Arian controversy occasioned this determination."[97]

'Constrained by circumstances,' 'constrained by circumstances' – what, exactly, does that phrase mean? A person cannot be faulted for drawing imaginary parallels, such as, "I was constrained by circumstances – I didn't have enough money for the necklace, so I stole it" or, "I was constrained by circumstances – the truth wouldn't work, so I lied." Hardly the most honorable of justifications.

In any case, the above quote references the pressures upon The Council of Nicaea to derive a solution to the Arian controversy-pressures sufficient to require the introduction of 'non-Biblical categories.' Arius, the aforementioned Christian priest of Alexandria,

---

97. *New Catholic Encyclopedia*. Vol 13, p. 426.

(2.B6) Doctrinal Differences / Christ Jesus, Son of God?

argued that the divine Triad was composed of three separate and distinct realities. Arius professed belief in Christ Jesus as being of created, finite nature. In other words, a man. His major work, *Thalia* (Banquet), was publicized in the year 323 CE. The famous Arian syllogism proposed that if Jesus was a man, then a person shouldn't suggest that he was God, and if Jesus was God, a person shouldn't say he died. Arius proposed that the God-Man concept doesn't stand up to critical analysis, and defies explanation.

The Arian challenges to Trinitarian theology would swamp and sink below the surface of relevant history if any single person could explain the God-Man concept. But 1,700 years of sifting the sand of apologetics have failed to yield a jewel of Trinitarian reason of sufficient brilliance to be spiritually illuminating to the majority of mankind. The challenges periodically waft through the porous walls of obstinate doctrine, posing such questions as, "When God reportedly became man, did He give up His Divine powers?" If He did, then He wasn't God anymore, and if He didn't, He wasn't man. If the God-Man died on the cross, does this mean God died? No, of course not. So who died? Just the 'Man' part? But in that case the totality of the person didn't die – only a part of him died. Just the man part dying makes as much sense as someone claiming to have eaten a salami sandwich...except for the bread, or to have eaten an egg...except for the yolk. The language satisfies the grammatical qualifications of a sentence, but boils down to a nonsensical description of snacking on salami slices or sections of egg white.

Furthermore, if it was a man who died, or the man-portion of a proposed union of humanity and divinity, then the sacrifice wasn't good enough, for the claim is that only a divine sacrifice would have been sufficient to atone for the sins of mankind. Hence, death of the man or of the man-portion of the proposed triune being would have contributed no more to the atonement of sins than would the death of a sinless man. Which leaves little option for explanation other than to revert to the claim that some element of divinity died. Strictly monotheistic Jews, Unitarian Christians and Muslims would no doubt contend that, as for those who say it was God who died, well, they can just go to Hell. The expectation is that God, who is living and eternal, will agree.

But to continue the thought, Trinitarian doctrine claims that God not only became man, but He remained God. Unitarian thought claims that such an assertion once again satisfies the grammatical requirements of the English language for a sentence, but is the literary equivalent of an Escher illusional painting – viewed with a critical eye, a person can take in the vision, but the impossible contortions can never a reality make. It is like claiming, "I burned a stick of wood to ashes, but it's still a tree," or "I shaped a ball of clay into a cube, but it's still round." Anyone who makes such a statement is bound to be viewed with a certain reserve, if not frankly sideways, by their peers. Similarly, the Unitarian declaration is that God is God and man is man. Those who confuse the two fail to recognize that God can not give up His Godliness, because His entity is defined by His Divine attributes. Neither does God need to experience human existence in order to understand the suffering of mankind. Nobody knows the plight of mankind better than The Creator, since He created mankind with comprehensive knowledge of everything from thermoreceptors to thoughts, from cilia to subconscious. God *knows* the problems, plight, and suffering of humankind – He created a universe whose complexities transcend such obvious dimensions of human experience.

(2.B6) Doctrinal Differences / Christ Jesus, Son of God?

The "But God can do anything" defense leaves a person to consider, "Well, if God can do anything then why didn't He make sense of Trinitarian doctrine – assuming it to be correct, that is?" If God can do anything certainly He could have presented a sensible explanation which would not require resorting to the introduction of "non-Biblical categories." God could have explained who lived, who died, and how to make sense of the so-called 'Trinity.' But He didn't. Why? Did God leave humankind to figure it out for themselves, or can a person safely assume that there is no basis in religious reality for that which God did not reveal?

The concept of God providing a theology which invites objections that lack satisfying answers grates painfully against the sensitive, innate understanding of God as All-Merciful, providing clear guidance to all mankind.

Standard Trinitarian response at this point? The assertion that a person would believe if only they understood the Trinity. Standard Unitarian response? Nobody understands the Trinity -- nobody. That is why it is called a religious mystery; a mystery being something nobody understands. Talk with Trinitarian clergy long enough, bring up the above objections (and those to follow) and sooner or later the confirmed Trinitarian will admit, "It's a mystery." The "You just have to have faith" defense is not far behind. The Unitarian typically points out, however, that moments earlier the Trinitarian proposed that a person would believe, if only he or she would understand. However, when a legitimate attempt is made to understand, by way of seeking answers to relevant questions, the claim transforms to one of a religious mystery (i.e. nobody understands!). In the absence of an acceptable explanation, the initially confident assertion morphs into an admission of ignorance admixed with the suggestion that, "The only way a person can believe is to have faith" (i.e., the only way to believe is to believe). If blind, unthinking faith is the methodology God wants mankind to follow, a person may wonder why He commands mankind to reason ("'Come now, and let us reason together,' says the Lord..." Isaiah 1:18).*

Returning to the above quote, Arius' rational challenges to established Church doctrine could not be answered by Biblical reference, occasioning the need for an official policy statement from church authorities. The Council of Nicaea was convened in 325 CE, two years following the public debut of Arius' *Thalia*. Not surprisingly, the issue of Arius' theology was the principal item on the agenda, having been the impetus behind the convening of this first ecumenical council. An objective analyst would not have difficulty concluding that the Church, rather than upset the status quo by conceding unfounded doctrines to the rational Arian arguments, resorted to assembling a foundation from non-Biblical sources to support previously accepted doctrines. Condemnation of Arius as a heretic was a matter of predictable reflex.

So what is a non-Biblical source? A person can safely assume that if it is not from scripture (i.e. not from God), then it must be from the minds of men (and what does that reduce to if not human imagination?). How much safer and easier would it have been to have modified Church doctrine in conformity with rational argument and,

---

* The problem with blind indoctrination is that it doesn't work when a person knows better. A hypochondriac might believe that a placebo is medicine, if convincingly presented as such. Through blind faith in the doctor, a hypochondriac's imagined symptoms may be overcome by conviction that the prescribed sugar pills are 'just what the doctor ordered.' On the other hand, if the hypochondriac has reason to believe that the placebo is just that, the fake medicine won't work. Unitarians argue that the 'Trinity' is a great doctrinal placebo swallowed by most of the world of Christianity. Believers embrace the doctrine on trust of the authority of their Church, not realizing they are being fed a manmade doctrine lacking Divine authority or scriptural substantiation. The Unitarian argument continues with the claim that once the lack of scriptural support for the Trinity is laid bare, a person comes to understand that the 'Trinity' is simply not the medicine which The Creator has prescribed in issuing guidance to mankind.

(2.B6) Doctrinal Differences / Christ Jesus, Son of God?

more importantly, scripture? No doubt adhering to Trinitarian notions cemented the job security of Trinitarian clergy, albeit upon questionable tenets of faith clothed in a somewhat suspect mantle of Church approval.

Likewise, no doubt confidence in Church teachings waned in the active minds of thinkers like Arius – thinkers who, in the present day, are supported by Christian sources which contribute to the understanding that Jesus never claimed sonship or partnership in divinity, and for that matter, neither did his disciples. Furthermore, the evidence suggests that neither did Paul.*

The body of the above quote goes on to outline some of the constructed doctrines, such as consubstantiality, begotten and not made, etc., followed by the unbelievably straight-faced assertion that Augustine sought the ideology most compatible with inbred human understanding (i.e., "Augustine sought in man's psychology or way of knowing the natural analogate for understanding the eternal generation of the Son."[98]). More than one person will read the above and mutter, "They...are...joking – they must be." After all, is this not the same doctrine responsible for the Medieval and Spanish inquisitions,

---

* This statement may come as a shock, for it is a common impression that Paul attributed divine sonship to Jesus. It is possible that he did, but given the evidence above and the fact that nobody stoned him to death for blasphemy, most likely he did not. The simple fact of the matter is that the evidence cited above applies to all authors of the New Testament. The confusion lies in differentiating the teachings of Paul from those of Pauline theology. Whereas Paul appears to have spoken of Christ Jesus as a 'son of God' in the metaphorical sense, typical of the idiom of his age, the designers of Pauline theology appear to have bent the words of Paul into service for a more literal interpretation. Hence, it would appear that it was not Paul who conceived Jesus to be a literal 'son of God,' but rather those who followed to design a theology in his name. In the end, it is a fine point and one which doesn't matter much, for the teachings of Jesus and those of Paul (as discussed in following chapters) were largely at variance with one another, and a person simply has to choose sides between the two.

98. *New Catholic Encyclopedia.* Vol 13, p. 426.

(SECTION 2) GOD

the eight waves of the Christian Crusades, and countless forced conversions of natives during the age of colonialism? The doctrine that makes so much sense that over twelve million died under torture in denial of the tenets of Trinitarian faith? *Twelve million!* The doctrine that makes so much sense that, to this day, African natives have to be coerced into conversion through baiting with food and medicine?

In startling contrast, torture is forbidden in the Islamic religion. Even capital punishment must be implemented quickly and humanely, and only when justified by the law. As a historical footnote the torture of the medieval inquisition was initiated not by Pope Gregory IX, who instituted the papal Inquisition in 1231, but, at the height of irony, by Pope *Innocent* IV, who issued the Bull *Ad extirpanda*, authorizing torture in the year 1252.[99] Authorizing torture under the direction of the inquisitors was the first step, which must have disappointed those of the clergy who wished to get their hands dirty, up close and personal. To accommodate such lofty Christian sentiments, "...in 1256 Pope Alexander IV gave them (the inquisitors) the right to mutually absolve one another and grant dispensations to their colleagues. With this legal and moral issue circumvented, one inquisitor could torture and his companion then absolve him."[100] The average man on the street will be led to conclude that if the need for torture and coercion to refresh memories is an index of innate understanding, someone needs to rewrite the textbooks of clinical psychiatry.

Sympathizers might take a moment to imagine an un-indoctrinated individual, anywhere in the world. Imagine this person enjoying a life in quiet contemplation of the perfect symmetry of creation, seeking the reality of God. Imagine the foreign natives of distant

---

99. *Encyclopaedia Britannica.* CD-ROM. (Under "Inquisition").

100. Burman, Edward. 1984. *The Inquisition, The Hammer of Heresy.* New York: Dorset Press. p. 62.

(2.B6) Doctrinal Differences / Christ Jesus, Son of God?

lands, the illiterate masses, the lone individual on a tropical island. How many of them can be imagined to one day snap their fingers, slap their forehead in sudden realization and spiritual awakening, and proclaim the Father, Son and Holy Spirit?

The likelihood is slim to none that Augustine's judgement was based on a prospective, double-blinded, controlled and randomized study. Should the hundreds of thousands of 'heretic' Unitarian Christians who were burned at the stake in intolerant Trinitarian judgement be asked, they could be expected to have some very reasonable objections. In the modern day, some of them might even reference the Qur'an, "Let there be no compulsion in religion…" (TMQ 2:256).

But to return to the immediate issue, one more difficulty which requires smoothing over in the interest of the 'son of God' doctrine concerns the following quotes:

> "In the Gospel of St. John, twice the title Son of God means nothing more than Messiah. Thus Nathanael's confession of faith, 'Rabbi, thou art the Son of God, thou art King of Israel!' (Jn 1:49) regards the two as equivalent (see also 11.27)."[101]

> "It is not always clear what the term (Son of God) means when spoken by the demons; it may mean only man of God (Mt 8.29 and parallels; Lk 8.28; Mk 3.11; Mk 1.25 and parallels: the Holy One of God), but in Lk 4.41 it clearly means the Messiah."[102]

> "Used by the centurion at the Crucifixion, it (Son of God) seems to have meant only a just man (cf. Mt 27.54 and Mk 15.39 with Lk 23.47)."[103]

---

101. *New Catholic Encyclopedia.* Vol 13, p. 430.
102. *New Catholic Encyclopedia.* Vol 13, p. 429.
103. *New Catholic Encyclopedia.* Vol 13, p. 429.

(SECTION 2) GOD

The above three quotes suggest one of two possible scenarios. In the first scenario, the term 'son of God' can be understood to mean Messiah, King of Israel, 'man of God,' 'holy one of God,' or simply a just (i.e. righteous) man, for parallel stories are encountered in the gospels relating these terms as if synonymous. For example, the demons were recorded as having identified Jesus as "the holy one of God" in one account and "Son of God" in another, and the centurion is recorded as having identified Jesus as the "Son of God" in Matthew 27:54 and Mark 15:39, but as "a righteous man" in Luke 23:47. So maybe they mean the same thing. In the second scenario, however, a person could not be faulted for suggesting that because the parallel accounts record the same events, but with different words, this variance represents a Biblical inaccuracy. In either case, there is a problem. If the terms are synonymous, and a person cannot trust the Bible enough to understand the meaning of 'Son of God' in one instance, how can anybody interpret the same phrase with confidence elsewhere? And if the disagreement in the reports represents a Biblical inaccuracy, in which one gospel author got it right and the other(s) got it wrong, then who wants to base salvation on the flip of a coin?

A further difficulty in the above quote is that two of the above-referenced gospels tell different stories, though witnessing the same event. Matthew 8:28-29 records two possessed men in the tombs and Luke 8:26-28 only one single possessed man. An ungodly Biblical inaccuracy or what? Even if a person defends the Bible as being the inspired word of God – not the actual word, but the inspired word – would God inspire inaccuracy?

Some might wonder why Christian authors smooth over Biblical discrepancies such as this, and such as those cataloged in the upcoming sections on the Old and New Testaments (Sections 3.A. and 3.B.). Others take a more jaundiced view. The Christian world would like to believe that Church authorities are sincere and pious individuals,

(2.B6) Doctrinal Differences / Christ Jesus, Son of God?

seeking truth and not deception. But how many people would bend the truth to gain 10% of the gross income of an entire congregation? Suspicion can be fairly high that, in the words of George Bernard Shaw, "A government which robs Peter to pay Paul can always depend on the support of Paul."[104] In other words, a church which tithes the congregation in order to pay the salary and living expenses of the clergy can always depend on the support of the clergy.

A follow-on question is, "how many Bible-toting, Sunday school-teaching, regular churchgoers would bend the truth under pressure of wealth?" The person who conceives of none is either daft or lying. Current affairs document countless priests and ministers who not only bend the truth, but the altar boys as well. Jesus warned about these false 'men of God' in Matthew 7:15-16: "Beware of false prophets, who come to you in sheep's clothing, but inwardly they are ravenous wolves. You will know them by their fruits..." And many of them have proven to be pretty fruity, all right. There has to be some reason why hundreds of Roman Catholic priests have contracted and died of AIDS, as reported in *The Kansas City Star* (Jan 30, 2000). According to the front-page article, priests are dying of AIDS at a rate somewhere between four and eleven times that of the general U.S. population. Deceptive and falsified death certificates disrupt analysis, but "...many priests and medical experts now agree that at least 300 priests have died." Some put the number closer to 1,000. Ruling out mosquito bites, a person has to conclude that a strong current of hypocrisy is coursing through the Roman Catholic clergy.* And yet, this is the quality of men who are chosen to be trusted leaders of congregations, counselors of faith, and absolvers of sins.

---

104. Shaw, George Bernard. 1944. *Everybody's Political What's What?* Ch. 30.

* In addition, approximately 5% of Catholic clergy are reported to be pedophiles, as per *Time Magazine*, 'Can the Church be Saved?,' April 1, 2002, p. 60.

(SECTION 2) GOD

The overshadowing dilemma, then, aside from all other considerations, returns to the discussion earlier in this chapter – namely what does 'Son of God' mean? And how would the original Hebrew translate? From '*ebed*' to 'slave' or 'son?' Even if the correct translation is 'son,' how is this different from all the other 'sons of God' who were clearly nothing more than righteous individuals or, at most, prophets? The *New Catholic Encyclopedia* states, in association with R. Bultmann's historical criticism of the New Testament, "Son of God has recently been denied a place in theology on the grounds that, as found in NT writings, it is part of the mythological garb in which the primitive Church clothed its faith....The problem confronting one constructing an adequate theological idea of Son of God is to determine the content that the idea expresses."[105] Religious freethinkers around the world may exclaim in unison, "Excuse me? The Catholic Church admits that even the world of Christianity cannot agree on the meaning of 'Son of God?'"

Given non-conformity in understanding, one comes to grasp the survival-based need of the early church to define one particular belief system, whether true or not. Enter the Council of Chalcedon in 451 C.E., which declared the dogmatic definition which since has come to dominate Christology: "...one and the same Christ, Son, Lord, only-begotten, known in two natures, without confusion, without change, without division, without separation."[106] Emphasis should be placed upon the "without confusion" and "without division" assertions. Anyone who embraces the evidence of this chapter readily recognizes that the above quote is a statement, but not a truth. Confusion, division and separation have plagued the seekers of truth in Christianity since the time of Jesus.

---

105. *New Catholic Encyclopedia.* Vol 13, p. 431.

106. *Catholic Encyclopedia.*CD-Rom; 1914 edition, under 'Council of Chalcedon.'

(2.B6) DOCTRINAL DIFFERENCES / CHRIST JESUS, SON OF GOD?

In the end, many people form opinions with their hearts more than with their minds. As Lehmann points out,

> "So the concept of "the son of God" led to a misunderstanding which had undreamed-of consequences. Anyone with only a superficial knowledge of the East knows that the Orientals like picturesque speech...A simple liar is a son of lies, and anyone who can go one better becomes a father of lies. The phrase "son of God" is on the very same level of speech and thought.
>
> In Semitic linguistic usage this description says nothing more than that a bond exists between a man and God. A Jew would never even dream of thinking that the son of God meant a genuine relationship between a father and a son. A son of God is a blessed man, a chosen vessel, a man who does what God wants. Any attempt to take this image literally and so deduce the divinity of the son contradicts the facts."[107]

Those who understand the expression 'son of God' to have metaphorical rather than literal meaning may achieve resolution to a multitude of parallel difficulties. In addition to resolving Christian doctrinal difficulties, recognizing 'son of God' to mean a prophet or a righteous individual, and nothing more, challenges the Christian with the focused Qur'anic teachings. In specific, Allah teaches, "...the Christians call Christ the Son of Allah. That is a saying from their mouths; (in this) they but imitate what the Unbelievers of old used to say. Allah's curse be on them: how they are deluded away from the Truth!" (TMQ 9:30).

---

107. Lehmann, Johannes. 1972. *The Jesus Report*. Translated by Michael Heron. London: Souvenir Press. pp. 138-9.

(Section 2) God

But lest a person misunderstand, the point is not that one book has it right and the others wrong. Not at all. The point is that all three books (OT, NT, Qur'an) have it right. Both books of the Bible, as well as the Holy Qur'an, teach the Oneness of God and the humanity of Jesus, thereby reinforcing one another. So all three have it right. What has it wrong is not the books of scripture, but the baseless doctrines which have been of such illegitimate origin as to require derivation from 'non-Biblical categories.'

(2.B) Doctrinal Differences

(2.B7) The Trinity

"The Three in One, the One in Three? Not so!
To my own God I go.
It may be He shall give me greater ease
Than your cold Christ and tangled Trinities."

– Monotheistic version of Rudyard Kipling's chapter heading to "Lispeth," *Plain Tales from the Hills.*

The Trinity is considered one of the greatest mysteries of the Christian faith. And there should be no surprise – the origin of the word itself is a mystery. The word 'Trinity' does not exist in the Bible, prompting *The New Westminster Dictionary of the Bible* to state, "The word does not occur in scripture..."[108] *The Encyclopedia of Catholicism* admits, "The doctrine of the Trinity as such is not revealed in either the OT or the NT..."[109]

The Greek for 'triad' was "A word first used of the Trinity in the Godhead by Theophilus of Antioch, who names as the Triad 'God

---

108. Gehman, Henry Snyder (editor). *The New Westminster Dictionary of the Bible.* 1970. The Westminster Press. p. 958.

109. McBrien, Richard P. (General Editor). 1995. *HarperCollins Encyclopedia of Catholicism.* New York: HarperCollins Publishers. p. 1270.

(SECTION 2) GOD

and His Word and His Wisdom'"[110] This, at the bare bones least, is a triad which makes semi-sense once a person accepts that God's words are an expression of His wisdom. Why Theophilus felt compelled to separate God from His attributes is a separate and largely irrelevant issue.

History indicates that the word 'Trinity' was first proposed by Tertullian, a third-century lawyer in Carthage, who put forth his theory on co-sharing of Divinity between God, Jesus, and the holy spirit. The fact that Tertullian was a lawyer tickles the fancy of those who have noticed that the evolutionary origin of incomprehensible words and insensible concepts frequently seems to stem from lawyers and politicians (many of whom are lawyers anyway, but with the added political requirement of lacking even the minimal ethics of the legal profession). A person wonders what was in Tertullian's fine print, and upon what evidence he based his theory. What spawned the theory which somehow escaped the astute and inspired minds of the gospel-writers, the disciples, and even Jesus himself? A person should not expect to find definitive scriptural reference, for, "The formal doctrine of the Trinity as it was defined by the great church councils of the fourth and fifth centuries is not to be found in the NT."[111] The best a person can hope for is passages which appear to suggest the Trinity, in concept if not in name.

The formal doctrines of the Trinity and Divine sonship of Jesus collectively sprung from the interpretation of the aforementioned council of Nicaea in the year 325 CE. These doctrines were incorporated into the Nicene Creed – "A profession of faith agreed upon, although with *some misgivings* because of its *non-Biblical* terminology, by the bishops at Nicaea I (325) to defend the true faith against

---

110. Cross, F. L. and E. A. Livingstone (editors). 1974. *The Oxford Dictionary of the Christian Church*. London: Oxford University Press. p. 1393.

111. Achtemeier, Paul J. p. 1099.

(2.B7) Doctrinal Differences / The Trinity

Arianism." (emphasis mine -- the 'faith' being 'true' only in the opinion of the authors of the referenced work).[112] This formula of one God existing in three co-equal persons was denied general acceptance at the time of initial conception. Born into the world of Christianity over three centuries following the ministry of Christ Jesus, many church 'fathers' could not recognize the features of the 'trinity' to be a doctrinal child conceived through the teachings of Jesus. The two dissenting bishops at the Council of Nicaea, along with Arius, were exiled to Illyricum, after which none of those in objection dared to deny the doctrine of Nicaea.[113] Only after overcoming the resistance of Arius, Athanasius of Alexandria, Hilary of Poitiers, and many other prominent church figures, were the Trinity and the Nicene creed formally ratified by the council of Constantinople in 381 CE.[114] A series of decrees penned between 380-392 CE by Emperor Theodosius I established Trinitarian Christianity as the only approved religion of the Roman empire. The Nicene Creed was subsequently made authoritative at the Council of Chalcedon in 451. The rest is history, and not a particularly attractive one at that.

History defends the understanding that the Trinitarian formula was agreed upon long after the time of Jesus and the disciples, by a group of people with self-appointed authority. Even then, the process of deriving the Trinitarian formula was so convoluted that,

> "It is difficult, in the second half of the 20th century, to offer a clear, objective, and straightforward account of the revelation, doctrinal evolution, and theological elaboration of the mystery of the Trinity. Trinitarian discussion, Roman Catholic as well as other, presents a somewhat unsteady silhouette."[115]

---
112. *New Catholic Encyclopedia*. Vol 10, p. 437.
113. *New Catholic Encyclopedia*. Vol 10, p. 433.
114. McManners, John. p. 72.
115. *New Catholic Encyclopedia*. Vol 14, p. 295.

(Section 2) God

Furthermore,

> "...the formula itself does *not* reflect the immediate consciousness of the period of origins; it was the product of 3 centuries of doctrinal development...It *is this contemporary return to the sources that is ultimately responsible for the unsteady silhouette.*" (emphasis mine) [116]

In other words, from the point of view of the Church, the problem is that educated laity are coming to trust source scriptures more than the dogmatic creed derived from the mix of creative minds and extra-Biblical sources. As if the above quote were not enough to make the point, the authors continued, seemingly for clarification and emphasis,

> "The formulation 'one God in three Persons' was not solidly established, certainly not fully assimilated into Christian life and its profession of faith, prior to the end of the 4th century. But it is precisely this formulation that has first claim to the title *the Trinitarian dogma.*
>
> Among the Apostolic Fathers, there had been *nothing even remotely* approaching such a mentality or perspective." (emphasis mine) [117]

Perhaps a person should not be surprised that, with the doctrine of the Trinity unknown to early Christians*, once proposed and approved by the Church councils, another several centuries had to

---

116. *New Catholic Encyclopedia.* Vol 14, p. 295.
117. *New Catholic Encyclopedia.* Vol 14, p. 299.
* For details as concerns the creeds of the Ante-Nicene Fathers and the evolution of the Trinity, see *The Mysteries of Jesus,* by Ruqaiyyah Waris Maqsood; Sakina Books, Oxford, pp. 194-200.

(2.B7) Doctrinal Differences / The Trinity

pass before this foreign 'Christian' concept gained acceptance. The *New Catholic Encyclopedia* observes that devotion to the Trinity was delayed until as late as the 8th century, at which time it began to take hold in monasteries at Aniane and Tours.[118]

In the midst of the growing 19th and 20th century awareness of the differences between Trinitarian doctrine and the period of origins, a person might be surprised to find one group who claim to be followers of Christ Jesus reading the following in the Holy Qur'an:

> "O People of the Book! Commit no excesses in your religion: nor say of Allah anything but the truth. Christ Jesus the son of Mary was (no more than) a Messenger of Allah, and His Word, which He bestowed on Mary, and a Spirit proceeding from Him: so believe in Allah and His Messengers. Do not say "Trinity": desist: it will be better for you: for Allah is One God: glory be to Him: (far Exalted is He) above having a son. To Him belong all things in the heavens and on earth. And enough is Allah as a Disposer of affairs" (TMQ 4:171).

And warning:

> "O People of the Book! Exceed not in your religion the bounds (of what is proper), trespassing beyond the truth, nor follow the vain desires of people who went wrong in times gone by – who misled many, and strayed (themselves) from the even Way." (TMQ 5:77)

One may wonder what, from the New Testament, separates these two groups by such a vast expanse of understanding. No doubt the key difference which divides Trinitarians from Unitarians, and Christians from Muslims, is Pauline theology. For centuries the argument has been put forth that Trinitarian Christians largely follow

---

118. *New Catholic Encyclopedia.* Vol 14, p. 306.

(SECTION 2) GOD

Pauline theology more than that of Jesus. This charge is difficult to deny, for Jesus taught the Law of the Old Testament, whereas Paul preached mysteries of faith, in denial of the Law which the prophets had suffered and struggled to convey. In disrespect to thousands of years of revelation conveyed through a long chain of esteemed prophets, and contrary to the teachings of the rabbi Jesus himself, Paul focused not on the life and teachings of Jesus, but upon his death. As Lehmann put it,

> "The only thing which Paul considers important is the Jew Jesus' death, which destroyed all hopes of liberation by a Messiah. He makes the victorious Christ out of the failed Jewish Messiah, the living out of the dead, the son of God out of the son of man."[119]

More than a few scholars consider Paul the main corrupter of Apostolic Christianity and of the teachings of Jesus;

> "What Paul proclaimed as 'Christianity' was sheer heresy which could not be based on the Jewish or Essene faith, or on the teaching of Rabbi Jesus. But, as Schonfield says, 'The Pauline heresy became the foundation of Christian orthodoxy and the legitimate church was disowned as heretical.'"[120]

Lehmann continues,

> "Paul did something that Rabbi Jesus never did and refused to do. He extended God's promise of salvation to the Gentiles; he abolished the law of Moses, and he prevented direct access to God by introducing an intermediary."[121]

Others elevate Paul to sainthood. Joel Carmichael, who commented as follows, very clearly is not one of them:

---

119. Lehmann, Johannes. pp. 125-6.
120. Lehmann, Johannes. p. 128.
121. Lehmann, Johannes. p. 134.

(2.B7) Doctrinal Differences / The Trinity

"We are a universe away from Jesus. If Jesus came "only to fulfill" the Law and the Prophets; If he thought that "not an iota, not a dot" would "pass from the Law," that the cardinal commandment was "Hear, O Israel, the Lord Our God, the Lord is one," and that "no one was good but God"....What would he have thought of Paul's handiwork! Paul's triumph meant the final obliteration of the historic Jesus; he comes to us embalmed in Christianity like a fly in amber."[122]

Many authors have pointed out the disparity in the teachings of Paul and Jesus; the best of them have avoided opinionated commentary and concentrated on simply exposing the elements of difference. Dr. Wrede comments,

"In Paul the central point is a divine act, in history but transcending history, or a complex of such acts, which impart to all mankind a ready-made salvation. Whoever believes in these divine acts – the incarnation, death, and resurrection of a celestial being, receives salvation.

And this, which to Paul is the sum of religion – the skeleton of the fabric of his piety, without which it would collapse – can this be a continuation or a remoulding of the gospel of Jesus? Where, in all this, is that gospel to be found, which Paul is said to have understood?

Of that which is to Paul all and everything, how much does Jesus know? Nothing whatever."[123]

And Dr. Johannes Weiss contributes,

---

122. Carmichael, Joel. p. 270.
123. Wrede, William. 1962. *Paul.* Translated by Edward Lummis. Lexington, Kentucky: American Theological Library Association Committee on Reprinting. p. 163.

(SECTION 2) GOD

> "Hence the faith in Christ as held by the primitive churches and by Paul was something new in comparison with the preaching of Jesus; it was a new type of religion."[124]

Which theology won the day, and why, and how, are questions left to the analyses of the above authors. Should a person come to recognize that the teachings of Paul and those of Jesus oppose one another, consideration should be given to the question: "If I had to choose between the two, to whom should I give priority – Jesus or Paul?" The question is so relevant that Michael Hart had the following to say in his scholastic tome, in which he ranks the 100 most influential men of history:

> "Although Jesus was responsible for the main ethical and moral precepts of Christianity (insofar as these differed from Judaism), St. Paul was the main developer of Christian theology, its principal proselytizer, and the author of a large portion of the New Testament."[125]

With regard to Paul's perspective,

> "He does not ask what led to Jesus' death, he only sees what it means to him personally. He turns a man who summoned people to reconciliation with God into the savior. He turns an orthodox Jewish movement into a universal religion which ultimately clashed with Judaism."[126]

The three main points where Pauline theology conflicts with that of Jesus are critical – elements so crucial that deviation from the truth threatens a person's salvation. In order of importance they rank:

---

124. Weiss, Johannes. 1909. *Paul and Jesus*. (Translated by Rev. H. J. Chaytor). London and New York: Harper and Brothers. p. 130.
125. Hart, Michael H. *The 100, A Ranking of the Most Influential Persons in History.* p. 39 of the 1978 edition by Hart Publishing Co.; p. 9 of the 1998 edition by Citadel Press. Go figure.
126. Lehmann, Johannes. p. 137.

(2.B7) Doctrinal Differences / The Trinity

(1) The divinity of Jesus alleged by Pauline theology versus the oneness of God taught by Christ Jesus; (2) Justification by faith, as proposed by Paul, versus Old Testament law, as endorsed by Christ Jesus; (3) Jesus having been a universal prophet, as per Paul, versus an ethnic prophet, as per the teachings of Christ Jesus.* Interestingly enough, these three points constitute the greatest doctrinal differences separating Christianity not only from Judaism, but also from Islam. Running a theological finger down the backbone of revealed monotheism, Trinitarian Christianity seems to stand out of joint.

To address the first of these points, Jesus is recorded as having taught the oneness of God, as in Mark 12:29: "Jesus answered him, 'The first of all the commandments is: "Hear, O Israel, the Lord our God, the Lord is one." Jesus reportedly continued with "And you shall love the Lord your God with all your heart, with all your soul, with all your mind, and with all your strength," finishing with emphasis upon the initial claim, "This is the first commandment." (Mark 12:30). Not only did Jesus stress importance by sandwiching his statement between the repeated and emphatic "This is the first commandment," but the importance of this teaching is equally stressed in Matthew 22:37 and Luke 10:27, and further complemented by the first commandment as recorded in Exodus 20:3 – "You shall have no other gods before Me." Jesus conveyed the above teaching

---

* Christ Jesus was one more prophet in the long line of prophets sent to guide the astray Israelites. As Christ Jesus so clearly affirmed, "I was not sent *except* to the lost sheep of the house of Israel." (Matthew 15:24) When Jesus sent the disciples out in the path of God, he instructed them in such a manner as to leave no uncertainty in this regard, for he told them, "Do not go into the way of the Gentiles, and do not enter a city of the Samaritans. But go rather to the lost sheep of the house of Israel." (Matthew 10:5-6) Throughout his ministry, Jesus was never recorded as having converted a single Gentile, and in fact is recorded as having initially rebuked a Gentile for seeking his favors, likening her to a dog (Matthew 15:22-28 and Mark 7:25-30). One wonders, what does that mean now, for those who have taken Jesus to be their 'personal savior' and presume to speak in his name?

(SECTION 2) GOD

from Deuteronomy 6:4-5 (as acknowledged in all reputable Biblical commentaries), yet Pauline theology somehow arrived at concepts which have been extrapolated to support what is now known as the Trinity. One wonders how. Jesus referred to the Old Testament – what did the Pauline theologins refer to? Significantly absent from the above teaching of Jesus is the association of himself with God. There never was a better time or place, throughout the New Testament, for Jesus to have claimed partnership in divinity, were it true. But he didn't. He didn't say, "Hear, O Israel, the Lord our God, the Lord is one – but it's not quite that simple, so let me explain..."

To pause and review, the relevant issues up to this point in the discussion are these:

1. The Trinitarian formula was conceived in the 3rd century and codified in the 4th, distant both in time and theology from the period of revelation.

2. The Trinitarian formula was completely unknown to the Apostolic Fathers.

3. The Trinity is not found in the Old or New Testaments, either in name or in formula.

4. The Trinitarian formula was conceived by men, relying upon the mysticisms of Paul and the theology which developed in his name.

5. And...Pauline theology is in direct conflict with the strict monotheism and accountability to the law conveyed both in the Old Testament and in the teachings of Christ Jesus.

Discussion continues, however, for analysis of the scriptural evidence (or lack thereof) reveals the flimsiness of Trinitarian theology.

The strongest evidence for the Trinity is often suggested to be the First Epistle of John, verses 5:7-8, which reads, "For there are three who bear witness in heaven: the Father, the Word, and the Holy Spirit; and these three are one, And there are three that bear witness on earth: the Spirit, the water, and the blood; and these three agree as one."

(2.B7) Doctrinal Differences / The Trinity

One problem – this phrase "the Father, the Word, and the Holy Spirit; and these three are one" has long been recognized as an interpolation (a misleading insertion) in the *King James Version* of the Bible, taking origin from a marginal note added to the scripture by one of the late manuscript copiers. *The Interpreter's Bible* comments, with regard to I John 5:7,

> "This verse in the KJV is to be rejected (with RSV). It appears in no ancient Greek MS nor is it cited by any Greek father; of all the versions only the Latin contained it, and even this in none of its most ancient sources. The earliest MSS of the Vulg. do not have it. As Dodd (*Johannine Epistles*, p. 127n) reminds us, 'It is first quoted as a part of I John by Priscillian, the Spanish heretic, who died in 385, and it gradually made its way into MSS of the Latin Vulgate until it was accepted as part of the authorized Latin text.'"[127]

Dr. C.J. Scofield, D.D., backed by eight other Doctorates of Divinity, states the above even more clearly in his footnote to this verse: "It is generally agreed that this verse has no manuscript authority and has been inserted."[128]

How I John 5:7 grew to popular acceptance is no mystery to students of divinity. Originally inserted by a scribe, whether opinionated and manipulative, or well intentioned but relying upon a faulty memory or illegitimate records, the insertion of this verse satisfied those who sought support for their ideology. In accordance with the proverb that people see the world not as it is, but as they are, this verse was bent into the service of those who desired substantiation regardless of source. In the words of E. Gibbon,

---

127. *The Interpreter's Bible*. 1957. Volume XII. Nashville: Abingdon Press. pp. 293-294.

128. Scofield, C. I., D.D. (Editor). 1970. *The New Scofield Reference Bible*. New York: Oxford University Press. P. 1346 (footnote to the verse of I John 5:7).

143

(SECTION 2) GOD

"The memorable text, which asserts the unity of the *Three* who bear witness in heaven, is condemned by the universal silence of the orthodox fathers, ancient versions, and authentic manuscripts....An allegorical interpretation, in the form, perhaps, of a marginal note, invaded the text of the Latin Bibles, which were renewed and corrected in a dark period of ten centuries. After the invention of printing, the editors of the Greek Testament yielded to their own prejudices, or to those of the times, and the pious fraud, which was embraced with equal zeal at Rome and at Geneva, has been infinitely multiplied in every country and every language of modern Europe."[129]

Having been recognized as lacking manuscript authority, this passage of I John 5:7 has been unceremoniously expunged from numerous more modern and reputable translations, to include the *Revised Standard Version* of 1952 and 1971, the *New Revised Standard Version* of 1989, the *New American Standard Bible*, the *New International Version*, *The Good News Bible*, *The New English Bible*, *The Jerusalem Bible*, and many others. Most striking, however, is not the number of translations which have removed this passage, but rather the number of translations which, once the lack of authenticity of these verses became thoroughly and unequivocally recognized, nonetheless retained the passage. Should a person conclude that such devotion is to truth or to doctrinal convention? The *New King James Version of the Bible*, seemingly reluctant to correct the 1611 version at risk of losing the paying audience, the congregation, and no doubt the support of the publisher, appears to fall into the doctrinal convention category.

So the interpolation has persisted for centuries, present in the 1611 *King James Version* for close to 400 years, and now perpetuated

---

129. Gibbon, Edward, Esq. Vol. 4, Chapter XXXVII, pp. 146-7.

(2.B7) Doctrinal Differences / The Trinity

in the *New King James Version*. Even the *New Scofield Reference Bible* retains the passage, despite the footnote advising the lack of manuscript authority. Even more striking is that although the *Scofield Reference Bible*, being a reference version designed to meet the needs of scholars and students of divinity, recognizes the illegitimacy of the verse, the *Scofield Study Bible*, being a version designed for the unsuspecting and religiously uneducated laity, retains the verse without even hinting at its dubious origin.

Translators of still other versions continue to present doctrinally prejudiced efforts. This does not speak favorably with regard to basic ethics unless a person believes, as many do, that lying is justified in the propagation of religious belief. Paul is quoted as having identified such individuals, with the clear suggestion that he may be amongst them, in the verse, "For if the truth of God hath more abounded through my lie unto his glory; why yet am I also judged as a sinner?" (Romans 3:7 – *King James Version*). *The American Standard Version* and NRSV read much the same. And the fact is that some Bible translators may operate on this lowly ethic – so much so, in fact, that many have attempted to change the translation of this verse itself. Yet those who insert wording such as "Someone might argue..." (NIV, NKJV) have the burden of proof upon them to show where they find such misleading words in the foundational Greek manuscripts. Nowhere? The words are plucked out of thin air and inserted out of expediency rather than accuracy? Well, if this is the work ethic of those who translate one part of the Bible, how much confidence can a person have in the rest of their work? More importantly, given the premise that Paul considered it acceptable to lie for the glory of God, how much confidence can a person have in anything written by Paul in the first place? The situation is one in which Paul admits to condoning lying in the path of religion, and yet most of the world of Christianity trust every word he wrote! The assumption that a man

(SECTION 2) GOD

who admitted a willingness to lie nonetheless told nothing but 'gospel truth' can only be made by those who lack cortical competence.

Some may assert that Paul was not speaking of himself in the above verse, but of others who embodied this poor evangelical ethic. Perhaps, and then again perhaps not. But even if that had been the case, who wrote the many books of the New Testament, gospels included, which are of unknown authorship? Answer: others. *The others?* Those who Paul identifies with Romans 3:7? Nobody knows, and how can they? Unknown authors evade credentialing; no reliable assessment of ethics, honesty or trustworthiness may be made.

Leaving evaluation of the degree of truthfulness of Paul's writings aside, the Islamic and the 'Paul-wasn't-right-on-everything' Christian perspective is that good does not follow from evil. A lie, even to glorify God, is nonetheless a lie and contrary to the code of truth to which humankind is bidden by our Creator. And God doesn't need man to lie in order to glorify Him. After all, if people must resort to lying in order to justify a belief system which encompasses a commandment not to bear false witness in the first place, how consistent and true can the religion be? Does it not make more sense for God to have given humankind the tools to derive truth *through* truth?

Regardless of a person's viewpoint, the primary scriptural justification of the Trinity (the First Epistle of John 5:7-8), as discussed above, lacks validation.

With regard to other scriptural evidences for the Trinity, the *New Catholic Encyclopedia* knowingly cites,

> "In the Gospels evidence of the Trinity is found explicitly only in the baptismal formula of Mt 28:19....The only place in the gospels where the three divine Persons are explicitly mentioned together is in St. Matthew's account of Christ's last command to his apostles, 'Go, therefore, and make disciples

(2.B7) Doctrinal Differences / The Trinity

of all nations, baptizing them in the name of the Father and of the Son and of the Holy Spirit (Mt 28.19).'"[130]

II Corinthians 13:14 complements this passage by recording the benediction, "The grace of the Lord Jesus Christ, and the love of God, and the communion of the Holy Spirit be with you all." However, a gaping chasm lies between the above quotes and the sheer and unyielding wall of Trinitarian doctrine – a chasm which requires a leap of faith unprotected by a net of evidence. The old "Lions and tigers and bears, oh my," line does not evoke the image of a strange mythological beast with features of all three creatures. Rather, separate and distinct entities are typically at the forefront of consciousness. Trinitarian doctrine enforces the belief, however, that the mention of three entities in the same sentence should evoke innate understanding of the same triune God which remains a metaphysical mystery of faith. The practical man and woman may point out that going to dinner at Joe and Frank and Luigi's restaurant should not inspire a person to expect a triune synthesis of humanity in restaurant ownership. Such belief may make things easier to figure come tax time, but not come the Day of Judgement.

More concrete objection to conclusions drawn from Matthew 28:19, as quoted above, is found in Mark 16:15-16. The latter verses describe the exact same 'Great Commission,' but the 'Father, Son, and Holy Spirit' formula found in Matthew 28:19 is conspicuously absent. So who recorded the words of Jesus correctly and who didn't? Or are both wrong? Both passages describe the same event, but while theologians have bent Matthew 28:19 into service as an evidence for the Trinity (or, as per quotation of the *New Catholic Encyclopedia* above, the *only* explicit evidence for the Trinity), Mark 16:15-16 rigidly withstands such manipulation. So who is telling the truth and

---

130. *New Catholic Encyclopedia.* Vol 14, p. 306.

(SECTION 2) GOD

how can a person tell? And once again, who wants to risk salvation on a coin-flip?

One standard by which truth can be measured is achieved by looking at what the disciples of Jesus actually did. The letters of Paul expose the fact that baptism in the early church was only done in the name of Jesus (examples include Acts 2:38, 8:16, 10:48, 19:5, and Romans 6:3.), and not "...in the name of the Father and of the Son and of the Holy Spirit." Assuming the disciples actually did as they were told, their actions endorse Mark 16:15-16 as the more faithful account of the 'Great Commission.' Similarly, their actions condemn the teaching of Matthew 28:19, and thereby condemn this evidence ("The only place in the gospels where the three divine Persons are explicitly mentioned together..."[131]) for the Trinity. On the other hand, if the *disciples* were not doing as they were told then a person has no basis to trust anything they are recorded as having said or done. And if the disciples are not to be trusted, how much less should Paul, who never even met Jesus, be trusted?

Another popular reference is John 10:38, which reads, "The Father is in me and I in the Father." John 14:11 reads much the same. But what do these words mean? If a person believes these verses support the concept of co-sharing of divinity, John 14:20 should be factored into the equation, reading, "At that day you (i.e., the disciples) will know that I am in my Father, and you in me, and I in you." Bearing in mind that Aramaic and Hebrew possess far greater capacity for metaphor than English, the only logical conclusion is that the language is metaphorical, and hence none of the above quotes can be used to defend Trinitarian doctrine. The only other option is the Hell-bent blasphemy that the council of Nicaea failed to recognize a dozen disciples as partners with both Jesus and God. Infinitely more reasonable is to admit that 2000 year-old colloquialisms are more likely to be just that – flowery phrases which, if taken literally, become

131. *New Catholic Encyclopedia.* Vol 14, p. 306.

(2.B7) Doctrinal Differences / The Trinity

distractions from reality. If language evolution is examined, the Old English of a short six or seven centuries ago is incomprehensible except to scholars. What, then, is known of 1,600 year old Greek texts which translate the dead Semitic languages of ancient Hebrew and Aramaic, much less their colloquialisms?

John 14:9 relates, "He who has seen me has seen the Father." Assuming the language to be literal rather than figurative, which is a bold assumption, a person still has to rectify John 14:9 with John 5:37, which reads, "You have neither heard His voice at any time, nor seen His form." John 1:18 is even more emphatic, stating, "No one has seen God at any time." Paul documents agreement as follows: "who (God) alone has immortality*, dwelling in unapproachable light, whom no man has seen or can see, to whom be honor and everlasting power." (I Timothy 6:16). The "unapproachable" and "no man has seen or can see" clauses certainly do not conform to the approachable and visible person of Jesus. The argument of John 14:9, when played out, reveals itself to be invalid. The one scriptural step forward slips three back when one learns that Jesus was recorded as having stood bodily in front of the eyes of the disciples, informing them with a voice audible to the gospel author, if to no one else, that "You have neither heard His voice at any time, nor seen His form."

John 10:30 relates Jesus as having said, "I and the Father are one." In the minds of many, that's it! All is settled; God and Jesus are one, and all who fail to grasp the concept are reckoned blind, stupid or obstinate. Such uncompromising opinions are the providence of those who trust the potentially 'wool over the eyes' English translation more than the untranslated Greek of the source documents. The Greek in this case reveals that the word which is translated to the English 'one' is '*heis*.'[132] This word, '*heis*,' is also found in John 17:11

---

* What about our 'no end of life' friend, Melchizedek, in Hebrews 7:3?
132. *Strong's Exhaustive Concordance of the Bible.* 1980. World Bible Publishers.

149

(SECTION 2) GOD

and 17:21-23. John 17:11 reads, "...Holy Father, keep through Your name those whom You have given me, that *they may be one* as we are" (emphasis mine). Literal or metaphorical? John 17:21 reinforces the metaphor with the words, "That they (all believers) *all may be one*, as You, Father, are in me, and I in You, that they (all believers) also *may be one in us*, that the world may believe that You sent me" (emphasis mine). If a person is faithful to the equation, the sum total adds up to a whole lot more than three-in-one; a person is either going to have to think bigger and more blasphemous, or do math in other than base 10, if the Trinity is to be preserved.

The above-quoted John 10:30, being a widely misapplied verse, deserves a closer examination for the sake of completeness. Trinitarian Christianity argues that Jesus declared, "I and my Father are one," whereupon the Jews prepared to stone him for blasphemy according to their accusation that, "You, being a Man, make yourself God" (John 10:33). The argument is that the Jews recognized Jesus' claim to being God, so all should understand John 10:30 similarly. This might seem reasonable at first glance, but only if the passage is taken out of context. The passage does not end there, but continues with Jesus correcting the misunderstanding -- a very believable scenario, for the entire mission of Jesus was to correct the errors of the Jews and redirect them to true faith. In fact, the Bible presents a long series of stories in which Jesus corrects the misunderstandings of the Jews, and this is only one such case.

To analyze the passage appropriately, a person might begin with the preceding verse, John 10:29, which emphasizes the separate and distinct natures of God and Jesus – The One the giver, the other the receiver. Many who subsequently read John 10:30 come away with the understanding that this verse dictates the metaphor to be that Jesus and God are in agreement, one in understanding, or one in purpose. Those who do not side with this perception might note Jesus' response to the Jews' accusation of blasphemy. Did Jesus

(2.B7) Doctrinal Differences / The Trinity

stand up with divine confidence once he perceived that the Jews believed him to have claimed divinity? Did Jesus insist, "You heard me right – I said it once, and I'll say it again!"? Quite the opposite, he pronounced that they heard him wrong – they misunderstood – and went on to quote Psalm 82:6 reminding the Jews that the phrases which are translated to "son of God" and even "you are gods" are metaphors. In the words of the Bible,

> "Jesus answered them, 'Is it not written in your law, "I (God) said, 'You are gods'?* If He called them gods, to whom the word of God came (and the Scripture cannot be broken), do you say of him whom the Father sanctified and sent into the world, 'You are blaspheming,' because I said, 'I am the son of God'?" (John 10:34-36). *Psalm 82:6

Jesus seems to have included himself with the group of those "to whom the word of God (i.e., revelation) came," who were identified in the referenced Psalm 82:6 as 'gods' with a small 'g' or 'children of God.' The beginning of the referenced section, Psalm 82:1, proclaims a bold 'in-the-face' metaphor when judges are identified as 'gods.' Not as righteous men, not as prophets, not as sons of god, but *as gods*. Furthermore, continuation of the passage in Psalm 82:6-7 leaves no doubt that 'sons of god' refers to mortal human beings – "I (God) said, 'You are gods, and all of you are children of the Most High. But you shall die like men, and fall like one of the princes'" (Psalm 82 6-7). And lastly, let us not forget that the Greek word '*huios*,' which is translated to 'son' in the above quote, was "...used very widely of immediate, remote or figurative kinship,"[133] leaving considerable ambiguity with regard to the translation of the above passage in the first place.

So once the passage is read as a whole, Jesus is seen to have iden-

---

133. *Strong's Exhaustive Concordance of the Bible.*

(SECTION 2) GOD

tified himself with other righteous mortals. Jesus further emphasized the metaphorical language of these passages as such, denied the claim of divinity, and behaved as would be expected of a flesh-and-blood prophet. After all, if Jesus were a partner in divinity, wouldn't a person reasonably expect him to have asserted his rank with confidence?

Similarly, for every verse held as an evidence of the Trinity, there are one or more which discredit or disqualify. Those who selectively adopt only those scriptural passages which suit their desire or doctrine make mockery of revelation, while those who accept the entire scripture discover the truth of its teaching.

In the meantime, the burden of Trinitarian proof continues to rest upon the Christian clergy. Much to the frustration of the Christian world, Biblical confirmation of Jesus teaching the Trinity is not just scarce, it is absent. If anything, as pointed out above, the opposite is in fact the case. Three times Jesus is recorded as having emphasized the first commandment as: "...the Lord our God, the Lord is one" (Mark 12:29; Matthew 22:37; and Luke 10:27). In none of these three instances does Jesus even hint at a more complex formula or understanding. And who has more Biblical authority than Jesus?

The Trinitarian argument that "Yes, God is one, but God is one in a triune being, like an egg is one, but one in three separate and distinct layers" sounds catchy, but fails to satisfy those who seek evidence and confirmation in the teachings of the prophets -- any of the prophets, for that matter.* It also fails to satisfy those who seek proof rather than explanation. There was a time when the world

---

* Analogies such as the egg and the triple point of water deserve rebuttal nonetheless. At the most basic level many refuse to demote the majesty of God to comparison with anything of creation, but especially to anything as low on the list as the product of a squawking hen's filthy cloacal tract. Furthermore, nothing known to man does exist in a triune state, for the triune state is not defined just as three elements making one whole, but of three elements

(contd. on page 153)

(2.B7) DOCTRINAL DIFFERENCES / THE TRINITY

accepted explanations of the Earth being flat, of all the planets revolving around the Earth, of the ability to transmute base substances into gold, and even of a fountain of perpetual youth. But good explanations do not a reality make. Whether or not a valid analogy to the concept of the Trinity exists, the question is not whether comparison to an element of the material world can be made. Rather, the question is whether the doctrine is valid in the first place, and did Jesus teach it? The answers, according to the information cited above, are 'no' and 'no.'

Consequently, in recent years defenders of Trinitarian doctrine have run out of arguments. With lack of Biblical evidence to substantiate the Trinity, some have asserted that Jesus taught this element of creed to his disciples, but in secret. Even this claim has an answer, for Jesus presented his message for all to hear, stating, "I spoke openly to the world. I always taught in synagogues and in the temple, where the Jews always meet, and in secret *I have said nothing*" (John 18:20 – emphasis mine).

So who is a person to believe, Jesus or Pauline theologins? Scripture or doctrine? What people read in scripture with their own two eyes, or what they are told by one held to be a religious authority (and quite possibly a cousin to the same corrupt religious authorities that Jesus reportedly condemned during the time of his ministry)? For those who seek closeness with Christ Jesus in this life

---

(contd. from page 152)

being consubstantial, coeternal, and coequal. Water at the triple point may be consubstantial – all of equivalent molecular structure. However, the intermolecular covalent bonds differ and the three states of steam, water, and ice are not coequal. Nobody can make tea with ice or sorbet with steam. Similarly, the three parts of an egg are neither consubstantial, coeternal, nor coequal. The yolk, white, and shell are of different substances, unequal in flavor, consistency, color, and nutrition. One cannot be substituted for the other. An omelet cannot be made with eggshells, or a meringue with yolks. Furthermore, those who put the 'coeternal' theory to the test on a hot summer day will likely find the hypothesis to stink after a while.

(SECTION 2) GOD

and in the hereafter, Jesus is recorded as having instructed his followers on how to do so: "For whoever does the will of my Father in heaven is my brother and sister and mother" (Matthew 12:50). And the will of God, as conveyed through His prophets, including Moses in the Old Testament and Christ Jesus in the New Testament, is to teach the oneness of God. A oneness of God, for that matter, which carries over into Islamic monotheism, for the teachings of the Holy Qur'an not only confirm the oneness of God (Allah), but refute the Trinity, as follows:

1. "...Do not say Trinity: desist..." (TMQ 4:171)

2. "They do blaspheme who say: God is one of three in a Trinity: for there is no god except one God (Allah)" (TMQ 5:73)

3. "...your God (Allah) is One God (Allah): whoever expects to meet his Lord, let him work righteousness, and, in the worship of his Lord, admit no one as partner" (TMQ 18:110)*

Many who view the clarity of such Islamic teachings juxtaposed to the tangled and indefensible web of Trinitarian ideology may question, "Well, what's wrong with Islam then?" Others continue to object, "But Jesus is God!" Upon the foundation of such opposing viewpoints are the lines of religious differences drawn.

---

* The impartial observer may be struck by the thought that the above quotes would have been an extremely bold assertion by a man claiming revelation if divine evidence for the Trinity did in fact exist – the claim of the Holy Qur'an as revelation would have been too easily refuted. Additionally, such an emphatic denial of the Trinity would seem to have been an extremely peculiar manner of appeal to the Christians of the time of Muhammad. On one hand the Qur'an acknowledges the virgin birth and prophethood of Christ Jesus, much to the alienation of Judaism. On the other hand the Qur'an denies the Trinitarian formula, much to the offence of Christianity. Allah condemns paganism in the Holy Qur'an in even stronger terms. If the Holy Qur'an was one man's attempt to gather a following, it certainly lacked tactical appeal to the overwhelming majority of Jews, Christians, and Pagans. But if the Holy Qur'an was not a man's attempt to gain a worldly following, one wonders what the secondary gain might then have been. If, that is, the assumption is that the Holy Qur'an originated in the mind of a man. However, if the Holy Qur'an truly is revelation from God, then lack of human motivations and secondary gains would be expected, and the presence of teachings in conflict with manmade doctrines would be consistent with the point of revelation (i.e., to correct the deviations which developed in pre-existing religions).

(2.B) DOCTRINAL DIFFERENCES
(2.B8) Divinity of Jesus?

"Man is made to adore and to obey: but if you will not command him, if you give him nothing to worship, he will fashion his own divinities, and find a chieftain in his own passions."
— Benjamin Disraeli, *Coningsby*, bk. 4, ch. 13

The critical element of contention between Jesus and Pauline theology rests in Pauline theology's elevation of Jesus to divine status – a doctrine that Jesus seemingly denies, as follows:

"Why do you call me good: No one is good but One, that is, God" (Matthew 9:17, Mark 10-18, and Luke 18:19);

"...My Father is greater than I" (John 14:28);

"I do nothing of myself, but as the Father taught me, I speak these things" (John 8:28);

"...Most assuredly, I say to you, the son can do nothing of himself..." (John 5:19);

"But I know Him, for I am from Him, and He sent me" (John 7:29);

(SECTION 2) GOD

"...he who rejects me rejects Him who sent me" (Luke 10:16);

"But now I go away to Him who sent me..." (John 16:5);

"Jesus answered them and said, 'My doctrine is not mine, but His who sent me'" (John 7:16);

"For I have not spoken on my own authority; but the Father who sent me gave me a command, what I should say and what I should speak" (John 12:49);

and Matthew 24:36, Luke 23:46, John 8:42, John 14:24, John 17:6-8 etc.

What does Pauline theology say? That Jesus is a co-sharer in divinity, God incarnate. So whom should a person believe? The following quotes are attributed to Jesus, complemented by elements of emphasis attributed to this author:

"The first of all the commandments is: 'Hear O Israel, The Lord *our* God, the Lord is one" (Mark 12:29);

"But of that day and hour no one knows, neither the angels in heaven, *nor the Son*, but *only* the Father" (Mark 13:32).

"'...You shall worship the Lord your God, and Him *only* you shall serve'" (Luke 4:8);

"...My food is to do the will of Him who sent me..." (John 4:34);

"I can *of myself* do nothing...I do not seek my own will but the will of the Father who sent me" (John 5:30);

"For I have come down from heaven, not to do my own will, but the will of Him who sent me" (John 6:38);

"My doctrine is *not mine*, but His who sent me" (John 7:16);

"I am ascending to *my* Father and your Father, and to my God and your God" (John 20:17)

(2.B8) Doctrinal Differences / Divinity of Jesus?

The bold print in the above quotes is not meant to imply that Jesus spoke with the above emphasis, although given the limitations of the written record, nobody can claim with certainty that he didn't. Rather, the points of emphasis are selected to illustrate the difficulty any open-minded and objective reader has with accepting the alleged divinity of Jesus based upon what Jesus himself is quoted as having taught. Jesus appears to have clearly, if not emphatically, established a zone of separation between himself and God in the above quotes. In the words of Joel Carmichael, "The idea of this new religion, with himself as its deity, was something he (Christ Jesus) could never have had the slightest inkling of. As Charles Guignebert put it, 'It never even crossed his mind.'"[134] So if Jesus did not lay claim to some element of divinity, then what is he? Having nothing more reliable to depend upon than the Biblical record, Jesus appears to answer the question as follows:

> "A *prophet* is not without honor except in his own country, among his own relatives, and in his own house" (Mark 6:4);
>
> "But Jesus said to them, "A *prophet* is not without honor except in his own country and in his own house." (Matthew 13:57)
>
> "...it cannot be that a *prophet* should perish outside of Jerusalem" (Luke 13:33).

If the masses of the present age do not grasp the 'prophet' concept, the masses of the past certainly seemed to have, for they recognized, "This is Jesus, the prophet from Nazareth of Galilee" (Matthew 21:11), and "A great prophet has risen up among us..." (Luke 7:16). The disciples recognized Jesus as, "...a prophet mighty in deed..." (Luke 24:19). See also Matthew 14:5, 21:46, and John 6:14. If

---

134. Carmichael, Joel. p. 203.

157

(SECTION 2) GOD

these assertions were inaccurate a person has reason to question why Jesus didn't correct the statements at the time they were made. Why didn't Jesus seize the opportunity to define his divinity if, that is, he truly was divine? Jesus had many opportunities to clarify his position, such as when the woman stated, "...Sir, I perceive that you are a prophet" (John 4:19). Why didn't he speak up? Why didn't he clear his throat, thank the lady for her lowly impression, but explain that there was more to his essence than just prophethood? Or was there?

Christ Jesus, a man? Could it be? A good part of the religiously introspective world wonders "Why not?" Acts 2:22 records Jesus as "Jesus of Nazareth, a *man* attested by God to you by miracles, wonders, and signs which *God did* through him in your midst, as you yourselves also know" (emphasis mine). Jesus himself is recorded as having said, "But now you seek to kill me, a *man* who has told you the truth which I heard *from God*..." (John 8:40—emphasis mine). Strikingly, a similar quote is found in the words of Jesus recorded in the Holy Qur'an, translated to, "He (Jesus) said: 'I am indeed a servant of Allah: He has given me Revelation and made me a prophet'" (TMQ 19:30). This also sounds very much like the words by which Allah instructed Muhammad to identify himself: "Say: 'I am but a man like you: it is revealed to me by inspiration, that your God is One God (Allah)...'" (TMQ 41:6).

The *only* New Testament verse which supports the doctrine of Incarnation is I Timothy 3:16. However, with regard to this verse (which states that "God was manifest in the flesh"), the following comment is offered:

> "This strong expression might be justified by the language of St. Paul (I Tim. iii. 16), but we are deceived by our modern Bibles. The word ὃ (*which*) was altered to θεὸς (*God*) at Constantinople in the beginning of the sixth century:

(2.B8) Doctrinal Differences / Divinity of Jesus?

the true reading, which is visible in the Latin and Syriac versions, still exists in the reasoning of the Greek, as well as of the Latin fathers; and this fraud, with that of the *three witnesses of St. John*, is admirably detected by Sir Isaac Newton."[135]

Given the above there should be little surprise that twentieth century Christianity has expanded to include those who deny the alleged divinity of Jesus. A significant sign of this realization is the following report of the London *Daily News*: "More than half of England's Anglican bishops say Christians are not obliged to believe that Jesus Christ was God, according to a survey published today."[136] Noteworthy is the fact that the above does not reference the opinion of lay clergy, but of bishops, leaving many head-scratching parishioners wondering who to believe, if not the majority opinion of the higher ranks of their own clergy.

Regardless of any devotee's romantic view of religious origins, the harsh reality is that all prophets but Adam were born in the bath of amniotic fluid which flushes each and every element of humanity from the womb of woman – Christ Jesus included. No doubt the mother of Jesus suckled him at her breast in the natural act of nurturing a human child, but in what would be an incongruous act for God, as the relationship would imply a dependence of God upon some element of His very own creation. A person would suspect that Jesus crawled on a dirt floor and grew up in a human fashion complete with worldly eating and worldly drinking (most certainly followed by the occasional trip to a worldly bathroom). His human hunger, thirst, anger, pain, fatigue, sorrow, anxiety and frustration are all well described in the Bible. Jesus slept, but God never sleeps (Psalm 121:4). Jesus was tempted by Satan (Luke 4:1-13), and yet James 1:13

---

135. Gibbon, Edward, Esq. Vol. 5, Chapter XLVII, p. 207.
136. London *Daily News*. June 25, 1984

(SECTION 2) GOD

tells mankind, "...God cannot be tempted with evil..." Jesus prayed and gave thanks (to Whom?), fasted (why?), carried the teachings of God, and in the end helplessly suffered humiliation and torture at the oppressive hands of misguided tyrants. A man oppressed by tyrant rulers or a god oppressed by the very creation He will Himself condemn on the Day of Judgement? Many (and not just Muslims) would argue that the Islamic view is more complimentary and noble of God as a supreme and transcendent God, and more realistic of Jesus as a prophet and a man.

The question begs an answer, "Why *must* Jesus be God? Is there any specific reason why he can't just be human?"

The exchange over this issue typically follows a predictable pattern, such as that which follows:

> Most of the world of Christianity asserts that mankind needed a sacrifice for the redemption of sin, but that a human sacrifice would not do – only a divine sacrifice would suffice. Strict Monotheists, be they Orthodox Jew, Unitarian Christian or Muslim may well object, "Oh. So you mean to say you believe God died?"
>
> Trinitarian Response: "No, no, perish the thought. Only the man died."
>
> Orthodox Jew/Unitarian Christian/Muslim (hereafter OJ/UC/M): "In that case the one sacrificed didn't need to be divine after all, if only the man-part died."
>
> Trinitarian: "No, no, no. The man-part died, but Jesus/God had to suffer on the cross to atone for our sins."
>
> OJ/UC/M: "What do you mean 'had to?' God is the source of all creation. God doesn't 'have to' anything."

(2.B8) Doctrinal Differences / Divinity of Jesus?

Trinitarian: "God needed a sacrifice and a human just wouldn't do. God needed a sacrifice big enough to atone for the sins of mankind, so He sent His only begotten son."

OJ/UC/M: "Then we have a different concept of God. The God we believe in doesn't exist in a state of need. Our God never finds Himself in a position where He wants to do something but can't because He needs something else to accomplish His desires. Our God never looks around saying, "Gee, I want to do this, but I can't. First I need this certain something. Let's see, where can I find it?" In that scenario God would be dependent upon another entity – namely whatever He would depend upon to satisfy His needs. In other words, God would have to have a higher god. For a strict monotheist that concept is just not possible, for God is One, supreme, self-sufficient, the source of all creation. God does not have needs; mankind has needs. Man and womankind need His guidance, mercy and forgiveness, but He doesn't *need* anything in exchange. He may desire servitude and worship, but there is a galaxy of difference between need and desire. God *desires* good for the human race, and instructs mankind through revelation on how to attain His reward through keeping His commandments – commandments regarding creed, such as recognizing God to be One God, alone and without partner, and commandments regarding worship, such as prayer."

Trinitarian: "But that's the point; with regard to prayer, man is a sinner and God is pure and holy. Men and women can't approach God directly because of the impurity of sin. Hence, men and women need an intercessor to pray to."

OJ/UC/M: "Did Jesus sin?"

161

(SECTION 2) GOD

Trinitarian: "Nope, of course not, he was sinless."

OJ/UC/M: "How pure was Jesus?"

Trinitarian: "100% pure. Jesus was (God/Son of God), so he was 100% holy."

OJ/UC/M: "But then the barrier to man's approach to God has not changed through taking Jesus as intercessor. If Jesus is 100% holy that puts the theology back to the starting point of the argument, for the original premise was that mankind cannot approach an entirely holy entity because of the incompatibility of sinful man and the purity of anything 100% holy. If Jesus was 100% holy then he is no more approachable than a 100% holy God, according to the premise of the argument. On the other hand, if Jesus was *not* 100% holy, then he was himself tainted and could not approach God directly, much less be God, the Son of God, or partner with God."

A fair analogy might be that of going to meet a supremely righteous man. A person might be told of a man who is the holiest person alive. Supposedly he reeks holiness; holiness radiates from his being, oozes from his pores. So a person goes to meet him, but is told the 'saint' won't agree to the introduction, and in fact can't stand to be in the same room with a sin-tainted mortal. The visitor can talk with his receptionist, but he's too holy to see the likes of laity. What does a person think now? Does the man sound holy, or does he sound crazy?

The common sense majority expect a holy person to be approachable – the more holy, the more approachable. Approachability goes hand-in-hand with holiness, so the need for an intermediary between man and God jumps the rails of reason and plummets over the precipice of presumption.

Frustration usually approaches critical mass for anyone who attempts to argue such issues, for it is often at this point that rational

(2.B8) Doctrinal Differences / Divinity of Jesus?

discussion gives way to emotionally-charged challenges. For example, when scriptural evidence is seen to fail, those who argue on the basis of extra-Biblical doctrine are forced to close the book from which they claim to take guidance (i.e., the Bible) and divert discussion to the mystical and intangible. Who can argue with such condescending questions as, "Haven't you ever felt the power of Jesus in your life?"

Whether or not a person (including the one asking) understands the question is a separate issue. Strict monotheists can be quick to answer in the affirmative, but with the amendment that the power of the truth Jesus taught is greater than the blasphemies which grew to dominate Christian thought subsequent to the time of his ministry. The strict monotheist, whether Orthodox Jew, Unitarian Christian, or Muslim, might also feel inclined to question what the power of the deceptiveness of Satan would feel like. A person might expect it to be pretty slick and persuasive, for how many adherents could Satan expect to win over if he did not appear in a cloak of righteousness? So how can a person tell the difference between the truth of God and the deception of Satan? If people choose a religion based on inner emotion and not on rational thought, how can they be assured of being on the right path? The God-given faculty of judgement is based upon cognitive reason – any other opinion must by necessity assume that a rational creation was given an irrational law. God reportedly directs humankind in Isaiah 1:18, "'Come now, and let us reason together,' says the Lord..." Nowhere does God appear to teach, "Feel your way along." The tools of the Satan – the stress-cracks of human weakness through which the forces of evil gain a handhold – consist of the base emotions, the lower desires. Nobody ever sits down over a hot cup of tea in the fading twilight of a pastel sunset illuminating a contemplative mood and tabulates the pros and cons of adultery/theft/avarice etc. Nobody ever arrives at sin through deductive reasoning – it just doesn't happen. Mankind arrives at sin through following base desires to the compromise of better (rational) judgement. Sins of the flesh are dangerous enough, from both worldly and after-worldly perspectives. How much more dangerous are errors of religious choice based upon the emotional appeal of proposals of spiritual exclusivity?

In the past such claims of spiritual exclusivity were largely limited to the domain of the Gnostics, who were burned at the stake as heretics right up until the time, or so it would seem, that Trinitarian doctrine found itself naked and defenseless in the woods of theological debate. Dependence upon the 'holy spirit' and 'guiding light' mystical religious defenses, though previously considered a trademark of Gnostic heresy, became a modern defense in the ranks of Christian orthodoxy, serving as the only straws to be clutched in an effort to resist the undertow of the overwhelming weight of Biblical evidence. The claim that a person lacks the 'Holy Spirit' if they do not accept a given ideology serves as the ultimate storm-wall of religious discussion, diverting the thrust of rational argument away from the ears of those who would prefer the evidence to go away rather than be confronted by the inconvenience of its force. The claim that a person will understand Jesus if they only accept the 'Holy Spirit' into their lives meets resistance from those who seek to avoid such Gnostic ideology – ideology which implies an arbitrary nature to God, Who grants mystical understanding to some while withholding it from others.

Strict monotheists may try to redirect discussion back to the main point of relevance. For example, many religious groups (Muslims included) accept Jesus, but as a prophet of God. They believe that which he taught, including the oft-repeated declaration of himself as nothing more than a prophet and a man, as discussed above. In contrast, many *don't* believe what Pauline theology taught, preferring to rely upon the clear truth of the prophets in preference to the murky and turbulent contradictions of those who followed in their wake. No matter how sincere Paul may appear to have been, all Muslims and

(2.B8) Doctrinal Differences / Divinity of Jesus?

many Unitarians point out that Paul was not a disciple, never met Jesus, and in fact persecuted, imprisoned, and killed his followers (Acts 22:19 and 26:9-11), consented to the stoning of Stephen (Acts 7:58-60 and 22:20), and made havoc of the Church (Acts 8:3). Many conceive that Paul may have had a mind-warping vision or dream, but assert that the engineer and voice behind the curtain-of-illusion on *that* yellow brick road to Damascus could not have origin in divinity if the alleged inspiration resulted in teachings contrary to those previously revealed. In the creed of the Muslim and many Unitarian Christians, God neither changes His mind nor manifests inconsistency.

Those who discredit Paul's claim to divine inspiration speculate that, following the alleged vision, Paul thereafter continued to make havoc of the Church, but this time from within. Some would call it subterfuge. Others, apparently, consider his actions sufficient for sainthood.

Any such exchange of ideas usually ends abruptly, because disagreement between fiery emotionalism and calm rationality is doomed to frustrate both parties. One side speculates on an imagined 'WWJD – What Would Jesus Do?' The other focuses on the documented 'WDJD – What *Did* Jesus Do?' The vast majority of Christians claim to follow Jesus, but to their own embarrassment follow what others have taught about Jesus in preference to that which he himself taught. Unitarian Christians and Muslims claim to follow Jesus, and then actually do so. Christians who claim to take their religious origins from the teachings of Jesus should feel some sense of humiliation when they find his teachings better exemplified in the manners of the Islamic community than in those of the Christians themselves.*

---

* The exercise is only valid when comparing practicing Muslims with practicing Christians. Unfortunately, the majority of those who claim the title of Islam in Western nations are either not practicing, or poor examples of Islamic virtues. Hence, to be fair, a person has to search out the best examples of Islamic piety in order to appreciate the following comparison.

(SECTION 2) GOD

Practical examples include the following:

Appearance:

1. The world acknowledges Jesus to have been bearded. Which religious groups emulate this example?

2. Jesus is commonly acknowledged to have dressed in modesty. Nobody imagines Christ Jesus in shorts and a tee-shirt, or even a form-fitting suit. If anyone attempts to construct a mental picture, the result typically involves flowing robes, from wrists to ankles, without any hint of even the shape of his body. When Jesus delivered his 'Sermon of the Mount,' did he have a paunch? We like to think not, but in fact nobody knows, and his loose clothes may be the reason for that. So, how many practicing Muslims does a person find dressed with Christ-like modestly? The traditional clothing of the Middle East and Indio-Pakistan subcontinent are perhaps the best examples. Now, how many Christians bear out this modesty?

3. The mother of Jesus covered, and the practice was maintained amongst the Christians of the Holy Land up to the middle of the 20th century. Any photograph of a Palestinian Christian parade or congregation prior to 1950 shows a field of headscarves. But which women of piety cover now – practicing Christians or practicing Muslims?

Manners:

1. Jesus placed emphasis on the next world, and was a man preoccupied with striving for salvation. How many 'righteous' Christians fit this 'It's not just on Sundays' profile? Now how many 'five prayers a day, every day of the year' Muslims?

2. Jesus spoke with humility and kindness. He was not known to 'showboat.' His image is not associated with theatrics. He was a simple man known for quality and truth. How many preachers and how many evangelists follow this example?

(2.B8) Doctrinal Differences / Divinity of Jesus?

3. Jesus taught his disciples to offer the greeting of 'Peace' (Luke 10:5). He then set the example several times by offering the greeting, "Peace be with you" (Luke 24:36, John 20:19, John 20:21, John 20:26). Who continues this practice to this day, Christians or Muslims? 'Peace be with you' is the meaning of the Muslim greeting, "Assalam alaikum." Interestingly enough, emphasis on this greeting is to be found in Judaism as well, in Genesis 43:23, Numbers 6:26, Judges 6:23, I Samuel 1:17 and I Samuel 25:6.

Religious Practices:

1. Jesus was circumcised (Luke 2:21). Paul taught it was not necessary (Rom 4:11 and Gal 5:2). Which religious group follows Jesus and which follows Paul?

2. Jesus did not eat pork, in keeping with Old Testament law (Leviticus 11:7 and Deuteronomy 14:8). How many Christians can make this claim?

3. Jesus did not give or take usury, in compliance with the Biblical commandment, "If you lend money to any of My people who are poor among you, you shall not be like a moneylender to him; you shall not charge him interest." (Exodus 22:25). Usury is forbidden in the books of the Old Testament and the Qur'an, as it was forbidden in the religion of Jesus.

4. Jesus did not fornicate, abstaining from extramarital contact with the opposite sex. How many Christians adhere to this example? Note: the issue surpasses fornication, extending to the least physical contact with the opposite sex. With the exception of performing religious rituals and helping those in need, Jesus is not recorded as ever having *touched* a woman other than his mother. Strictly practicing Orthodox Jews maintain this practice to this day in observance of Old Testament law. Likewise, *practicing* Muslims do not even shake hands between the sexes. Can Christian 'hug your neighbor' and 'kiss the bride' congregations make the same claim?

(SECTION 2) GOD

Religious Practices Associated with Worship:

1. Jesus purified himself with washing prior to prayer, as was the practice of the religion and of the pious prophets preceding him (see Exodus 40:31-32 in reference to Moses and Aaron).

2. Jesus prayed in prostration (Matthew 26:39), like the other prophets – (see Nehemiah 8:6 with regard to Ezra and the people, Joshua 5:14 for Joshua, Genesis 17:3 and 24:52 for Abraham, Exodus 34:8 and Numbers 20:6 for Moses and Aaron). Who prays like that, Christians or Muslims?

3. Jesus fasted for more than a month at a time (Matthew 4:2 and Luke 4:2). Jesus was following an example set by the pious who preceded him (Exodus 34:28, I Kings 19:8). So who follows the example of Jesus, if not those who annually fast the month of Ramadan?

4. Jesus made pilgrimage for the purpose of worship, as all orthodox Jews aspire to do. In his day pilgrimage (as recorded in the Bible) was directed to Jerusalem (Acts 8:26-28). Muslims, if able, make pilgrimage to Makkah as directed by Allah in the Holy Qur'an. Should Christians have difficulty accepting the change of pilgrimage sites from Jerusalem to Makkah, Muslims cite Matthew 21:42-43. In Matthew 21:42 Jesus reminded his followers of Psalm 118:22, 23 as follows:

"The stone which the builders rejected has become the chief cornerstone. This is the Lord's doing, and it is marvelous in our eyes."

Matthew 21:43 then records Jesus as having predicted,

"Therefore I say to you, the kingdom of God will be taken from you and given to a nation bearing the fruits of it."

The first quote references 'the rejected,' who for 2,000 years have been understood by Jews and Christians alike to be the Ishmaelites – the bloodline of Muhammad and the majority of the Arab Muslims. Jesus foretells the kingdom of God being taken from the Jews and

(2.B8) Doctrinal Differences / Divinity of Jesus?

given to a more deserving nation. Muslims assert that no people could be more deserving than those who embrace the teachings and follow the example of all the prophets, Jesus and Muhammad included.

Furthermore, Muslims point out that Makkah is not without mention in the Bible. 'Makkah' is pronounced 'Bakka' in one of the Arabic dialects. Thus, the Holy Qur'an mentions 'Makkah' as 'Makkah' in one passage (48:24) and as 'Bakka' in another verse, which reads, "The first house (of worship) appointed for men was that at Bakka; full of blessing and of guidance for all kinds of beings." (TMQ 3:96). Psalm 84:5-6 provides the remarkable link between Old Testament and Qur'an: "Blessed *is* the man whose strength *is* in You, whose heart *is* set on *pilgrimage. As they* pass through the Valley of Baca, they make it a spring…" The sacred 'spring' of the well of Zamzam in Bakka/Makkah is well known. Additionally, as noted in the form of an editor's comment in E. Gibbon's work, "Mecca cannot be the Macoraba of Ptolemy; the situations do not agree, and till the time of Mahomet, it bore the name of Becca, or the House, from its celebrated temple. It is so called even in some parts of the Koran."[137]

Matters of Creed:

1. Jesus taught the oneness of God (Mark 12:29-30, Matthew 22:37 and Luke 10:27), as conveyed in the first commandment (Exodus 20:3).

2. Jesus declared himself a man and a prophet of God (see above), and nowhere claimed divinity or divine sonship. Which creed are the above two points more consistent with, the Trinitarian formula or the absolute monotheism of Islam?

Practical questions in this regard arise. Questions like, "What was the religion of Jesus?" and "If Jesus lived, preached, and completed his ministry faithful to the religious law of his time, why are those who

---

137. Gibbon, Edward, Esq. Vol. 5, Chapter L, p. 442.

claim to follow in his name not living by his example?" After all, the book of Acts documents how strict the practices were amongst the early followers of Christ Jesus. Acts 10:14 documents Peter's avoidance of unclean animals, 11:2-3, 15:1, and 15:5 the emphasis upon circumcision, 6:7 and 15:5 the conversion of priests and Pharisees into the faith, and 21:20 emphasizes the zeal of the thousands of believers "for the Law." In this regard, Carmichael notes,

> "The above passages are astonishing; they indicate that for a whole generation after Jesus' death his followers were pious Jews and proud of it, had attracted into their fold members of the *professional* religious classes, and did not deviate *even* from the burdensome ceremonial laws."[138]

So that was the first generation of followers. Yet despite the presented scriptural evidences, many Christians prefer to follow the teachings of Paul, the Pope, or select priests and ministers over the recorded teachings of Jesus. As a result, common ground for discussion between the true followers of Jesus and the followers of 'what somebody says about Jesus' is frequently found to be lacking. And although some think this to be a fairly recent disagreement, it is in fact an old division which Paul noted within his lifetime by commenting,

> "Now I say this, that each of you says, "I am of Paul," or "I am of Apollos," or "I am of Cephas," or "I am of Christ."
> (I Corinthians 1:12)

So Paul, Apollos (an Alexandrian Jew), Cephas (Peter), and Christ Jesus all had their own separate and distinct group of followers, each according to his teachings and example. History weeded out the two groups in the middle, leaving a clean separation between those

---

138. Carmichael, Joel. p. 223.

(2.B8) Doctrinal Differences / Divinity of Jesus?

who live "of Paul" and those who are "of Christ." Whereas Christ Jesus proclaimed the Kingdom of God, Paul proclaimed the mysteries which were to prove to be the foundation of the church and modern Christology.

Since Paul had such formative influence upon Trinitarian doctrine, a person wonders what brought him to the mysteries of his belief. Reportedly a light from the heavens, a voice, a convincing message (Acts 9:3-9). But in II Corinthians 11:14-15 even Paul admits that, "...Satan himself transforms himself into an angel of light. Therefore it is no great thing if his ministers also transform themselves into ministers of righteousness..." So whom was Paul talking to? An angel of light or Satan?

Perhaps Paul *thought* he had a divine vision, but how can mankind trust that Paul could tell the difference between an apparition from God and a convincing ploy of the Satan? Paul didn't seem to question the authority that he was to act upon, despite the advice, "Beloved, do not believe every spirit, but test the spirits, whether they are of God; because many false prophets have gone out into the world." (1st Epistle of John 4:1). Regardless of who authored Paul's vision, he was a changed man. And although many a soul has reformed through religious observance, this is simply not the example seen with Paul. Rather, Paul appears to have transitioned from fighting Christianity openly to impacting the Church from within by contradicting the concrete and accepted teachings of Moses *and* Jesus. A person reads of James, the younger brother of Jesus and head of the new church, admonishing Paul for his blasphemous teachings ("but they have been informed about you that you teach all the Jews who are among the Gentiles to forsake Moses, saying that they ought not to circumcise their children nor to walk according to the customs" [Acts 21:21]). James continued by warning Paul of the meeting of the assembly to decide his punishment ("What then? The assembly must

(SECTION 2) GOD

certainly meet, for they will hear that you have come"[Acts 21:22]). Therefore, James directed him to make repentance, purify himself of sacrilege, and thereafter "walk orderly and keep the law," while he still had the chance ("Therefore do what we tell you: We have four men who have taken a vow [which necessitates the purification rituals]. Take them and be purified with them, and pay their expenses so that they may shave their heads, and that all may know that those things of which they were informed concerning you are nothing, but that you yourself also walk orderly and keep the law." [Acts 21:23-24]). Paul's purification didn't last for long. The brother of Jesus – a true disciple and head of the Church – admonished Paul for his blasphemies, to which Paul quickly returned after completing the purification rituals.

A person wonders, *WWJD* -- What *Would* Jesus Do? No doubt he would not concede his revelation to the contrary opinions of Pauline theology. That being the case, why do some people continue to consider Jesus to be divine?

Having reached the halfway point of this chapter, let us summarize some of the above points:

1. Jesus differentiated between himself and God.

2. Jesus exalted God, but defined himself as nothing more than a man and a prophet.

3. The disciples agreed, also acknowledging Christ Jesus as a man and a prophet.

4. The only New Testament verse (I Timothy 3:16) held to support the doctrine of Incarnation is corrupted.

5. The Bible describes the life and history of Jesus in terms which can only be associated with humanity.

6. Rational arguments for the humanity of Jesus overwhelm the emotional defenses of those who seek to support the Incarnation.

(2.B8) Doctrinal Differences / Divinity of Jesus?

7. The example of Jesus, in appearance, manners, religious practices and creed, is better exemplified in the lives of practicing Muslims than in the lives of practicing Christians.

8. Pauline theology and that of Christ Jesus are separate and divergent, having resulted in different schools of thought. So much so that, from the time of Paul, a person had to choose between being a person 'of Paul' or 'of Christ.'

Lacking an explicit Biblical verse to support the theory of Incarnation, the Christian world is forced to justify the theology on the basis of what they consider to be suggestive evidences. What follows, then, is a list of the evidences held to be supportive of the theory of Incarnation, in combination with rebuttal.

'Evidence' #1: Some associate Jesus with divinity because he performed miracles. Many Unitarian Christians and all Muslims disagree on the grounds that Jesus did indeed perform miracles, but by the will of God and not through any divine powers of his own. To repeat the above quote of Acts 2:22, "Jesus of Nazareth, a *man* attested by God to you by miracles, wonders, and signs which *God did* through him in your midst, as you yourselves also know" (emphasis mine). In conformity with both Biblical and Qur'anic teachings, Muslims contend that the miracles of Jesus were performed by the power of God through the vehicle of the person of Christ Jesus. The Holy Qur'an conveys,

> "Then will Allah say: "O Jesus the son of Mary! Recount My favor to you and to your mother. Behold! I strengthened you with the holy spirit, so that you spoke to the people in childhood and in maturity. Behold! I taught you the Book and Wisdom, the Law and the Gospel. And behold! You made out of clay, as it were, the figure of a bird, by My leave, and you breathed into it, and it became a bird by My leave, and

(SECTION 2) GOD

you healed those born blind, and the lepers, by My leave. And behold! You brought forth the dead by My leave." (TMQ 5:110).

The Islamic perspective is that miracles can be God-given signs to convince mankind that just as a prophet's actions bear divine endorsement, likewise he speaks with divine authority. However, taken individually the performance of miracles cannot be considered a sign of divinity, for many Biblical characters are recorded as having performed miracles similar to those of Jesus. For example, multiple traditions relate hundreds of miracles of Muhammad with greater historical authenticity than Biblical manuscripts. While the science of authenticating hadith* (traditions relating the words, deeds, appearance, and approvals of Muhammad) is regarded as a wonder of historical record keeping, the Bible does not satisfy many of the most basic requirements of accuracy in the historical record. For example, authors of many of the books (including the Gospels) are unknown, the time period in which they were written is ill-defined, and the source of much of the related information is ambiguous. These issues will be discussed at greater length in subsequent sections, but a small teaser is to examine the story of Judas' betrayal of Jesus to the chief priests. Where did the writer get his information? Nobody knows. Who witnessed the betrayal? Doesn't say. Was the gospel writer there? Would hardly make sense. Was the passage revealed by God? Nothing in the Gospels seems to indicate so.

The Jesus Seminar is perhaps one of the most objective and sincere attempts in modern history of an ecumenical council of Christian

---

* For a brief discussion of hadith methodology, see the author's website, www.leveltruth.com, under appendices to the book. For more in-depth study, the reader is referred to *Hadith Literature: Its Origins, Development and Special Features*, by Muhammad Zubayr Siddiqi (Islamic Texts Society, London, 1993), and *Studies in Hadith Methodology and Literature,* by Muhammad Mustafa Azami (American Trust Publications, Indianapolis, 1977).

(2.B8) Doctrinal Differences / Divinity of Jesus?

scholars to determine the authenticity of the recorded acts and sayings of Jesus. Yet their methodology involves casting votes. Two thousand years after the ministry of Jesus, nearly two hundred scholars are formulating a collective Christian opinion regarding the reliability of the quotes and historical reports of Jesus by casting colored beads. For example, as regards the reported words of Jesus, the definitions of the bead colors are as follows:

> "Red – Jesus said it or something very close to it. Pink – Jesus probably said something like it, although his words have suffered in transmission. Gray – these are not his words, but the ideas are close to his own. Black – Jesus did not say it; the words represent the Christian community or a later point of view."[139]

Other Christian committees have attempted authentication of the canonized Bible text by similar methodologies. Hence, a person finds,

> "By means of the letters A, B, C, and D, enclosed within 'braces' { } at the beginning of each set of textual variants the Committee has sought to indicate the relative degree of certainty, arrived at the basis of internal considerations as well as of external evidence, for the reading adopted as the text. The letter A signifies that the text is virtually certain, while B indicates that there is some degree of doubt. The letter C means that there is a considerable degree of doubt whether the text of the apparatus contains the superior reading, while D shows that there is a very high degree of doubt concerning the reading selected for the text."[140]

---

139. Funk, Robert Walter. 1996. *Honest to Jesus, Jesus for a New Millennium.* Polebridge Press. p. 8.

140. Aland, Kurt, Matthew Black, Carlo M. Martini, Bruce M. Metzger & Allen Wikgren (Editors). 1968. *The Greek New Testament.* Second Edition. United Bible Societies. pp. x-xi.

(SECTION 2) GOD

These ranking systems are probably about the best to be contrived given the material at hand, and do serve the useful purpose of exposing the strengths and weaknesses of the Biblical text. However, next to the exquisitely refined authentication system of hadith methodology, these classification systems suffer significant embarrassment.

The issue of accuracy of historical record-keeping is relevant, for when a person hears a story – even a believable story at that – the first question should always be, "Where did you hear that?" Any reasonable set of historical standards includes the identification and verification of sources. The Holy Qur'an and many traditions of Muhammad satisfy the highest degrees of authentication, but the majority of Biblical passages do not.

The issue at hand, however, is that Jesus is not the only historical figure reported to have been a prophet and to have great miracles enter the world through his person – certainly the miracles which occurred through the person of Muhammad are no less numerous or impressive, and are witnessed by a historical record which puts all other records of similar time period to shame. Just as the miracles of Moses, Elisha, and Muhammad do not elevate them to divine status, Jesus should not be considered as sharing divine office due to the miracles performed during his ministry.

For example:

(A) Jesus reportedly fed thousands with a few fish and loaves of bread. And by the will of God Elisha fed a hundred people with twenty barley loaves and a few ears of corn (II Kings 4:44); granted a widow such abundance of flow from a jar of oil that she was able to pay off her debts, save her sons from slavery, and live on the profits (II Kings 4:1-7); and gave increase to a handful of flour and spot of oil such that he, a widow and her son had enough to eat for many days, after which "The bin of flour was not used up, nor did the jar of oil run dry..." (I Kings 17:10-16). So what does that make Elisha?

(2.B8) Doctrinal Differences / Divinity of Jesus?

The historical record of Muhammad feeding the masses with just a handful of dates on one occasion, a small pot of milk on another, and just enough meat for a small party on still another are equally miraculous. Likewise are the stories of his watering the masses (1,500 people on one occasion) with just a small bowl of water. Yet Muslims do not elevate Muhammad above the rank of human prophethood.

(B) Jesus healed the lepers. But likewise did Elisha heal Naaman (II Kings 5:7-14). For that matter, the disciples were bidden to such service in Matthew 10:8. What does that make them?

(C) Jesus cured a blind man. Elisha not only dealt blindness to his enemies, but restored vision to the blind through prayer (II Kings 6:17-20). Muhammad is reported to have cured blindness through prayer as well.

(D) Jesus raised the dead. Once again, Elisha preceded this feat by raising a child who was dead for a short time (I Kings 17:22) as well as another child who was dead for a long time (II Kings 4:34). Even the dead bones of Elisha reportedly revived a dead man whose corpse was temporarily hidden in Elisha's tomb. As soon as the dead man's body touched the bones of Elisha, he revived (II Kings 13:21). Furthermore, the disciples were also bidden to raise the dead (Matthew 10:8). So once again, what does that make them?

(E) Jesus walked on water. Had he been around in the time of Moses, he might not have had to.

(F) Jesus cast out devils. So did his disciples (Matthew 10:8). So did the sons of the Pharisees (Matthew12:27 and Luke 11:19). So, for that matter, do the wayward followers whom Jesus will reportedly disown (see Matthew 7:22) – an item of interest and concern to all who feel faith bolstered by priests and ministers who produce such theatrics, even if real.

(SECTION 2) GOD

'Evidence' #2: The Old Testament predicted the coming of Jesus. Yes, and Christian scholarship acknowledges that the Old Testament predicted the coming of John the Baptist in the book of 'Malachi.' There are also Old and New Testament predictions of a prophet to come which do not fit the profile of either John the Baptist or Jesus (see 'Messengers'—section 4).

'Evidence' #3: The Bible describes God as 'Saviour' and Jesus as 'saviour.' Conclusion? God is 'Saviour,' Jesus is 'saviour,' therefore Jesus is God? The conflict with this concept is that Othniel, Ehud, Shamgan, Gideon, and other anonymous 'saviours' deserve invitation to the party. Why? The Hebrew word by which God is identified as saviour in the Old Testament is *yasha*.' This word *yasha* appears 207 times in the Old Testament Hebrew, amongst which are references to Othniel (Judges 3:9), Ehud (Judges 3:15), Shamgan (Judges 3:31), Gideon (Judges 8:22), and anonymous individuals (2 Kings 13:5, Neh 9:27, Oba 1:21). Why is this word *yasha* translated differently for these individuals than for Jesus and for God? Only the translators know for sure, but the motivations appear less than honorable. The end result is that the selective mistranslation shelters the unsuspecting public from recognizing the application of this word to be far from exclusive.

'Evidence' #4: Jesus is recorded in John 8:58 as having said, "...before Abraham was, I AM" and Exodus 3:14 records God as having informed Moses, "I AM WHO I AM." First of all, according to the words of Jesus, is a person to conclude that Jesus had a pre-human existence? According to Jeremiah 1:5, so did Jeremiah. According to the Islamic religion, so did all mankind. Next, is a person to draw a parallel between the 'I AM' attributed to Jesus and that attributed to God? Once again the foundational text pokes fun at the translation. Jesus is *not* recorded to have said "...I AM" in capital 'makes-me-look-like-God' letters. Jesus is *translated* as having said

(2.B8) DOCTRINAL DIFFERENCES / DIVINITY OF JESUS?

"...I AM" in a 'looks-like-God's-words-in-Exodus, think-they'll-buy-it?' effort at textual synchronization. What Jesus *is* recorded to have said is *'eimi'* in small, humble, uncapitalized, unprepossessing and non-exclusive (found 152 times in the New Testament) Greek letters which don't justify capitals *or* comparison with the supposed words of God in Exodus (which themselves are not capitalized, either in the Hebrew *'hayah'* or the Greek Septuagint *'ho ohn'*). By no means can the New Testament Greek *'eimi'* attributed to Jesus be compared with the Old Testament Greek *'ho ohn'* attributed to God in the Septuagint. By no means of honesty or accuracy, that is. Likewise, neither can either one of these phrases honestly be capitalized "I AM," especially in light of the 151 other instances of *'eimi'* being translated to the uncapitalized, "I am." Why is *'eimi'* capitalized once and not capitalized 151 times, if not due to the selective desires of the translators? To their own credit, most reputable Bibles avoid this textual games-playing, and translation of the words of Jesus are not capitalized to 'I AM' in the *New International Version*, the *Revised Standard Version*, the *New Revised Standard Version*, the *American Standard Version*, and many others.

'Evidence' #5: Mark 16:19 and Luke 22:69 report that Jesus was received into heaven, where he sat at the right hand of God. Of initial significance is that Mark 16:9-20 is under question and has been rejected from many Bibles, for the reason that Mark 16:9-20 is of doubtful scriptural authority.[141] Barring the consideration that the entire passage may not have been revealed in the first place, the argument that closeness to God makes one equal to, partners with, or part of God breaches clear from the waters of reason. The Bible says Jesus sat with God. The conclusion that God sat beside Himself, on his own right side is a true stretch of the imagination. In conflict

---

141. See *New Catholic Encyclopedia*, Vol 2, p. 395, where Mark 16:9-20 is listed amongst the "doubtfully authentic deuterocanonical sections" included in the Bible canon by the decree of Trent. Also see footnote to these verses in the NRSV.

(SECTION 2) GOD

with this bizarre thought is Isaiah 44:6, which reads, "Thus says the Lord…'I am the First and I am the Last; besides Me there is no God.'" Isaiah 43:11 reinforces with, "I, even I, am the Lord, and besides Me there is no savior." So what is the argument again? That Jesus sat beside Himself, Theirselves, Godselves, whatever – but he sat beside God *without* sitting beside God because, "Besides Me there is no God," and "…besides me there is no savior."? A true dilemma arises – either Jesus sat beside God and therefore is neither God *nor* savior, or he didn't sit beside God as reported and the Bible is unreliable. Both conclusions support the humanity of Jesus, and neither suggests partnership with God. So what is a person supposed to believe? The Bible also says, "And Enoch *walked* with God…" (Genesis 5:24). So what does that make him?

'Evidence' #6: Some Christians attribute divinity to Jesus because they believe that Jesus forgave sins. Luke 5:20 reads, "So when he saw their faith, he said to him, "Man, your sins are forgiven you'" and Luke 7:47-48 states something similar, "Therefore I say to you, her sins, which are many, are forgiven….And he said to her, 'Your sins are forgiven.'" The claim is that, by these words, Jesus forgave the sins of the people concerned. Others suggest that the wording is more indicative of Jesus informing the individuals that their sins were forgiven than of Jesus actually forgiving sins of his own initiative. Significantly, Jesus did not pronounce, "I forgive your sins." Passing on the forgiveness of The Creator, of which knowledge Jesus was no doubt privileged through revelation, is consistent with John 12:49 – "For I have not spoken on my own authority, but the Father who sent me gave me a command, what I should say and what I should speak." Furthermore, assuming that Jesus forgave sins on his own initiative contradicts the statement, "I can of myself do nothing…" (John 5:30).

A deeper question is not whether Jesus was recorded as having

(2.B8) Doctrinal Differences / Divinity of Jesus?

power to forgive sins, but whether or not such an attribute would make Jesus equal to God. The Pharisees are reported as having thought so, but Jesus is recorded as having corrected them. Luke 5:21 records, "And the scribes and the Pharisees began to reason, saying, 'Who is this who speaks blasphemies? Who can forgive sins but God alone?'" Again, the argument is that the Pharisees thought Jesus laid claim to being God, so we should too. However, it's a peculiar argument – that the people who hated Jesus, the people who defied him and obstructed his mission, lied against him, fabricated evidence at his trial, plotted the humiliation, beating, and murder of Jesus, *they* knew him best. Jesus is recorded as having stated that the Jews *didn't* understand him. Consistent with this observation is the fact that Jesus is recorded in the very next verse, Luke 5:22, as having rebuked the Pharisees for their suggestion with the words, "…'Why are you reasoning in your hearts?'" (as opposed to reasoning with their minds), which is the rough scriptural equivalent of having told the Pharisees that they didn't know what they were talking about, for they were allowing their emotions to override rational judgement.

And again, what better place for Jesus to have asserted his divinity with authority, if, that is, he were in fact divine? What better place for Jesus to have affirmed the suggestion of the Pharisees and to have explained the alleged triunity of God? But he didn't do that, and a person has to assume he had good reason not to, for in fact he stated the exact opposite.

'Evidence' #7: So perhaps the fact that God was called 'Lord' (Greek '*kurios*,') and Jesus was also called 'lord' can be bent into service. This argument also doesn't work, for a whole lot of other people were likewise called 'lord.' However, once again, selective capitalization of the translation of '*kurios*,' where it suits the doctrinal purpose of the translators, becomes evident. 'Lord' is a title of respect, and as evidenced by numerous stories throughout the Bible,

181

(SECTION 2) GOD

including Matthew 18:23-34 and Luke 19:11-21, the title 'Lord' does not, of itself, imply divinity. For example, Sarah called Abraham 'lord' (I Peter 3:6). Nonetheless, John 20:28 is held up as evidence, quoting Thomas as having identified Jesus as "My Lord and my God!" I Corinthians 8:6 seems somewhat at odds with this verse, reading, "Yet for us there is only one God, the Father...and one Lord Jesus Christ...." 'Lord' and 'God' are defined as separate and distinct entities in one passage, but one and the same in another – two descriptions which a person would think to be mutually exclusive. Exodus 4:16 evokes a certain interest in this regard. The Greek literally translates to Moses being *Elohim* (God) to Aaron. Substitution of the word 'as' to distort the translation to read 'as God' has no basis in the manuscript, but it does throw laity off the unmistakable scent of an overwarmed theology gone bad. In a book where pagan gods (e.g., Ex. 12:12; 18:11; 20:3), judges (Psalms 82:1&6), angels (Psalm 8:5), and prophets (Exodus 4:16) are identified with the same *'Elohim'* as The One True God, beside Whom there is no other, who can trust a doctrine based on human interpretations of ancient colloquialisms?

'**Evidence' #8**: People 'worshipped' Jesus, and he did not object. Well, that's not quite true, is it? What the foundational Greek manuscripts record is that people *'proskuneo'ed'* Jesus, and he did not object. The word *'proskuneo'* has a selective translation in some Bibles to 'worship,' 'worshipped,' etc., but the full range of meanings is as follows:

> "*proskuneo, pros-koo-neh'-o*; from G4314 and a prob. der. of G2965 (mean. to kiss, like a dog licking his master's hand); to fawn or crouch to, i.e., (lit.or fig.) prostrate oneself in homage (do reverence to, adore): – worship."[142]

---

142. *Strong's Exhaustive Concordance of the Bible.*

(2.B8) DOCTRINAL DIFFERENCES / DIVINITY OF JESUS?

One would think it to be a fair assumption that few, if any, conceive the faithful to have licked the hand of Jesus like a dog licking the hand of it's master. Kissing the hand of Jesus might make more sense but assuming, for the sake of argument, that some of the faithful prostrated to Jesus, a person might then question the significance of such a gesture. Matthew 18:26 records the story of a slave who '*proskuneo*'ed' his master begging for forgiveness of his debts. Mark 15:16-20 records the humiliation of Jesus prior to the alleged crucifixion as follows:

> "Then the soldiers led him away into the hall called Praetorium, and they called together the whole garrison. And they clothed him with purple; and they twisted a crown of thorns, put it on his head, and began to salute him, "Hail, King of the Jews!" Then they struck him on the head with a reed and spat on him; and bowing the knee, they worshiped (*proskuneo*'ed) him. And when they had mocked him, they took the purple off him, put his own clothes on him, and led him out to crucify him."

Acts 10:25 records: "As Peter was coming in, Cornelius met him and fell down at his feet and worshiped (*proskuneo*'ed) him." Old Testament references include 1 Samuel 25:23, in which Abigail "fell on her face before David, and bowed down to the ground." 2 Kings 4:37 speaks of a Shunammite woman who, after having her child revived through the prayers of Elisha, "…fell at his feet, and bowed to the ground…" Genesis 50:18 and 2 Samuel 19:18 weigh into the equation as well.

Taken in total, the word '*proskuneo*' can only imply divinity if Peter, David, and Elisha, among others, are invited to the party. Otherwise, selective translation must be assumed, for when the mocking soldiers prostrated, theirs was a noteworthy posture, but

(SECTION 2) GOD

devoid of any true devotion. Likewise, there should be little doubt that when others prostrated to Peter, David, Elisha, the slave-master, etc., theirs was a gesture of respect common to the customs of their time. Extending such a gesture of respect to Jesus seems to have been a matter of course. However, the main question is, "Did the people revere Jesus as God in so doing?" Noteworthy is that nobody is recorded as having prayed to Jesus, and the rights due to God were directed to God and to Him alone. Jesus is recorded as having taught: "You shall worship the Lord your God, and Him only you shall serve." (Luke 4:8) Intriguing to note is that the only duty which is restricted to God alone in the above teaching is not the word translated to 'worship,' but rather that translated to 'serve.' The latter is the Greek '*latreuo*,' which bears the following definition:

> "latreuo, lat-ryoo'-o; from latris (a hired menial); to minister (to God), i.e., render religious homage: – serve, do the service, worship (-per)."[143]

The definition of '*latreuo*' is relatively narrow. There is little or no room for manipulation to alternate understandings, as is the case with the aforementioned '*proskuneo*.' And significantly, out of a grand total of 22 uses in the New Testament, the word '*latreuo*' nowhere applies to Jesus. Consequently, the point may be made that while some people seem to have prostrated to Jesus in accordance with the customs of their day, they did not '*latreuo*,' or render religious homage, to Jesus. Both Jesus and his followers not only prostrated to God, but also reserved their servitude for Him alone, according to the laws He prescribed. Who is the Lord and Master of Creation, and who is His servant, seems clear.

'Evidence' #9: Some attribute divinity to Jesus based upon his alleged resurrection. This subject is critical, for the keystone of

---

143. *Strong's Exhaustive Concordance of the Bible.*

(2.B8) Doctrinal Differences / Divinity of Jesus?

Christianity is the belief that Jesus died for the sins of mankind. The concepts of the crucifixion, resurrection and atonement are discussed more fully in following sections. However, for now the point deserves to be made that even amongst first-century Christians the crucifixion and resurrection were controversial topics. They have remained so to this day. The reason for this controversy relates to the fact that none of the gospels is an eyewitness account – they are all based on second or third-hand information, as recognized by Joel Carmichael, who commented upon what the Gospels record as the last words of Jesus, "It may be legitimate to doubt the historic authenticity of these words as coming from Jesus' own mouth; who could the witnesses have been?"[144] and further clarifies, "Not only do they (the disciples) 'all forsake' Jesus and flee; they do not – even more surprisingly – reappear during Jesus' trial nor are they present at his execution, nor are they the ones who bury him."[145]

Many scholars – predominantly those whose salaries are not directly proportional to the Sunday tithe – agree that the gospel writers worked off nothing but hearsay evidence in recording the supposed crucifixion. Even the *New Catholic Encyclopedia* admits, "The four Evangelists differ slightly in the wording of the inscription (on top of the cross), which shows that they were citing from memory and hearsay evidence."[146]

The grim fact is that this has been well recognized since the time of Jesus, but thoroughly covered up by those who would have humankind believe the authors of the gospels had front row seats and photographic memories. In reality, all of the disciples deserted Jesus at the garden of Gethsemane as recorded in Mark 14:50 -- "Then they all forsook him and fled." Peter may have followed Jesus at a distance,

---

144. Carmichael, Joel. p. 202.
145. Carmichael, Joel. p. 206.
146. *New Catholic Encyclopedia*. Vol 4, p. 486.

(SECTION 2) GOD

but only as far as the courtyard of the high priest Caiaphas. Here 'The Rock' (on which Jesus promised to build his church, complete with the promise of the keys of heaven -- Matthew 16:18-19) thrice denied (Did Jesus say 'rock?' Perhaps what he really meant to say was 'Satan' and 'an offense,' as pronounced by Jesus just a scant *five* verses later in Matthew 16:23. A greater reversal of fortunes would be hard to imagine, but such is the shaky endorsement of the man Catholics hold to have been the first pope of the Catholic Church) knowing Jesus. Anyway, Peter is not acknowledged to have been one of the gospel authors. So where were *they*? Matthew 27:55 and Luke 23:49 point out that the observers were distanced from the crucifixion, so no answer can be given except on pure speculation.

Regarding the supposed resurrection, nobody seems to agree on what happened following the crucifixion. The four gospels (Matthew 28, Mark 16, Luke 24, and John 20) read as follows:

Who went to the tomb?
Answer:
    Matthew: "Mary Magdalene and the other Mary"
    Mark: "Mary Magdalene, Mary the mother of James, and Salome"
    Luke: "The women who had come with him from Galilee" and "certain other women"
    John: "Mary Magdalene"

Why did they go to the tomb?
    Matthew: "To see the tomb"
    Mark: they "brought spices, that they might come and anoint him"
    Luke: they "brought spices"
    John: no reason given

(2.B8) Doctrinal Differences / Divinity of Jesus?

Was there an earthquake (something a person expects would not easily go unnoticed)?
    Matthew: Yes
    Mark: no mention
    Luke: no mention
    John: no mention

Did an angel descend (again, a significant enough event that a person would not expect any self-respecting gospel writer to have missed or forgotten it)?
    Matthew: Yes
    Mark: no mention
    Luke: no mention
    John: no mention

Who rolled back the stone?
    Matthew: The angel
    Mark: unknown
    Luke: unknown
    John: unknown

Who was at the tomb?
    Matthew: "an angel"
    Mark: "a young man"
    Luke: "two men"
    John: "two angels"

Where were they?
    Matthew: The angel was sitting on the stone, outside the tomb.
    Mark: The young man was inside the tomb, "sitting on the right side."
    Luke: The two men were inside the tomb, standing beside them.
    John: The two angels were "sitting, one at the head and the other at the feet, where the body of Jesus had lain."

(SECTION 2) GOD

By whom and where was Jesus first seen?
  Matthew: Mary Magdalene and the "other Mary," on the road to tell the disciples.
  Mark: Mary Magdalene only, no mention where.
  Luke: Two of the disciples, en route to "a village called Emmaus, which was about seven miles from Jerusalem."
  John: Mary Magdalene, outside the tomb.

Little or no consistency to the stories, which leads a person to question what the Bible is – a book of viewpoints, or a book of God. Heinz Zahrnt concludes his analysis as follows:

> "The days of the unhistorical doctrine of verbal inspiration as held by Old Protestant theology are over. From now onwards the Bible is understood as an historical book, written and transmitted by men and therefore subject to the same laws of tradition, the same errors, omissions and alterations as any other historical source. The men who produced it were no automata, instruments of God, but individual writers, men of flesh and blood who had their own decided aims and tendencies in writing, who lived within the limited horizons of their time and were moulded by the ideas of their environment."[147]

Many who examine the evidence with an objective and open mind find themselves inclined to agree. After all, the details of each of the above four accounts being correct would constitute the impossible, while the concept of revelation at odds with itself would constitute the ungodly. If the Bible is to be considered a book of God a person's concept of God is challenged – does a person conceive God to be characterized by inconsistencies such as the above? If the

---

147. Zahrnt, Heinz. 1817. *The Historical Jesus.* (Translated from the German by J. S. Bowden). New York: Harper and Row. p. 42.

(2.B8) Doctrinal Differences / Divinity of Jesus?

Bible is to be considered a book of human viewpoints then no person can be faulted for any opinion they construct around the loose and jumbled framework of contradictory teachings found therein. A person can assert that despite the differences, all four gospels teach the crucifixion, and this is true. Many people find such thoughts sufficient to satisfy beliefs. Others wonder what alternative viewpoints were reduced to ashes in the destruction of the estimated 250 to 2,000 acts, epistles, and gospels which the council of Nicaea excluded from canonization, and why the alleged crucifixion was debated amongst early first century Christians (i.e., What did they know that we don't?). With regard to the present issue, none of these points matter. Even if the story of the crucifixion were true, being raised from the dead would not imply divinity of Jesus any more than it does for the children raised through the prayers of Elisha, the dead man revived through touching Elisha's bones, or Lazarus resurrected at the hands of Jesus. For that matter, God promises to raise all mankind come the Day of Judgement – what will that make us?

'Evidence' #10: Some attribute divinity to Christ Jesus because he spoke of things to come (i.e., he had foreknowledge of certain events in the future). However, isn't that the job of a prophet? To prophesy? And isn't that the example of all the prophets, for that matter, for how else was the coming of Jesus predicted in the Old Testament? Importantly, prophets only have foreknowledge of that which is revealed to them, whereas the knowledge of God is absolute. Were Christ Jesus the son of God or some element of divinity, a person would expect his knowledge to have been comprehensive. Yet we encounter teachings which counter this expectation, such as,

> "Particularly difficult to explain would be the logion of Mk 13.31 concerning the Last Day: 'But of that day or hour no one knows, neither the angels in heaven, nor the Son, but the

(SECTION 2) GOD

Father only.' The authenticity of this passage can hardly be questioned, for a community bent on exalting its Lord would scarcely have constructed a saying in which He confesses ignorance."[148]

Summary of 'Evidences': Some people consider that, despite the objections, the sheer number of the above 'evidences' suggests the divinity of Jesus. This assertion betrays a misunderstanding of logic. A large number of evidences could certainly suggest a specific conclusion, but only if each evidence brings something to support the conclusion. It doesn't have to be a lot, but there has to be some buoyancy in order to float the argument. Either a couple big logs or a million tiny twigs bundled together will bear a man down a river. An ounce of gold can be gained from one huge nugget, or from a hundred chunks of crude ore with gold laced into the matrix. A court case can be concluded with one perfect photo or a hundred suggestive testimonies, but a million worthless testimonies won't support a verdict. Basing a doctrine on ten, or a hundred, or even a thousand 'evidences,' each one of which brings nothing to support the conclusion, is as futile as trying to float a raft of rocks, or smelt salt for gold. Add more rocks to the raft, smelt more salt, the desired result will remain elusive, just as a conclusion evades a million 'evidences,' each one of which lacks the slightest validity.

Do any other 'evidences' for the presumed divinity of Jesus remain? When all else fails some clergy claim that Jesus was filled with the holy spirit, and therefore he must be divine. But does the Church assert that Jesus was filled with the holy spirit in some manner different from Peter (Acts 4:8), Stephen (Acts 6:5 and 7:55), Barnabas (Acts 11:24), Elizabeth (Luke 1:41), and Zacharias (Luke 1:67)?

---

148. *New Catholic Encyclopedia*. Vol 13, p. 428.

(2.B8) Doctrinal Differences / Divinity of Jesus?

Some set Jesus apart from the above individuals, claiming that Jesus was filled with the holy spirit since before birth. Others point out that John the Baptist was not associated with divinity, though Luke 1:15 records, "...He (John the Baptist) will also be filled with the holy spirit, even from his mother's womb."

Some regard the holy spirit as an integral with God. Others struggle to grasp the concept, certain only that whatever the 'holy spirit' is, it is sent to all of the righteous of mankind as is written, "And we are His witnesses to these things, and so also is the holy spirit whom God has given to those who obey Him" (Acts 5:32). The conclusion that the holy spirit is given to all who obey God has the clear ring of reason, and at least this concept stands up to scripture. The question then arises, "What is this 'holy spirit?'"

(2.B) Doctrinal Differences

(2.B9) Holy Spirit

"Free from desire, you realize the mystery.
Caught in desire, you see only the manifestations."
— Lao-Tzu, *Tao Te Ching*

'Holy Spirit' is yet one more term which deserves definition prior to discussion. However, for most people 'Holy Spirit' or 'Holy Ghost' conceptually defies confinement to words. What comes from most mouths, clergy and laity alike, usually reflects an individualized blend of parroted doctrinal teachings and personal imagination, if not wishful thinking. The product is typically an easily separated mix of personal opinion and ambiguous, though doctrinally sanctioned, apologetics. Like oil and water, such a mixture separates into immiscible components in the minds of many, and as such fails to gel into a solid and homogeneous reality. The Islamic understanding, on the other hand, is remarkably concrete, teaching that the 'Holy Spirit' is Gabriel, the angel of revelation. When a person comes to '*Rûh-ul-Qudus*' in the Holy Qur'an (see ayah 2:87), some (like Yusuf Ali) translate 'holy spirit,' others (like Muhammad Al-Hilali and Muhammad Khan) translate 'Gabriel' and still others (like Saheeh International) offer both 'holy spirit' and 'Gabriel,' reflecting the fact that in the creed of the Muslim the two terms are synonymous.

(2.B9) Doctrinal Differences / Holy Spirit

While Qur'an and Hadith teach that the scripture of Jesus no longer exists in the purity of the original, and that the Bible is to one degree or another corrupted, many Muslims still contend that the truth of Islam can be found *in the Bible*. And since Muslims frequently attempt to justify Islamic ideology on the basis of Biblical teachings, one might well question, "How does a Muslim explain the use of 'Holy Spirit' in the Bible?" For a person can *not* substitute 'Angel Gabriel' for 'Holy Spirit' in all cases and have it make sense."

At first glance the question may appear to be a valid challenge to Islamic proselytizing, for 'Angel Gabriel' truly cannot be substituted for the words 'Holy Spirit' in every instance, without rendering certain passages of the Bible implausible or insensible. The challenge, then, is for Muslims to either make sense of each and every point of contention between Islamic and Christian creed, *from a Biblical perspective*, or to stop arguing Islam on the basis of the Bible completely. This would seem to be an ultimately fair challenge, for otherwise Muslims can be reasonably accused of the same disingenuousness with which they charge the Christian world – namely that of selectively employing only those Bible quotes which suit their purpose, while dismissing without legitimately discrediting all verses which prove ideologically uncomfortable. However, at least two points need to be considered in order to understand the Islamic perspective. The first concerns the questionable reliability of the Bible, which will be addressed in the chapters devoted to that subject (sections 3.A. and 3.B.). The second point interdigitates with the first, lying in an analysis of intentions, for Muslims do not claim the Bible to be unadulterated revelation from God pointing the way to the Holy Qur'an and Islam. Rather, Muslims consider the Bible to be very much adulterated, polluted with teachings which have been unfaithfully inserted or manipulated by men while the hillocks of divine truth visibly rise clear and identifiable above the jungle of

(Section 2) God

contradictory human insertions. That which is from God is understood to be demonstrable as such whereas that which is from man bears the earmarks of suspicion, signaling the need for canonical caution. Recognizing the possibility that literary license has been assumed by Bible translators, who are under suspicion for having tailored translation to suit doctrinal desires, is of key importance.

The thrust of Unitarian Christian and Muslim argument, then, focuses not only upon faithful adherence to substantiated truth, wherever it may be found, but also upon the casting out of illegitimate conclusions, whether allegedly Bible-based or otherwise.

With regard to the word 'spirit,' a case can be made to support the claim that the translation is an inaccurate distortion of the foundational Greek manuscripts. Various voices of Islam would be expected to agree, but Christian opinion is far more convincing as evidenced by such statements as, "The term 'spirit' translates Hebrew (*ruach*) and Greek (*pneuma*) – words denoting 'wind,' 'breath,' and, by extension, a life-giving element."[149] Should a person research 'spirit' in Kittel and Friedrich's *Theological Dictionary of the New Testament*, the researcher will encounter reference to the Greek '*pneúma*,' as mentioned above. However, an interesting complication to unquestioning doctrinal acceptance develops, for the accepted meanings of '*pneúma*' are listed to include: *Wind, Breath, Life, Soul, Transferred* (i.e., Metaphorical) Sense of Spirit, Mantic pneúma (the spirit that stirs and inspires), *Divine pneúma* (about which the authors comment "But there is in Greek no sense of a personal holy spirit."), the *pneúma* of Stoicism (to which few, in the modern day, subscribe), and *Non-Greek Development of Meaning* (which is to say, 'unauthentic,' for even the Greek is not the language of Christ Jesus).[150]

---

149. Achtemeier, Paul J. p. 401.

150. Kittel, Gerhard and Gerhard Friedrich. pp. 876-877.

(2.B9) Doctrinal Differences / Holy Spirit

If a person reads the above carefully, he or she may notice that considerable literary license has been assumed in translating '*pneúma*' to 'spirit.' Saying the same thing in different words, in the above list the correct and direct translation of '*pneúma*' is nowhere 'holy spirit.' According to the above text (which is widely considered to be one of the most authoritative and scholarly references on this subject worldwide), the word '*pneúma*' bears diverse possibilities in translation. Of course, 'holy wind' or 'holy breath' do not support Trinitarian doctrine as does 'holy spirit,' and the concept of working to objectively discover the truth of God's message does not afford the same peer approval as manipulating the supposed words of revelation to support institutional decrees.

Also noteworthy is the startling coincidence between 'John' being dramatically more poetic than any of the other gospels and 'John's' apparently unique utilization of the Mantic '*pneúma*,' as described above. So great is the disparity that one author comments, "The paucity of statements about the Spirit in Mark and Matthew is surprising."[151] Couple this find with the fact that the doctrines of the Trinity and divine sonship of Jesus primarily stem from strained interpretations of the poeticisms of 'John,' with little, if any, scriptural support from other gospels, and critical concern buckles forth from the overstressed foundation of the proposed doctrines.

Undeniably, there is ample room for healthy skepticism and alternative understanding of Biblical scripture. There are those who read the Bible and understand 'Holy Spirit' to be an indefinable third element of divinity, in line with the '*pneúma*' of Stoicism or the unauthentic meaning developed following the period of revelation. Others understand God to be One, without partner or subdivision, and search for that which is rational and justified according to logic. For this latter group 'Holy Spirit' can not be understood except in reference to a concrete entity separate and distinct from God.

---
151. Kittel, Gerhard and Gerhard Friedrich. p. 886.

(SECTION 2) GOD

An example of how the Bible suffers in translation, and why conclusions vary as consequence, is the following: the Greek 'paraclete' can mean "helper, defender, mediator, consoler."[152] Elsewhere it is translated "advocate, helper."[153] Harper's concurs with "advocate."[154] Why is this important? Because,

> "The word Paraclete occurs only five times in the Bible, and all five occurrences are in the supposed writings of St. John: 1st Epistle of John 2:1; and the Gospel according to John 14:16, 14:26, 15:26, 16:7."[155]

Should a person assume that this word slipped the minds of the other three gospel writers? If so, one would suspect that it must not have been very important…but on the contrary, these five passages are *critical*. In fact, Trinitarian emphasis on the need to accept the 'Holy Spirit' hinges on these few quotes. A person can appreciate the peculiarity of this incongruity, for if the concept of the 'Paraclete' is so crucial to the creed God wants man to gain from revelation, one wonders why it didn't make enough of an impression on the other three gospel authors to be worthy of mention. Even once.

Whatever the motivations, *'paraclete'* is one more term which is frequently mistranslated as 'Holy Spirit' or 'Holy Ghost.' Modern translation of the Bible is tending toward greater honesty, accuracy, and academic integrity, and yet *'paraclete'* is still often mistranslated as 'counselor,' or 'comforter'. The correct translation as 'helper, defender, mediator, consoler,' or 'advocate, helper' (as quoted above) would imply an actual physical entity, which would be consistent with the notion that "Some trace the origin of the use of *parakletos* in the

---

152. *New Catholic Encyclopedia*. Vol 10, p. 989.
153. Kittel, Gerhard and Gerhard Friedrich. p. 782.
154. Achtemeier, Paul J. p. 749.
155. *New Catholic Encyclopedia*. Vol 10, p. 989.

(2.B9) Doctrinal Differences / Holy Spirit

Johannine works back to the concept of heavenly helpers."[156] And who could be a greater 'heavenly helper' than Gabriel, the angel of revelation himself?

Similarly,

"In 1st cent. Greek, *Parakletos* was a legal term used mainly of advocate, defender, or intercessor. True to its basic meaning one 'called out to stand beside, defend, advise or intercede,' it was used of legal counsel and witnesses alike."[157]

The above quote defines what the word meant in the time of the revelation. But somewhere in the passage of time, select theologians claimed to have known better, and consequently developed a disparate understanding. Association of *'parakletos'* with a material and physical entity proved inconvenient, and appears to have been avoided at great ethical cost.

And so, to review:

(1) The definition of 'holy spirit' is elusive in Christianity, but concrete in Islam (i.e., synonymous with the angel of revelation, Gabriel).

(2) The definitions of *'pneúma'* (translated to 'spirit' in the Bible) are diverse, but is not correctly translated 'holy spirit' anywhere in the original meaning of the Greek.

(3) Only according to the derived and unauthentic, 'non-Greek development of meaning' is *'pneúma'* translated to 'holy spirit.'

(4) Christian theology regarding the 'holy spirit' depends virtually entirely on the gospel and first epistle of 'John.'

(5) The 'Paraclete' verses in the gospel and first epistle of 'John' are absolutely critical to the Christian teaching of the need to accept the 'holy spirit.'

---

156. Kittel, Gerhard and Gerhard Friedrich. p. 783.
157. Hastings, James. *Dictionary of The Bible.* p. 183.

(Section 2) God

(6) The 'Paraclete' is not mentioned in any of the other gospels or epistles of the New Testament.

(7) The word 'Paraclete' is itself frequently mistranslated, and nowhere is 'holy spirit.'

(8) Correct translation of 'Paraclete' appears to imply a material, human entity.

With these points firmly in mind, what remains is to trace the meaning of 'Paraclete' in the five NT verses which contain this term (1st Epistle of John 2:1; and the Gospel of 'John' 14:16, 14:26, 15:26, and 16:7). Taken in order:

1. The 1st epistle of John, 2:1 (I Jn 2:1) identifies Christ Jesus as a *'paraclete,'* frequently translated as *'advocate,'* as in, "...And if anyone sins, we have an advocate with the Father, Jesus Christ the righteous." So whatever a *'paraclete'* is – advocate, helper, comforter, *whatever* – Jesus was one according to this verse.

2. John (the gospel this time) 14:16-17 reads,

> "And I will pray the Father, and He will give you another helper (i.e., *'paraclete'*), that he may abide with you forever, even the Spirit of truth, whom the world cannot receive, because it neither sees him nor knows him; but you know him, for he dwells with you and will be in you."

One key to understanding the above quote of John 14:16-17 is not the word *'paraclete,'* herein translated 'helper;' rather, the crucial word of the above passage is the qualifying adjective, 'another.' The word for 'other' in ancient Greek is either *'allos'* or *'heteros,'* and the word used in this passage is *'allos,'* the meaning of which is "...'the other,' strictly where there are many, as distinct from *'heteros,'* where there are only two..."[158] The wording is specific and leaves little or no room for interpretation, as one might expect from revelation – the

---

158. Kittel, Gerhard and Gerhard Friedrich. p. 43.

(2.B9) Doctrinal Differences / Holy Spirit

point of revelation being to guide rather than to confuse. According to this definition, Jesus seems to have advised his disciples (and all humankind by extension) to anticipate another *'paraclete'* (e.g. helper) following his ministry. Not just another helper, but one characterized by qualities which Muslims are quick to point out as being consistent with the prophet of Islam, Muhammad. Jesus speaks of another *'paraclete'* characterized by:

i. Honesty (i.e., 'the spirit of truth' -- such a familiar quality of Muhammad that he was known, even amongst his *enemies* during his lifetime [Christians and Jews included] as 'As-Saadiq Al-Ameen' -- 'As-Saadiq' meaning 'the truthful;' 'Al-Ameen' meaning 'the trustworthy')

ii. Being recognized by the faithful (remembering all the Jewish rabbis, Christian monks, clergy and scholars who have converted to Islam for no other discernible reason than sincere belief)

iii. And bringing a message that will last forever (the Qur'an, to this day, being unchanged letter for letter).

Jesus identifies the *'paraclete'* to come as *another* (i.e. the same as him -- the "other, strictly where there are many.") Nobody can fault a person for concluding that this passage describes a prophet who would follow in the long line of prophets and bring a final, eternal message. Such a conclusion provides a more comfortable and legitimate fit than the strained claim that this passage describes some mystical 'holy spirit,' as derived from an unauthentic, 'non-Greek development of meaning.' On the other hand, the conclusion that Jesus is unique in a 'begotten, not made, son of God' sense if there is another, "...strictly where there are many...," all of whom bear the exact same description as Jesus (i.e. the description of *'paraclete'*) is not just unfounded. Indeed, it is contrary to scripture.

Lest there be any confusion over this point, the New Testament confirms that the Greek *'pneúma,'* herein translated 'spirit,' is not restricted to mystical beings but can refer to flesh and blood humans, both good and bad. For example, 1st Epistle of John 4:1-3 records,

(SECTION 2) GOD

> "Beloved, do not believe every spirit, but test the spirits, whether they are of God; because many false prophets have gone out into the world. By this you know the Spirit of God: every spirit that confesses that Jesus Christ has come in the flesh is of God, and every spirit that does not confess that Jesus Christ has come in the flesh is not of God. And this is the spirit of the Antichrist, which you have heard was coming, and is now already in the world."

The above verse not only clarifies the human nature of some 'spirits' (i.e., *pneúma*) but Muslims claim that this verse admits Muhammad into the equation as well, for *every* spirit that "... confesses that Jesus Christ has come in the flesh is of God." Muhammad said it, all Muslims affirm it, The Holy Qur'an documents it – in the minds of a billion Muslims, the fact that the Bible says of such people that they are "of God" settles it.

3 & 4. The third reference to *'paraclete'* is in John 14:26, which reads,

> "But the helper (*paraclete*), the holy spirit, whom the Father will send in my name, he will teach you all things, and bring to your remembrance all things that I said to you."

The fourth reference, John 15:26, carries the same message. Once again, Trinitarians may justify the mysticism of their belief with the above passage. Others perceive reference to a prophet who will mention Jesus with respect, reminding the world of the God-given message Jesus *really* brought, as opposed to the misdirections which developed in the minds, beliefs, and doctrines of later generations. Consideration can once again be given to Muhammad and the Holy Qur'an. The union of the two comments,

(2.B9) Doctrinal Differences / Holy Spirit

"He will bear witness to the truth of what Jesus did and said and was,"[159]

and

"...even though this divine Advocate is the very 'Spirit of truth' (John 14:16; 15:26; 16:13), the world will not listen to him (14:17)"[160]

would make perfect sense if the prophethood of Muhammad were assumed to be true, for the witness is borne, and yet the majority of the world's population turn a deaf ear.

5. The final mention of *'paraclete'* is found in John 16:7 –

"Nevertheless I tell you the truth. It is to your advantage that I go away; for if I do not go away, the helper will not come to you; but if I depart, I will send him to you."

This last reference to the *'paraclete,'* like a small but high-velocity projectile, lays waste to surrounding doctrines with cavitation energy far in excess of the innocent appearance of the entrance wound. Trinitarians may continue to assert that *'paraclete'* refers to the mystical 'Holy Spirit,' but John 16:7 negates that possibility. In the above verse Jesus is recorded as having stated that unless he goes away the *'paraclete'* will not come; even though multiple, multiple passages of the Bible speak of the presence of the 'holy spirit' in or before the time of Jesus (see I Samuel 10:10, I Samuel 11:6, Isaiah 63:11, Luke 1:15, 1:35, 1:41, 1:67, 2:25-26, 3:22, John 20:21-22). Both cannot be true, and the most logical conclusion, if the Bible is to be trusted, seems to be that 'holy spirit' and *'paraclete'* are anything but synonymous. The issue at hand then becomes one of searching out the true, human *'paraclete,'* as predicted by Jesus.

---

159. *New Catholic Encyclopedia.* Vol 10, pp. 990.
160. *New Catholic Encyclopedia.* Vol 10, pp. 989.

Compounding the confusion is the fact that Jesus is recorded as having contradicted himself in John 14:17. The *'paraclete'* being described as pre-existent – "...but you know him (i.e. the *'paraclete'*), for he dwells with you and will be in you," makes sense considering the fact that Jesus himself is identified as *'paraclete'* in I John 2:1. However, seating this verse side-by-side with John 16:7, "...if I do not go away, the helper (i.e., the *paraclete*) will not come to you; but if I depart, I will send him to you," the researcher unexpectedly head-butts the rock-hard reality of the conflict. Church conclusion? "The Paraclete is another Paraclete in whom Jesus comes but who is not Jesus (14:18, 16:7)."[161] Some accept that explanation. Others counsel that Jesus spoke of himself in one case and of a prophet to follow in the other. Billions of Muslims have voted Muhammad as the fulfillment of this prophecy, a few million Mormons vote John Smith, a smattering of Ahmadi'ites side with Mizra Ghulam Ahmad, the Baha'i with *Bab* Mirza Ali Muhammad and Mirza Husain Ali, and small handfuls have pledged faith to the claims of David Koresh, Jim Jones, Luc Jouret, Marshall Applewhite and similar cultists in their day (and look at what happened to them). The critical decision for each individual, then, may not be over whether or not Jesus predicted a prophet to follow, but rather over which of the many claimants to the title lived in divinely ordained fulfillment of the prophecy.

---

161. Kittel, Gerhard and Gerhard Friedrich. p. 892.

(2.B) Doctrinal Differences
(2.B10)
Crucifixion

"The report of my death was an exaggeration."
– Mark Twain, Letter to the *New York Journal* in response
to rumors of his death while in Europe

The primacy of the alleged crucifixion in Christian belief needs little or no introduction. However, if the world of Christianity expects others to adopt their belief, the demand for supporting evidence has relevance. Everyone knows the story of the crucifixion has been related by billions of faithful Christians over two thousand years of proselytizing canonized belief. Everyone knows the Biblical record relates several roughly parallel stories of the alleged crucifixion of Jesus. But everyone also knows that many other fallacious myths have been propagated over longer periods of religious history than this, and the duration and popularity of a deception does not validate a myth. So while most Christians accept the theory of the crucifixion without question, many others are not satisfied. Such individuals read, "...that Christ died for our sins according to the Scriptures" (I Corinthians 15:3), and question, "Umm, according to exactly *which* scriptures?" For, as Carmichael comments,

> "For that matter the whole insistence, in the Gospels as well as in Paul's Epistles, that everything had been accomplished in

(Section 2) God

fulfillment of the Scriptures seems puzzling. No such belief —
in the death and resurrection of the Messiah — is recorded
among the Jews at all, and certainly not in the Hebrew
Scriptures."[162]

Paul himself invited criticism of the concept of the crucifixion and of the mysteries constructed thereabout, having stated,

> "For Jews request a sign, and Greeks seek after wisdom; but we preach Christ crucified, to the Jews a stumbling block and to the Gentiles (Greeks) foolishness." (I Corinthians 1:22-23).

Or, in other words, "We preach something without signs and without wisdom – who is with us?"

No surprise, then, that so many find the proposal of Jesus having been crucified incompatible with their concept of God's mercy, His majesty, and His methodology. Muslims, for example, believe Jesus was saved from crucifixion, in accordance with the following, "…but they did not kill him (Jesus), nor crucified him, but so it was made to appear to them, and those who differ therein are full of doubts, with no (certain) knowledge, but only conjecture to follow, for of a surety they did not kill him:-Nay, Allah raised him up unto Himself; and Allah is Exalted in Power, Wise..." (TMQ 4:157-158).

Should a person believe Jesus to have been God, one wonders why God would permit death to overtake Him when He had the power to save Himself. Should a person believe Jesus to have been the 'Son of God,' why would God not answer the prayer of His son, when Jesus is recorded as having said, "Ask, and it will be given to you; seek, and you will find; knock, and it will be opened to you. For everyone who asks receives, and he who seeks finds, and to him who knocks it will be opened" (Matthew 7:7-8)? Jesus reportedly *did* ask (to the point of sweating "like great drops of blood" in prayer [Luke 22:44]),

---

162. Carmichael, Joel. p. 216.

(2.B10) DOCTRINAL DIFFERENCES / CRUCIFIXION

he clearly sought to be saved, and nowhere is Jesus quoted as having said, "everyone who asks receives, except for me." Matthew 7:9 contributes, "Or what man is there among you who, if his son asks for bread, will give him a stone?" Put another way, who imagines that God would answer a prophet's plea for rescue with a short weekend on a cross instead? Plenty of sunshine and all the vinegar a person can sip from a sponge? There is an incompatibility issue here – if people believe God, or the son of God, was born in a bath of his own urine (which is exactly what amniotic fluid consists of), then they will have no problem believing that God committed suicide (and what else would the act of allowing Oneself to die be called when, being omnipotent, able to save Oneself?). Similarly, such people will have no difficulty believing that God turned His back on His Son in the time of greatest need. The rest of the world wonders "Whose concept of God is this compatible with, anyway?"

Well, Tertullian,* for one. The comment has been offered that,

> "Tertullian enjoyed paradox. To him the divine character of Christianity was vindicated not by its reasonableness but by the very fact that it was the kind of thing no ordinary mind could have invented. The crucifying of the Son of God sounds ridiculous and scandalous: 'I believe because it is outrageous.'"[163]

Certainly the alleged crucifixion of Jesus sounds "ridiculous and scandalous" to many. This same group may be greatly shocked to find the founder of the 'Trinity' justifying an integral element of the doctrine he himself invented simply on the basis of it being outrageous and unbelievable. No doubt a person may wish to reconsider

---

* The aforementioned originator of the proposal of the Trinity, and a formative influence on the development of Trinitarian Christianity.

163. McManners, John. p. 50.

(SECTION 2) GOD

the teachings of anyone who states, "It makes no sense, and even I can't understand it. But we should all believe it because a human mind could never have derived such a ridiculous idea. Therefore it must be from God." The blade of such belief gouges deeply as it chatters across the end-grain of reason. If such is the methodology of God, is not mankind justified to believe each and every outrageous theory of divinity – the more silly and ridiculous the better?

Somewhere, someone is bound to respond, "But Jesus had to die for our sins!" One wonders, "Why? Because God is not big enough to forgive mankind without a blood sacrifice?" This is not what the Bible teaches. Jesus himself is reported as having taught the meaning of Hosea 6:6, "I desire mercy, and not sacrifice." Once was not enough – the lesson was important enough to be worthy of two mentions, the first in Matthew 9:13, the second in Matthew 12:7. Why, then, are clergy teaching that Jesus had to be sacrificed? And if he was sent for this purpose, why did he pray to be saved?

Furthermore, why does a person have to believe in order to be redeemed? On one hand, Original Sin is held to be binding, whether a person believes in it or not. On the other hand, salvation is held to be conditional upon belief (i.e., acceptance) of the crucifixion and atonement of Jesus. In the first case belief is held to be irrelevant, in the second case belief is required. The question arises, "Did Jesus pay the price or not?" If he paid the price, then the sins of man are forgiven, whether a person chooses to believe or not. If he didn't pay the price, it doesn't matter either way. Lastly, forgiveness doesn't *have* a price. If a man forgives another's debt, he forfeits the right to ask for his money back. Nowhere is there a person who can reasonably state, "Remember that money you owe me? I forgive it. Now...pay me!" The argument that God forgives, but only if given a sacrifice which He says He doesn't want in the first place (see Hosea 6:6, Matthew 9:13 and 12:7) drags a wing and cartwheels down the

(2.B10) Doctrinal Differences / Crucifixion

runway of rational analysis. From whence, then, does the formula come? By the scripture it clearly did not come from Jesus. So do people believe teachings *about* the prophet in preference to those *of* the prophet himself? The gospels themselves condemn such inverted priorities, for Matthew 10:24 records Jesus as having declared, "A disciple is not above his teacher, nor a servant above his master."

A person can reasonably question, then, what should be understood from the verse, "Then he said to them, 'Thus it is written, and thus it was necessary for the Christ to suffer and to rise from the dead the third day" (Luke 24:46)? Whether a person assumes literal or metaphorical interpretation is a matter of personal choice, but only the metaphor makes sense if the message that God does not desire sacrifice, and that Jesus needed to 'die' for the sins of man, are to be reconciled with one another. Furthermore, Biblical reference to death is frequently metaphorical (as in Paul's statement of his suffering as, "…I die daily" – I Corinthians 15:31). Perhaps 'rising from the dead' does not mean to rise from the literal state of *being* dead, but to rise from the metaphorical state of death, such as:

    i. Having been unconscious or sleeping (as in 'He slept like a dead man')

    ii. Having been suffering (as in the many Biblical analogies between suffering and death)

    iii. Having been incapable (as in "He couldn't do a thing last night, he was just dead")

    iv. or having been in the tomb, left for dead, but in fact alive (as in "He recovered miraculously – he came back from the dead).

Who can say with certainty?

In any case, Jesus was recorded as having taught that it was necessary for him to at least suffer and return following the third day. Matthew 12:40 clarifies, "For as Jonah was three days and three nights in the belly of the great fish, so will the Son of Man be three days and three nights in the heart of the earth." This simple verse opens the gates to a relatively uncharted territory of thought. "Three days and three nights" must be assumed to mean exactly what it says, for otherwise a person would expect it would not be stated with such clarity and specificity of detail. However, if a person believes the story as told in the Bible, Jesus is recorded as having spent only one day and two nights – Friday night, Saturday day, and Saturday night – in the sepulchre following the alleged crucifixion. Does this pose a difficulty? A person would think so, because the above quote is Jesus' response to the request for a sign, to which Jesus reportedly answered, "An evil and adulterous generation seeks after a sign, and no sign will be given to it except the sign of the prophet Jonah. For as Jonah was three days and three nights in the belly of the great fish, so will the Son of Man be three days and three nights in the heart of the earth" (Matthew 12:38-40). The above, "...no sign will be given to it except..." declares, in no uncertain terms, that this is the *only* sign which Jesus offers. Not the healing of the lepers, not the curing of the blind, not even the raising of the dead. Not the feeding of the masses, not the walking on water, not even the calming of the storm. No, Jesus commented that *no* sign will be given but the sign of Jonah.

Many Christians base faith on some version of a perceived 'miracle,' whether of those related in the Bible, of those linked to Christianity in contemporary times, or of those borne of personal experience. And yet, Jesus strikingly isolates the sign of Jonah as the only sign to be given. Not the crying statues, not the visions of Mary, not the faith healing. Not the speaking in tongues, not the exorcising of spirits, not the receiving of the Holy Ghost. Just the sign of Jonah. That's all. If a person chooses to adopt a different sign, they are free to make that choice. But they must understand they are doing so against the teaching of Jesus, as related in the Bible. Considering the sign of Jonah to have such priority in the opinion of Jesus, it demands examination.

(2.B10) DOCTRINAL DIFFERENCES / CRUCIFIXION

Christian tradition reports Jesus as having died for the sins of the world shortly prior to Friday sunset, leading to the celebration of 'Good Friday.' This also explains why the Jews were under pressure to expedite the death of the three crucified before sunset, for the Friday sunset ushers in the Jewish Sabbath (according to the Hebraic lunar calendar, the day ends at sunset. Hence, Friday sunset heralds the beginning of Saturday, the Jewish Sabbath). The problem facing the Jews was that a crucified man can live for days on the cross, or he can die much sooner than expected, for the rapidity by which crucifixion kills relates to an individual's psychological strength as well as to his physical fitness, and hence is somewhat unpredictable. Hanging on a cross with the body weight suspended on outstretched arms fatigues the muscles of respiration, to the point where an individual can no longer breathe. The mechanism of death, therefore, is slow asphyxiation – slower in individuals with greater endurance, fitness, and mental commitment to the struggle for life. Most crucifixes were constructed with small seats, enough to partially bear the weight of the body in order to prolong the torture; in the case of Jesus, Christian tradition reports the feet having been nailed. The reason for this brutality is that a dying individual would be forced to partially support his weight on impaled feet, greatly compounding the agony preceding death. However, when death was to be expedited, the Romans would break the legs. Losing the ability to brace the body with the legs accelerated the fatiguing of the chest muscles, exhaustion, and death.

The Jews, not knowing whether the three crucified would survive the Sabbath, were faced with an Old Testament Catch-22. Jewish law dictates that the dead body of the crucified be removed from the cross, and not allowed to hang overnight, for, "If a man has committed a sin worthy of death, and he is put to death, and you hang him on a tree (crucify him), his body shall not remain overnight on the tree, but you shall surely bury him that day, so that you do not defile the land

(SECTION 2) GOD

which the Lord your God is giving you as an inheritance; for he who is hanged (crucified) is accursed of God" (Deuteronomy 21:22-23). However, the removal and burial of the corpse would have been forbidden work on the Sabbath. Therefore, had any one of the crucified died on the Sabbath, Jewish law forbade either leaving the corpse hanging, or removing and burying it. The only practical solution was to speed the death of those crucified, eliminating not only the condemned, but the dilemma as well.

Accordingly, the Bible records Jesus as having been removed from the cross and placed in the sepulchre late Friday afternoon, just prior to sunset. Sunday morning, *before sunrise*, Mary Magdalene returned to the tomb, having rested the Sabbath in accordance with the law (Luke 23:56 and John 20:1), and found it empty. At the tomb she is told that Christ is risen (Matthew 28:6, Mark 16:6, Luke 24:6). The arithmetic works out to one night (Friday sunset to Saturday sunrise) plus one day (Saturday sunrise to sunset) plus one night (Saturday sunset to slightly before Sunday sunrise) equaling two nights and one day – a far cry from the "three days and three nights" referenced in the sign of Jonah. Once again, a person either has to accept the evidence that something is very wrong, or do math in other than base ten.

One more piece of this scriptural puzzle deserves consideration. The above "For as Jonah..." (or, as the *New Revised Standard Version* records, "For *just* as Jonah..." [emphasis mine]) compares the state of Jesus with that of Jonah. Even school children know that Jonah was alive from the time his friends reduced the ship's ballast by the measure of his weight, to the somewhat rough moment of regurgitation onto the sandy shore. With Jonah having been alive throughout the entire ordeal, a person could speculate that Jesus, "...just as Jonah..." was alive throughout as well. It is of interest to note that when the tomb was visited on Sunday morning each of the gospels describes

(2.B10) Doctrinal Differences / Crucifixion

Jesus as 'risen,' which is hardly surprising given the fact that cold rock slabs, unlike warm, wave suppressed waterbeds, don't exactly invite a person to sleep in. What is missing from the Bible, however, is the statement that Jesus was *resurrected*. Jesus is reported to have said, "I came forth from the Father and have come into the world. Again, I leave the world and go to the Father" (John 16:28). But where does Jesus say he would die and be resurrected in the process? The word 'resurrected' is nowhere to be found. 'Risen from the dead' is mentioned a handful of times, but never from the lips of Jesus himself.

The above chain of logic may not change any one person's way of thinking, but it should at least illustrate the reasonableness of the different viewpoints which can be gained from the Bible, especially if a person gives priority to the recorded words of Jesus over all other Biblical opinions. The Islamic understanding is one such viewpoint – one which affirms the prophethood of Jesus while pointing out that the scriptural teachings of Jesus not only discredit many elements of established 'Christian' doctrine, but reinforce Islamic ideology as well.

In recent years, many have found their doubts strengthened by a trail of engaging theories in books of critical Christian challenge. One such work, *The Jesus Conspiracy* by Holger Kersten and Elmar R. Gruber, is of interest with regard to the subject of this chapter, for research presented therein suggests that whoever was wrapped in the shroud of Turin did not die, and that the organized church has made extensive effort (including falsifying carbon dating tests) to discredit the authenticity of the shroud. The suggestion is offered that the Catholic church recognized that the shroud of Turin documents the survival of whoever was crucified and enshrouded therein, and since that is absolutely the *last* fact they wish to see surface, they deliberately discredited their own religious relic. This theory may annoy some individuals by nature of suggesting a conspiracy, but it does leave a person to wonder why, if the Catholic church has now discredited the authenticity of the shroud of Turin, why do they continue to object to independent testing? Such as independent carbon dating? After all, if not authentic, what value could the shroud possibly have to them now? Why not take it out, shave off some insignificant snippets and pass them around? But no, the custodians of the shroud are not that forthcoming. Why, if not that the authenticity of the shroud threatens their theology?

Muslims believe, as stated above, that Jesus was never crucified in the first place, "...but so it was made to appear..." (TMQ 4:157). If the proposal sounds extravagant to those who have been raised to think the opposite, the doctrine of the crucifixion sounds even more odd when placed beside Deuteronomy 22:23, which states "...he who is hanged (crucified) is accursed of God." Synchronous claims to divine inerrancy of the Bible and to the crucifixion of Jesus cast a truly peculiar light on anyone who supports such beliefs, for the inescapable conclusion can be none other than the obvious. Either Jesus was not crucified, the Bible is errant, or, according to the scripture, Jesus was accursed of God. To hold that God's prophet, son, or partner (however a person happens to conceptualize Jesus) is also accursed of God can only achieve acceptance amongst those with synaptic sterility. The above pieces simply do not fit into the proposed package. Something has to give -- one or more of the non-conforming elements need to be recognized and cast out. Otherwise, the package as a whole bears the impossible qualities characteristic of make-believe, or perhaps a person should say, 'make-belief.'

Similarly confounding is Hebrews 5:7, which relates that because Jesus was a righteous man, God answered his prayer to be saved from death, as follows: "In the days of his flesh, Jesus offered up prayers and supplications, with loud cries and tears, to the one who was able to save him from death, and he was heard because of his reverent submission" (Hebrews 5:7, NRSV). What does "God heard his prayer"

(2.B10) DOCTRINAL DIFFERENCES / CRUCIFIXION

mean? That God heard and ignored? No, it means God answered his prayer. It certainly can't mean that God heard and refused the prayer, for then the phrase "because of his reverent submission" would be nonsensical, along the lines of, "God heard his prayer and refused it because he was a righteous man."

As mentioned above, Muslims are among those who deny the crucifixion of Jesus. However, the fact that *someone* was crucified is not denied. Who, then, do Muslims conceive to have been crucified in the place of Jesus? It's a moot point, and not terribly important. Some suggest that Allah altered the features of Judas to resemble those of Jesus, with the end result that Jesus was raised up and Judas was crucified in his place, to the deception of those in attendance. Well, maybe. But then again, maybe not. There is no compelling evidence to support this opinion, even though it does conform to the OT, NT, and Qur'anic principle of people reaping what they sow.

Notably, some would object to the suggestion of Judas having been crucified on the basis that, as per Matthew 27:5, Judas threw his ill-gotten silver back at the priests and "...went and hanged himself." So some would object. The author of 'Acts' (commonly held to have been Luke the evangelist) would likely be one of them, for Acts records that Judas "...purchased a field with the wages of iniquity; and falling headlong, he burst open in the middle and all his entrails gushed out." (Acts 1:18) So if the author of 'Acts' and the author of the gospel of 'Matthew' cannot agree on the matter, what truly happened could be anybody's guess.

On the other hand, if the proposal of Judas having been crucified in place of Jesus sounds technically strained, it shouldn't; God is described as having restrained the eyes of two disciples (i.e., intimate companions who should have readily recognized their teacher) when they met the supposedly 'risen' Jesus on the road to Emmaus, "...so that they did not know him" (Luke 24:16). Another Biblical example

(SECTION 2) GOD

would be that Mary Magdalene is reported to have failed to recognize Jesus outside of the tomb, "...supposing him to be the gardener..." (John 20:15). A person could reasonably expect Mary Magdalene to have known better, under normal circumstances. On the other hand, if the concept of another crucified in place of Jesus sounds foreign to Christianity, it isn't. Amongst early Christian groups the Corinthians, the Basilidians, the Paulicians, and the Carpocratians all believed Christ Jesus to have been spared. The Basilidians, in specific, believed that Simon of Cyrene was crucified in his place. Typical of such dissenting groups, all of the above were judged to have been Gnostics and/or heretics by the orthodox Church, and were violently suppressed by a Trinitarian majority who systematically burned dissenters into oblivion for the first fifteen centuries of Roman Catholic rule (the most recent roasting having taken place in Mexico in 1,850 CE).

To be fair, Gnostic ideology did have a place in many, if not most or even all groups regarded to be dissenters from orthodoxy. But then again, Gnosticism has a place in Orthodoxy as well, for what is 'gnosis' if not the belief that initiates possess some esoteric but essential knowledge necessary for salvation, but which can neither be explained nor justified? And what else has the discussion of the preceding pages exposed, if not the lack of scriptural foundation for the canon of Trinitarian Orthodoxy?

Of the above groups, the Paulicians (initially known as 'Paulinians,' likely due to taking guidance from Paul of Samosata) hold special interest. Paul of Samosata reportedly took his teaching from Diodorus, head of the Nazarene Church in Antioch. His teachings in turn branched off the trunk of apostolic ideology through individuals such as Lucian (who in turn taught Arius), Eusebius of Nicomedia, and even Nestorius (whose sphere of influence expanded from Eastern Europe as far east as China and as far south as Abyssinia). The Paulician influence eventually spread to occupy most, if not all, of Europe and North Africa. Yet so complete was their

(2.B10) DOCTRINAL DIFFERENCES / CRUCIFIXION

annihilation by the Roman Catholic Church during the period of persecution, that both they and their books were virtually completely destroyed. Only in the mid-nineteenth century was one of their sacred books, *The Key of Truth*, discovered in Armenia and translated. From this document a view of the practices and beliefs responsible for the popularity of this group can be appreciated.

The Paulicians may invite condemnation for their dualistic ideology, acceptance of suicide, and excess of asceticism. Notable is the peculiar Paulician concept of Christ Jesus having been a phantasm, and not a man. On the other hand, the Paulicians did adhere to belief in Divine Unity, the Immaculate Conception, baptism, and other creeds and practices which date from the apostolic age. Included in the list of their particulars is the apparent lack of an organized priesthood or hierarchy of clergy. The leaders married and had families. The services were characterized by simplicity of worship and the lack of sacraments – not even holy water was accepted in their services. The Paulicians refused to adopt any visible object of worship – no relics, no images, not even the cross. All images, whether paintings or sculpture, were viewed as idolatrous, foreign to the teachings of Jesus, and in violation of the second commandment. The doctrine of Incarnation appears to have been denied, as were the doctrines of Original Sin and the Trinity, all rejected on the basis of lacking scriptural foundation. The Paulicians denied the alleged crucifixion of Jesus, and consequently rejected the doctrines of Resurrection, Atonement, and Redemption of Sins.

The Paulicians also shunned infant baptism as an innovation distant from the teachings and practice of Jesus, claiming that baptism without mature faith and repentance was of little or no value. Celebration of Christmas was likewise avoided on the grounds of being a manmade holiday constructed as a concession of the Catholic Church to coincide with the pagan festival of *Sol Invictus* (celebration of the return of the Sun-god [i.e., *Sol invictus* – the Invincible Sun]

(SECTION 2) GOD

every year on December 25, which coincides with the winter solstice). Tithes were neither solicited nor accepted. Strict diet was maintained, devotion to worship in all aspects of life stressed, and cleanliness of temper, thoughts, work and words aspired to.

One inquisitor described such heretics under the following umbrella:

> "Heretics are recognizable by their customs and speech, for they are modest and well regulated. They take no pride in their garments, which are neither costly nor vile. They do not engage in trade, to avoid lies and oaths and frauds, but they live by their labour as mechanics — their teachers are cobblers. They do not accumulate wealth, but are content with necessaries. They are chaste and temperate in meat and drink. They do not frequent taverns or dances or other vanities. They restrain themselves from anger. They are always at work; they teach and learn and consequently pray but little. They are to be known by their modesty and precision of speech, avoiding scurrility and detraction and light words and lies and oaths."[164]

A better model based upon the mold of the carpenter-King might be difficult to find. St. Bernard was quoted as having commented,

> "If you interrogate them, nothing can be more Christian; as to their conversation, nothing can be less reprehensible, and what they speak they prove by deeds. As for the morals of the heretic, he cheats no one, he oppresses no one, he strikes no one; his cheeks are pale with fasting, he eats not the bread of idleness, his hands labour for his livelihood."[165]

---

164. Lea, Henry Charles. 1958. *A History of The Inquisition of The Middle Ages.* Vol. I. New York: Russell & Russell. p. 85.

165. Lea, Henry Charles. Vol. I, p. 101.

(2.B10) DOCTRINAL DIFFERENCES / CRUCIFIXION

But for their creed, they were killed. Over a period of centuries the Paulicians were hounded wherever they were to be found. The reign of Empress Theodora during the 9th century was known for the re-establishment of image worship in Constantinople and, as E. Gibbon notes,

> "Her inquisitors explored the cities and mountains of the Lesser Asia, and the flatterers of the empress have affirmed, that, in a short reign, one hundred thousand Paulicians were extirpated by the sword, the gibbet, or the flames."[166]

The Paulicians eventually were driven from Armenia to Thrace, and on to Bulgaria. From Bulgaria they spread to Serbia, Bosnia and Herzegovinia, then north to Germany; west to France, and south into Italy. By sea they found routes to Venice, Sicily and Southern France. The rapid expansion of the Paulicians, who also became known as the 'Catharii' (meaning 'the Pure'), became a threat to the Roman Catholic Church, and they were condemned at the Councils of Orleans in 1022, of Lombard in 1165, and of Verona in 1184. Not until the Medieval Inquisition of the thirteenth century was the church able to act upon their condemnation of the Paulicians, but then, opening floodgates on the dammed-up hostility of several centuries, they applied the full force of their vehement hatred with a vengeance sufficient to sever their lineage. The loss of the Paulicians, and of the various other Christian sects cloned from similar ideological germ cells, testifies to the terrible efficacy of the religious cleansing of the Medieval Inquisition and subsequent periods of persecution. F. C. Conybeare comments,

> "It was no empty vow of their elect ones, 'to be baptized with the baptism of Christ, to take on themselves scourgings, imprisonments, tortures, reproaches, crosses, blows, tribula-

---

166. Gibbon, Edward, Esq. Vol. 6, Chapter LIV, p. 242.

tion, and all temptations of the world.' Theirs the tears, theirs the blood shed during more than ten centuries of fierce persecution in the East; and if we reckon of their number, as well we may, the early puritans of Europe, then the tale of wicked deeds wrought by the persecuting churches reaches dimensions which appal the mind. And as it was all done, nominally out of reverence for, but really in mockery of, the Prince of Peace, it is hard to say of the Inquisitors that they knew not what they did."[167]

That the Catholic Church was so effective in eliminating their opposition is of no surprise to those who study their methodology. The degree of savagery did not even spare their own people, at times sacrificing members of the orthodoxy to insure complete elimination of the Unitarians. For example, the mixed population of Catholics and Unitarians of the people of Beziers, in the South of France, were attacked in the following manner:

"From infancy in arms to tottering age, not one was spared – seven thousand, it is said, were slaughtered in the Church of Mary Magdalen to which they had fled for asylum – and the total number of slain is set down by the legates at nearly twenty thousand."[168]

The full horror of the callous cruelty of the leader of this massacre comes into focus in consideration of the fact that:

"A fervent Cistercian contemporary informs us that when Arnaud was asked whether the Catholics should be spared, he feared the heretics would escape by feigning orthodoxy,

---

167. Conybeare, Fred. C., M.A. 1898. *The Key of Truth*. Oxford: Clarendon Press. Preface, p. xi.

168. Lea, Henry Charles. Vol. I, p. 154.

(2.B10) DOCTRINAL DIFFERENCES / CRUCIFIXION

and fiercely replied, 'Kill them all, for God knows his own!' In the mad carnage and pillage the town was set on fire, and the sun of that awful July day closed on a mass of smouldering ruins and blackened corpses – a holocaust to a deity of mercy and love whom the Cathari might well be pardoned for regarding as the Principle of Evil."[169]

The use of torture by the inquisitors was equally horrific, for it did not end at confession. Once confession was offered torture was renewed to extract names of associates. Following this information, torture was again continued to ensure the last drop of information was squeezed from the mangled husk of what had once been a human being.

Once accused, the pitiful defendant was bound to suffer. Torture yielded an invariable result, if not out of truth, then out of desperation to bring an end to the pain. Horrifically, protestations of innocence and even the oath of orthodoxy did not bring relief, for suspects professing orthodox belief were committed to suffer a test of faith, of which the Church was creative. Trials by water and fire were popularized and sanctioned by the Catholic Church for the testing of a person's faith by way of *'Judicium Dei'* – 'Judgement of God.' The concept was based upon the belief that the purity of water would not accept a guilty body into its midst (i.e., floaters were judged guilty and executed, sinkers were considered innocent, and if rescued before drowning, spared), while earthly fire, like the fire of Hell, would be forbidden to harm those who (in their view) were the faithful Christians bearing the promise of paradise. The 'Hot Iron Test' was the most commonly employed, as it was simple and readily available. In this test the accused was required to carry a red-hot piece of iron for a certain number of steps, usually nine. Judgement

---

169. Lea, Henry Charles. Vol. I, p. 154.

(Section 2) God

was offered either at the time of the test (those burned were judged guilty) or several days later (those whose wounds were healing were considered innocent, whereas those whose wounds showed signs of infection were judged guilty). Other variations existed, such as determining whether or not a person suffered a burn when an arm was immersed up to the elbow in boiling water or boiling oil.

Lest a person presume such methods rarely employed, the Council of Rheims in 1157 decreed that such trials by ordeal be employed to satisfy all cases of suspected heresy.[170]

Now, why all this discussion about what is now a little known and dead sect? Well, the intent is neither to glorify any religious sect beyond the merits of its ideology, nor to evoke sympathy for their cause. Rather, the above discussion is intended to call home the realization that alternate Christian ideologies occupied a position of significance in religious history – a position which has for the most part become obscure in the shadow of prevailing Trinitarianism. The Corinthians, the Basilidians, the Paulicians, and the Carpocratians may be little known today, but they had a place in history. History, however, has not only been written by those who prevailed, but systematic effort to erase the record of all scriptures contrary to those of the Roman Catholic Church was largely successful in the first millennium of Roman Catholic rule. Additionally, historical attempts to villainize all other religions or sects of Christianity has prejudiced the minds of much of the populace. So successful were these efforts that the records and holy books of those who appear to have been closest to the worship of the apostolic fathers have been largely lost. Similarly, those closest to embodying the practices and creed of the prophet Jesus have come to be regarded as 'heretics,' not for any error inherent to their beliefs, but simply because they do not embrace the 'evolved' doctrines of that religious body which gained official

---

170. Lea, Henry Charles. Vol. I, p. 306.

(2.B10) Doctrinal Differences / Crucifixion

sanction. In other words they became condemned for non-conformity – non-conformity with views which, though lacking scriptural authority, were selected by men of position and propagated for reason of political expediency.

One of the curious elements of Trinitarian history lies in the fact that almost everywhere it went in the Christian world, it had to be imposed upon a previously Unitarian people. The Donatists and the Arians, the Visigoths and the Ostrogoths, the Vandals and the Paulicians all had to be muscled aside prior to the imposition of lasting Trinitarian rule. Even in England and Ireland there is suspicion that, contrary to official historical accounts, a good portion of the population were Unitarian Christian prior to receiving Trinitarian influence. Whereas Unitarians attempted to spread faith through example and invitation, the Roman Catholic Church spread Trinitarian faith by shearing the populace with the wickedly sharp blades of compulsion and elimination. Once the land was theirs, the torture marks and scars where the blades had bitten too deeply were covered with a thick ointment of claims of heresy and alterations in the accuracy of recorded history, for the satisfaction of those who would otherwise question the vicious methodology.

Reviewing what can be surmised from unprejudiced historical accounts, opposing views to those of Trinitarian Christianity are seen to have been voiced by a large population of the religious, and spanning the known world. And the opinions of those who denied the crucifixion and death of Christ Jesus were not necessarily either a minority in their time or incorrect in their claim. All that not withstanding, many would argue that from a gut level it makes more sense for God to have punished Judas for his treachery than to have tortured Jesus for his innocence. The argument would become more convincing if the doctrines of atonement and original sin could be shown to be invalid, for these two doctrines hinge off the doorframe

(SECTION 2) GOD

of the alleged death of Jesus. The first hurdle for many people in considering such revolutionary thoughts straddles the ages old assertion that Christ Jesus was the "Lamb of God who takes away the sins of the world" (John 1:29), for in the mind of the Trinitarian, this verse can have no relevance other than to that of the doctrine of atonement. Unitarians, however, conceive Jesus to have lived a life of sacrifice in order to bear a purifying teaching which, if adopted, would cleanse the world of deviation.

(2.B) DOCTRINAL DIFFERENCES
(2.B11)
Lamb of God

"The response is to the image, not to the man....
It's not the man we have to change, but rather
the received impression."

– Ray Price (White House speechwriter),
New York Times, October 31, 1993

Many devout Christians consider the translation of John 1:29, in which Christ Jesus is labeled the "Lamb of God who takes away the sins of the world," to constitute unequivocal proof of the concepts of the crucifixion and atonement. Others are more speculative, and perhaps for good reason.

Many may choose to reserve judgement based on nothing more than the simple fact that, once again, the Christian world itself does not agree on the meaning or significance of this concept of 'lambness.' Others question the Bible translation and canonization while still others encounter difficulty coupling Old and New Testament 'lamb of God' references to form a reasonable chain of logic. And there should be no surprise – even John the Baptist, from whose mouth the term supposedly took origin, seemed to have trouble with the term. The Christian claim is that John the Baptist knew who Jesus was,

(SECTION 2) GOD

and positively identified him as the 'lamb of God' in John 1:29. But if John the Baptist knew Jesus so well as to identify him with certainty in John 1:29, why, then, did he question Jesus years later, "Are You the Coming One, or do we look for another?" (Matthew 11:3)

Amongst those who have difficulty rectifying Old and New Testament references are the Catholic clergy themselves. The *New Catholic Encyclopedia* admits inability to determine the origin of the title 'Lamb of God,' for although attempts are made to trace the term through Isaiah (chapter 53) by way of Acts 8:32, "...this text is incapable of explaining the expression..."[171]

Another source contributes the following:

> "amnos. Attested from classical times and used in the LXX, this word occurs four times in the NT, always with reference to Jesus as the innocent lamb who suffers vicariously for others (Jn. 1:29, 36; Acts 8:32; 1 Pet. 1:19). Since Judaism does not call the Redeemer a lamb, two derivations have been sought: first, in the fact that the servant of the Lord in Is. 53:17 (cf. Acts 3:13; 4:27) is compared to a lamb (cf. Acts 8:32), and second, in that Jesus was crucified at the Passover and thus came to be seen as the paschal lamb (1 Cor. 5:7). The Aramaic might also offer a basis with its use of the same word for both "lamb" and "boy or servant." Thus the Baptist in Jn. 1:29, 36 might have been describing Jesus as the *servant* of God who takes away the sin of the world in vicarious self-offering (Is. 53)."[172] (emphasis mine)

Of acute interest is the comment that the word '*amnos*' may be mistranslated, for translation to 'boy' or 'servant' could equally apply. Were that the case, any link between Old and New Testament

---

171. *New Catholic Encyclopedia.* Vol 8, p. 338.
172. Kittel, Gerhard and Gerhard Friedrich. p. 54.

(2.B11) Doctrinal Differences / Lamb of God

references to 'lamb of God' would shred faster than ticker-tape in a turbo prop. Hence, it is with great interest that one encounters the *New Catholic Encyclopedia* agreeing that the Aramaic word *talya'* can be translated to boy or servant, as well as to lamb.[173] Furthermore, the proposal that the phrase uttered by the Baptist was "Behold the Servant of God," and not "Behold the Lamb of God" is, in their words, "very plausible" and "much easier to explain."[174]

Consequently, a person finds translation of the word '*amnos*' to 'servant' to be equally, if not more acceptable than 'lamb.' As with '*pais theou*,' the first translation of which is 'servant of God,' the translation of '*amnos*' appears to be more affected by doctrinal preference than by objective evidence — which in this case suggests the inability to accept any firm conclusion in the absence of corroborating evidence.

Finally, there is the now-familiar pattern of Jesus bearing the label of '*amnos*' in the gospel of John and in none of the other gospels, which once again implies some degree of unimportance, or at the very least, lack of substantiation. Perhaps the terminology was judged by three out of four gospel writers not to be of sufficient significance to warrant mention. Perhaps it was never said in the first place, or perhaps it was not stated with the meaning into which the Greek has been translated. Assuming the phrase was stated in the first place, had the original meaning been 'servant of God' instead of 'lamb of God,' the other three gospel authors are to be applauded for having refused to corrupt the message into an abstract recipe of 'lambness.' Alternatively, if the Bible is to be trusted as the word of God, a person is forced to conclude that God did not see fit to reveal or inspire this knowledge to three of the four gospel authors. Considering the expected objective to be one of spreading the word of revelation as

---

173. *New Catholic Encyclopedia.* Vol 8, p. 339.
174. *New Catholic Encyclopedia.* Vol 8, p. 339.

widely and precisely as possible, such a scenario would hardly seem likely.

As with all other elements of creed discussed herein, each person is expected to adopt whatever understanding gels from the individual blend of personal desire, preconditioning, and research. The sadness is that for centuries only one school of thought has predominated over Christian theology, to the exclusion of other alternatives. For those who would consider the issue in the context of Christian creed as a whole, the plausibility of the doctrines of Original Sin, the Crucifixion and Atonement must be factored into the analysis. After all, what is a sacrificial lamb for if not sacrifice, with an eye to the benefit to be gained thereby?

(2.B) Doctrinal Differences
(2.B12) Original Sin

"He that falls into sin is a man;
that grieves at it, is a saint;
that boasteth of it, is a devil."
— Thomas Fuller, *The Holy State and the Profane State*

The concept of Original Sin is completely foreign to Judaism and Eastern Christianity, having achieved acceptance in only the Western Church. Furthermore, Christian and Islamic concepts of sin are virtual opposites in many respects. On one hand, the core of human nature rebels against the Christian proposal that evil thoughts and equivalent actions are equally sinful. There is no such concept of 'sinning in the mind' in Islamic ideology; in Islam an evil thought is conceived to be converted into a *good* deed simply by refusing to act upon it. The act of overcoming and dismissing the evil suggestions which forever assail the minds of humankind is held to be deserving of reward rather than punishment. Islamically speaking, an evil thought only becomes sinful when ratified by an act of fulfillment.

Conceiving good deeds is commendable, but frequently contrary to the base nature of man. Since the creation of the human race, mankind, if not bound by the restrictions of societal or religious mandates, has historically dined on the banquet of life with lust and abandon. The orgies of self-indulgent sins which have carpeted the corridors of history envelop not only individuals and small communities, but even major world powers which ate their full of deviancy, to the point of self-destruction. Sodom and Gomorrah may top most lists, but the greatest powers of the ancient world, to include the Greek, Roman and Persian empires, as well as those of Genghis Khan and Alexander the Great, certainly bear mention alongside those which degenerated into debauchery, and from thence into decay. And whereas examples of such communal decay are innumerable, cases of individual corruption are by far more common.

Individuals unrestrained by religious morals are far more frequently encountered on the path of selfish and sinful hedonistic delights than on the path of selfless and righteous good behavior.

So good thoughts are not always the first instinct of mankind. As such, the Islamic understanding is that the very conception of good deeds is to be rewarded – even if not acted upon. The physical fulfillment of a good deed is an act of obedience to our Creator and may even be an act of worship, if dedicated to His pleasure. As such, good deeds are believed to be rewarded many times more than the actual value of the deed, with the proportion of the reward dependant upon factors known best to Allah. These factors may relate to such elements as sincerity of intention, level of difficulty, and amount of personal sacrifice involved therein. But no doubt the greatest multiplier is the loving grace and beneficence of Allah.

Belief in the concept of 'Original Sin' simply does not exist in Islam. And never has. For the Christian audience, the question is not whether the concept of Original Sin exists in the present day, but rather whether or not the concept existed in Christianity during the period of origins. Specifically, is the concept of Original Sin to

(2.B12) DOCTRINAL DIFFERENCES / ORIGINAL SIN

be found in the teachings of Jesus? The answer is, "Apparently not." Whoever dreamt up the concept of original sin, it certainly does not appear to have come from Jesus, for he is quoted as having taught, "Let the little children come to me, and do not forbid them, for of such is the kingdom of heaven" (Matthew 19:14). A person may wonder how "for of such" could be "the kingdom of heaven" if the unbaptized are all bound for Hell. Children are either born with the stain of 'Original Sin' upon them, or they are bound for "the kingdom of heaven." The Church can have one, but not both. Ezekiel 18:19-20 records,

> "Yet you say, 'Why should the son not bear the guilt of the father? Because the son has done what is lawful and right, and has kept all My statutes and done them, he shall surely live. The soul who sins shall die. The son shall not bear the guilt of the father, nor the father bear the guilt of the son. The righteousness of the righteous shall be upon himself, and the wickedness of the wicked shall be upon himself."

Deuteronomy 24:16 repeats the point. The objection may be raised that this is Old Testament, but it's not older than Adam! If 'Original Sin' dated from Adam and Eve, a person wouldn't find the above in *any* scripture of *any* age!

Islam teaches that each person is born in a state of spiritual purity, oriented towards submission to God and with correct belief in His Unity – His Oneness. Following birth, any given individual's convictions may fall prey to the seductive misguidance which surrounds mankind, whether it be manifest in wayward peers, parents, culture, or simply the allure of worldly things. The Islamic understanding, then, is that all humankind are born knowing the reality of God, but experience and upbringing may layer thick piles of alternative teachings and prejudiced propaganda into a stratified compost which drowns truth in the ferment of a polluted consciousness. However, for those whom Allah wills, the hearts and minds remain receptive of truth, when made clear.

Islam teaches that sins are not inherited and, for that matter, not even Adam and Eve will be punished for their sins, for God has forgiven them. Each individual will be judged according to his or her own deeds, with good deeds counting towards salvation and sins counting against, for "...man can have nothing but what he strives for" (TMQ 53:38-39) and, "Who receives guidance, receives it for his own benefit: who goes astray does so to his own loss: no bearer of burdens can bear the burden of another..." (TMQ 17:15). On the Day of Judgement each person will bear personal responsibility for his or her actions, trusting Allah to be fair and just, to reward the good deeds, and to forgive the sins for which repentance was made. But no baby and nobody goes to Hell for being unbaptized and burdened with sin as a birthright (or should a person say 'a birthwrong?').

(2.B) Doctrinal Differences
(2.B13) Atonement

"Must then a Christ perish in torment in every age to save those that have no imagination?"
— George Bernard Shaw, *Saint Joan*, epilogue

The Atonement -- what a concept. Who would not like someone else to pick up the check for their every indulgence and transgression? Who, if committing a crime, would not like someone else to go to jail for them? If theories were validated on the basis of beauty and desirability, there would very likely be no greater truth than the theory of the atonement of Jesus. However, desire for something to be true and the beauty of the telling as to why it would be nice, were it true, do not a reality make. So no matter how much a person wants to rely upon the atonement for an easy salvation, the critical question is simply whether or not the concept has a basis in revealed reality. In other words, will the concept of The Atonement be there when a person seeks the safety net of an effortless salvation on the Day of Judgement? Or will the plain of anxious human souls be filled with untold billions of downcast faces when God pronounces that He never said that? When the humans who promised such doctrines will abandon the followers who trustingly served them during their lifetimes, and flee from a falsehood which will have no possible support in the face of Divine disavowal, where and to whom will a person turn?

(SECTION 2) GOD

There are those who conceive that an apology to God in such a place and time will be accepted. Others understand life to be a proving ground for the hereafter, and that a person's book of deeds is closed upon death. After all, if an apology on the Day of Judgement will be sufficient to achieve salvation, what need for Hell? For who will not claim faith and offer sincere repentance when the reality of God's punishment will be laid bare for all to see? And what weight would such an apology have when life is past, and no sacrifice is required in the offering of faith? A righteous life demands denial of many sinful pleasures, and sacrifice of time, effort and worldly priorities. Compromise of hedonistic delights in pursuit of God's pleasure testifies to a person's faith – a faith sufficient to seek God's satisfaction through servitude and worship. That testimony will have weight. That testimony will be deserving of reward. What weight will a person's testimony and repentance have when faced with an undeniable reality which even the greatest of devils amongst mankind will be forced to recognize, and in a place and time where witness to the obvious will shoulder no cost or compromise to the individual?

The promise of salvation through the alleged atonement of Jesus is either the greatest blessing to mankind or a false assurance to those who lack the sincerity to commit to a life of righteousness. If false, this doctrine will be found to have no more value than a forged contract, which gives satisfaction when imagined to be authoritative but proves valueless when presented for fulfillment.

The critical question, then, is who authored the concept of the atonement? If God, then mankind would be foolish not to close on the offer of an easy salvation. But if conceived by humans, the person who expects a penthouse suite in the highest heaven based on this doctrine would be well advised to question the authority of the one who claims to speak for God, if not a prophet.

Analogies may be drawn, such as the case of a court falsely

(2.B13) Doctrinal Differences / Atonement

convicting an innocent person for a crime. Is there any scenario in which the true criminal is no longer liable for punishment? After all, the time has been served, right? Not by the responsible person, but it's been served. Therefore the true criminal goes free when the error in judgement is discovered? The chain of responsibility is clear in this life. Both Biblical and Qur'anic teachings support the fact that each individual is responsible for his or her own deeds, and nobody bears the burden of another's iniquities. So where does *Jesus* mention his persecution to be an exception? And certainly, if Jesus was never crucified in the first place (the evidence for which is discussed above in section 2.B.10) the doctrine of atonement falls apart at the foundation.

So some choose to enjoy the corruption of this world conceiving that whatever degree of disobedience they embody will be forgiven as a consequence of Jesus having paid the price. Others consider such an attitude to be one of deluded irresponsibility. And, like all delusions, like all wishful thinking, adherents to such ideologies often become violently disposed to those who lift the veil which cloaks a distasteful and contrary reality.

Those who find satisfaction in the loose interpretation of the alleged words of the disciples, Paul, and other para-prophet personages may research their individual codes of life and religion no further. Those who find firmer footing on the teachings of the prophets perceive that God promises nothing of good in the hereafter to those who duck accountability to Him. Jesus is quoted as having addressed the fact that belief, in and of itself, is *not* sufficient for salvation – "Not everyone who says to me, 'Lord, Lord,' shall enter the kingdom of heaven, but he who does the will of my Father in heaven" (Matthew 7:21). Furthermore, when questioned on how to achieve salvation, Jesus is recorded as having taught, "But if you want to enter into life (eternal life, that is – i.e., salvation) keep the

(SECTION 2) GOD

commandments" (Matthew 19:17), and love God and fellow men (Luke 10:27). But where is Jesus recorded as having counseled his followers that they could relax, for in a few days he would pay the price and they could all go to Heaven on nothing more than belief? It didn't happen -- it just didn't happen. The concerned skeptic is forced to question, "Why? Could it be that it's not true? Could it be that someone is scribbling wishful thoughts in the margins of scripture?"

A person wonders where the concept of The Atonement came from in the first place. Few are surprised to hear the name, "Paul." Another questionable doctrine coming from the same questionable source? So it would seem. Acts 17:18 reads,

> "Then certain Epicurean and Stoic philosophers encountered him (Paul). And some said, 'What does this babbler want to say?' Others said, 'He seems to be a proclaimer of foreign gods,' because he preached to them Jesus and the resurrection."

Paul directly claims to be the originator of the doctrine of resurrection as follows, "Remember that Jesus Christ, of the seed of David, was raised from the dead according to my gospel" (II Timothy 2:8). Sure enough, the concept of Christ Jesus dying for the sins of mankind is found in the epistles of Paul (for example, see Romans 5:8-11 and 6:8-9), and nowhere else. Nowhere else!?!? Not from Jesus? Not from the disciples? Is it possible to consider that their schedules were so busy that they neglected to teach the critical details upon which Christian faith rests? "'Curiouser and curiouser!' cried Alice."[175]

At this junction discussion should properly return to the law, for nobody can be faulted for suspecting that someone played fast and loose with ideology in the design of Christian thought. With

---

175. Carroll, Lewis. *Alice's Adventures in Wonderland.* ch. 2.

(2.B13) Doctrinal Differences / Atonement

regard to the law Jesus, being a Jew, lived by Old Testament (Mosaic) law. He is recorded as having taught, "Do not think that I came to destroy the Law or the Prophets. I did not come to destroy but to fulfill" (Matthew 5:17). The very next verse emphasizes that not the smallest element, not even a single letter of the law will change as long as heaven and earth exist, "For assuredly, I say to you, till heaven and earth pass away, one jot (i.e. Greek *Iota*—the ninth letter of the Greek alphabet) or one tittle (i.e. a stroke or dot) will by no means pass from the law till all is fulfilled" (Matthew 5:17-18). Some apologists assert that all was 'fulfilled' upon the alleged death or resurrection of Jesus, allowing the laws to be restructured in the period of time following. But that reasoning doesn't work, for every Christian testifies that Christ Jesus will return to vanquish an anti-Christ at a point in time in close proximity to the Day of Judgement. So, if the mission of Jesus upon planet Earth is regarded as the endpoint, all has not yet been fulfilled. More likely, however, 'all being fulfilled' refers to exactly what a person would instinctively assume, meaning the totality of events of all creation from the beginning of existence to the Day of Judgement. However a person understands the phrase, planet Earth remains whole and unrent, the heavens intact, and no sign of a returned Jesus on the horizon. Yet 2,000 years ago Paul said that not just a jot or a tittle, but the entire law has changed.

Paul's amendment to the teaching of Moses *and* Jesus reads, "...and by him (Christ Jesus) everyone who believes is justified from all things from which you could not be justified by the law of Moses" (Acts 13:39). A more permissive blanket statement would be hard to conceive. A person can easily imagine the voice of the collective public screaming, "Please, let's have some more of that!" And here it is: "But now we have been delivered from the law, having died (i.e., suffered) to what we were held by, so that we should serve in the newness of the Spirit and not in the oldness of the letter" (Romans

7:6). Which reads not at all unlike, "But now I tell you to forget this old law, the inconveniences of which we have lived with for too long, and begin to live by the new religion of our desires, and not by the old, uncomfortable mandates of revelation." According to Paul, the law was good enough for Moses and Jesus but not for the remainder of humankind.

There should be little wonder that a person who considered himself qualified to negate the message of the prophets also considered himself to be all things to all people, as he so clearly stated:

> "For though I am free with respect to all, I have made myself
>   a slave to all, so that I might win more of them;
> To the Jews I became as a Jew, in order to win Jews.
> To those under the law I became as one under the law (though
>   I myself am not under the law) so that I might win those
>   under the law.
> To those outside the law I became as one outside the law
>   (though I am not free from God's law but am under
>   Christ's law) so that I might win those outside the law.
> To the weak I became weak, so that I might win the weak.
>   I have become all things to all people, that I might by all
>   means save some." (NRSV; I Corinthians 9:19-23).

And what is wrong with trying to be all things to all people? What is wrong is that when a man tries to be all things to all people he fails to be the most important thing to the most important person – he fails to be true to himself. The scenario is best known to the field of politics, where the man with the greatest success is the one who sells himself to the largest number of interest groups. The problem is that he typically sells his soul in the process. Ultimately, the man who begins by deceiving others ends deceived himself, thinking himself popular by nature of gaining the winning vote, and not realizing that

(2.B13) Doctrinal Differences / Atonement

the people approve the falsehood of his image and not the truth of his person. And if the populace only approves the person when deceived as to his nature, how, then, can the approval of God be expected, for He is never deceived?

In the end, whereas the true prophets, Christ Jesus included, promised a hereafter worth the effort of adhering to God's laws as conveyed through revelation, Paul promised worldly enjoyment unrestricted by commandments, complemented by the insecure assurance of an easy salvation. Little wonder that Paul gained a following.

James taught that faith alone was *not* sufficient for salvation. James 2:14-26, entitled 'Faith Without Works is Dead,' contains a passage in which James sarcastically compares those of faith, but lacking good works, with demons, saying, "You believe that there is one God. You do well. Even the demons believe – and tremble!" (James 2:19). Modern words might read more like, "You believe in God? So what? So does Satan. He believes with such certainty that he trembles – how are you different from him?" The defining feature of a righteous person is "...that a man is justified by works, and not by faith only" (James 2:24). Why? Because, "For as the body without the spirit is dead, so faith without works is dead also." (James 2:26)

Christ Jesus was a man who confidently persisted upon the truth, without compromising *his* values in order to appeal to the people. He taught simplicity and sense, such as, "...as the Father gave me commandment, so I do..." (John 14:31) and, "If you keep *my* commandments, you will abide in my love, just as I have kept my Father's commandments and abide in His love" (John 15:10). To repeat, "If you keep *my* commandments...(emphasis mine)." Yet, nowhere did Jesus command belief in divine sonship, begotten nature, the Trinity, the crucifixion, resurrection, atonement, and many other critical elements of Trinitarian dogma. In fact, Christ Jesus, if anything, is recorded as having taught exact opposites.

(SECTION 2) GOD

Furthermore, in stark contrast to Paul, Jesus does not appear to have tried to have been all things to all people. He appears to have tried to have been *one* thing to all people -- a prophet bearing the truth of God. He does not appear to have been afraid to voice the harsh truth, to speak his mind, to convey revelation without putting a more appealing and acceptable spin on it. In the short passage of Matthew 23:13-33, Jesus chastises the Pharisees with the label 'hypocrites' no less than eight times, 'blind' five times, 'fools' twice, topped off with 'serpents' and 'brood of vipers.' *That* is the forthright example of a true prophet. But now there are those who view Paul as the main voice of revelation, despite the clarity of the message, "A disciple is not above his teacher, nor a servant above his master" (Matthew 10:24).

So why are the writings of Paul, who was not even a disciple, given priority over those of 'the teacher' despite scriptural directive to the contrary? And what does mankind get from Paul with regard to the doctrine of atonement? Not just an amendment to the teachings of Jesus, it's a whole new religion, and a whole new law! It is so easy and attractive, a person *wants* to believe it. And given the bloody history of Roman Catholic intolerance, a person *had* to believe it, *or else*! Consequently, the Church appears to have succeeded in mixing a seemingly innocent hardener of satisfying falsehoods into the resinous minds of the receptive masses, catalyzing a cementing of convictions upon an unsupported creed distanced far from Jesus' teaching, "Most assuredly, I say to you, he who believes in me, the works that I do he will do also..." (John 14:12). One wonders, did Jesus mean things like living according to revealed law, keeping the commandments, praying *directly* to God -- things like that?

The sincere person of God might be a little concerned about what Jesus will have to say, upon his return, should he find his followers preferring the teachings of Paul and the Council of Nicaea to those of

(2.B13) Doctrinal Differences / Atonement

his own. Perhaps Jesus will address the issue of Paul by quoting Jeremiah 23:32, "'Behold, I am against those who prophesy false dreams,' says the Lord, 'and tell them, and cause My people to err by their lies and by their recklessness. Yet I did not send them or command them; therefore they shall not profit this people at all,' says the Lord." Whatever else Jesus might say or do, a person can safely assume that his return will catch a lot of people by surprise.

(2.B) DOCTRINAL DIFFERENCES

(2.B14) Return of Jesus

> ""If Jesus Christ were to come today, people would not even crucify him. They would ask him to dinner, and hear what he had to say, and make fun of it."
> – D.A. Wilson, *Carlyle at his Zenith*

There is one thing that Christians and Muslims agree upon, and that is the return of Christ Jesus. Interestingly enough, both religions expect Jesus to return in a victory of faith, during which he will defeat the anti-Christ, correct the deviancies in religion, and establish the purity of the message of revelation throughout the world. Christians expect this purity of revelation to echo their evolved doctrines of Christianity, whereas Muslims expect Christ Jesus to remain consistent with the revelation he conveyed during the time of his ministry, to refute the alterations of others who falsely claimed to follow in his name, and to validate both his message and that conveyed by the final prophet he himself predicted. In short, Muslims expect Christ Jesus to validate Muhammad as the final messenger, and to endorse pure submission to God (Islam) as the religion for all mankind, as revealed in all three of the Abrahamic religions.

(2.B14) DOCTRINAL DIFFERENCES / RETURN OF JESUS

In the mind of the Muslim, the return of Jesus will go hard on those who have chosen to embrace the doctrines of men in preference to the teachings of the prophets. Those who chose to persist upon the blasphemy of associating a son and partner with God, after the denial of such doctrine by Jesus himself, will be deserving of punishment.

The Holy Qur'an records that Jesus will be questioned in this regard as follows:

> "And behold! Allah will say: 'O Jesus the son of Mary! Did you say to men, "Worship me and my mother as gods in derogation of Allah"?' He will say: "Glory to You! Never could I say what I had no right (to say). Had I said such a thing, You would indeed have known it. You know what is in my heart, though I do not know what is in Yours. For You know in full all that is hidden. Never said I to them anything except what You commanded me to say, to wit, 'Worship Allah, my Lord and your Lord'; And I was a witness over them whilst I dwelt amongst them; when You took me up, You were the Watcher over them, and You are a Witness to all things." (TMQ 5:116-117)

Until such time as Jesus returns with *prima facie* evidence – namely his irrefutable human reality – one question assaults the doctrinal defense system. It is same question, perhaps, that Jesus will ask of those who will claim to have followed 'in his name' – "Where in the Bible is Jesus recorded as having said, in *clear* and *unambiguous* terms, 'I am God, worship me?'" Nowhere. So why is he considered divine? Would he have forgotten to pass on such an essential teaching, if it were true? Unlikely. If Jesus never claimed to be God, and the doctrine of his divinity was contrived by men who followed 'in his name,' then this sounds like dangerous territory, perhaps relating to Matthew 15:9, "These people draw near to me with their mouth, and honor me

(SECTION 2) GOD

with their lips, but their heart is far from me. And in vain they worship me, teaching as doctrines the commandments of men." One wonders what doctrines are more the "commandments of men" than the man-made doctrines of the Trinity, Divine sonship of Jesus, Divinity of Jesus, Original sin, and Atonement. And what does Jesus say of those who adopt such doctrines? "In vain they worship me."

The question posed by Jesus in Luke 6:46 similarly seems to threaten a favorable judgement -- "But why do you call me 'Lord, Lord,' and not do the things which I say?" In other words, why would a person call Jesus 'Lord,' but then follow the teachings of others in preference to those of Jesus? In Luke 6:49, Jesus describes the ruin of those who build their houses upon such foundations to be 'great.' And is there any surprise? According to the scripture, such people should be fearful of being disowned by Jesus in the hereafter and denied the mercy of The Creator, in line with the aforementioned prediction of Jesus, "And then I will declare to them, 'I never knew you; depart from me, you who practice lawlessness!" (Matthew 7:23).

Of course, there are those who assert that faith is faith -- it is not to be pushed, manipulated, or reasoned with. Belief in any particular doctrine and/or religious mystery is held to be a gift of faith. Such a scenario returns to the assumption of an arbitrary God, Who grants this gift of faith to some and withholds it from others. Those who think along these lines often imagine that the more unfounded things they believe, the greater their reward in the hereafter -- simply because they believed without proof. Mark Twain summed up such attitudes with the observation, "It was the schoolboy who said, 'Faith is believing what you know ain't so.'"[176] A frequent observation, however, is that there is a big difference between believing *in* God without proof, and believing doctrines *about* God which are not only lacking proof,

---

176. Twain, Mark. *Following the Equator.* ch. 12. "Pudd'nhead Wilson's New Calendar."

but for which there is evidence to the contrary in the teachings of the prophets. Herein lies a dormant and torpid problem, somnolently hibernating for the season of reckoning. Herein also may lie those referred to in Matthew 13:13 -- "...seeing they do not see, and hearing they do not hear, nor do they understand."

Furthermore, scripture directs mankind to base belief upon proof rather than hunches and emotions; the Bible directs, "Test (some versions say 'prove') all things; hold fast what is good" (I Thessalonians 5:21). Isaiah 1:18 conveys, "'Come now, and let us reason together,' says the Lord." Nowhere does God add, "...but some things are beyond reason," or "...but some things can't be tested." So a person should thank God for the gift of faith in Him. But after that, truth should be sought in the teachings of His prophets. Accept and follow those teachings, and a person will be submitting to God's will through obedience to Him. Submit to the teachings of others or to personal design and desires, and a person takes another for guidance over God. The Bible cautions, "'If you are willing and obedient, you shall eat the good of the land; but if you refuse and rebel, you shall be devoured by the sword'; for the mouth of the Lord has spoken." (Isaiah 1:19-20)

The sincere seeker, then, will climb the smooth staircase of stacked evidences, holding firmly to the handrail of reason. Mankind is bidden to faith and trust in God, and commanded to reason through scripture. Recognizing that although, in the words of Shakespeare, "The devil can cite Scripture for his purpose,"[177] truth becomes evident through examination of scripture as a whole. The conclusion as to just which devils have been citing precisely which scriptures for their purpose will no doubt vary from one individual to another. Thousands of years of disagreement should not be expected to be resolved to the satisfaction of all people in the present age, no

---

177. Shakespeare, William. *The Merchant of Venice*. I.iii.99.

(SECTION 2) GOD

matter how comprehensive the analysis. So, despite all that which has been presented above, many Christians will continue to adhere to their faith. Muslims, however, will continue to assert that the man-made falsehoods of Trinitarian doctrine stand on an undermined sand-cliff of Biblical snippets, none of which can withstand the forceful and repetitive waves of comprehensive analysis. On the contrary, analysis of the Bible as a whole exposes a purely monotheistic understanding of God, complete with the prediction of a prophet to follow in fulfillment of both Old and New Testament prophecies. He is worth both looking and praying for.

Section 3
Books of Scripture

"There is only one religion, though there are a hundred versions of it."

– George Bernard Shaw,
Plays Pleasant and Unpleasant, Vol. 2, preface

(SECTION 3) BOOKS OF SCRIPTURE

The common theme which runs through all religions is that if a person believes in God and submits to His decree – practicing the commanded and avoiding the forbidden, and turning to Him in repentance if having transgressed limits -- a person will achieve salvation. The difference in opinion, however, lies in defining God's decree. Jews consider the Old Testament to be the endpoint of revelation at present, whereas Christians and Muslims alike contend that should the Jews follow their scripture, they would accept Jesus as a prophet and embrace his teachings. But most Jews, so they say, were and are Jews – too bonded with Jewish tradition and the elitist concept of being the 'chosen people' to recognize the error of their obstinacy.

Muslims continue the thought by asserting that anybody (Jewish, Christian, or otherwise) who *does* embrace the prophethood of Jesus has to face the reality of Jesus calling to strict monotheism, to Old Testament law, and to seeking a prophet to follow himself. But most who claim to be followers of Jesus are in fact followers not of what *Jesus* taught, but rather of what *others* taught *about* Jesus. Principal amongst those of influence is Paul of Tarsus, followed by those who persisted in the abstract interpretation of his teachings, in preference to those of Jesus. The Old Testament cautions,

246

(Section 3) Books of Scripture

"Whatever I command you, be careful to observe it; you shall not add to it nor take away from it. If there arises among you a prophet or a dreamer of dreams, and he gives you a sign or a wonder, and the sign or the wonder comes to pass, of which he spoke to you, saying, 'Let us go after other gods' – which you have not known – 'and let us serve them,' you shall not listen to the words of that prophet or that dreamer of dreams, for the LORD your God is testing you to know whether you love the LORD your God with all your heart and with all your soul. You shall walk after the LORD your God and fear Him, and keep His commandments and obey His voice; you shall serve Him and hold fast to Him." (Deuteronomy 12:32 – 13:4)

Despite the above caution, the creed of modern day Christianity is more heavily influenced by the writings of Paul (which proclaim a new construct of God which, as stated above, "you have not known"), than by the teachings of Jesus (which emphasize The One true and indivisible God as taught by all preceding prophets). The theological morass derived from the mystical teachings of Paul is unavoidably thick, confusing and, unfortunately for those who venture too far therein, often entangling. For simplicity, many choose to trust a charismatic leader (pastor, priest, pope, etc.) who predictably enjoins acceptance of all that which aligns with established doctrine. That choice having been made, the follower becomes confirmed upon a religious construct of men, most frequently in rejection of the simple and direct teachings of the prophet Jesus himself. Faithful monotheists, on the other hand, will progress in faith through adherence to scripture, rather than resting comfortably on the interpretations and teachings of men, many of whom, like those preceding them, are charismatic and convincing, but astray.

(Section 3) Books of Scripture

Judaism and Christianity call a person to the acceptance of specific ideologies and dogma. Should a person question the basis of the many unfounded elements of Judaic or Christian canon, there are a number of mechanisms in place which serve to emotionally bludgeon the too-deep thinker into unwilling acceptance. Manipulations such as accusations of spiritual inferiority and threats of withholding sacraments, or of being ostracized from the community, leverage many 'on the edge' followers into uneasy compliance. This low level of initial commitment transmutes to resigned acceptance over time. Eventually, when the degree of personal investment grows beyond that which a person can bring his- or herself to abandon, entrenchment within established dogma becomes complete.

The Islamic religion also teaches accepted beliefs, to be sure, but with the claim of not overstepping the boundaries of reason. The dominant call of the Islamic religion is for all people to study the evidences around them and seek truth rather than dogma. Jews and Christians are entreated to study their own scripture more seriously – the Jew is encouraged to become a better follower of Moses, and the Christian a better follower of Jesus. In the process, submission to the teachings of the prophets is expected to take precedence over unfounded doctrines propagated by the process of religious indoctrination.

The Islamic claim is that should a person seek truth rather than dogma, he or she will eventually recognize God as one God and submit to His teachings as conveyed through revelation and the examples of the prophets. Objective study of the scriptural basis of all other religions will lead the serious seeker to recognize the errors and the unacceptable, ungodly elements of all books which precede the Holy Qur'an. Furthermore, the sense of the chain of revelation, the evidences of Divine origin of each link in this chain, and the clear teachings of Islam at the core of all revealed religions will clear a

(SECTION 3) BOOKS OF SCRIPTURE

pathway to understanding. The traveler on this spiritual path will soon come to recognize 'submission to the will of God' as the only possible code of life acceptable to The Creator.

The Islamic claim is that true and sincere people of God should not feel threatened, for the Islamic religion claims nothing more than a revival and completion of the teachings of all the prophets – a confirmation of the core message of all prior revelations, and a conclusion to the chain of revelation and God's guidance to mankind. As stated in the Holy Qur'an, "This Qur'an is not such as can be produced by other than Allah; on the contrary, it is a confirmation of (revelations) that went before it, and a fuller explanation of the Book – wherein there is no doubt – from the Lord of the Worlds." (TMQ 10:37) Committed followers of Moses are expected to recognize both Christ Jesus and Muhammad as prophets who followed, while strict adherents to the teachings of Jesus will find the call to Islam and the prediction of the final prophet Muhammad in their own scripture.

On the other hand, whereas sincere Jews and Christians should not feel threatened as individuals, the institutions of Judaism and Christianity are very much threatened, for the Islamic religion claims to expose the false foundations upon which these institutions have constructed their infirm edifices.

On the level of the individual, the Islamic belief is that all people of all time were born with innate understanding that God is one, Lord and Creator of humankind, to be worshipped alone, without partner or intercessor. In the Islamic religion this baseline, innate knowledge of God is part of the inborn nature of humankind, known as '*fitrah*.' *Fitrah* includes knowledge of the lordship and unity of God, the innate ability to discriminate between good and evil, and the healthy instincts and inclinations gifted as birthright to all humans. Those of sincerity and God-fear are expected to act upon their *fitrah*, to seek to

(Section 3) Books of Scripture

embrace the truth they encounter during their worldly lives, to recognize the truth of God as and when it comes to them, and to progress in purity and piety. Those who seek deviancy are expected to deny their *fitrah*, not only as regards acknowledgement of Lordship of the Creator, but also as regards recognition and respect of the basic laws of good and evil, defiling themselves through the process of disobedience.

Consistent with the justice of God, each and every man, woman, and child will enter the hereafter for judgement with a record of deeds built upon the foundation of *fitrah*. Some individuals will pass from the plane of worldly existence treasuring the joyous accomplishment of having accepted and acted upon the truths to which they were exposed. Others will bear the heavy burden of having denied the clarity of revelation and man's duty to God, beginning with denial of the very foundation of belief, which is to say God Himself.

Islam teaches that in the days of oral tradition, but preceding written language, God sent a prophet to each nation so that none would live and die without receiving the offer of salvation. When God gifted the recording of His teachings to man in the form of written language, the books of scripture supplanted the need for further prophets. The message of God reached subsequent generations through the combination of oral tradition, written scripture, and religious men and women who served as pious examples and inspiring reminders to their communities.

God is recorded as having gifted mankind with a series of scriptures, revealing the Suhuf (Sheets) to Abraham, the Zaboor (Psalms) to David, the Tawraat (Torah) to Moses, the Injeel (Gospel) to Jesus, and the Qur'an to Muhammad. Each book replaced the preceding record once the pristine message of God's revelation became sufficiently adulterated to warrant correction and purification.

(Section 3) Books of Scripture

Such claims demand a heavy burden of proof. Initially, a person might point out that nobody can deny the numerous individuals throughout history who selectively applied the teachings of God in accordance with deviant (although sometimes seemingly well-intentioned) personal, political, and cultural desires. In regard to these individuals, Allah teaches,

> "There is among them a section who distort the Book with their tongues, (as they read) you would think it is a part of the Book, but it is no part of the Book; and they say, 'That is from Allah,' but it is not from Allah: it is they who tell a lie against Allah, and (well) they know it!" (TMQ 3:78)

and,

> "Then woe to those who write the Book with their own hands, and then say: 'This is from Allah,' to traffic with it for a miserable price! – woe to them for what their hands do write, and for the gain they make thereby." (TMQ 2:79)

The historical result is that of a common theme running through the scriptural remnants of the Abrahamic religions, with both the Old and New Testaments diverging from preceding books of revelation according to the whims and agendas of scribes and translators. All the same, the Old Testament, New Testament and Holy Qur'an are all consistent in regard to the basic creed – namely to recognize God and to worship Him and Him alone, to keep His commandments, and to obey His messengers.

The deviancies crept in (and continue to creep in) when the job of recording, translating, or canonizing fell into the hands of those who sought to design religion closer to their own hearts' desire. Consider, for example, the Psalms of David. If anyone believes that what remains in the hands of man is a complete and unadulterated

(SECTION 3) BOOKS OF SCRIPTURE

book of guidance, as revealed to David, and that it is capable of standing on it's own merit, they better have another read. Next consider the Old Testament, which (as discussed shortly) is so filled with errors and contradictions as to render the entire work suspect. Then consider the New Testament, which represents the canonization of four gospels to the exclusion of somewhere between an estimated 250 and 2,000 non-canonical acts, epistles and gospels (which were discarded and burned with only a handful of 'apocryphal' survivors).* One wonders about the character of the men who made *that* editing choice, their intention and religious orientation, and their willingness to compromise truth in order to support group ideology.

---

* The history of the apocrypha is interesting, for, as per the *Encyclopaedia Britannica* (CD-ROM), "The history of the term's (apocrypha) usage indicates that it referred to a body of esoteric writings that were at first prized, later tolerated, and finally excluded." It is interesting to note that the apocrypha, though initially 'prized,' eventually fell from grace in the eyes of the religious community to the station of simply being tolerated, and subsequently to being rejected outright. The assertion that the exact same sequence of religious evolution ultimately resulted in the rejection of the pure teachings of Christ Jesus himself does not exactly remain distant. And how can it, when the very history of early 'Christianity' is shaded in doubt? To quote from the *Encyclopaedia Britannica* once again,

> "The writers of the four Gospels included in the New Testament were bearing witness to assured truths that the faithful ought to know, and *no convincing reconstruction of historical facts* is possible from these books of the New Testament. The only avowedly historical book in it is the Acts of the Apostles. The New Testament as a whole represents merely a selection from the early Christian writings. It includes *only* what conformed to the doctrine of the church when, later on, that doctrine became fixed in one form. Between the Acts of the Apostles, dating probably from the late 1st century, and the writings of Eusebius of Caesarea (died c. 340) and his contemporaries in the first quarter of the 4th century, there is an almost complete gap in Christian historiography" (above emphasis mine).

So the question arises once again, "What did the early first, second, and third century 'Christians' know that we don't?"

(Section 3) Books of Scripture

For those who wish to evaluate scripture in a more pragmatic fashion, examination of some of the contradictions and inaccuracies in the Old and New Testaments is overdue. The list is long enough to make any reasonable and objective observer skeptical with regard to the Bible being the unadulterated word (or, as some claim, the inspired word) of God. What is meant by the list being 'long enough?' Well, it's greater than one. After all, God is infallible, so the smallest single mistake is enough to prove ungodly origin of that passage in specific and pollution of the scripture as a whole. Assuming the smallest single mistake sufficient to prove corruption of the revelation as a whole, the many listed contradictions and/or inaccuracies are expected to be considered not just significant, but conclusive. For if a person is unable to trust one part of the book, which parts *are* to be trusted?

Two main objectives subsequently need to be addressed – the first being an equivalent evaluation of the Holy Qur'an as revelation, and the second being consideration of evidence suggestive of the Holy Qur'an having been revealed in continuity with Old and New Testaments.

(3.A)
The Old Testament

"(The Bible) has noble poetry in it; and some clever fables; and some blood-drenched history; and a wealth of obscenity; and upwards of a thousand lies."

— Mark Twain, *Letters from the Earth,* vol. II

How much evidence of tampering, pollution of truth, and adulteration of reality does a person need?

Here is a partial list, with the relevant points emphasized in bold italics:

(1) Genesis 6:19-20 (*two* of *each* animal), versus Genesis 7:2-3 (*seven* of *clean* animals, *two* of *unclean* animals)?

Genesis 6:19-20: And of every living thing of all flesh you shall bring *two* of *every* sort into the ark, to keep them alive with you; they shall be male and female. Of the birds after their kind, of animals after their kind, and of every creeping thing of the earth after its kind, *two* of *every* kind will come to you to keep them alive.

Genesis 7:2-3: You shall take with you *seven* each of every clean animal, a male and his female; *two* each of animals that are unclean, a male and his female; also *seven* each of birds of the air, male and female, to keep the species alive on the face of all the earth.

(2) Genesis 6:3 and Genesis 11:11 – Life limited to 120 years or not?

Genesis 6:3: And the LORD said, "My Spirit shall not strive with man forever, for he is indeed flesh; yet his days shall be *one hundred and twenty* years."

Genesis 11:11: After he begot Arphaxad, Shem lived *five hundred* years, and begot sons and daughters.

(3) Genesis 6:3 and Genesis 9:29 – Life limited to 120 years or not?

Genesis 6:3: And the LORD said, "My Spirit shall not strive with man forever, for he is indeed flesh; yet his days shall be *one hundred and twenty* years."

Genesis 9:29: So all the days of Noah were *nine hundred and fifty* years; and he died.

[Note: Some theologians state that the foretold '120 years' referred to the predicted time of the flood, when the lives of so many of mankind were destined to end. This also doesn't work, for placing Genesis 5:32 (which, preceding Genesis 6:3 in sequence, must have been revealed prior to Genesis 6:3) next to Genesis 7:6 shows that a hundred years or less passed between the revelation of Genesis 6:3 and the flood, as noted in the quoted verses below:]

Genesis 5:32: And Noah was *five hundred years old*, and Noah begot Shem, Ham, and Japheth.

Genesis 7:6: Noah was *six hundred years old* when the floodwaters were on the earth.

(4) Genesis 16:16, 21:5, 21:8 and the passage of Genesis 21: 14-19

Genesis 16:16: Abraham was *eighty-six years old* when Hagar bore Ishmael to Abraham.

Genesis 21:5: Now Abraham was *one hundred years old* when his son Isaac was born to him.

(3.A) THE OLD TESTAMENT

Genesis 21:8: So the child *grew* and was *weaned.*

So Ishmael was 14 when Isaac was born, and Isaac was weaned (which, in the Middle East, and preceding the modern age of formula and instant cereal, takes two years according to ethnic custom) prior to Ishmael being cast out by Sarah. The difference between Genesis 16:16 and 21:5 establishes the age difference to be 14 years, and the weaning of Isaac, described in Genesis 21:8, adds another two years, at least.) Yet the story of Genesis 21:14-19 portrays a helpless infant rather than an able-bodied, sixteen year old Ishmael, as follows:

> Genesis 21:14-19: So Abraham rose early in the morning, and took bread and a skin of water; and putting it on her shoulder, he gave it and *the boy* to Hagar, and sent her away. Then she departed and wandered in the Wilderness of Beersheba. And the water in the skin was used up, and she *placed the boy under one of the shrubs.* Then she went and *sat down across from him* at a distance of about a bowshot; for she said to herself, "Let me not see the *death of the boy.*" So she sat opposite him, and lifted her voice and wept.
>
> And God heard the voice of *the lad.* Then the angel of God called to Hagar out of heaven, and said to her, "What ails you, Hagar? Fear not, for God has heard *the voice of the lad* where he is. Arise, *lift up the lad* and *hold him with your hand,* for I will make him a great nation."
>
> Then God opened her eyes, and she saw a well of water. And she went and filled the skin with water, and *gave the lad a drink.*

The list of incongruities in the above passage is lengthy. To begin with, to describe a sixteen year-old as a 'boy' or a 'lad' is clearly peculiar. In a time and place when sixteen year-old males were

257

commonly married and awaiting their second or third child while supporting a growing family, in addition to being hunters, soldiers, and, albeit rarely, even kings on occasion, a sixteen year old male could be considered nothing less than a man. Exactly how does a father give a sixteen year-old man to his wife, and how, in turn, does she leave him under a shrub? The statement that "she went and sat down across from him" clearly implies that he lacked the physical capability of standing up and walking to the side of his mother, and the following appeal of the mother not to "see the death of the boy" complements the impression of incapacitation on the part of Ishmael. However, would a sixteen year-old youth/man of the desert not have been more fit and expected to outlive his aging mother, especially under conditions of exposure? Would he have been expected to have cried ("the voice of the lad")? And how, precisely, does a mother "lift up" a sixteen year-old man of the desert and "hold him with your hand"? Lastly, is a person truly expected to believe that Ishmael was of such frail constitution that he required his mother to give him a drink, for he was unable to get a drink of water himself?

(5) Genesis 26:34 and Genesis 36:2-3 – who were the wives?

Genesis 26:34: When Esau was forty years old, he took as wives *Judith* the daughter of Beeri the Hittite, and *Basemath* the daughter of Elon the Hittite.

Genesis 36:2-3: Esau took his wives from the daughters of Canaan: *Adah* the daughter of Elon the Hittite; *Aholibamah* the daughter of Anah, the daughter of Zibeon the Hivite; and *Basemath*, Ishmael's daughter, sister of Nebajoth.

(6) Genesis 32:30, Exodus 33:11 and Exodus 33:20 – Jacob and Moses' lives preserved? They saw God's face or not?

Genesis 32:30: So Jacob called the name of the place Peniel: "For I have seen God *face to face*, and *my life is preserved.*"

(3.A) The Old Testament

Exodus 33:11: So the LORD spoke to Moses *face to face*, as a man speaks to his friend.

Exodus 33:20: But He (God) said, "*You cannot see My face;* for *no* man shall see Me, and live."

(7) Numbers 23:19 and Genesis 6:6-7 – Does God repent or not?

Numbers 23:19: "God is not a man, that He should lie, nor a son of man, that He should repent."

Genesis 6:6-7: And the LORD *was sorry* that He had made man on the earth, and He was grieved in His heart. So the LORD said, "I will destroy man whom I have created from the face of the earth, both man and beast, creeping thing and birds of the air, *for I am sorry* that I have made them."

(8) II Samuel 6:23 and II Samuel 21:8 – Did Michal have children or not?

II Samuel 6:23: Therefore *Michal* the *daughter of Saul* had *no children to the day of her death.*

II Samuel 21:8: So the king took Armoni and Mephibosheth, the two sons of Rizpah the daughter of Aiah, whom she bore to Saul, and the *five sons of Michal* the *daughter of Saul,* whom she brought up for Adriel the son of Barzillai the Meholathite.

(9) II Samuel 8:4 and I Chronicles 18:4 – 700 or 7000 horsemen?

II Samuel 8:4: David took from him one thousand chariots, *seven hundred horsemen*, and twenty thousand foot soldiers.

I Chronicles 18:4: David took from him one thousand chariots, *seven thousand horsemen*, and twenty thousand foot soldiers.

[Note: Numbers in ancient Hebrew were written *longhand*. Seven Hundred in the Hebrew was '*sheba*' *me'ah*'. Seven Thousand was '*sheba*' *eleph*.' The error is the difference between '*me'ah*' and '*eleph*,' so numerical errors in the Old and New Testaments are not simple copying errors of leaving off a zero here or there, but actual word disparities.]

(Section 3) Books of Scripture

(10) II Samuel 8:9-10 and I Chronicles 18:9-10 – Toi or Tou? Joram or Hadoram?

II Samuel 8:9-10: When Toi king of Hamath heard that David had defeated all the army of Hadadezer, then Toi sent *Joram* his son to King David, to greet him and bless him, because he had fought against Hadadezer and defeated him (for Hadadezer had been at war with *Toi*); and *Joram* brought with him articles of silver, articles of gold, and articles of bronze.

I Chronicles 18:9-10: Now when *Tou* king of Hamath heard that David had defeated all the army of Hadadezer king of Zobah, he sent *Hadoram* his son to King David, to greet him and bless him, because he had fought against Hadadezer and defeated him (for Hadadezer had been at war with *Tou*); and *Hadoram* brought with him all kinds of articles of gold, silver, and bronze.

(11) II Samuel 10:18 and I Chronicles 19:18 – 700 or 7000 charioteers? 40,000 horsemen or footmen? Captain's name?

II Samuel 10:18: Then the Syrians fled before Israel; and David killed seven *hundred* charioteers and forty thousand *horsemen* of the Syrians, and struck *Shobach* the commander of their army, who died there.

I Chronicles 19:18: Then the Syrians fled before Israel; and David killed seven *thousand* charioteers and forty thousand *foot soldiers* of the Syrians, and killed *Shophach* the commander of the army.

(12) II Samuel 17:25 and I Chronicles 2:17 – Israelite or Ishmaelite?

II Samuel 17:25: This Amasa was the son of a man whose name was *Jithra*, an *Israelite*, who had gone in to Abigail the daughter of Nahash, sister of Zeruiah, Joab's mother.

I Chronicles 2:17: Abigail bore Amasa; and the father of Amasa was *Jether* the *Ishmaelite*.

(3.A) The Old Testament

[Note: 'Jithra' and 'Jether' are cross-referenced in the Biblical text as referring to the same individual, although, once again, differing in the spelling of the name. With regard to the issue of 'Israelite' versus Ishmaelite,' if the authors couldn't get that one straight, a person might question how much more might they have been inclined, being Jewish, to calculated name-switching in the case of Abraham sacrificing his 'only begotten son,' Isaac? The above section 2.B.5 discusses the fact that at no time was Isaac the only begotten son of Abraham. And a person sees here that the authors of the Old Testament substituted 'Israelite' with 'Ishmaelite' when there was no obvious motivation. How much more likely would they have been to have switched names when the supposed superiority of the Jews and the birthright and covenants of God were at stake? Incidentally, once this contradiction became known it was creatively hidden in many modern versions of the Bible. For example, the *New Revised Standard Version* translates the Hebrew *'yisre'eliy'* in II Samuel 17:25 to 'Ishmaelite.' A discrete footnote acknowledges that the correct translation would be 'Israelite,' but that 'Ishmaelite' was substituted, presumably in order to conform with the *'yishma'eliy'* of I Chronicles 2:17. Conflict was thereby avoided in the translation, but not in the foundational, source documents. One may presume that the authors attempted to achieve consistency in the translation at the expense of accuracy and faithfulness to the source documents – a sly attempt to cover up the internal contradiction of the untranslated text. Those who note the disingenuity would do well to remember this example, for future Bible translations will likely embody many creative efforts at making the errors discussed herein disappear. The following is a big one, and likely to be the first to be addressed.]

(13) II Samuel 24:1 and I Chronicles 21:1 – God or Devil? (How does a scripture possibly confuse the two?)

II Samuel 24:1: Again the anger of the **LORD** was aroused against Israel, and He moved David against them to say, "Go, number Israel and Judah."

261

I Chronicles 21:1: Now *Satan* stood up against Israel, and moved David to number Israel.

(14) II Samuel 23:8 and I Chronicles 11:11 – Tachmonite or Hachmonite? 300 or 800?

II Samuel 23:8: These are the names of the mighty men whom David had: Josheb-Basshebeth the *Tachmonite*, chief among the captains. He was called Adino the Eznite, because he had killed *eight hundred* men at one time.

I Chronicles 11:11: And this is the number of the mighty men whom David had: Jashobeam the son of a *Hachmonite*, chief of the captains; he had lifted up his spear against *three hundred*, killed by him at one time.

[Note: Once again, the Bible itself cross-references the two disparate names of Josheb-Basshebeth and Jashobeam, leaving no uncertainty to the fact that both passages describe the same person.]

(15) II Samuel 24:9 and I Chronicles 21:5 – 800,000 or 1,100,000?

II Samuel 24:9: Then Joab gave the sum of the number of the people to the king. And there were in Israel *eight hundred thousand* valiant men who drew the sword, and the men of Judah were *five hundred thousand* men.

I Chronicles 21:5: Then Joab gave the sum of the number of the people to David. All Israel had *one million one hundred thousand* men who drew the sword, and Judah had *four hundred and seventy thousand* men who drew the sword.

(16) II Samuel 24:13 and I Chronicles 21:11,12 – 7 or 3 years?

II Samuel 24:13: So Gad came to David and told him; and he said to him, "Shall *seven years* of famine come to you in your land? Or shall you flee three months before your enemies, while they pursue you? Or shall there be three days' plague in your land? Now consider and see what answer I should take back to Him who sent me."

(3.A) THE OLD TESTAMENT

I Chronicles 21:11-12: So Gad came to David and said to him, "Thus says the LORD: 'Choose for yourself, either *three years of famine*, or three months to be defeated by your foes with the sword of your enemies overtaking *you*, or else for three days the sword of the LORD—the plague in the land, with the angel of the LORD destroying throughout all the territory of Israel.' Now consider what answer I should take back to Him who sent me."

(17) I Kings 4:26 and II Chronicles 9:25 – 40,000 or 4,000?

I Kings 4:26: Solomon had *forty thousand* stalls of horses for his chariots, and twelve thousand horsemen.

II Chronicles 9:25: Solomon had *four thousand* stalls for horses and chariots, and twelve thousand horsemen...

(18) I Kings 15:33 and 2 Chronicles 16:1 – Did Baasha die in the 27th 'year of Asa, king of Judah' or did Baasha 'come up against Judah' in the 36th 'year of the reign of Asa'?

I Kings 15:33: In the *third year* of Asa king of Judah, Baasha the son of Ahijah became king over all Israel in Tirzah, and *reigned twenty-four years*.

2 Chronicles 16:1: In the *thirty-sixth year of the reign of Asa*, Baasha king of Israel came up against Judah and built Ramah, that he might let none go out or come in to Asa king of Judah.

(19) I Kings 5:15-16 and II Chronicles 2:2 – 3,300 or 3,600?

I Kings 5:15-16: Solomon had seventy thousand who carried burdens, and eighty thousand who quarried stone in the mountains, besides *three thousand three hundred* from the chiefs of Solomon's deputies, who supervised the people who labored in the work.

II Chronicles 2:2: Solomon selected seventy thousand men to bear burdens, eighty thousand to quarry stone in the mountains, and *three thousand six hundred* to oversee them.

(Section 3) Books of Scripture

(20) I Kings 7:26 and II Chronicles 4:5 – 2,000 or 3,000 baths?

I Kings 7:26: It was a handbreadth thick; and its brim was shaped like the brim of a cup, like a lily blossom. It contained ***two thousand*** baths.

II Chronicles 4:5: It was a handbreadth thick; and its brim was shaped like the brim of a cup, like a lily blossom. It contained ***three thousand*** baths.

(21) II Kings 8:26 and II Chronicles 22:2 – 22 or 42 years old?

II Kings 8:26: Ahaziah was ***twenty-two years old*** when he became king, and he reigned one year in Jerusalem. His mother's name was Athaliah the granddaughter of Omri, king of Israel.

II Chronicles 22:2: Ahaziah was ***forty-two years old*** when he became king, and he reigned one year in Jerusalem. His mother's name was Athaliah the granddaughter of Omri.

[Note: The answer to this discrepancy is that Ahaziah's age must have been 22, because II Chronicles 21:20 through II Chronicles 22:2 teaches that the king died at the age of 40, and was succeeded by his son, who was 42. A man fathers a child two years older than himself? Arithmetic, according to Mickey Mouse, is "Being able to count up to twenty without taking off your shoes." But between the reader's toes and all appendages of the family cat, there is simply no way to make these figures add up. While the logical conclusion approaches ramming speed, II Chronicles 22:1 points out that Ahaziah, the successor, was the *youngest* son. If the youngest son was two years older than the father, how many years did the older sons have on their father? So assigning an age of 42 to the son was a copying error, no doubt, but that's not the point. Isaiah 40:8 claims that, "...the word of our God stands forever." This passage in Isaiah doesn't excuse copying errors, or any other error for that matter, regardless how slight. In fact, according to this criterion, any 'word' which has not 'stood forever' is immediately disqualified as having been from God.]

(3.A) The Old Testament

(22) II Kings 24:8 and II Chronicles 36:9 – 18 or 8 years old? 3 months or 3 months and 10 days?

II Kings 24:8: Jehoiachin was *eighteen* years old when he became king, and he reigned in Jerusalem *three months*.

II Chronicles 36:9: Jehoiachin was *eight* years old when he became king, and he reigned in Jerusalem *three months and ten days*.

(23) Ezra 2:65 and Nehemiah 7:67 – 200 or 245 singers?

Ezra 2:65: ...besides their male and female servants, of whom there were seven thousand three hundred and thirty-seven; and they had *two hundred men and women singers*.

Nehemiah 7:67: ...besides their male and female servants, of whom there were seven thousand three hundred and thirty-seven; and they had *two hundred and forty-five men and women singers*.

Comparison of II Kings, chapter 19 with Isaiah, chapter 37 reveals a sequence of 37 verses which correspond virtually to the letter. The correspondence is so exact as to have prompted several Bible critics to have suggested plagiarism by one of the authors, or copying from a common source document. And while this charge of plagiarism may have validity, a more generous suggestion might be that these two chapters exemplify the exquisitely accurate consistency which should be expected of a book of God. Whether the story be retold once, twice, or a thousand times, as long as the origin of the tradition lies in revelation from the All-Mighty, the story should not change, not even in the smallest detail. The fact that the remainder of the Old and New Testaments lack such accuracy of parallel testimonies threatens the boldness of the claim to an inerrant Biblical record, leaving a person to contemplate the significance of contradictory scriptural entries, such as those listed above.

And then there are the simple questions. Questions like, "Does anybody really believe that Jacob wrestled with God, and Jacob prevailed (Genesis 32:24-30)?" The Creator of a Universe

240,000,000,000,000,000,000,000 miles in diameter with all its intricacies, with the measly planet Earth alone weighing in at a middle weight of 5,976,000,000,000,000,000,000,000 kg, and someone believes that a paltry blob of protoplasm not only wrestled with The One who created him, but prevailed?

Another simple question: God is recorded as having warned Adam, "but of the tree of the knowledge of good and evil you shall not eat, for in the day that you eat of it you shall surely die" (Genesis 2:17), and "but of the fruit of the tree which is in the midst of the garden, God has said, 'You shall not eat it, nor shall you touch it, lest you die'" (Genesis 3:3). So which is it? Did Adam bite the apple or didn't he? The way the story is told, he bit the apple and lived. Yet God promises death the *very same day*. So did he bite it or not? If he did he should have died, and if he didn't mankind should still be in paradise. Is the 'die' part an error of translation or a metaphor? If an error, then let the translators admit it. If a metaphor, then once again a person can emphasize the metaphorical nature of Hebrew idiom and suggest that Jesus, similarly, didn't 'die' any more than Adam did.

Next point – who wrote the Old Testament? Tradition states that Moses wrote the Pentateuch, but a person can assume that Moses would have encountered slight technical difficulty recording his own obituary in Deuteronomy 34:5-12. No doubt Moses had to pass on writing the record of his own death, burial, wake, and aftermath. So who was the author of these passages, is he/she to be trusted, and what does this say about authorship of the Old Testament as a whole?

Then there are the tales of naked drunkenness, incest and whoredom which no man or woman of modesty and integrity could read to their mother, much less to their own children. And yet, some very large portion of the world population put their trust in a book which records that Noah "...drank of the wine and was drunk, and became uncovered (naked) in his tent" (Genesis 9:22), and that Lot

(3.A) The Old Testament

"...went up out of Zoar and dwelt in the mountains, and his two daughters were with him; for he was afraid to dwell in Zoar. And he and his two daughters dwelt in a cave. Now the firstborn said to the younger, 'Our father is old, and there is no man on the earth to come in to us as is the custom of all the earth. Come, let us make our father drink wine, and we will lie with him, that we may preserve the lineage of our father.' So they made their father drink wine that night. And the firstborn went in and lay with her father, and he did not know when she lay down or when she arose. It happened on the next day that the firstborn said to the younger, 'Indeed I lay with my father last night; let us make him drink wine tonight also, and you go in and lie with him, that we may preserve the lineage of our father.' Then they made their father drink wine that night also. And the younger arose and lay with him, and he did not know when she lay down or when she arose. Thus both the daughters of Lot were with child by their father." (Genesis 19:30-36)

Tales of debauchery and deviancy include adultery and prostitution (Genesis 38:15-26), more prostitution (Judges 16:1), wholesale and open depravity (II Samuel 16:20-23), whoredom beyond description (Ezekiel 16:20-34 and 23:1-21), and whoring spiced with adultery (Proverbs 7:10-19). The rape and incest of II Samuel 13:7-14 is described in a sequence of verses which bears a most interesting moral to the story, for the victim of the incestuous rape was counseled to "hold her peace," for, as regards the rapist, "He *is* your brother; (so) do not take this thing to heart." (II Samuel 13:20) The concept that such 'pearls of wisdom' are the fruits of revelation can only be the stuff of deviant dreams.

On the subject of dreaming, II Timothy 3:16 reads, "All scripture is given by inspiration of God, and is profitable for doctrine, for

267

reproof, for correction, for instruction in righteousness." Makes sense – that's the way it should be. But can anyone conceive the 'profit, reproof, correction, or instruction in righteousness' conveyed in the above passages? The person who thinks they can probably should be in prison.

Another curiosity which arises from the above snippets of the Old Testament begs resolution. According to Genesis 38:15-30, Perez and Zerah were born to Tamar after incestuous and extramarital fornication with her father-in-law, Judah. Passing over the fact that, according to Leviticus 20:12, both of them should have been put to death (and prophets are not above the law), one wonders what the lineage of Perez and Zerah were. After all, the proposed 'word of God' tells us, "One of illegitimate birth shall not enter the congregation of the Lord; even to the tenth generation none of his descendants shall enter the congregation of the Lord." (Deuteronomy 23:2) So who was the tenth generation from Zerah? Doesn't matter. Who was the tenth generation from Perez? Somebody named Solomon. His father (the ninth generation) also has a familiar sounding name – David. Trusting Matthew 1:3-6, David was the ninth generation of a bastard, and as such, according to the Old Testament, should by no way enter the 'congregation of the Lord.' The same goes for Solomon. And yet they are both held to have been righteous men of God, if not prophets – either one of which, in light of the above condemnation, would present an awkward understanding, at best.

David's son, Solomon, was not only the tenth generation of illegitimacy through Perez but also the first generation of illegitimacy through David's adulterous and illicit union with Bathsheba, the wife of Uriah (II Samuel 11:2-4), if the Old Testament is to be believed. Once again, breezing past the death penalty which remained unfulfilled (Leviticus 20:10), Solomon is portrayed as having a double-dose of unacceptability against him. Or does he? Something doesn't sound

(3.A) The Old Testament

right here – something must be wrong somewhere. Either David and Solomon were not prophets or the Old Testament is not to be trusted. The pieces of God-given revelation should not require reshaping and force in order to fit together, but should slide together with the slickest of conformity in congruence with the perfection of The One who created the heavens and Earth in perfect harmony. That is the way it should be, and the average Christian suggests that such is precisely the case with the New Testament.

However, such an assertion deserves inspection. Having examined the above, a person can readily understand why the author of 'Jeremiah' bewails, "How can you say, 'We are wise, and the law of the Lord is with us?' Look, the false pen of the scribe certainly works falsehood." (Jeremiah 8:8) The *New Revised Standard Version*, unlike the *New King James Version*, doesn't soften their words, recording the same passage in 'Jeremiah' as, "How can you say, 'We are wise, and the law of the Lord is with us,' when in fact, the false pen of the scribes has made it into a lie?" So that is the Old Testament – so full of errors that even one of the authors bemoans the scriptural corruption generated by the "false pens of the scribes."

Many claim that similar problems plague the New Testament – weaknesses, inconsistencies and contradictions surface, demanding explanation. If so, Christians face the challenge, "Are you a person of God, or are you a person of Christianity?" The question demands testimony in the audience of The Creator. The followers of God, His prophets (Jesus included) and His revelation will submit to God-given truths, when made clear, while the adherents of any man-made religion will defend their doctrine against logic, reason, and revelation. Discussion of the frail or nonexistent foundation of the most passionately defended Christian doctrines has already been offered. The remaining question of primary importance relates to the authority of the New Testament.

(3.B)
The New Testament

"Be sure that you go to the author
to get at his meaning, not to find yours."
– John Ruskin, Sesame and Lilies

William Blake, in *The Everlasting Gospel,* commented:

"Both read the Bible day and night,
But thou read'st black where I read white."

The above is a beautiful statement of that which is known to all. There is so much room for interpretation and so many inconsistencies in the New Testament as to have spawned a myriad of varied belief systems. So much so as to have prompted one author to opine,

"You can and you can't,
You shall and you shan't,
You will and you won't,
And you will be damned if you do,
And you will be damned if you don't."[178]

Why do so many varying viewpoints exist? First and foremost, definitive understanding of which writings should be included/excluded

---

178. Dow, Lorenzo. *Reflections on the Love of God.*

(3.B) The New Testament

from the Bible is lacking. Secondly, even amongst those books which are canonized, the many variant manuscripts lack uniformity, so much so that such a respected reference as *The Interpreter's Dictionary of the Bible* states, "It is safe to say that there is not one sentence in the NT in which the MS tradition is wholly uniform."[179]

The degree of non-conformity of the many Bible manuscripts is well known to anybody of scholarship. The severity of the resultant uncertainty, even amongst canonized books, is exemplified by the verse of Acts 8:37, which has been dropped from many modern Bible translations, including the *New International Version* and the *New Revised Standard Version*, for reason that this verse is not to be found in the most ancient of manuscripts. As such, the verse appears to be a later insertion, and consequently several respected translations enumerate the verse of Acts 8:37, but leave it completely blank. Such is just one minor example of the lack of consensus with regard to Bible content. According to *Harper's Bible Dictionary*, "The NT canon also has an uneven and complex history....no canonical lists appear before around AD 150..."[180] John Reumann, in the Oxford Bible Series entitled *Variety and Unity in New Testament Thought*, comments,

> "The canon as a collection becomes more problematical when one sees how varied are the writings that have been included (and how some of those left out are by no means intrinsically inferior in style or later in date) or how opinions differed over some of these writings in the patristic centuries."[181]

And Graham Stanton (also in the Oxford Bible Series) adds, "The early church retained four gospels in spite of regular embarrassment

---

179. Buttrick, George Arthur (Ed.). 1962 (1996 Print). *The Interpreter's Dictionary of the Bible*. Volume 4. Nashville: Abingdon Press. pp. 594-595 (Under Text, NT).
180. Achtemeier, Paul J. p. 111.
181. Reumann, John. 1991. *Variety and Unity in New Testament Thought*. Oxford University Press. p. 281.

over the differences..."[182]

Nonetheless, the *New Catholic Encyclopedia* claims,

"All the books in the canon are inspired, but it is debated whether or not there is or could be any inspired book that, because of its loss, is not in the canon. The Church has not settled the question. The more general opinion is that some inspired books probably have been lost."[183]

Why this lurking suspicion that some of the books have been lost? Biblical evidence -- "In 1 Cor 5.9, St. Paul refers to a previous letter of his, and in 2 Cor 2.3-9; 7.8-12 he refers to an earlier letter different from 1 Corinthians."[184] Paul also speaks of the 'epistle from Laodicea' in Col 4:16 – where is that? And furthermore, between 1 Chr 29:29, 2 Chr 9:29 and 2 Chr 12:15 a total of six lost books are also disclosed in the Old Testament.[185] So, it would seem, material most certainly has been lost; how much has been inappropriately *added* is yet another subject of debate.

Besides those books which appear to have been lost, five books (i.e., 2 Peter, 2 John, 3 John, James, and Jude) suffered reversals in acceptance, the canonicity of 'Hebrews' and 'Apocalypse' was debated on the basis of unknown authorship, and canonicity was claimed for many others which have since sunk into the obscurity of the apocrypha.[186] Even following the 'Final Stabilization' in the 5th century, 'Hebrews,' 'Apocalypse,' and many of the Catholic Epistles remained controversial through the Middle Ages.[187] This controversy remained so problematic that an end was sought, and so, after well

---

182. Stanton, Graham. p. 135
183. *New Catholic Encyclopedia*. Vol 2, p. 386.
184. *New Catholic Encyclopedia*. Vol 2, p. 386.
185. *New Catholic Encyclopedia*. Vol 2, p. 386.
186. *New Catholic Encyclopedia*. Vol 2, p. 391.
187. *New Catholic Encyclopedia*. Vol 2, p. 395.

(3.B) The New Testament

over a thousand years of indecision and debate, the Council of Trent was convened, and dogmatic definition of the Biblical canon laid down on April 8, 1564 in the decree, *De Canonicis Scripturis*.[188]

A person might wonder on what authority such canonization was made, almost 16 centuries following the ministry of Jesus. The Catholic Church takes the stand that,

> "The decree of Trent, repeated by Vatican I on April 24, 1870, is the infallible decision of the magisterium. In the decree, certain doubtfully authentic deuterocanonical sections are also included with the books (*cum omnibus suis partibus*): Mk 16.9-20; Lk 22.19b-20, 43-44; and Jn 7.53-8.11."[189]

Of note are the back-to-back claims of magisterial infallibility and doubtful authenticity, which may lead some to conclude that such claims to infallibility can be little more than papal propaganda. A person can fairly express concern over the claim that Abraham sinned, Moses sinned, but every pope for the last two millennia was infallible.

Concern becomes heightened when one learns that Pope Honorius I, who ruled the Vatican for the thirteen years between the end of October, 625 CE until his death Oct. 12, 638, was posthumously anathematized for the alleged heresy of Monophysitism (teaching that Christ has one single nature rather than two), and Monothelitism (the claim that Christ has only one will). The sentence of anathema on the basis of heresy was passed by the third Council of Constantinople (the sixth ecumenical council) in 680, and Pope St. Leo II subsequently confirmed the condemnation two years later, in 682.[190, 191]

---

188. *New Catholic Encyclopedia*. Vol 2, p. 395.
189. *New Catholic Encyclopedia*. Vol 2, p. 395.
190. *Encyclopaedia Britannica*. CD-ROM.
191. *New Catholic Encyclopedia*. Vol 7, pp. 123-125.

(SECTION 3) BOOKS OF SCRIPTURE

Now, here is a pope whose views were so popular as to have been sanctioned by the Synod of Constantinople in the year of his death as "truly agreeing with the apostolic preaching."[192] Yet 44 years later Pope St. Leo II, with the support of the same church which previously endorsed Honorius, declared Pope Honorius anathema because he "...did not, as became the apostolic authority, extinguish the flame of heretical teaching in its first beginning, but fostered it by his negligence" and "...allowed the immaculate rule of apostolic tradition, which he received from his predecessors, to be tarnished."[193] The Trullan Synod, as well as the seventh and eighth ecumenical councils, formalized the condemnation.[194] One wonders, exactly which of the two opposing popes in this scenario is infallible? Because someone has to be wrong – either Pope Honorius was fallible and deserved to be declared anathema according to the rules of the church, or Pope Honorius was correct and Pope St. Leo II erred in declaring him anathema. Either way, a person cannot be faulted for concluding that one pope was right, one pope was wrong, and nobody is infallible, despite the tiresome repetition of the claim.

Skimming the chronicles of papal history, a person encounters similar accounts which raise more than a few contemplative eyebrows. Pope Pius IX convened the first Vatican Council in 1869-1870, and defined the doctrine of papal infallibility – a doctrine which was so self-evident as to have evaded authoritative definition for over fifteen centuries. The delay in formalization of the doctrine is understandable, given the history of the papacy. The 600's witnessed the intrigue surrounding Pope Honorius I, as described above. The mid-900's introduced John XII, whose crimes against humanity and religion

---

192. Chapman, Dom John. 1907. *The Condemnation of Pope Honorius*. London: Catholic Truth Society. p. 25.

193. Chapman, Dom John. pp. 114-115.

194. Chapman, Dom John. p. 115.

(3.B) The New Testament

were of such breadth, depth, and perversity as to prompt one author to declare him a Christian Caligula, adding,

> "...the charge was specifically made against him that he turned the Lateran into a brothel; that he and his gang violated female pilgrims in the very basilica of St. Peter; that the offerings of the humble laid upon the altar were snatched up as casual booty. He was inordinately fond of gambling, at which he invoked the names of those discredited gods now universally regarded as demons. His sexual hunger was insatiable – a minor crime in Roman eyes. What was far worse was that the casual occupants of his bed were rewarded not with casual gifts of gold but of land. One of his mistresses was able to establish herself as a feudal lord 'for he was so blindly in love with her that he made her governor of cities— and even gave to her the golden crosses and cups of St. Peter himself.'"[195]

Benedict IX assumed the chair of St. Peter in 1032, only to sell the papacy to his godfather, Giovanni Gratiano, for the impressive sum of 1,500 pounds of gold.[196] Similar debacles were to come to light in subsequent years, such as when the chair of St. Peter became uncomfortably overloaded by the trinity of popes Benedict XIII, Gregory XII and John XXIII (himself an ex-pirate, as if the situation demanded even more intrigue) all occupying the office of the papacy at the same time in the early 1400's.[197]

Perhaps the most noteworthy peculiarity is that of the thirteenth century Pope Celestine V, about whom the *New*

---

195. Chamberlin, E. R. 1993. *The Bad Popes.* Barnes & Noble, Inc., p. 43-44. The subquote is attributed to Liudprand of Cremona, *Liber de Rebus Gestis Ottonis*, translated by F. A. Wright. London, 1930. Chapter x.
196. Chamberlin, E. R. p. 70-71.
197. Chamberlin, E. R. p. 158.

(SECTION 3) BOOKS OF SCRIPTURE

Catholic Encyclopedia notes, "Celestine's reign was marked by an unfortunate subservience to Charles II and by administrative incompetence....Realizing his incompetence, Celestine issued a constitution (December 10) declaring a pope's right to resign, and on December 13 freely resigned."[198] A more interesting twist to the tale would be hard to find – here is a pope who recognized his own incompetence and resigned. The Catholics claim that a pope can't do anything wrong, but here is one who, so it would seem, couldn't do anything right. Infallible but incompetent – a truly peculiar proposition.

More recently, in 1962 Pope John XXIII convened the Vatican II council, which ultimately issued the *Nostra Aetate*, proclaimed by Pope Paul VI (the successor to Pope John XXIII) on October 28, 1965; the *Nostra Aetate* is a document which exonerated the Jews of the alleged crime of crucifying Christ Jesus. Not only that, but the document asserts that "Indeed, the Church believes that by His cross Christ, Our Peace, reconciled Jews and Gentiles, making both one in Himself."[199] A collective "Now, wait a minute" was voiced around the world, and has echoed through the canyons of Christian consciousness ever since. Whether or not Christ Jesus ever was in fact crucified holds no relevance to this topic – what is of importance is the observation that a view held and supported by every pope since the inception of the Roman Catholic Church is opposed by one pope and his council in the twentieth century, and then endorsed by all popes who followed. So, were all preceding popes wrong not to have recognized the proposed innocence of the Jews, or did Pope John XXIII, Pope Paul VI, and Popes John Paul I and II endorse politically correct ideologies from the dark side of reality? The Jews, most certainly, rejoice in this professed exoneration, for the practical implication is an end to nearly two millennia of Catholic anti-Semitism.

---

198. *New Catholic Encyclopedia*. Vol 3, p. 365.
199. *Nostra Aetate*. 28 October 1965. Item #4. Official publication of the Vatican website, www.vatican.va

(3.B) The New Testament

Pope John Paul II has called for the Church to do "*tshuva*" (Hebrew for repentance) for its protracted history of anti-Semitism, and for all Catholics to henceforth refrain from harassment and discrimination against the Jews on the basis of their being considered accursed and condemned. However, just as the other 'infallible' popes of history clearly did not agree, neither do all members of the present day orthodoxy, for,

> "During the Vatican Council debate on the declaration dealing with the Jews, the Holy Synod of the Coptic Orthodox Church communicated to Rome its forthright understanding that "the Holy Bible gives a clear testimony that Jews have crucified Lord Jesus Christ and bore the responsibility of His Crucifixion." The communication recalled that "the Jews repeatedly said to Pontius Pilate: 'Crucify him, crucify him (Luke 23:21).' 'His blood be on us and our children (Matthew 27:25).'" The Coptic Orthodox Church then provided documentation for the view that the Jews stand "condemned" according to the New Testament. "Said St. Peter the Apostle: 'but ye denied the Holy One and the Just and desired a murderer (Barabbas) to be granted unto you; and killed the Prince of Life (Acts 3:14-15).'" Furthermore, the condemnation rests upon all Jews in their collective existence whether in ancient days or in this time. "This condemnation does not include a specific group and not others; for St. Peter addressed the Jews 'of every nation under Heaven (Acts 2).'"[200]

Returning to the original train of thought (i.e., the evolution of the Biblical canon and Council of Trent), the Christian public is asked to believe that the pious companions and followers couldn't agree upon the canon of Christian scripture a month, a year, two years

---

200. Gilbert, Arthur. 1968. *The Vatican Council and The Jews*. New York: The World Publishing Company. p. 7.

(SECTION 3) BOOKS OF SCRIPTURE

following the ministry of Jesus, but somehow some extraordinarily enlightened clergy distilled the purity of the truth of Christology from the scriptures 1,564 years later. Perhaps a person should be concerned over the risk of trusting the collective opinion of the rather progressive clergy who ushered so many religious innovations down the aisles of traditional worship. Innovations such as the cross, the crucifix, paintings, religious icons, stained glass portrayals, etc. Of course, many people love these elements of worship and defend them on the basis of their beauty, their inspiring and emotionally evocative nature, or the simple fact that they serve as religious reminders. That may be so. But what human judgement outweighs the commandments of God on the scales of opinion? What 'person of God' feels so superior as to say, "Well, yeah, God forbids it -- but I think it's okay"? The supreme arrogance is to believe that somehow God failed to consider all the angles, and we as human beings have the right to veto His decree based upon our own caprice.

Some form of negligence to the commandments certainly appears to have been apparent with regard to the aforementioned items of worship. For example, the most familiar symbols of Christianity are the naked cross and the crucifix. A person might assume that wear, display, and use of these items in religious services originated from the time of Jesus. Nothing could be further from the truth. In fact, adoption of both the cross and the crucifix into Christian life and rituals was innovated centuries after the ministry of Jesus. Representation of the bare cross, not surprisingly, came first, during the period of Constantine in the fourth century.[201] The earliest crucifixion scenes date from the 5th century, while the image of Christ crucified on a crucifix date from the 6th century; not until the 13th century did the cross appear on the altar table.[202] The *New Catholic Encyclopedia* comments,

---
201. *New Catholic Encyclopedia*. Vol 4, p. 486
202. *New Catholic Encyclopedia*. Vol 4, pp. 485-6.

(3.B) The New Testament

"The representation of Christ's redemptive death on Golgotha does not occur in the symbolic art of the first Christian centuries. The early Christians, influenced by the Old Testament prohibition of graven images, were reluctant to depict even the instrument of the Lord's Passion."[203]

Rarely are two sentences so rich in information. A person learns from the above quote that the Christians of the first centuries respected the Old Testament. One wonders what happened between then and now? The early Christians avoided any depiction of humans, even Christ Jesus, out of respect for the commandment of God to shun graven images. Only when softened up by four hundred years of religious 'progressiveness' did artists begin to challenge the boundaries of their religion.

Further innovations such as the commissioning of statues, paintings and stained glass portrayals subsequently became commonplace. These being the fruits of those who claimed to follow in the name of Jesus – turning Jesus the iconoclast into Jesus the icon – the religious purist can hardly be blamed for pointing out the lack of conformity with his example and teaching. Some people no doubt applaud the movement away from harsh and restrictive Old Testament laws; others shudder in contemplation of the ramifications for those who seek a path other than that which God prescribes. Men and women of God will seek scriptural clarification to secure their beliefs. Men and women of institutions, however, will seek the reassurances of clergy, which by this point should be considered suspect, if not in many cases completely corrupt.

For those who seek clarification from God, examination of the authority of the New Testament is of paramount importance. Should clear and identifiable errors be discovered, a search for a final and amending revelation should be considered reasonable.

---

203. *New Catholic Encyclopedia.* Vol 4, p. 486.

(SECTION 3) BOOKS OF SCRIPTURE

The following identifies (in bold italics) some of the more glaring New Testament conflicts:

(1) Matthew 1:12 and Luke 3:27 – Who was Salathiel's father?

Matthew 1:12: And after they were brought to Babylon *Jechonias* begot Salathiel, and Salathiel begot Zorobabel.

Luke 3:27: ...the son of Zorobabel, which was the son of Salathiel, which was the son of *Neri*...

(2) Matthew 1:16 and Luke 3:23 – Who was Joseph's father?

Matthew 1:16: And *Jacob* begot Joseph the husband of Mary, of whom was born Jesus who is called Christ.

Luke 3:23: Now Jesus himself began his ministry at about thirty years of age, being (as was supposed) the son of Joseph, the *son of Heli*...

(3) Matthew 2:14 and Luke 2:39 – To Egypt or Nazareth?

Matthew 2:14: When he arose, he took the young child and his mother by night and departed for *Egypt*, and was there until the death of Herod...

Luke 2:39: So when they had performed all things according to the law of the Lord, they returned to Galilee, to their own city, *Nazareth*.

(4) Matthew 4:3-9 and Luke 4:3-11 – stones to bread, throw himself down, *then* worship Satan, or stones to bread, worship Satan, *then* throw himself down?

(5) Matthew 6:9-13 and Luke 11:2-4 – compare the 'Lord's Prayer' (See section 6.B. of this book)

(6) Matthew 7:7,8 and Luke 13:24 – all who seek will find, or not?

Matthew 7:7,8: "Ask, and it will be given to you; seek, and you will find; knock, and it will be opened to you. For *everyone who asks receives*, and he who seeks finds, and to him who knocks it will be opened."

(3.B) THE NEW TESTAMENT

Luke 13:24: "Strive to enter through the narrow gate, for many, I say to you, *will seek* to enter and *will not be able.*"

(7) Matthew 8:5 and Luke 7:3-7 – the centurion came himself, or sent messengers?

Matthew 8:5: Now when Jesus had entered Capernaum, a centurion came to him, pleading with him...

Luke 7:3-7: So when he heard about Jesus, *he sent elders* of the Jews to him, pleading with him to come and heal his servant. And when they came to Jesus, they begged him earnestly, saying that the one for whom he should do this was deserving, "for he loves our nation, and has built us a synagogue." Then Jesus went with them. And when he was already not far from the house, *the centurion sent friends* to him, saying to him, "Lord, do not trouble yourself, for I am not worthy that you should enter under my roof. Therefore *I did not even think myself worthy to come to you.* But say the word, and my servant will be healed.

(8) Matthew 8:28 and Luke 8:27 – one or two men?

Matthew 8:28: When he had come to the other side, to the country of the Gergesenes, there met him *two demon-possessed men,* coming out of the tombs, exceedingly fierce, so that no one could pass that way.

Luke 8:27: And when he stepped out on the land, there met him *a certain man* from the city who had demons for a long time. And he wore no clothes, nor did he live in a house but in the tombs.

(9) Matthew 9:18 and Mark 5:22-23 – Dead or not?

Matthew 9:18: While he spoke these things to them, behold, a ruler came and worshiped him, saying, "My daughter *has just died,* but come and lay your hand on her and she will live."

Mark 5:22-23: And behold, one of the rulers of the synagogue came, Jairus by name. And when he saw him, he fell at his feet and begged him earnestly, saying, "My little daughter *lies at the point of* *death*. Come and lay your hands on her, that she may be healed, and she will live."

(10) Matthew 10:2-4 and Luke 6:13-16 – Who was a disciple, Lebbeus (whose surname was Thaddeus) or Judas the son of James?

Matthew 10:2-4: Now the names of the twelve apostles are these: first, Simon, who is called Peter, and Andrew his brother; James the son of Zebedee, and John his brother; Philip and Bartholomew; Thomas and Matthew the tax collector; James the son of Alphaeus, and ***Lebbaeus, whose surname was Thaddaeus***; Simon the Cananite, and Judas Iscariot, who also betrayed him.

Luke 6:13-16: And when it was day, he called his disciples to himself; and from them he chose twelve whom he also named apostles: Simon, whom he also named Peter, and Andrew his brother; James and John; Philip and Bartholomew; Matthew and Thomas; James the son of Alphaeus, and Simon called the Zealot; ***Judas the son of James***, and Judas Iscariot who also became a traitor.

(11) Matthew 10:10 and Mark 6:8 – Bring a staff or not?

Matthew 10:10: ...nor bag for your journey, nor two tunics, nor sandals, ***nor staffs***; for a worker is worthy of his food.

Mark 6:8: He commanded them to take nothing for the journey *except a staff*—no bag, no bread, no copper in their money belts...

(12) Matthew 11:13-14, 17:11-13 and John 1:21 – John the Baptist was Elijah or not?

Matthew 11:13-14: For all the prophets and the law prophesied *until John*. And if you are willing to receive it, ***he is Elijah who is to come.***

Matthew 17:11-13: Jesus answered and said to them, "Indeed, Elijah is coming first and will restore all things. But I say to you that ***Elijah has come already,*** and they did not know him but did to him whatever they wished. Likewise the Son of Man is also about to suffer at their hands." Then the disciples understood that ***he spoke to them of John the Baptist.***

(3.B) THE NEW TESTAMENT

John 1:21: And they asked him (i.e., John the Baptist), "What then? Are you Elijah?" He said, "*I am not.*"

(13) Matthew 12:39 (the sign of Jonah being the *only* sign) versus Mark 8:12 (no sign to be given) versus Luke 7:22 and 11:20 (holding up miracles to be signs). Which is it?

Matthew 12:39: But he answered and said to them, "An evil and adulterous generation seeks after a sign, and no sign will be given to it *except the sign of the prophet Jonah.*"

Mark 8:12: But he sighed deeply in his spirit, and said, "Why does this generation seek a sign? Assuredly, I say to you, *no sign* shall be given to this generation."

Luke 7:22: Jesus answered and said to them, "Go and tell John the things you have seen and heard: that the blind see, the lame walk, the lepers are cleansed, the deaf hear, the dead are raised, the poor have the gospel preached to them."

Luke 11:20: "But if I cast out demons with the finger of God, surely the kingdom of God has come upon you."

(14) Matthew 15:22 and Mark 7:26 – The woman was from Canaan or Greece?

Matthew 15:22: And behold, a woman of *Canaan* came from that region and cried out to him, saying, "Have mercy on me, O Lord, Son of David! My daughter is severely demon-possessed."

Mark 7:26: The woman was a *Greek*, a Syro-Phoenician by birth, and she kept asking him to cast the demon out of her daughter.

(15) Matthew 20:29-30 and Mark 10:46-47 – One or two beggars?

Matthew 20:29-30: Now as they went out of Jericho, a great multitude followed him. And behold, *two blind men* sitting by the road, when they heard that Jesus was passing by, cried out, saying, "Have mercy on us, O Lord, Son of David!"

Mark 10:46-47: As he went out of Jericho with his disciples and a great multitude, ***blind Bartimaeus***, the son of Timaeus, sat by the road begging. And when he heard that it was Jesus of Nazareth, he began to cry out and say, "Jesus, Son of David, have mercy on me!"

(16) Matthew 21:1-2 and Mark 11:1-2 – A donkey present or not? Bring 'him' (the colt) or 'them' (the colt and the donkey)?

Matthew 21:1-2: Now when they drew near Jerusalem, and came to Bethphage, at the Mount of Olives, then Jesus sent two disciples, saying to them, "Go into the village opposite you, and immediately you will find a ***donkey*** tied, and ***a colt with her***. Loose ***them*** and bring ***them*** to me.

Mark 11:1-2: Now when they drew near Jerusalem, to Bethphage and Bethany, at the Mount of Olives, he sent two of his disciples; and he said to them, "Go into the village opposite you; and as soon as you have entered it you will find a ***colt*** tied, on which no one has sat. Loose ***it*** and bring ***it***.

(17) Matthew 26:74-75 and Mark 14:72 – Before the cock crows once or twice?

Matthew 26:74-75: Then he began to curse and swear, saying, "I do not know the Man!" ***Immediately a rooster crowed.*** And Peter remembered the word of Jesus who had said to him, "***Before the rooster crows,*** you will deny me three times." So he went out and wept bitterly.

Mark 14:72: ***A second time the rooster crowed.*** Then Peter called to mind the word that Jesus had said to him, "***Before the rooster crows twice***, you will deny me three times." And when he thought about it, he wept.

(18) Matthew 27:5 and Acts 1:18 – How did Judas die?

Matthew 27:5: Then he threw down the pieces of silver in the temple and departed, and went and ***hanged himself.***

(3.B) The New Testament

Acts 1:18: Now this man purchased a field with the wages of iniquity; and *falling headlong*, he burst open in the middle and all his entrails gushed out.

(19) Matthew 27:11-14 (Jesus answered Pilate "It is as you say," and *not one word more*) or John 18:33-37 (Jesus and Pilate held a conversation).

Matthew 27:11-14: Now Jesus stood before the governor. And the governor asked him, saying, "Are you the King of the Jews?" Jesus said to him, "It is as you say." And while he was being accused by the chief priests and elders, *he answered nothing*. Then Pilate said to him, "Do you not hear how many things they testify against you?" But he answered him *not one word*, so that the governor marveled greatly.

John 18:33-37: Then Pilate entered the Praetorium again, called Jesus, and said to him, "Are you the King of the Jews?" Jesus answered him, "Are you speaking for yourself about this, or did others tell you this concerning me?" Pilate answered, "Am I a Jew? Your own nation and the chief priests have delivered you to me. What have you done?" Jesus answered, "My kingdom is not of this world. If my kingdom were of this world, my servants would fight, so that I should not be delivered to the Jews; but now my kingdom is not from here." Pilate therefore said to him, "Are you a king then?" Jesus answered, "You say rightly that I am a king. For this cause I was born, and for this cause I have come into the world, that I should bear witness to the truth. Everyone who is of the truth hears my voice."

(20) Matthew 27:28 (scarlet robe) vs. John 19:2 (purple robe)

Matthew 27:28: And they stripped him and put a *scarlet robe* on him.

John 19:2: And the soldiers twisted a crown of thorns and put it on his head, and they put on him a *purple robe*.

(21) Matthew 27:34 and Mark 15:23 – gall or myrrh in the wine? Tasted it or not?

(Section 3) Books of Scripture

Matthew 27:34: ...they gave him sour wine *mingled with gall* to drink. But when he had *tasted it*, he would not drink.

Mark 15:23: Then they gave him wine *mingled with myrrh* to drink, but he *did not take it*.

(22) Mark 15:25 and John 19:14-15 – Jesus crucified before the third hour or after the sixth hour?

Mark 15:25: Now it was the *third hour*, and they crucified him.

John 19:14-15: Now it was the Preparation Day of the Passover, and *about the sixth hour*. And he said to the Jews, "Behold your King!" But they cried out, "Away with him, away with him! Crucify him!"

(23) Luke 1:15, 1:41, 1:67, 2:25 and John 7:39 – the 'Holy Ghost/Spirit' given or not?

Luke 1:15: He (John the Baptist) will also be *filled with the Holy Spirit*, even from his mother's womb.

Luke 1:41: And it happened, when Elizabeth heard the greeting of Mary, that the babe leaped in her womb; and Elizabeth was *filled with the Holy Spirit*.

Luke 1:67: Now his father Zacharias was *filled with the Holy Spirit*...

Luke 2:25: And behold, there was a man in Jerusalem whose name was Simeon, and this man was just and devout, waiting for the Consolation of Israel, and the *Holy Spirit was upon him*.

John 7:39: But this he spoke concerning the Spirit, whom those believing in him would receive; for the Holy Spirit *was not yet given*, because Jesus was not yet glorified.

(24) Luke 2:10-14 and Luke 12:49-53 – a prophet announced by angels as heralding peace on Earth, good will to men, or one who brings fire and division?

Luke 2:10-14: Then the angel said to them, "Do not be afraid, for behold, I bring you good tidings of great joy which will be to all

(3.B) The New Testament

people. For there is born to you this day in the city of David a Savior, who is Christ the Lord. And this will be the sign to you: you will find a babe wrapped in swaddling cloths, lying in a manger." And suddenly there was with the angel a multitude of the heavenly host praising God and saying: "Glory to God in the highest, and *on earth peace, goodwill toward men!*"

Luke 12:49-53: "I (Christ Jesus) *came to send fire on the earth*, and how I wish it were already kindled! But I have a baptism to be baptized with, and how distressed I am till it is accomplished! *Do you suppose that I came to give peace on earth?* I tell you, *not at all*, but rather division. For from now on five in one house will be divided: three against two, and two against three. Father will be divided against son and son against father, mother against daughter and daughter against mother, mother-in-law against her daughter-in-law and daughter-in-law against her mother-in-law."

(25) Luke 23:39-40 and Mark 15:31-32 – one thief defended Jesus or not?

Luke 23:39-40: Then one of the criminals who were hanged *blasphemed him*, saying, "If you are the Christ, save yourself and us." *But the other, answering, rebuked him*, saying, "Do you not even fear God, seeing you are under the same condemnation?

Mark 15:31-32: Likewise the chief priests also, mocking among themselves with the scribes, said, "He saved others; himself he cannot save. Let the Christ, the King of Israel, descend now from the cross, that we may see and believe." *Even those who were crucified with him reviled him.*

(26) Luke 14:26 and I John 3:15 – to hate one's brother or not?

Luke 14:26: "If anyone comes to me (Christ Jesus) and *does not hate* his father and mother, wife and children, *brothers* and sisters, yes, and his own life also, he cannot be my disciple."

I John 3:15: *Whoever hates his brother* is a murderer, and you

(SECTION 3) BOOKS OF SCRIPTURE

know that no murderer has eternal life abiding in him.

(27) Luke 23:26, Matthew 27:32, Mark 15:21 versus John 19:17 – Who carried the cross, Simon or Jesus?

Luke 23:26: Now as they led him away, they laid hold of a certain man, *Simon a Cyrenian*, who was coming from the country, and on him they laid the cross that he might bear it after Jesus.

Matthew 27:32: Now as they came out, they found *a man of Cyrene, Simon by name.* Him they compelled to bear his (Christ Jesus) cross.

Mark 15:21: Then they compelled a certain man, *Simon a Cyrenian*, the father of Alexander and Rufus, as he was coming out of the country and passing by, to bear his (Christ Jesus) cross.

John 19:17: And *he (Christ Jesus), bearing his cross,* went out to a place called the Place of a Skull, which is called in Hebrew, Golgotha...

(28) Luke 23:43 and John 20:17 – ascended or not?

Luke 23:43: And Jesus said to him, "Assuredly, I say to you, *today* you will be with me in Paradise." (Stated to one of the other two crucified on the evening of his own crucifixion, predicting ascension *that very same day*)

John 20:17: Jesus said to her, "Do not cling to me, *for I have not yet ascended* to my Father." (Stated to Mary Magdalene on the *second* day following the crucifixion)

(29) Luke 23:46 versus John 19:30 – were the last words of Jesus "Father, 'into Your hands I commit my spirit'" or were they "It is finished"?

Luke 23:46: And when Jesus had cried out with a loud voice, he said, "Father, *'into Your hands I commit my spirit.'*" Having said this, he breathed his last.

John 19:30: So when Jesus had received the sour wine, he said, "*It is finished!*" And bowing his head, he gave up his spirit.

(3.B) The New Testament

(30) John 1:18, I John 4:12, I Timothy 6:16 (God *cannot* be seen) *versus* Genesis 12:7, 17:1, 18:1, 26:2, 32:30; Exodus 3:16, 6:2-3, 24:9, 33:11, 33:23, Numbers 14:14, Amos 9:1 (God *seen*)

For example, **John 1:18** and **I John 4:12** both read: "No one has seen God at *any* time."

Genesis 12:7: Then the Lord *appeared to Abram* and said...

Genesis 32:30: So Jacob called the name of the place Peniel: "For I have *seen God face to face*, and my life is preserved."

Exodus 6:2-3: And God spoke to Moses and said to him: "I am the LORD. *I appeared* to Abraham, to Isaac, and to Jacob, *as God Almighty,* but by My name LORD...

(31) John 5:31 and John 8:14 – Was Jesus' record true or not?

John 5:31: "If I (Jesus) bear witness of myself, my witness *is not* true."

John 8:14: Jesus answered and said to them, "Even if I bear witness of myself, my witness *is* true, for I know where I came from and where I am going..."

(32) Acts 9:7 and Acts 22:9 – Fellow travelers heard a voice or not?

Acts 9:7: And the men who journeyed with him stood speechless, *hearing a voice* but seeing no one.

Acts 22:9: "And those who were with me indeed saw the light and were afraid, but they *did not hear the voice* of him who spoke to me."

(33) Acts 9:7 and Acts 26:14 – Paul's companions fell to the ground or remained standing?

Acts 9:7: And the men who journeyed with him *stood speechless*, hearing a voice but seeing no one.

Acts 26:14: And when *we all had fallen to the ground*, I heard a voice speaking to me and saying in the Hebrew language, 'Saul, Saul, why are you persecuting me? It is hard for you to kick against the goads.'

(SECTION 3) BOOKS OF SCRIPTURE

The alleged vision and conversion of Paul, as discussed in points #32 and 33 above, is a critical keystone upon which Trinitarian ideology depends, for if Paul's testimony were discredited, from which other author of the Bible would Trinitarian ideology take origin? The fact that the three accounts of Paul's vision lack consistency, as noted in the above list, may be regarded with great concern by those who consider such contradictions to be signposts of falsehood. Those who do not harbor such suspicions nonetheless must face the fact that no one particular Biblical description can be validated as authentic, for at most only one account can be correct, leaving two in error in at least some of the details.

Furthermore, a person should not forget the differences among all four gospels with regard to the events following the alleged crucifixion, as described above in section 2.B.8.

Lastly, Matthew 1:6-16 and Luke 3:23-31, which record 26 and 41 generations, respectively, in the lineage between David and Joseph, simply don't match up. No two names correspond *in sequence* except for the last (i.e., Joseph, who by no stretch of the imagination really was the father of Jesus). Furthermore, God's name is left out (if Jesus really were the 'Son of God' in some special sense, would God have left His name out of the lineage, not once but twice?).

This last inconsistency deserves further examination. The mismatch in the list of names is as follows (from the *New King James Version*):

	MATTHEW 1:6-16	LUKE 3:23-31
	DAVID	DAVID
(1)	SOLOMON	NATHAN
(2)	REHOBOAM	MATTATHAH
(3)	ABIJAH	MENAN
(4)	ASA	MELEA
(5)	JEHOSHAPHAT	ELIAKIM

(3.B) THE NEW TESTAMENT

(6)	JORAM	JONAN
(7)	UZZIAH	JOSEPH
(8)	JOTHAM	JUDAH
(9)	AHAZ	SIMEON
(10)	HEZEKIAH	LEVI
(11)	MANASSEH	MATTHAT
(12)	AMON	JORIM
(13)	JOSIAH	ELIEZER
(14)	JECHONIAH	JOSE
(15)	SHEALTIEL	ER
(16)	ZERUBBABEL	ELMODAM
(17)	ABIUD	COSAM
(18)	ELIAKIM	ADDI
(19)	AZOR	MELCHI
(20)	ZADOK	NERI
(21)	ACHIM	SHEALTIEL
(22)	ELIUD	ZERUBBABEL
(23)	ELEAZAR	RHESA
(24)	MATTHAN	JOANNAS
(25)	JACOB	JUDAH
(26)	JOSEPH (husband to Mary)	JOSEPH (no relation to Mary)
(27)		SEMEI
(28)		MATTATHIAH
(29)		MAATH
(30)		NAGGAI
(31)		ESLI
(32)		NAHUM
(33)		AMOS
(34)		MATTATHIAH
(35)		JOSEPH (no relation to Mary)

291

(36)	JANNA
(37)	MELCHI
(38)	LEVI
(39)	MATTHAT
(40)	HELI
(41)	JOSEPH (husband to Mary)

Christian apologists defend this imbalance with the claim that one lineage is that of Jesus through his mother, and the other is that of Jesus through his mother's husband, Joseph. However, many view this defense to be just one more of the unacceptable 'believe what I say, not what you see with your own two eyes' claims, for the Bible clearly states in both cases that each lineage defines the ancestors of Jesus through the virgin Mary's husband, Joseph.

What happened is clear, but distasteful to those who would have revelation end with the Bible. Scholars acknowledge that the synoptic gospels of Matthew, Mark, and Luke most likely shared a common source document – known hypothetically as the 'Q' (short for '*quella*,' meaning 'sources' in German). Whoever wrote the gospel according to Matthew must have presumed the first 'Joseph' to be *the* 'Joseph,' whereas the author of the gospel according to Luke recognized the earlier 'Josephs' (numbers 26 and 35) as referring to ancestors bearing a common name, but not referring to Joseph, the husband of Mary. Alternatively, the two authors utilized different source documents to begin with, at least with regard to this passage. Whatever the case may be, the two lists both attempt to define the lineage of Joseph through the fraternal line, and they simply do not match – by a long shot.

The reader may notice the cautious reference to the authors of the gospels in the above paragraph. The reason why the authors are not mentioned by name is that the authorship of the gospels is

(3.B) THE NEW TESTAMENT

unknown, and Biblical scholars rarely, if ever, assert that 'Matthew,' 'Mark,' 'Luke,' and 'John' were actually written by the disciples who bore those names. Well, perhaps 'disciples' is not the right word. Luke 6:14-16 and Matthew 10:2-4 list the twelve disciples, and although these two lists differ with regard to two entries (Judas the son of James, and Lebbaeus), Mark and Luke are not amongst the listed disciples in either account. For that matter, speculation is offered that not even the author of 'John' makes the list. This is a point of confusion for some, for the list in Matthew 10:2-4 includes a disciple named 'John.' However, modern scholarship acknowledges that there is no evidence, other than questionable testimonies of second century authors, to suggest that John, the son of Zebedee, was the author of 'John' the gospel.[204, 205] Furthermore, John the disciple was believed to have died on or around 98 CE,[206] whereas the gospel known as 'John' was written circa 110 CE.[207] So whoever Luke (the physician), Mark (the ambiguous), and John (the unknown, but certainly not the long-dead one) were, there appears to be some distance, both physical and temporal, between their personages and that of Jesus to begin with.

Nonetheless, the gospels are attributed to these four, despite the fact that modern Christian scholarship is in doubt as to the names of the real authors. Graham Stanton affirms, "...the gospels, unlike most Graeco-Roman writings, are anonymous. The familiar headings

---

204. Kee, Howard Clark (Notes and References by). 1993. *The Cambridge Annotated Study Bible, New Revised Standard Version.* Cambridge University Press. Introduction to gospel of 'John.'
205. Butler, Trent C. (General Editor). *Holman Bible Dictionary.* Nashville: Holman Bible Publishers. Under 'John, the Gospel of'
206. Easton, M. G., M.A., D.D. *Easton's Bible Dictionary.* Nashville: Thomas Nelson Publishers. Under 'John the Apostle.'
207. Goodspeed, Edgar J. 1946. *How to Read the Bible.* The John C. Winston Company. p. 227.

293

(SECTION 3) BOOKS OF SCRIPTURE

which give the name of an author ('The Gospel according to...') were not part of the original manuscripts, for they were added only early in the second century."[208] Later in the same book, Stanton questions, "Was the eventual decision to accept Matthew, Mark, Luke, and John correct? Today it is generally agreed that neither Matthew nor John was written by an apostle. And Mark and Luke may not have been associates of the apostles."[209]

Even if the gospel authors were from amongst the disciples, Jesus made it clear that he did not feel the disciples were able to handle everything he wished to tell them (e.g. John 16:12 – "I still have many things to say to you, but you cannot bear them now."). Jesus recognized them to be of little faith (Matthew 8:26, 14:31, 16:8, and Luke 8:25), lacking understanding (Matthew 15:16), and, in fact, despaired over having to bear with that "...faithless and perverse generation..." (Luke 9:41). The misalignment was pervasive, for even those who should have known Jesus best (i.e., his own relatives) thought him crazy (Mark 3:21 and John 8:48), and the very people to whom he was sent rejected him (John 1:11). So regardless of who the true gospel authors were, and even if the gospels were penned by the disciples, the question of reliability remains an unavoidable issue.

To use the book of 'Matthew' as an example, there are several passages which serve to raise the eyebrows of the speculative reader. Matthew 2:15 asserts that Jesus was taken to Egypt "to fulfill what had been spoken by the Lord through the prophet, 'Out of Egypt I have called my son.'" Well, that is the proposal. However, exactly which scripture was the detainment of Jesus in Egypt supposed to be in fulfillment of? Hosea 11:1. So what does Hosea 11:1 actually read? "When Israel was a child, I loved him, and out of Egypt I called my son." In short, it appears to be a scriptural match – a match made

---

208. Stanton, Graham N. p. 19.
209. Stanton, Graham N. pp. 134-135.

(3.B) The New Testament

in heaven. But only if a person stops reading there. The full passage, continuing into Hosea 11:2, reads, "When Israel was a child, I loved him, and out of Egypt I called my son. The more I called them, the more they went from me; they kept sacrificing to the Baals, and offering incense to idols." (Hosea 11:1-2, NRSV) Taken in context, a person can only apply the referenced passage to Christ Jesus if, at the same time, asserting that Jesus was an idol-worshipper.

Similar errors abound. A short two verses later, Matthew 2:17 comments on Herod's genocide of the infants of Bethlehem with the words, "Then was fulfilled what had been spoken through the prophet Jeremiah: 'A voice was heard in Ramah, wailing and loud lamentation, Rachel weeping for her children; she refused to be consoled, because they are no more'" (Matthew 2:17, NRSV). One minor problem. The referenced Old Testament passage (Jeremiah 31:15) refers to an actual event in history, namely the abduction of Rachel's children, as well as those of the Israelite community, by Sargon, the king of Assyria. The scriptural parallel is not just strained and stressed, it is non-existent. So too with Matthew 27:10, which references Jeremiah 32:6-9. The referenced quote is not to be found. Furthermore, one verse describes a potter's field, the other Hanamel's field. One field priced out at thirty pieces of silver, the other at 17 shekels of silver. Both were actual transactions seperate in time and place. Any effort to claim 'fulfilment' of previous scripture is capricious at best.

And the list goes on.

Efforts to align the New and Old Testaments with one another, thick with claims of the New Testament fulfilling predictions of the Old, are understandable in the context of authors who bore a message for which they sought validation. Most of mankind are familiar with the tendency of evangelists to attempt to project legitimacy through referencing known and respected works. However, when the claimed references are found to be faulty, misapplied, or frankly non-existent, the legitimacy of the document, as well as of the author himself, becomes sadly suspect.

Despite all that has been mentioned above, many Christians continue to assert that the Bible is the unadulterated word of God. The above should constitute sufficient evidence to refute this claim, but if not, Paul had something to say. In I Corinthians 7:12, Paul stated, "But to the rest I, not the Lord, say...," indicating that what follows was from him, and not from God. So if nothing else, this section of the Bible, by Paul's own admission, is not the word of God. I Corinthians 1:16 points out that Paul could not remember if he baptized anybody other than Crispus, Gaius, and the household of Stephanas as follows: "...Besides, I do not know whether I baptized any other." Those who defend the Bible as God's literal words should be questioned, "Does this sound like God talking?" Would God say, "Paul baptized Crispus, Gaius, and the household of Stephanas, and there may have been others. But that was a long time ago, and, well, you know, so much has happened since then. It's all kind-of fuzzy to Me right now."?

I Corinthians 7:25-26 records Paul as having written, "Now concerning virgins: I have no commandment from the Lord; yet I give judgement as one whom the Lord in His mercy has made trustworthy. *I suppose* therefore that this is good because of the present distress..." (emphasis mine), and II Corinthians 11:17 reads, "What I speak, I speak not according to the Lord, but as it were, foolishly..." Again, does anybody believe that God talks like this? Paul admitted that he answered without guidance from God and without Divine authority, and that he personally believed himself to be divinely trustworthy in one case but speaking foolishly in the other. Paul justified his presumption of authority when he stated an opinion "...according to my judgement—and I think I also have the Spirit of God."

(3.B) The New Testament

(I Corinthians 7:40), only a few short verses after manifesting uncertainty with the insecure words, as quoted above, "I suppose..." The problem is that a whole lot of people have claimed to be filled with the 'Spirit of God,' while all the time doing some very strange and ungodly things. So should Paul's confidence be admired or condemned? However a person answers this question, the point is that whereas a common symptom of the duality of man is for overconfidence to be manifest at times, uncertainty at others, such is not the case with The All-Knowing Creator. Hence, whereas one man may have assumed "perfect understanding of all things," lifted pen and authored a gospel because "it seemed good to me" (Luke 1:3), lots of people have written on religion assuming 'perfect understanding' and because it 'seemed good to them.' However, such lofty sentiments do not, in and of themselves, a scripture make.

The fallback position of the Bible defendant, then, is to assert that the New Testament is not the literal word of God, but the *inspired* word of God. Such an assertion takes support from II Timothy 3:16, which states the obvious – "All scripture is given by inspiration of God..." However, that is not to say that something becomes scripture just by naming it as such. Just because an ecumenical council holds up four books to be the truth, to the exclusion (and destruction) of the other thousand or so gospels, this does not make any one of them scripture. The proof is not in the opinion of men, even if unanimous, but in the divinity of origin, as indicated by the internal and external evidence. Those books which fail the tests of divine origin and/or inspiration can be assumed to either have been impure from the outset, or even if pure in the original revelation, altered at some later point in time and therefore corrupted. It is simply not harmonious with the perfection of God either to reveal or to inspire errors.

Isaiah 40:8 helps to define one measure by which authenticity of revelation may be determined, for this verse states, "The grass withers,

297

(SECTION 3) BOOKS OF SCRIPTURE

the flower fades, but the word of our God stands forever." A person need not question the source of Isaiah 40:8, for regardless of origin the truth of the statement is self-evident, timeless and undeniable – the teachings of God *do* stand forever. The point, however, is that not all *books* 'stand forever,' as is obvious from the above exposition. And if "the word of our God stands forever" means it doesn't get lost, where is the original gospel of Jesus, if not lost? There is not a true Biblical scholar alive who would dispute the fact that not even a single page of the original Gospel of Jesus is known to exist. Scholars aside, any person can realize this conclusion on their own by recognizing that Jesus spoke Aramaic, not Greek. The oldest known manuscripts canonized as the 'Gospel truth' are commonly acknowledged to date from the fourth century CE, and are predominantly written in a anguage foreign to Jesus -- a language he never spoke – *Koiné* Greek! Largely written by unknown authors, with unknown motivations and peppered with identifiable and unGodly mistakes, the void left by the loss of the original gospel of Jesus is readily apparent and poorly compensated.

The mistakes and inconsistencies encountered in even the oldest surviving manuscripts are so numerous as to have prompted C. J. Cadoux, Mackennal Professor of Church History at Oxford, to write,

"In the four Gospels, therefore, the main documents to which we must go if we are to fill-out at all that bare sketch which we can put together from other sources, we find material of widely-differing quality as regards credibility. So far-reaching is the element of uncertainty that it is tempting to 'down tools' at the outset, and to declare the task hopeless. The historical inconsistencies and improbabilities in parts of the Gospels form some of the arguments advanced in favour of the Christ-myth theory. These are, however, entirely outweighed – as we have shown – by other considerations. Still, the discrepancies

(3.B) The New Testament

and uncertainties that remain are serious – and consequently many moderns, who have no doubt whatever of Jesus' real existence, regard as hopeless any attempt to dissolve out the historically-true from the legendary or mythical matter which the Gospels contain, and to reconstruct the story of Jesus' mission out of the more historical residue."[210]

Professor Cadoux is not alone in his opinion. Any serious religious amateur quickly becomes aware of the considerable frustration which exists amongst Christian theologians, largely owing to the lack of original scripture, identifiable authors, and, in two words, definitive guidance.

For example, in the words of Robert W. Funk, the originating scholar of the *Jesus Seminar,*

"To add to the problem, no two copies of any of the books of the New Testament are exactly alike, since they were all handmade. It has been estimated that there are over seventy thousand meaningful variants in the Greek manuscripts of the New Testament itself. That mountain of variants has been reduced to a manageable number by modern critical editions that sort, evaluate, and choose among the myriad of possibilities. The critical editions of the Greek New Testament used by scholars are in fact the creations of textual critics and editors. They are not identical with any surviving ancient manuscript. They are a composite of many variant versions."[211]

Professor Dummelow of Cambridge sheds an interesting light on how so many variants of the text came into being, with the following comment on the ethics of scriptural record keeping:

---

210. Cadoux, Cecil John. 1948. *The Life of Jesus*. Middlesex: Penguin Books. p. 16-17.
211. Funk, Robert Walter. 1996. *Honest to Jesus, Jesus for a New Millennium*. Polebridge Press. pp. 94-95.

(SECTION 3) BOOKS OF SCRIPTURE

"A copyist would sometimes put in not what was in the text, but what he thought ought to be in it. He would trust a fickle memory, or he would even make the text accord with the views of the school to which he belonged. Besides this, an enormous number of copies are preserved. In addition to the versions and quotations from the early Christian Fathers, nearly four thousand Greek MSS* of the New Testament are known to exist. As a result the variety of readings is considerable."[212]

Lest the above be taken as personal opinion, the above quote is taken from a work derived from the combined scholarship of 42 Christian doctorates of divinity and scholars of international repute. A person might fairly question why such a group of distinguished scholars would talk down their own book of guidance if not out of dedication to truth.

Interesting and supportive comments are found in the following:

"The speeches in the Fourth Gospel (even apart from the early messianic claim) are so different from those in the Synoptics, and so like the comments of the Fourth Evangelist himself, that both cannot be equally reliable as records of what Jesus said: Literary veracity in ancient times did not forbid, as it does now, the assignment of fictitious speeches to historical characters: the best ancient historians made a practice of composing and assigning such speeches in this way."[213]

Rev. Findlay goes so far as to note:

---

* MSS, meaning 'manuscripts'

212. Dummelow, Rev. J. R. (editor). 1908. *A Commentary on the Holy Bible*. New York: Macmillan Publishing Co., Inc. Introduction, p. xvi.

213. Cadoux, Cecil John. p. 16.

(3.B) The New Testament

"None of the evangelic writings thus produced, not even those now in the New Testament, claimed on their appearance to have canonical authority; all alike were the offspring of the desire to present what was known or believed about Christ with the aim of satisfying the religious needs of the communities for which they were severally written."[214]

Later commenting on the nature of the Apocryphal Gospels, the same author offers the following observation, remaining mute on the obvious conclusion that, based upon his previous assertion (stated a short two pages before and as quoted above), the same considerations could equally apply to the canonized gospels:

"The desire would naturally arise for a presentation of the evangelic facts which would be in harmony with prevailing thought and feeling. If this desire was to be satisfied, some manipulation of the generally accepted tradition was necessary, but that did not seem a serious matter in an age which had little conscience for the obligation of depicting things as they actually were. Thus Gospels were produced which clearly reflected the conceptions of the practical needs of the community for which they were written. In them the traditional material was used, but there was no hesitation in altering it or in making additions to it or in leaving out what did not suit the writer's purpose."[215]

In fact, recognition of the fact that the gospel authors modified their sources is so well accepted amongst scholars as to have spawned a particular methodology of gospel analysis, known as redaction criticism. Through redaction criticism, New Testament scholars

---

214. Findlay, Rev. Adam Fyfe, M.A., D.D. 1929. *The History of Christianity in the Light of Modern Knowledge.* London: Blackie & Son, Ltd. p. 318.

215. Findlay, Rev. Adam Fyfe. p. 320

(SECTION 3) BOOKS OF SCRIPTURE

attempt to guess each gospel author's intentions, theological stance and evangelical purpose through analysis of the gospel form and editorial modifications (including insertions, deletions, reinterpretations and rearrangements) made to the sources from which each gospel was derived.[216]

Whether or not a person agrees with the above view of gospel and Biblical history, this challenge, if incorrect, deserves rebuttal. Silence of Church authorities can otherwise be safely assumed to imply assent. But whatever the reason for the vast variability of the scriptural accounts, the fact remains that they *do* differ. Whatever the mechanism of the misalignment, the lack of uniformity remains a malignant difficulty which grossly disfigures the claim of inerrancy.

The argument can nonetheless be made that the 'word of God' is still to be found in the Bible. *This* may be true! The problem is, a lot of other teachings of questionable origin are found as well. And this is very likely one explanation for the growing interest in the Islamic religion within Western nations – so much so that Islam is presently the fastest growing religion in America and the World.[217]

The Islamic proposal is that the serious and sincere, whose hearts and minds are open to evidence and not boarded up by the plywood of preconception, will be inclined to recognize both the Godly *and* the human elements of the Bible. The human elements of the Bible drive the sincere to search for God's refinement and correction of what has become corrupted, while the Godly elements serve as a scriptural skeleton of ethics, morals, and codes of conduct. This framework suffices the individual until such time as the Qur'an and the religion of Islam are encountered. For such individuals,

---

216. For more information, see Stanton, Graham N. 1989. *The Gospels and Jesus*. Oxford University Press. pp. 24-26.
217. *Guinness Book of Knowledge*. p. 195.

(3.B) The New Testament

the familiarity and recognition of the Islamic teachings are often welcomed as the body of revelation which fills out the framework of truths found scattered throughout the corrupted texts of previously revealed scriptures.

Translation of the Holy Qur'an reads,

> "It is He Who sent down to you (step by step), in truth, the Book, confirming what went before it; and He sent down the Law (of Moses) and the Gospel (of Jesus) before this, as a guide to mankind, and He sent down the Criterion (of judgement between right and wrong)." (TMQ 3:3)

Many people infer from the above passage that the Qur'an endorses the Jewish and Christian Bibles (the Old and New Testaments) as scripture. Not true. The Qur'an teaches that there is truth *amongst* the books of the Christians and Jews, and that God did indeed send down the 'Law of Moses' and the 'Gospel of Jesus.' Just where the 'Law of Moses,' the 'Gospel of Jesus,' and the truths therein are to be found – in which passages, and whether in books of the Bible, the apocrypha, or elsewhere – the Qur'an does not specify.

Perspective is an issue here. A person might read "the Law (of Moses) and the Gospel (of Jesus)" and reflexively leap to equating this reference with the Old and New Testaments. The association is understandable given the influence of Western media and religions, yet the preceding analysis should suffice to convince even the most committed devotee that wherever the scriptures of Moses and Jesus are, they are certainly not preserved in the Bible in the purity in which they were revealed. Hence the need for revelation to confirm the truth of "what went before," to refute the scriptural corruptions of men, and to function as a "…Criterion (of judgement between right and wrong)." Hence, also, the need for a revelation bearing the welcome announcement,

(SECTION 3) BOOKS OF SCRIPTURE

"O People of the Book! There has come to you Our Messenger, revealing to you much that you used to hide in the Book, and passing over much (that is now unnecessary): There has come to you from Allah a (new) light and a perspicuous Book, – Wherewith Allah guides all who seek His good pleasure to ways of peace and safety, and leads them out of darkness, by His Will, unto the light, - guides them to a Path that is Straight." (TMQ 5:15-16)

The unfortunate mixture of man-made scriptural insertions and true revelation in the books of the Jewish and Christian Bibles has resulted in loss of ability to judge the difference without clarification by The Author. Some of the resultant misunderstandings are of a relatively minor nature, others catastrophic. For example, 'Born Again' Christians want the world to believe, as recorded in the *King James Version,* "...unless one is born again, he cannot see the kingdom of God," (John 3:3) and "...You must be born again" (John 3:7). This modern sect depends upon an ideology which hinges off the words 'born again,' – words which are, in fact, a mistranslation of the Greek *'gennao anothen,'* which means generated, or begotten, from above.[218] According to the true translation, *all* mankind are *'gennao anothen,'* whether a person wants it or not, for where is the person who is 'generated from below?' Some more modern Biblical translations are more faithful to the true definitions, others not (One wonders what the pressure of knowing that changing two words will impact sales by a few million copies feels like). For example, the *New International Version* goes halfway, translating *'gennao anothen'* as 'born from above.' In consequence, there are literally millions of souls who have departed this worldly life with their hopes for salvation pinned on a key phrase, and the concept constructed there-about, which in fact is non-existent in the meaning of the Greek.

---

218. *Strong's Exhaustive Concordance of the Bible.*

(3.B) The New Testament

A plethora of such misunderstandings have blossomed from the fertile field of the last 12 verses of the gospel of 'Mark,' which have long been in dispute, and for good reason. The two most ancient manuscripts (Vatican MS. No. 1209 and the Sinaitic Syriac codex) date from the fourth century and end at the eighth verse of the sixteenth (and last) chapter of 'Mark.' The last 12 verses of 'Mark' are not found in any known papyri prior to the sixth century CE, and even then, in a Syriac version of 616 CE, these 12 verses exist only as a marginal note (as can be confirmed in the marginal references of Nestle, *Novum Testamentum Graece*). As acknowledged in a footnote to the ending verse of 'Mark' in the 1977 RSV, "Some of the most ancient authorities bring the book to a close at the end of verse 8."[219] The *Interpreter's Bible* comments,

> "Attempts have been made to recover the 'lost ending' of Mark in the remaining sections of Matthew or Luke, or even John or Acts; but none of these has been generally approved, and it is doubtful if Luke's and Matthew's copies of Mark went beyond 16:8. The problem is a fascinating one for research; but it is probably insoluble at present."[220]

Hope is offered that "Further discoveries of early MSS may help toward a solution,"[221] but in the meantime debate rages and this passage, though most likely penned by the second-century presbyter Ariston,[222] has long been included in both the Catholic Vulgate and *King James* Bibles. Consequently, these verses have come to be virtually universally accepted by the Christian public. A person might ask, "What's the harm?" Just this – these last 12 verses of

---

219. *The Bible, Revised Standard Version*. 1977. New York: American Bible Society. Footnote at end of 'Mark.'
220. *The Interpreter's Bible*. p. 915.
221. *The Interpreter's Bible*. p. 915.
222. *The Interpreter's Bible*. p. 915.

(SECTION 3) BOOKS OF SCRIPTURE

'Mark' contain some of the key verses which are selectively employed to support evangelism, baptism, exorcism, speaking in tongues, and even testing faith by handling rattlesnakes in 'snake' cults. Faithfulness to the most ancient textual sources would bring the faithful one step closer to sleeping late Saturdays, ceasing to agonize over the fate of the unbaptized deceased, untying twisted tongues for noble and intelligible speech, and putting kids to bed without the fuel of nightmares seasoned by the smell of snake slime on the hands.

To return to II Timothy 3:16, the point is that God's scripture is inspired of Him, and as such is divinely inerrant. However, mankind has excelled at losing what was revealed, adding what wasn't, and twisting whatever remained in an attempt to derive a more appealing construct. Muslims assert that whenever the recorded 'word of God' faded into impurity at the hands of man, God, in His mercy, maintained His 'word' through delivering new, clarifying, pristine revelation. Meanwhile, the true 'word of God' (i.e. the laws and creed) remained in force throughout all time, albeit obscured under a shifting pile of confusing human corruptions and malignant misinterpretations. Only by renewing revelation has the 'word of God' stood forever, replacing that which stood 'only for a while.' The final, unaltered book in the series is promised to be the last book of revelation, and to be divinely protected against alteration until the end of time.

But before analyzing that claim, one final point: each and every doctrinal belief of the Trinitarian Creed (and many of the different Unitarian Churches as well) is based on the manipulation and/or misunderstanding of one or more ambiguous, questionable, rare or isolated passages buried in relative seclusion within the New Testament. In every case these passages lack support from the other books or epistles of the New Testament, as discussed above. Now, a person could reasonably expect that God would not hide the most important and critical elements of true belief, as the point of

(3.B) THE NEW TESTAMENT

revelation is to *reveal*. Any teacher will testify that the bulk of teaching is repetition. Hence, the ingredients of true faith can be expected to have been conveyed in clear and unambiguous terms, and with emphasis by way of repetition of key doctrinal points. The Muslim could easily assert that, with regard to the Bible, the above is precisely the case. The most repeated, consistent, and verifiable teachings of the Old and New Testaments convey the oneness of God and the mandate to obey Him, which incidentally includes the directive to accept the final messenger and the revelation with which he was sent.

Now, many well-read Christians will be quick to point out that the Bible ends with a strong warning in *Revelation*. Never mind that, "*Hebrews* was for long under suspicion in the West, and *Revelation* was usually excluded in the fourth and fifth centuries where the school of Antioch held sway."[223] No, never mind that, but just consider this: the last verses of the Bible (Revelation 22:18-19) warn against anyone adding or taking away from "this book" – a warning which should prompt the question, "Ummmm, which book?" The Bible is a collection of books. That's how it got the name – from the Latin '*Biblia*,' literally meaning 'the books.'[224] The word refers to a collection of books. Hence 'bibliography' for a list of books, 'bibliophile' for a lover of books, 'biblioteque' for 'library,' and 'Bible' for the collection of books known thereby.

F. F. Arbuthnot comments:

> "Another short journey takes us back to the fourteenth century, when people began to say 'The Bible.' The simple fact that we call this collection of books 'The Bible,' as if it were one book and not a collection of books, is a very important fact—a fact that has been fruitful of misunderstanding. We

---

223. Kelly, J. N. D. 1978. *Early Christian Doctrines*. San Francisco: Harper & Brothers Publishers. p. 60.
224. *New Catholic Encyclopedia*. Vol 2, p. 381.

(SECTION 3) BOOKS OF SCRIPTURE

naturally think of one book as having one author, or one directing genius....

Prior to the fourteenth century it was not called 'The Bible.' It was not thought of as one book. In Greek it was not *Ton Biblion*, but *Ta Biblia*—the books. And prior to the fifth century these were not called books at all, but writings—Hebrew and Christian writings."[225]

A person might find interest in noting that the books of the Bible are *not* compiled in chronological order. The book of *Revelation* was *not* the last book written chronologically. However, strategic placement at the end of the Bible serves to confirm the faith of those ignorant of the chronology. Many 'books' of the Bible, to include James, the 1st, 2nd and 3rd Epistles of John, the gospel of John, Jude, 1st and 2nd Timothy, Titus, and 2nd Peter were all written between an estimated 5 to 65 years *after* the book of *Revelation*.[226] *Revelation* is reported to have been written circa 95 CE, whereas 1st and 2nd Timothy and Titus are reported to have been written circa 150 CE, and 2nd Peter was written circa 160 CE.[227] A difference of two seconds, much less 55 years, would violate the 'thou shalt not add to' clause, *if* the above verses of *Revelation* are thought to apply to the Bible as a whole. But they do not, and can not.

The oldest known bound version of the Bible (sequestered with pride in the Vatican) dates from the 400's and contains the book, *The Shepherd of Hermas*. *The Shepherd of Hermas* was removed and placed in the apocrypha subsequent to inclusion in this oldest known bound Bible, and the Protestant Bible further eliminated not just one, but seven more books, as well as portions of accepted books, to include

---

225. Arbuthnot, F. F. 1885. *The Construction of the Bible and the Korân*. London: Watts & Co. pp. 8-9.
226. Goodspeed, Edgar J. pp. 226-7.
227. Goodspeed, Edgar J. pp. 226-7.

(3.B) The New Testament

Esdras I and II, Tobit, Judith, the additions to the book of Esther, the Wisdom of Solomon, Ecclesiasticus, Baruch, the Letter of Jeremiah, the Prayer of Azariah and the Song of the Three Young Men, Susanna, Bel and the Dragon, the Prayer of Manasseh, Maccabees I and II – the removal of which would have violated the 'thou shalt not take away' clause in each and every instance, had the teachings of *Revelation* applied to the Bible as a whole. Hence, the 'book' which the last line of *Revelation* refers to can be none other than itself, the *book* of *Revelation*, and the book of *Revelation* alone. Otherwise, the principal violators of the warning regarding deletions and insertions are the Christian Clergy themselves, for quite a lot has both been added to and removed from the *Biblia*, or collection of books as a whole.

The above arguments are not foreign to the clergy of Christianity. These problems are well recognized, but largely hidden from the eyes of the lay public, most of whom lack sufficient interest and motivation to wage the intellectual battle necessary to confront established Christian authorities with the baselessness, and in many cases frank falsehood, of their assertions. All the same, the above-mentioned sources are all Christian, and the most respected amongst them admit some amazing things. For example, no Christian scholar of significant worth considers Greek to have been the original language of Jesus – many just say it, knowing that if respected clergy speak of the 'original Greek' frequently and consistently, public imitation will follow. In time, the reality of the case will slip from the consciousness of the congregation, becoming submerged beneath layers of ingrained, unquestioning preconception…as has already happened with so many currently accepted Christian sacraments such as the cross, the crucifix, and the representational art which was considered open blasphemy by the first 500 years of pious predecessors. However, if asked directly, most clergy are honest enough to admit the fact that Jesus spoke Aramaic and ancient Hebrew, but not the *Koiné* Greek in which the

(Section 3) Books of Scripture

foundational manuscripts of the Bible are recorded. Reverend J. R. Dummelow of Queen's College fame (Cambridge, England), is just one of many who readily volunteer such information.[228] Running countercurrent to the overwhelming flow of evidence and scholarly opinion, a small handful of alleged theologians have recently struggled to suggest that Jesus did in fact speak *Koiné* Greek…but with the passage of 70,000 respected variants in the Greek manuscripts under the low-slung bridge of Christian scrutiny, suspended between the solid stanchions of 2,000 years of scholarly consensus, the crosshairs of skepticism should by all rights be fixed squarely between the eyes of those who attempt to reverse-engineer deficiencies of the New Testament.

The challenge of Judaism, then, is to refuse the prophethood of Christ Jesus, despite the overwhelming evidence of his divinely appointed office.

The challenge of 'Christianity' is to accept untenable tenets of faith, despite evidence which assaults every wall of the infirm castle of Trinitarian belief, right down to the very foundation, which is to say, the Bible.

The challenge of Islam is to accept Moses and Jesus as human prophets (but nothing more), to understand the capriciousness and infidelity of those who molded Judaism and Christianity to their present forms, to recognize Muhammad as the final prophet predicted in both Old and New Testaments, and to respect the revelation with which he was sent. Muslims claim this revelation to be consistent with previous scripture, congruent with human nature, and in conformity with the realities of worldly existence. They claim this revelation withstands the highest levels of critical analysis, being Godly in content, design, and complete perfection. They claim this revelation to be the Holy Qur'an.

---

228. Dummelow, Rev. J. R. Introduction, p. xvi.

(3.C)
The Holy Qur'an

"When Satan makes impure verses,
Allah sends a divine tune to cleanse them."
— George Bernard Shaw,
The Adventures of the Black Girl in Her Search for God

(3.C1) Brief History of The Qur'an

"One reason that history repeats itself is that so many people were not listening the first time." – Margaret Hussey

The Holy Qur'an was revealed at the beginning of the seventh century, approximately 600 years following the ministry of Christ Jesus. Muslims contend that, word for word, the revelation was placed in the mind and mouth of the prophet Muhammad throughout the latter 23 years of his life. Conversely, nonbelievers charge Muhammad with a full bouquet of profiles of false prophethood. Claims of scriptural plagiarism, deception, outright lying, and delusional thinking have all been advanced, as has the theory of Muhammad having been a man of extraordinary intelligence and insight, but nothing more. Some authors have even gone so far as to suggest that Muhammad was epileptic, and that the Holy Qur'an is in fact a compilation of his mutterings while in the throes of seizure.

(SECTION 3) BOOKS OF SCRIPTURE

The description of the alteration in Muhammad's outward appearance on the occasion of receiving revelation is no stranger to the historical record. His beloved wife, A'ishah, noted that he broke out in a sweat when receiving revelation, even on a cold day. Those who search to summarily execute the character of the man Muhammad can fashion whatever garment of conclusions suits their taste from such scraps of evidence. However, those who presume Muhammad's sincerity and face the circumstance with circumspection might be drawn to consider that an alteration in appearance might not only be excused, but rather expected, of any mortal confronted with the spiritual load of direct revelation. Any who have experienced the pounding pulse, crawling skin, rising hair, spinal chill, and quickening of senses which occur when faced with a spiritual abnormality can imagine the impact a moment of contact with The Creator, or even His representative, might have. Certainly a focused attention to the exclusion of all else, a sweat on the brow, an intensity of concentration written on the face of the messenger would be in no way unexpected. Far more unreasonable would be to assume that any mortal would converse with the angel of revelation in casual and comfortable terms, much like relaxing over coffee at the local gentleman's club. Many people break out in a sweat simply facing their boss. How much tighter their wound-up nerves might be stretched should they face The Creator of *all* bosses is hard to predict. Furthermore, anybody who has witnessed grand mal seizures knows that an epileptic does not produce intelligible speech, and in fact cannot communicate during the post-apoplectic period of recovery of senses. W. Montgomery Watt commented,

> "Opponents of Islam have often asserted that Muhammad had epilepsy, and that therefore his religious experiences had no validity. As a matter of fact, the symptoms described are not identical with those of epilepsy, since that disease leads to

(3.C1) The Holy Qur'an / Brief History

physical and mental degeneration, whereas Muhammad was in the fullest possession of his faculties to the very end. But, even if the allegation were true, the argument would be completely unsound and based on mere ignorance and prejudice; such physical concomitants neither validate nor invalidate religious experience."[229]

Hartwig Hirschfeld, a man who echoed no shortage of unfounded slanders in a much flawed and strongly biased attempt to argue against the Qur'an as revealed scripture, a man who exposed his prejudice in the preface to his *New Researches into the Composition and Exegesis of the Qoran* with the words, "The *Qoran*, the textbook of Islam, is in reality nothing but a counterfeit of the Bible,"[230] nonetheless concluded,

> "What remains now of epileptic or hysterical influence on the origin of Islam? Absolutely nothing. Never has a man pronounced a sentence with more circumspection and consciousness than Muhammed did in the *iqra'*. Should he have proclaimed it with nothing but prophetic enthusiasm, he must have been the greatest genius that ever lived."[231]

Of course, Muslims assert that Muhammad pronounced the *iqra'* (*surah* 96) completely devoid of circumspection, for he only repeated what was revealed to him. Hirschfeld, though in clear disagreement with the Muslim viewpoint, nonetheless dismissed the charge of epilepsy as too blatant a slander to be contained within the envelope of endorsement.

---

229. Watt, W. Montgomery. 1953. *Muhammad at Mecca*. Oxford: Clarendon Press. p. 57.
230. Hirschfeld, Hartwig, Ph.D. 1902. *New Researches into the Composition and Exegesis of the Qoran*. London: Royal Asiatic Society. Preface, ii.
231. Hirschfeld, Hartwig. p. 32

(SECTION 3) BOOKS OF SCRIPTURE

Delusional thinking similarly should be dismissed, for the reason that Muhammad did not appear to fully understand or believe what he was experiencing when he first received revelation. So traumatic was the initial encounter with the angel Gabriel that Muhammad required convincing. In words borrowed from the *New Catholic Encyclopedia*, "Mohammed himself was frightened, incredulous, and unsure of the meaning of the experience. It required persuasion from his wife and friends before he was convinced and believed that he had actually received a revelation from God."[232] A deluded person readily believes all that in which he or she is deluded. That is what delusion implies – a readiness to accept the absurd or implausible due to some warpage in the thought process. Furthermore, a significant period of time passed (some say as little as 40 days, others as much as 2 years) between the first and subsequent revelation. A deluded person's mind summons up bizarre ideas on a frequent basis. That is simply the nature of those who are psychologically disturbed – their mangled minds conjure up the peculiar with a regular and frequent periodicity. The bent mentation of a crazy person simply does not go on vacation for a couple of days, much less a week, much less 40 days or more. Just as delusional thinking is always betrayed by self-evident weaknesses, neither deception nor lying ever withstand the trials of logic and time – as the pleated fabric of history unfolds, events come to be realized, and lies to be recognized.

History having cleared Muhammad of such charges, no true scholar entertains such slanders. For example, Thomas Carlyle comments,

> "How he (Muhammad) was placed with Kadijah, a rich widow, as her steward, and traveled in her business, again to the fairs of Syria; how he managed all, as one can well

---

232. *New Catholic Encyclopedia*. Vol 9, p. 1001.

(3.C1) The Holy Qur'an / Brief History

understand, with fidelity, adroitness; how her gratitude, her regard for him grew: the story of their marriage is altogether a graceful intelligible one, as told us by the Arab authors. He was twenty-five; she forty, though still beautiful. He seems to have lived in a most affectionate, peaceable, wholesome way with this wedded benefactress; loving her truly, and her alone. It goes greatly against the impostor-theory, the fact that he lived in this entirely unexceptionable, entirely quiet and commonplace way, till the heat of his years was done. He was forty before he talked of any mission from Heaven. All his irregularities, real and supposed, date from after his fiftieth year, when the good Kadijah died. All his 'ambition,' seemingly, had been, hitherto, to live an honest life; his 'fame,' the mere good-opinion of neighbours that knew him, had been sufficient hitherto. Not till he was already getting old, the prurient heat of his life all burnt out, and *peace* growing to be the chief thing this world could give him, did he start on the 'career of ambition;' and, belying all his past character and existence, set up as a wretched empty charlatan to acquire what he could now no longer enjoy! For my share, I have no faith whatever in that.

Ah no: this deep-hearted Son of the Wilderness, with his beaming black eyes, and open social deep soul, had other thoughts in him than ambition. A silent great soul; he was one of those who cannot but be in earnest; whom Nature herself has appointed to be sincere....We will leave it altogether, this impostor-hypothesis, as not credible; not very tolerable even, worthy chiefly of dismissal by us."[233]

---

233. Carlyle, Thomas. 1841. *On Heros, Hero-Worship and the Heroic in History.* London: James Fraser, Regent Street. pp. 86-87, 89.

(Section 3) Books of Scripture

More remains to be said, and discussion of this topic will continue in the section devoted to the character of the man Muhammad. With regard to the other charges against Muhammad, and attempts at disqualification of the revelation he claimed, analysis of the Qur'an itself should suggest either validity or implausibility of such concerns.

To begin with, the word 'Qur'an' does not refer to a book, but to a revelation. Islamic tradition holds that this revelation was transmitted verbally to the prophet Muhammad by the angel of revelation, Gabriel. And so it has been maintained – as an oral tradition preserved to this day in the hearts and minds of devout *hafith* (memorizers, or 'protectors,' of the Qur'an), whose number in the present day, by conservative estimate, is unlikely to be less than 30 million.

The Qur'an was also recorded in written form by scribes, who faithfully transcribed each element of revelation at the time it was revealed, making the Holy Qur'an the only book of scripture recorded at the time of revelation and preserved unchanged to the present day. Writing material for the original scribes was scarce, as it was for the scribes of the Old and New Testaments, who largely relied upon parchment and ox-hides. As a result, the revelation of the Holy Qur'an was originally recorded on whatever was immediately available, to include palm leaves, sheets of leather, and shoulder blades of large animals. This bulky and inconvenient record was copied and compiled into an official *mushaf* (book), at the commission of Abu Bakr (the first Caliph), roughly two years after the death of Muhammad. The project was overseen by Zaid Ibn Thabit, one of Muhammad's faithful scribes. Between four and eight copies were subsequently completed during the caliphate of Uthman, and each copy was dedicated to one of the territories of the Islamic world. Two of these books are still known to exist – one in Tashkent, Uzbekistan, the other in Istanbul, Turkey. These 'originals' continue to serve as

(3.C1) THE HOLY QUR'AN / BRIEF HISTORY

written records for the remainder of mankind. Any record of the Qur'an, anywhere in the world, can be authenticated against these 'originals' to demonstrate the absolute integrity and preservation of the sacred book of Islam. It is this very preservation which has been regarded by some as a miraculous proof of the sanctity of the Holy Qur'an. Dr. Laura Vaglieri adds this element to her list of evidences with the comment,

> We have still another proof of the divine origin of the Quran in the fact that its text has remained pure and unaltered through the centuries from the day of its delivery until today..."[234]

Professor Arthur J. Arberry, Professor of Arabic at Cambridge University 1947-1969, contributes:

> "Apart from certain orthographical modifications of the originally somewhat primitive method of writing, intended to render unambiguous and easy the task of reading the recitation, the Koran as printed in the twentieth century is identical with the Koran as authorized by Uthman more than 1300 years ago."[235]

Respected voices from the past, such as that of Sir William Muir, state the following:

> "The recension of Othman has been handed down to us unaltered....There is probably in the world no other work which has remained twelve centuries with so pure a text."[236]

---

234. Vaglieri, Dr. Laura Veccia. Translated from Italian by Dr. Aldo Caselli, Haverford College, Pennsylvania. Originally published in Italian under the title: *Apologia dell' Islamismo* (Rome, A. F. Formiggini, 1925). 1980. *An Interpretation of Islam.* Zurich: Islamic Foundation. pp. 41-42.

235. Arberry, Arthur J. 1964. *The Koran Interpreted.* London: Oxford University Press. Introduction, p. ix.

236. Muir, Sir William. 1923. *The Life of Mohammad.* Edinburgh: John Grant. Introduction, pp. xxii – xxiii.

(SECTION 3) BOOKS OF SCRIPTURE

Whereas a more contemporary opinion can be found in the research of Adrian Brockett,

> "The transmission of the Qur'an after the death of Muhammad was essentially static, rather than organic. There was a single text, and nothing significant, not even allegedly abrogated material, could be taken out nor could anything be put in. This applied even to the early caliphs....The transmission of the Qur'an has always been oral, just as it has always been written."[237]

The written record of the Holy Qur'an was arrived at by unanimous approval of the tens of thousands of *sahaba* (Muslims who lived and interacted with the prophet Muhammad). All of these *sahaba* memorized portions of the Qur'an and many were *hafith*, having memorized the Qur'an in entirety. When the Qur'an was compiled in the form of a book, as described above, many *sahaba* possessed personal copies of their own recording. Many (if not all) of these copies were incomplete and others (such as those of Abdullah Ibn Masud, Ubay Ibn Kab and Ibn Abbas), while correct in one reading, did not leave room for the multiple possible readings which constitute one of the miracles of the Qur'an. Consequently, these partial records did not receive acknowledgement, *even from their possessors*, as complete and authoritative versions. The only written record of the Qur'an to be accepted by unanimous approval (including Abdullah Ibn Masud, Ubay Ibn Kab, Ibn Abbas, and all other scribes and memorizers) was the officially adopted *mushaf* compiled by Zaid Ibn Thabit under the commission of Abu Bakr. To prevent confusion and the possibility of division in future generations, all other written

---

237. Rippin, Andrew (editor). 1988. *Approaches to the History of the Interpretation of the Qur'an.* Chapter: 'Value of Hafs and Warsh Transmissions,' by Adrian Brockett. Oxford: Clarendon Press. Pp. 44-45.

(3.C1) The Holy Qur'an / Brief History

records were voluntarily turned in and, along with the remnants of the bones, animal skins and papyrus, destroyed. Had this not been done, future generations may have fallen prey to ignorance or pride, preferring one of the incomplete works passed down in a family or tribe to the true and complete revelation. Tribal solidarity and fractionation of the religion almost certainly would have resulted. The pious *sahaba* appear to have recognized and eliminated this risk by preserving only the total and complete revelation, discarding the bits and pieces which, at the very least, could have become sources of confusion.

Muslims are fond of pointing out that there was not a single person from amongst the contemporaries of Muhammad who disagreed with the text of the official *mushaf*. Not a single man or woman from amongst the *sahaba* claimed that a passage was left out or a different passage inserted which was not part of the revelation. Most important is the fact that what was gathered and destroyed were incomplete records and not differing records. The possessors voluntarily gave up their copies for destruction because the completeness of the *mushaf* compiled by Zaid Ibn Thabit included the contents of all pre-existing partial records. There simply were no accurate records which were not represented therein. Furthermore, as stated above, the Qur'an has primarily been preserved not in written form, but in the memories of the faithful. Memorizers cross-checked and confirmed the official written record of the Qur'an, validating the completeness and accuracy thereof. Not a single *hafith* dissented. And they numbered in the thousands.

The existence of even a few memorizers of the Qur'an, after 1,400 years, is extraordinary. The existence of tens of millions is considered by Muslims to be a gift from Allah. There are a billion Christians and many million Jews in the world, according to recent census statistics, but not one of them holds the original scripture of their religion in memory. A rare Rabbi may have memorized the Torah -- not as it was revealed, but as reconstructed in the period around 400 BC, following the destruction of the original during the 586 BC sacking of the Temple of Solomon by the conquering Babylonian empire (II Kings 25:8-17). The only known version of the Old Testament, whether in memory or in print, contains the ungodly errors discussed in the relevant chapter above. An *extremely* rare Christian has memorized the entire New Testament, in the translation of just one of the thousands of versions known to exist. Even more rare, if not completely nonexistent, is a memorizer of just one of the several thousand extant Greek manuscripts. But nowhere in the world and nowhere in history has anyone ever been known to have memorized the original Gospel of Jesus. Had they done so, the Christian world would cease struggling to make sense of the thousands of extant Greek manuscripts, and would face the world with the confident satisfaction of possessing the original Aramaic.

The Qur'an, then, appears to be unique as the only book of scripture which was recorded at the time of revelation and maintained in the purity of the original to the present day. There may be different translations into non-Arabic languages, but there is only one original. There is no confusion, such as exists with the plethora of versions of the Bible. There is no frustration, such as that which comes from lacking a definitive original scripture upon which to base a translation. There is no uncertainty, such as wondering what truths are sequestered away from the public eye in the private library of the Vatican or in the unreleased translation of the Qumran (Dead Sea) scrolls. Nobody need wonder how much the predominantly *Koiné* Greek differs from the spoken Aramaic of the prophet Jesus. Should the errors of translation from Aramaic and ancient Hebrew to *Koiné* Greek have been as numerous and grave as the previously mentioned errors translating *Koiné* Greek to English, all hope of Bible accuracy should reasonably have been dismissed well before this age.

(3.C1) The Holy Qur'an / Brief History

One huge difference between the Bible and the Qur'an is simply that the Qur'an was always in the hands of the people, whereas the Bible was not. Anybody who ever wanted a Qur'an could have one. The Bible, however, did not begin to exist in its present form -- meaning with the present table of contents – until canonized at the council of Trent in the year 367 CE. Even then, the Bible was maintained in the Latin Vulgate for more than a millennium. John Wycliffe's English translation of the New Testament in 1382 was followed by that of William Tyndale (completed by Miles Coverdale and edited by John Rogers) and Martin Luther's translation of the Bible into German – both of which were translated only as recently as the 16th century. Tyndale's reward? As noted in the foreword to this book, death – burned at the stake in 1536. Roger's? Same fate, different stake, year 1555. Their predecessor, Wycliffe, escaped the execution but not the fire, for the ecumenical Council of Constance condemned him posthumously in 1415, and his bones were exhumed and publicly burned. Had it not been for the intercession of Denmark, Miles Coverdale would have been similarly condemned. And like their authors, Wycliffe's and Tyndale's translations were publicly burned.

So for over 1500 years the Christian scriptures were available only in Greek or Latin, and only the educated class and certain of the more knowledgeable clergy could read them, for it is a fact that many of the Catholic clergy themselves were illiterate with regard to their own scripture. Furthermore, the educated class could only read the Bible if they had one, and the combination of the great expense and scant availability (all Bibles, of necessity, having been copied by hand), along with the harsh laws prohibiting possession of Bibles by laity (many of which prescribed death, especially in cases of possession of translations in the vernacular, or of unauthorized translations considered to be aligned with heresies, of which the Protestant Bibles were considered to have qualified) severely curtailed Bible acquisition.

(Section 3) Books of Scripture

Not until the invention of the Gutenberg printing press in the 1450's was a method of mass production feasible, and not until the Protestant Reformation of the sixteenth century was the Bible not only translated into languages of the literate laity (i.e., German and English), but mass produced and permitted to the public.

For the first time in Christian history, the sixteenth century witnessed periods where the production of Bibles translated into the vernacular, combined with the growth of non-Catholic sects endorsed by a sympathetic monarchy, overwhelmed the ability of the Catholic church to burn both books and dissenters. Responding to the pressures of Protestant reforms, the translation of the Bible into the vernacular being just one, the Catholic church produced the Douay-Rheims Bible, which represented the translation of the Latin Vulgate into English, with the New Testament portion completed in Rheims, France in 1582, and the Old Testament completed in Douay in 1609-10. All the same, even with mass production available from the 1450's, availability of the Bible was severely constrained, for, "...it was calculated that there must have been about 25,000 printed Bibles in circulation in western Europe around 1,515, one third of them in German, for about fifty million inhabitants; i.e., one Bible for every 2,000 souls."[238] The practical implication is that for over 1,500 years the common citizen could not verify the teachings of the Christian scriptures for lack of literacy as well as for lack of Bibles themselves. For an even greater period of time the laity could not question the canonized doctrines which were forced upon them, for fear of a 'bloodless death,' by which name burning at the stake came to be known.

Catholics argue that restriction of religious education to the offices of the church was necessary in order to maintain orthodox

---

238. Fossier, Robert (editor). 1986. *The Cambridge Illustrated History of The Middle Ages*. Cambridge: Cambridge University Press. Vol. 3, p. 495.

understanding, and to prevent the proliferation of heresies which was expected should individual interpretation of the scriptures be allowed. The intricacies of the Christian mysteries, according to the Catholic church, were such that they were unlikely to be comprehended through independent study, requiring explanation by representatives gifted with understanding. Indoctrination was trusted more than the deductive reasoning and conclusions of laity. Or even of scholars, for that matter. As Pope Innocent III stated in 1199,

> The mysteries of the faith are not to be explained rashly to anyone. Usually in fact, they cannot be understood by everyone, but only by those who are qualified to understand them with informed intelligence....The depth of the divine Scriptures is such that not only the illiterate and uninitiated have difficulty understanding them, but also the educated and the gifted.[239]

The Protestant stand, however, was that whatever the reason for the lack of previous Bible availability, whether well or ill-intentioned, all humans were created with brains and the ability to interpret the Christian scriptures for themselves. Protestants argue that once people were able to read the Bible in their own language, and freely analyze it for defects, those who sought Biblical truth came to be able to discern the fact that Biblical teachings and those of the Catholic church were frequently at variance with one another. Once the errors of Catholicism were laid bare, and the foundation of Catholic theology exposed as predominantly (and in many cases, entirely) extra-Biblical, gravitation to Protestantism was a matter of course. Muslims take the argument one step further, asserting that the weaknesses of the Christian scriptures, once evident, should drive a person not from one Christian sect to another, both still basing beliefs upon

---

239. Denzinger, Henricus & Schonmetzer, Adolfus. 1973. *Enchiridion Symbolorum, Definitionum et Declarationum de Rebus Fidei et Morum.* Barcinone: Herder. p. 246.

a scripture peppered with demonstrable errors and inconsistencies. Rather, Muslims suggest that those who seek the truth of God with sincerity should recognize the need for The Creator to have completed the truth of His revelation. Hence, a scripture revealed subsequent to the Bible should be sought – one which evidences a perfection and consistency consonant with that of The Creator.

Claiming this final revelation to be The Holy Qur'an, Muslims point out that the Qur'an was always in the hands and minds of the people. The Qur'an has been recited out loud in the daily prayers of the Muslims ever since revelation. Every year, in the month of Ramadan, the Qur'an is recited in entirety, out loud, in virtually every mosque in the world. Any Muslim listening could voice correction, but for 1,400 years there has never been so little as a single letter in dispute amongst orthodox (Sunni) Muslims. At the present day, that adds up to a billion unanimous votes. Amazingly enough, over time there have been many factions amongst the Sunni Muslims, some of them at war with one another. Uthman, the third Caliph, was assassinated while reading the Qur'an, and his dried blood is still to be seen on the pages. However, amongst all of these differing Muslim groups, and throughout all of these various centuries, the authenticity of the Qur'an has never been questioned. Certainly the same cannot be said of the Bible. As F.F. Arbuthnot commented,

> "From a literary point of view, the *Korân* is regarded as a specimen of the purest Arabic, written in half poetry and half prose. It has been said that in some cases grammarians have adapted their rules to agree with certain phrases and expressions used in it, and that, though several attempts have been made to produce a work equal to it as far as elegant writing is concerned, none have as yet succeeded.
>
> It will thus be seen, from the above, that a final and complete text of the Korân was prepared within twenty years after the

(3.C1) THE HOLY QUR'AN / BRIEF HISTORY

death (A.D. 632) of Muhammad, and that this has remained the same, without any change or alteration by enthusiasts, translators, or interpolators, up to the present time. It is to be regretted that the same cannot be said of all the books of the Old and New Testaments."[240]

The Qur'an, furthermore, exists in a living language, comprehended by hundreds of millions of devout followers even to the present day. The Bible exists primarily in the dead language of *Koiné* Greek, with snippets of equally necrotic ancient Hebrew (not the modern Hebrew spoken today) and Aramaic. In the entire world there are only a few scholars with partial understanding of these dead languages, and even they don't agree on translation. Evidence of the difficulty is found in the Preface to the *Revised Standard Version* of the Bible, which was authorized by vote of the National Council of the Churches of Christ in the U.S.A. in 1951. The RSV appears to have subsequently enjoyed the widest popular acceptance throughout the Christian world, both domestic and abroad. Nonetheless, despite the ecumenical scholarship and global acceptance, the RSV admits,

> "Many difficulties and obscurities, of course, remain. Where the choice between two meanings is particularly difficult or doubtful, we have given an alternative rendering in a footnote. If in the judgement of the Committee the meaning of a passage is quite uncertain or obscure, either because of corruption in the text or because of the inadequacy of our present knowledge of the language, that fact is indicated by a note. It should not be assumed, however, that the Committee was entirely sure or unanimous concerning every rendering not so indicated."[241]

---

240. Arbuthnot, F. F. pp. 5-6.
241. *The Bible, Revised Standard Version*. 1977. Preface, p. v.

325

(SECTION 3) BOOKS OF SCRIPTURE

Understanding of Biblical manuscripts increases with each new discovery, as evidenced by the motivation of Church authorities to revise the *King James Version* of 1611 to the *American Standard Version* of 1901, and subsequently to the *Revised Standard Version* fifty years later. The motivation for such revisions lay, as stated in the Preface of the RSV, in that

> "Yet the King James Version has grave defects....The King James Version of the New Testament was based upon a Greek text that was marred by mistakes, containing the accumulated errors of fourteen centuries of manuscript copying."[242]

And while understanding of the Greek New Testament continues to be refined, it is far from comprehensive at the present time, and is unlikely ever to be. In such a climate of uncertainty, mistranslation – whether malignant, accidental, or well-intentioned – is easily conveyed to those who lack the linguistic faculty by which to know better. The same is not true if the language is understood by the followers, who thereby have the ability to recognize and correct even the slightest of errors, and such is precisely the case with the Arabic language and the Holy Qur'an.

A person may wonder, then, how Muslims support the assertion that the Qur'an is unique and unchanged. Unsubstantiated claims are not acceptable. Most of humanity have been asked, nay, *forced* to blind belief for too long. The intelligent laity are tired of the appealing but unsubstantiated lines, sprinkled slick with the spittle of the proselytizers, and spiritually cold to the bone. Sincere seekers need a blanket of evidence to warm their convictions. Not just a cover which looks nice at a distance, but one which does the job. The following conglomerate of Qur'anic facets constitutes much of the quilt of evidences with which Muslims comfort their convictions.

---

242. *The Bible, Revised Standard Version.* 1977. Preface, p. iii.

(3.C) THE HOLY QUR'AN
(3.C2) Evidences: Introduction

"When speculation has done its worst,
two and two still make four."

– Samuel Johnson

The lack of references in the following discussion may seem surprising to those unfamiliar with Islamic history, but in fact is reflective of the common knowledge, in Islamic circles, of the presented information. The following elements of Islamic history and Qur'anic constitution are so well known as to be considered baseline knowledge amongst educated Muslim laity. Consequently, just as such well-known statements as, "The Bible is the foundational book of Christianity and contains the gospels attributed to Matthew, Mark, Luke, and John" needs no reference, neither does the majority of that which follows.

Nonetheless, confirmation of details can be obtained through a

(SECTION 3) BOOKS OF SCRIPTURE

multitude of respected source books of Muslim authorship, a few of the most respected works in this field being *Manaahil al-'Irfaan fee 'Uloom al-Qur'an* by Shaykh Muhammad 'Abd al Adheem az-Zarqaanee, *al-Madkhal li Dirasaat al-Qur'an al-Kareem* by Muhammad Abu Shahbah, and two books, both by the title of *Mabaahith fee 'Uloom al-Qur'an*, one authored by Dr. Subhee al-Saalih, the other by Dr. Mannaa' al-Qattaan. Whereas the above are written in the Arabic language, and are yet to be translated into English, two excellent books do exist in the English language. *'Ulum Al-Qur'an: An Introduction to the Sciences of the Qur'an*, by Ahmad Von Denffer, is a nice, though superficial, introduction to the subject. A far more scholarly and comprehensive work is *An Introduction to the Sciences of the Qur'aan*, by Abu Ammaar Yasir Qadhi.*

On the other hand, the conclusions of many, if not most, of the critical works of non-Muslim authorship are heavily tainted by the influence of religious prejudice. The majority of these critical works rate so low on the scale of objective scholastic value as to have been cast out not only by Muslims, but by educated clergy, orientalists, and religious scholars as well, leading one author to lament,

> "The totally erroneous statements made about Islam in the West are sometimes the result of ignorance, and sometimes of systematic denigration. The most serious of all the untruths told about it are, however, those dealing with facts; for while mistaken opinions are excusable, the presentation of facts running contrary to the reality is not. It is disturbing to read blatant untruths in eminently respectable works written by authors who *a priori* are highly qualified."[243]

---

* This last book is available through Al-Hidaayah Publishing, P.O. Box 3332, Birmingham, U.K. B10 9AW

243. Bucaille, Maurice, M.D. 1977. *The Bible, the Qur'an and Science.* Lahore: Kazi publications. pp. 110-111.

(3.C2) The Holy Qur'an / Evidences: Introduction

Of greatest impact is that many so-called 'scholastic works' are discredited by the author's own educated co-religionists. For the most part, however, the following details of verifiable Islamic history are simply omitted from presentation in such books, presumably because discussion of the subject is uncomfortable, if not overwhelming, to those who stand in denial of the signs suggestive of validity of the Islamic revelation.

On the other hand, there is virtually zero disagreement throughout the Muslim world on the following subjects, and verification thereof is relatively easy considering the accuracy of historical record-keeping typical of the Islamic sciences and traditions.

Admittedly, some modern books of Muslim authorship also suffer inaccuracies, not from anti-Islamic prejudice but from the opposite pole of overzealous attempts to glorify the religion. All the same, the commonly accepted elements of Qur'anic history are found to course through most such works with remarkable consistency. It is just these commonly accepted elements of Qur'anic integrity which will be discussed in this present work. Items of personal, sectarian, deviant (such as Ahmadi'ite, Shi'ite and Nation of Islam), or minority opinion are avoided herein, being left for those who wish to explore the less mainstream tributaries of religious controversy on their own.

(3.C) THE HOLY QUR'AN

(3.C3) Evidences –1: Innate Appeal

"All truth, in the long run, is only common sense clarified."
—Thomas Henry Huxley, *On the Study of Biology*

On the most superficial level the truth of the Qur'an is held by Muslims to be evident in the simple fact that it makes sense, precisely conforming to the template of innate understanding of God and His methodology. But what religion lacks this claim? No proof satisfies all mankind, as evidenced by the fact that the world is not Muslim. However, on the individual level the proof is in the exposure. Many who read the foundational books of the variety of religions find themselves inexplicably drawn to one specific book and the ideologies expressed therein. The Qur'an is no different. A person simply has to sit down and listen to/read it.

Should a person choose to do so, they will encounter a book of strikingly different character than those which remain with the other Abrahamic faiths. Whereas the Old Testament is largely a book of laws, lengthy 'begat' lists and dry history, and lacking spiritual richness, the New Testament bathes a person in spirituality while lacking

(3.C3) The Holy Qur'an / Evidences–1

concrete guidance on the significant issues of life, such as law, politics, family structure, etc. The Holy Qur'an, on the other hand, provides the foundation not only for the Islamic religion, but also for Islamic law, government, social conduct, family structure, and every element within both personal and social realms. H. G. Wells commented on the teachings conveyed by Muhammad as follows:

> "...they established in the world a great tradition of dignified fair dealing, they breathe a spirit of generosity, and they are human and workable. They created a society more free from widespread cruelty and social oppression than any society had ever been in the world before....It (Islam) was full of the spirit of kindliness, generosity, and brotherhood; it was a simple and understandable religion; it was instinct with the chivalrous sentiment of the desert; and it made its appeal straight to the commonest instincts in the composition of ordinary men. Against it were pitted Judaism, which had made a racial hoard of God; Christianity talking and preaching endlessly now of trinities, doctrines, and heresies no ordinary man could make head or tail of; and Mazdaism, the cult of the Zoroastrian Magi, who had inspired the crucifixion of Mani. The bulk of the people to whom the challenge of Islam came did not trouble very much whether Muhammad was lustful or not, or whether he had done some shifty and questionable things; what appealed to them was that this God, Allah, he preached, was by the test of the conscience in their hearts, a God of righteousness, and that the honest acceptance of his doctrine and method opened the door wide in a world of uncertainty, treachery, and intolerable divisions to a great and increasing brotherhood of trustworthy men on earth, and to a paradise not of perpetual exercises in praise and worship, in which saints, priests, and anointed kings were still to have the upper

(SECTION 3) BOOKS OF SCRIPTURE

places, but of equal fellowship and simple and understandable delights such as their soul craved for. Without any ambiguous symbolism, without any darkening of altars or chanting of priests, Muhammad had brought home those attractive doctrines to the hearts of mankind."[244]

The keystone of Islamic faith, as emphasized over and again in the Holy Qur'an, is the simple message of monotheism – a message which Muslims propose to have the greatest innate appeal of *all* knowledge, owing to the fact that The Creator instilled knowledge of His Unity and unique attributes into the mind, heart and soul of each and every human being. Thus, no person (unless preconditioned in life to do so) can be imagined to object when first encountering the message of the Oneness of The Creator, His many unique names and perfect attributes, and the fact that all people should focus their words and actions towards achieving His pleasure.

With regard to the Oneness of Allah, Islamic ideology is explicit on this point, conveying the clarification that Allah is One, Eternal and Absolute, not begotten and not begetting, without partner or co-sharer in divinity:

"Say: He is Allah, The One and Only;
Allah, The Eternal, Absolute;
He begets not, nor is He begotten;
And there is none like unto Him."
(TMQ 112:1-4)

It is upon this absolute clarification of Allah's uncompromised Unity which Trinitarian Christians raise objection, for Trinitarian ideology expresses the belief that God is indeed One, but three in One. The arguments of Trinitarian ideology having been discussed above,

---

244. Wells, H. G. Volume 2, pp 686-688.

(3.C3) The Holy Qur'an / Evidences–1

an interesting test of innate understanding can be proposed. Should a person assume that embracing inherent understandings brings comfort of convictions, whereas embracing teachings in conflict with inborn knowledge results in stress from the conflict, a test of correct beliefs becomes readily apparent. Predictably, those people living upon confirmation of innate understanding will be at ease with explaining their convictions, for their explanation will match not only their own inherent template of understanding, but that of their audience as well. In essence, such people convey certain knowledge to those who, in their heart of hearts, already know the truth, but just haven't heard it yet. On the other hand, those living with notions in conflict with inborn knowledge will encounter frustration, dissatisfaction and stress in attempting to explain their dogma, for such explanations will have to pass two innate belief barriers (both their own, and that of their audience) in order to gain acceptance. In essence, this second category of people must face two conflicts – the first being the internal conflict of having accepted doctrines at odds with their own innate understanding, the second being the effort of convincing an audience whom they already know will only embrace their beliefs if the force of indoctrination and religious conditioning are brought to bear. Those upon the truth will, as a result, be pleased and comfortable to discuss their beliefs anywhere and any time, and their relaxed and sensible presentation will be both evident and appealing. Those living in self-deception, however, will tend to avoid discussion of the relevant issues and, if forced to face such issues, will manifest confusion, frustration, stress and, ultimately, inability to explain themselves by any process approaching logic. Resort to emotional appeals, plays at self-righteousness, and histrionics are the hallmarks of those who fail in rational debate.

Secondary to creed, the Holy Qur'an presents many teachings regarding the practicalities of life. Fairness and equality, mercy and

(SECTION 3) BOOKS OF SCRIPTURE

love are underlying Qur'anic themes which at times give way to a system of justice which is fair but harsh against all those whose evil threatens the peace of Islamic society. No laws in the history of man have been more successful in restricting the evils of murder, rape, theft, adultery, fornication, homosexuality, alcohol and drugs. Cheating, lying, bribery, usury, prejudice, and all forms of injustice are condemned, giving way to a social reform which, if implemented, would likely unite all colors of mankind under The One God.

The practice of polygamy, while not preferred by the majority of mankind (Muslims included), is permitted and provides a lawful avenue for satisfaction of those individuals who otherwise might be driven to the sin of adultery. Women, on the other hand, are protected, and were given rights 1,400 years ago which were denied in Western society and Old and New Testament religions up until the 20th century (e.g. rights to property, inheritance, religion and education). Manners are corrected, with an emphasis on modesty and a middle path between the extremes to which a person can be drawn on both sides. Even use of money, time, and energy is addressed, again with a focus on a balanced application to person, family, religion and society. Miserliness is condemned, but being a spendthrift is likewise discouraged. Even war is regulated, with laws laid down to foster honorable conflict, beginning with war being allowed only in circumstances where all other options are exhausted and conflict forced. Even then the predominant theme of war is for Muslims not to abuse an advantage won, and to be merciful as much as the situation permits.

As the Holy Qur'an emphasizes the merits of freeing slaves, so also it frees the mind – correcting wrong beliefs propagated in previous societies and religions, and encouraging free thought. Objective truth is given clear priority over personal opinion, societal customs, family tradition, canonized institutional teachings, and all prejudicing

(3.C3) The Holy Qur'an / Evidences–1

outside influences. Compulsion of religion is forbidden in all circumstances. In addition, the Qur'an challenges and stimulates the intellect while soothing the spirit to satisfaction. In short, the Qur'an may be viewed as giving mankind what it needs and what would be expected of a 'final testament' – a balanced guidance in all facets of life.

Should a person be drawn to Islamic beliefs, the message and its supportive evidences will be perceived as undeniable. Should the Holy Qur'an leave a person feeling unfulfilled, this claim to innate appeal will appear false. So how do Muslims rectify this riddle? On one hand the claim is that the Qur'an precisely matches the innate understanding of God and His methodology instilled in every human soul; on the other hand a majority portion of mankind have denied, and continue to deny, the message.

Resolution of this apparent conflict boils down to the Islamic belief that any person possessing a mind free of prejudiced preconceptions will find the teachings of the Holy Qur'an to match innate convictions. Like a fertile field, such open minds will best cultivate that which they were created to receive. On the other hand, those who have allowed the receptive field of their minds to go to the weeds, sown with the seeds of the fallible teachings of man and irrigated with the approval of those to whom divine authority is falsely attributed, may be found to have minds closed and hearts sealed, the ears blocked and the vision veiled. By analogy, a blind person will find discussion of the photon theory of light, prismatic effects on the visible spectrum, neutral density filters in photography, etc. to be of limited relevance to life as he or she knows it. Likewise, those whose hearts and minds are closed to Islam are not expected to appreciate any value from discussions of Islamic evidences. But Muslims would assert that like light in relation to a blind person, failure to perceive does not negate reality – it just fails to convince those who lack appreciation of it. Who will receive and who will deny the message can only be tested by exploration of the evidences. Those who find strength therein will understand the Islamic viewpoint; those who don't, won't.

In support of the above, Allah tells mankind that He could have ordered creation to all be of one mind ("If your Lord had so willed, He could have made mankind one People: but they will not cease to dispute —TMQ 11:118), but for reasons best known to Him, He didn't. The obvious implication is that God guides some and leaves others to stray, and this is exactly what the Qur'an teaches with the words, "…'Truly Allah leaves to stray, whom He will; but He guides to Himself those who turn to Him in penitence'" (TMQ 13:27). The fact that God chooses to guide some while others are denied the recognition of His message is far from arbitrary, being the result of each individual's actions and receptiveness, for "We send the Messengers only to give good news and to warn: so those who believe and mend (their lives), – upon them shall be no fear, nor shall they grieve. But those who reject Our Signs, – punishment shall touch them, for that they did not cease from transgressing." (TMQ 6:48-49) and "Whatever of good reaches you, is from Allah, but whatever of evil befalls you, it is from yourself." (TMQ 4:79)

In other words, those who believe in God and are deserving of guidance receive it, while those who deny The Creator bear responsibility for slamming the door in the face of God's guidance. The fact that God does not guide those who deny Him is no less understandable than the fact that teachers only help those students who attend class. A gas attendant only gives street directions to those who ask. Those who do not seek knowledge or direction are left in the state of ignorance which they themselves choose, and those who actively work towards misguidance may find themselves confirmed thereupon.

The above teaching is encountered not only in the Qur'an, but in Old and New Testaments as well, providing one more strand in the cable of continuity. The Old Testament teaches, "They do not

(3.C3) The Holy Qur'an / Evidences–1

know nor understand; For He has shut their eyes, so that they cannot see, *And* their hearts, so that they cannot understand." (Isaiah 44:18), and the New Testament effectively repeats this teaching in Mark 4:11-12 and Matthew 13:11-15.

The burden of choice, then, is upon the individual. The person who is guided aright is the one who answers the call to righteousness whereas those who choose to go astray have nobody to blame but themselves. That Allah guides those who turn to Him with sincerity and belief is a manifestation of His mercy; that Allah leaves astray those who repeatedly deny Him is an understandable manifestation of His justice.

The Islamic viewpoint expressed above may seem elitist, but then again so are all religions. The world of religion is a heterogeneous mix of 'our-sect-is-saved-by-the-grace-of-God-and-all-others-will-burn-in-hell' factions. All revealed religions paint themselves to be the select of God, and propose reasons why they, and only they, are acceptable to The Creator. Most such fancies fall short not in consideration of why the group is 'saved,' the explanation of which always sounds good to those who belong, but rather in the inability to explain why some of mankind are *not* 'saved.' The difference between the Islamic religion and others in this regard is that Islam provides a concrete and acceptable explanation. Other religions largely fail to address the subject, leaving a person to question why God would guide some and not others. The concept of an arbitrary God is simply not acceptable in the minds of most.

Muslims claim that, for those exposed to the evidences which follow, one or more will appeal. Furthermore, this is held to be consistent with the expected methodology of revelation, being that Allah provided something for everyone – some thing or some things from amongst all the evidences to convince each and every individual of the divine origin of His revelation. Recognition is easy; refusal requires

(Section 3) Books of Scripture

obstinacy. None of humankind can blame God if he or she chooses to turn away in defiance, for Allah made mankind and instilled an innate understanding of Him, and He revealed a message which matches the inborn template of human understanding. Allah has delivered the truth of revelation on a metaphorical silver platter – He has done everything but place mankind directly in paradise. Now the decision is with man. People will either do their part by acknowledging the truth Allah has conveyed, or stand witness against themselves. As Allah teaches:

> "We send the Messengers only to give good news and to warn: so those who believe and mend (their lives), – upon them shall be no fear, nor shall they grieve. But those who reject Our Signs, – punishment shall touch them, for that they did not cease from transgressing." (TMQ 6:48-49)

(3.C) THE HOLY QUR'AN

(3.C4) Evidences –2: The Language of The Qur'an

"Language, as well as the faculty of speech, was the immediate gift of God."

– Noah Webster

The Holy Qur'an exists in one written form but ten different but complementary readings or recitations, and in seven different dialects. A person may wonder how this is possible. The answer lies in the intricacy of the Arabic language which, unlike English, maintains an extraordinarily malleable utility owing to the fact that the alphabet does not contain short vowel letters. Vowels in Arabic are designated by diacritical marks (distinguishing signs, like slashes) above or below consonants. So, for example, the Arabic letter equivalent to "b" in English would be pronounced "ba" if a slash is above the letter, but "bi" if the slash is below the letter. Other formulations may render the letter "bu", "baan," "been," "buun," "baa," "bii," "buu," "bai," "bau," etc. Certain words, written without diacritical marks, can bear construction with a variety of formulas of vowel signs, each of which renders the word a sensible, though different, meaning. For example,

(SECTION 3) BOOKS OF SCRIPTURE

the words for 'owner' and 'king' differ by only one vowel point. Context helps to determine the appropriate meaning of many such words, when not specified in the text.

The oral revelation and the original *mushaf* (book) of the Qur'an lack diacritical marks, allowing for ten officially recognized readings or recitations in seven different dialects, dependant on how vowel points are assigned to the unvowelled text. One of the miracles of the revelation is held to be that all of the readings of the Qur'an are consistent and complementary, as is the case with the appropriate descriptions 'Owner' and 'King' for Allah. The result is that Qur'anic recitation, to a person endowed with comprehensive knowledge of Arabic, does not convey one specific lesson but rather evokes a kaleidoscope of imagery and a rich avalanche of understanding.

Jews and Christians who find difficulty with the concept of an unvowelled scripture should recognize the common ground between the Bible and the Qur'an in this respect, for the foundational manuscripts of the Old Testament are similarly unvowelled. As per the *Encyclopaedia Britannica*:

> "Since texts traditionally omitted vowels in writing, the Masoretes introduced vowel signs to guarantee correct pronunciation. Among the various systems of vocalization that were invented, the one fashioned in the city of Tiberias, Galilee, eventually gained ascendancy. In addition, signs for stress and pause were added to the text to facilitate public reading of the Scriptures in the synagogue."[245]

Concentrically, of the many different readings of the Qur'an, the original books were recorded in the *Hafs 'an 'Aasim* recitation in order to 'correct pronunciation' and 'facilitate public reading' in the mosque. Were a copy of the original gospel of Jesus available, an

---

245. *Encyclopaedia Britannica*. CD-ROM.

(3.C4) THE HOLY QUR'AN / EVIDENCES-2

unvowelled text would be expected, for the Aramaic and ancient Hebrew native to the tongue of Jesus, like the Arabic of the Holy Qur'an, lack vowel letters. The Preface of the *Revised Standard Version* of the Bible notes the following, with regard to the Old Testament:

> "The vowel signs, which were added by the Masoretes, are accepted also in the main, but where a more probable and convincing reading can be obtained by assuming different vowels, this has been done."[246]

A certain freedom for textual manipulation becomes evident. The thought teases the imagination: prior to standardization by the Masoretes, the Hebrew text lacked punctuation marks, vowels, capital letters, and even word spaces. Just for fun, a person can run the words of any sentence in any language together, reduce capital letters to small case, remove all punctuation, vowel letters and diacritical marks, and then see how many different meanings can be derived from the remaining string of consonants. The teaching, 'God is One' becomes 'gdsn,' which can be expanded to anything from the farcical 'good sin' to the blasphemous 'God-Son' to the original 'God is One.' The most critical teaching of Jesus, as stated in Mark 12:29-30, Matthew 22:37 and Luke 10:27 is "the Lord is One...This is the first commandment." Yet, by the above process, 'the Lord is One' becomes 'thlrdsn,' which can be re-expanded to everything from the correct meaning to 'The Lord's one,' or even 'The Lord's son' (for, following the rules of Semitic languages, a single consonant, such as the 's' in this case, can be doubled). Such small differences in composition, such critical variants in theological posture.

Punctuation is critical as well, as pointed out by F. F. Arbuthnot, who relates the amusing story of a member of British Commons forced to issue a retraction after calling another member a liar. The

---

246. *The Bible, Revised Standard Version.* 1977. Preface, p. iv.

formal retraction was stated, "I said the gentleman lied, it is true; and I am sorry for it." However, the following morning the retraction appeared in the local paper as, "I said the gentleman lied. It is true; and I am sorry for it."[247] A reversal in meaning can result from a mistake in a single punctuation point in such circumstances.

A person can fairly question, then, who determined what constituted a 'more probable and convincing reading' of the unvowelled, unpunctuated, uncapitalized Hebrew scriptures? Was that decision based upon doctrinal prejudice or objective research? And if the vowel system of the Masoretes was trustworthy enough to be accepted as the scriptural support for an entire religion, why the need to alter the meaning in certain places in order to obtain 'a more probable and convincing reading'? For that matter, how trustworthy can the Masoretic system be when, by consensus of Jewish scholars, the correct pronunciation of the proper name of God has been lost for over a millennium? Lastly, why did the authors of the above quote restrict audience awareness to the rarely-read preface rather than place wake-up notes at the controversial decision points in the text? The conditions rightfully evoke no small degree of concern on the part of those who recognize the potential for adjusting translation to conform with doctrinal preference. The Preface continues as follows:

> "Sometimes it is evident that the text has suffered in transmission, but none of the versions provides a satisfactory restoration. Here we can only follow the best judgement of competent scholars as to the most probable reconstruction of the original text."[248]

---

247. Arbuthnot, F. F. p. 10.
248. *The Bible, Revised Standard Version.* 1977. Preface, pp. iv-v.

(3.C4) The Holy Qur'an / Evidences–2

The fact that what appears to be the most universally accepted Bible in history admits to the text having "suffered in transmission" does not necessarily imply any fault of modern scholarship, but it does imply an uncertainty of foundation.

So while both the Bible and the Qur'an were recorded in consonantal texts, the two vary greatly in reliability. The Qur'an was revealed and maintained as an oral tradition until the present day, so pronunciation and meaning has never been in question. The various readings of the Qur'an are all complementary, unlike the Bible where the "more probable and convincing reading" seeks definition, since the various verbal possibilities differ significantly in meaning. The Qur'an has been maintained unchanged to the present day, whereas "For the New Testament we have a large number of Greek manuscripts, preserving many variant forms of the text."[249] No single one of which is universally regarded as authoritative.

The context in which the literary miracle of the Qur'an was revealed is important in this regard, for each prophet appears to have been endowed with signs which were uniquely impressive to the people to whom he was sent. The skill most revered by ancient Egyptians was magic, and that most respected by Jews, doctoring. No surprise, then, that Moses was given miracles which stunned Pharaoh's court sorcerers into submission. Equally, there should be no surprise that Jesus was given the miracle of healing. In His mercy, Allah clothed the prophets in piety and righteousness, and credentialed them with the most impressive 'perk up and listen' works for the target population to which they were sent. Those who accepted the extraordinary works as signs of prophethood were successful. Those who rejected bore the weight of remaining in obstinate denial of the clear signs rapping on the closed door of their consciousness.

---

249. *The Bible, Revised Standard Version.* 1977. Preface, p. iv.

(Section 3) Books of Scripture

A person may then question what the highest skill and most respected art of the Arabs was. The answer is poetry, and eloquence of the spoken word. The complexity of the Arabic language stems from a profusion of dialects honored by a specificity of language unappreciated by those who, stunted by the limits of less exacting tongues enfolded within the superficiality of literacy in the modern age, lack capacity to appreciate a language which, "...could diversify the fourscore names of honey, the two hundred of a serpent, the five hundred of a lion, the thousand of a sword, at a time when this copious dictionary was intrusted to the memory of an illiterate people."[250]

So devoted were the Arabs to the impact of the spoken word that they held annual festivals, described as follows:

> "Thirty days were employed in the exchange, not only of corn and wine, but of eloquence and poetry. The prize was disputed by the generous emulation of the bards; the victorious performance was deposited in the archives of princes and emirs, and we may read, in our own language, the seven original poems which were inscribed in letters of gold, and suspended in the temple of Mecca."[251]

R. Bosworth Smith comments,

> "What the Olympic Games did for Greece in keeping up the national feeling, as distinct from tribal independence, in giving a brief cessation from hostilities, and acting as a literary center, that the annual fairs at Okaz and Mujanna were to Arabia. Here tribes made up their dissensions, exchanged prisoners of war, and, most important of all, competed with one another in extempore poetic contests. Even in the 'times of ignorance,' each tribe produced its own poet-laureate; and

---

250. Gibbon, Edward, Esq. Vol. 5, Chapter L, p. 452.
251. Gibbon, Edward, Esq. Vol. 5, Chapter L, p. 453.

(3.C4) The Holy Qur'an / Evidences–2

the most ready and the best saw his poem transcribed in letters of gold, or suspended on the wall of the entrance of the Kaaba, where it would be seen by every pilgrim who might visit the most sacred place in the country."[252]

In short, the Arabs liked their poetry.

The consistency plays out, for as Moses surpassed the magicians of Pharoah's court with the miracles sent as signs to an obstinate court, and as Christ Jesus humiliated the physicians of the period of his ministry with the miracles of healing sent through his person, Muhammad presented a revelation composed in the most beautiful expression of the Arabic language ever known to man. One passage of the Holy Qur'an can reduce hardened desert dwellers to tears, while another can elevate the spirits of the faithful to heights of ecstasy. Michener writes:

> "The Koran is probably the most often read book in the world, surely the most often memorized, and possibly the most influential in the daily life of the people who believe in it. Not quite so long as the New Testament, written in an exalted style, it is neither poetry nor ordinary prose, yet it possesses the ability to arouse its hearers to ecstasies of faith."[253]

The miraculous beauty of the Qur'an is so affecting as to have spawned a plethora of testimonies. Most weighty is the historical record of the *enemies* of Muhammad, many of whom were so drawn by the beauty of the Qur'an that they used to sneak through the thick, occlusive ink of desert darkness to steal an audience at night-

---

252. Smith, R. Bosworth, M.A. 1986. *Mohammad and Mohammadanism*. London: Darf Publishers Ltd. pp. 64-65.
253. Michener, James A. p. 70.

time recitations. On one such occasion, a number of these men bumped into each other in the dark on the way home from the reading. Identifying one another as the *leaders* of the enemies of Muhammad (Abu Sufyan and Abu Jahl being two of the three), they vowed an oath never to return. The next night they bumped into one another under the same circumstances again. This time they *really* swore not to return, pledging an oath by their idols in testimony to their sincerity. The next night they caromed off one another in the darkness once again.[254] Muslims regard this story as evidence of the irresistible beauty of the Holy Qur'an – a beauty so affecting that it drew the ears and imaginations of even the most hardened of detractors, the most staunch of enemies.

The conversion of Umar, one of the greatest warriors of his time and, up to the moment of his conversion, a greatly feared opponent of Islam, is frequently cited. Heading out with the intention of killing Muhammad, he was diverted to his sister's home where, upon hearing the beauty of the recitation of just one *surah*, he converted on the spot.

Other exemplary cases are to be found in the examples of Unays al-Ghifaaree and Al-Kindii, two of the greatest Muslim poets of the time of Muhammad. Unays al-Ghifaaree commented upon his first encounter with Muhammad as follows: "I have met a man of your religion in Makkah who claims to be sent by Allah. The people claim that he is a poet, or a sorcerer, or a magician. Yet, I have heard the words of sorcerers, and these words in no way resemble those uttered by a sorcerer. And I also compared his words to the verses of a poet, but such words cannot be uttered by a poet. By Allah, he is the truthful, and they are the liars!"[255] Al-Kindii, when asked to compose

---

254. Muhammad Ibn Ishaq Ibn Yasar. 1963. *Seerat An-Nabi*. Maydan Al Azhar (Cairo): Muhammad Ali Sabi'eh & Children. Vol. 1. p. 207

255. Narrated by *Muslim*.

(3.C4) The Holy Qur'an / Evidences–2

a passage like that found in the Qur'an, attempted, but surrendered to the inability to do so, admitting that such an accomplishment was simply not possible. Al-Kindii indicated that he would need to write books in order to convey the meaning of just a few lines of the Qur'an. His inability to match the beauty and content of the Qur'an is held by Muslims as testimony to the divine nature of Allah's challenge to mankind – "And if you (Arab pagans, Jews and Christians) are in doubt concerning that which We have sent down (i.e., the Qur'an) to Our slave (Muhammad), then produce a *surah* (chapter) of the like thereof and call your witnesses (supporters and helpers) besides Allah, if you are truthful" (TMQ 2:23). The reader is reminded that the 'We' and 'Our' in the above quote are English translations of the 'royal plural,' and not the plural of numbers. Having said that, the above quote benefits from closer examination.

Allah is recorded as having challenged mankind to attempt to match the Qur'an no less than five times. The first challenge (in order of revelation, not in order of the chapters) was to write an entire book equal to that of the Qur'an (*surahs* 17:88 and 52:33-34). When the greatest poets of the Arabic language could not even produce a single contestant, Allah issued a second challenge to write just 10 chapters the like of the Qur'an (*surah* 11:13). When the Arabian nation hung its head in abject literary humiliation, Allah reduced the challenge to that of producing one lone *surah* (chapter) the like of that found in the Qur'an (*surah* 10:38, followed by *surah* 2:23). For 1,400 years native Arabic-speaking Jews, Christians, pagans, and atheists have struggled to disprove the Qur'an for religious, political, and personal reasons. And Arabic is the native tongue of these antagonists. Something seems almost surreal about this scenario, for the shortest *surah* in the Qur'an is Al-Kauthar, number 108, weighing in at a power-packed, meaning-filled three lines. Three. Three lines totaling a scant ten words. So why have mankind been unable to write three

(SECTION 3) BOOKS OF SCRIPTURE

lines equal or better for the past 1,400 years? Why has mankind been unable to "...produce a *surah* of the like thereof?"

Muslims answer this question by pointing out that human standards are easily broken. 'Impossible' barriers are routinely transgressed, unbeatable records beaten, and previously unimagined successes achieved. The four minute mile has been mastered, the speed of sound shattered, the moon trod upon, the atom split, and electrons frozen. But nobody can ever accomplish that which God prohibits. Why have all of mankind been unable to write the like of the Qur'an? After 1,400 years? It's not for lack of time to think about it, that's for sure.

Al-Waleed Ibn al-Mughera, a lifelong antagonist of Islam and a poet in his own right, admitted, "By Allah, I heard a speech (the Qur'an) from Muhammad now; it is not from men or jinn (spirits) -- it is like sweetness. It is like the highest fruit in a tree growing in rich soil, and nothing can be above it."[256] When the best poets and the strongest enemies admit the supremacy of the revelation, despite personal refusal to adopt the teachings, a person might suspect that such opinions should be valued.

While some assert that Muhammad was just a very great poet, Muslims point out that one character trait of great artists is that when they finish cutting their ears off, they always see the flaws of their work more clearly than anyone else. Would a person expect Beethoven to challenge the world to write better music, or Michelangelo to challenge the world to make a better statue? Beethoven discarded some of his most respected compositions, only to have them surface after his death. Michelangelo was his own greatest critic, malleting his statues to shards because he felt they weren't good enough. History

---

256. *Manaahil Al-Irfaan fi Uluum Al-Qur'an (Wells of Knowledge of the Sciences of the Qur'an)*. 1988. Muhammad Abdul-At-Theem Az-Zarqaani. Dar Al-Kutub Al-Ilmee'a. Vol 1. p. 216.

testifies that the greatest of artists were always the most critical of their own achievements – throwing away spectacular compositions, painting over multi-million dollar 'masterpieces,' and reducing representational carvings to unrecognizable fragments. The point is that no man or woman of achievement and sanity would be likely ever to suggest such a cocky and over-confident challenge, for the greatest of perfectionists have always been the most critical of their own works, the most dissatisfied with their own efforts. Such a bold challenge could only be made, with confidence, by The One Who orders creation and Who knows that He will never allow the challenge to be met. And so, 1,400 years later, as noted by numerous authors, the challenge still stands. Professor A. J. Arberry states:

> "The Koran undeniably abounds in fine writing; it has its own extremely individual qualities; the language is highly idiomatic, yet for the most part delusively simple; the rhythms and rhymes are inseparable features of its impressive eloquence, and these are indeed inimitable."[257]

Dr. Laura Vaglieri contributes,

> "The Miracle of Islam *par excellence* is the Quran, through which a constant and unbroken tradition transmits to us news of an absolute certainty. This is a book which cannot be imitated. Each of its expressions is a comprehensive one, and yet it is of proper size, neither too long nor too short. Its style is original. There is no model for this style in Arab literature of the times preceding it. The effect which it produces on the human soul is obtained without any adventitious aid through its own inherent excellences. The verses are equally eloquent all through the text, even when they deal with topics, such as

---

257. Arberry, A. J. 1953. *The Holy Koran – An Introduction with Selections.* London: George Allen & Unwin Ltd. p. 28.

(SECTION 3) BOOKS OF SCRIPTURE

commandments and prohibitions, which must necessarily affect its tone. Stories of Prophets, descriptions of the beginning and the end of the world, enumerations and expositions of the divine attributes are repeated but repeated in a way which is so impressive that they do not weaken the effect. The text proceeds from one topic to another without losing its power. Depth and sweetness, qualities which generally do not go together, are found together here, where each rhetoric figure finds a perfect application....We find there vast stores of knowledge which are beyond the capacity of the most intelligent of men, the greatest of philosophers and the ablest of politicians."[258]

And A. Guillaume sums up as follows:

"The Qur'an is one of the world's classics which cannot be translated without grave loss. It (The Holy Qur'an) has a rhythm of peculiar beauty and a cadence that charms the ear. Many Christian Arabs speak of its style with warm admiration, and most Arabists acknowledge its excellence....indeed it may be affirmed that within the literature of the Arabs, wide and fecund as it is both in poetry and in elevated prose, there is nothing to compare with it."[259]

One notable point about the language of the Qur'an is that Muhammad started receiving revelation when he was 40 years old. People knew his character, his walk, his talk, his ethics, his morals. They *knew* his speech. The observation is frequently made that habits and personality traits do not markedly change past the age of thirty. An ancient Chinese proverb correctly states, "With men as with silk, it is most difficult to change colors once the dye has set." By the age

---

258. Vaglieri, Dr. Laura Veccia. pp. 40-41.
259. Guillaume, Alfred. pp. 73-74.

(3.C4) The Holy Qur'an / Evidences-2

of forty, most of mankind has congealed into a solid framework of concrete character traits. Not only had Muhammad proved himself no author (a point referred to in the verse, "And you were not [able] to recite a Book before this [Book came], nor are you [able] to transcribe it with your right hand; in that case, indeed, would the talkers of vanities have doubted." [TMQ 29:48]), but the language of Muhammad was identifiably on a much lower, human plane, than that of the Qur'an. Furthermore, Muhammad was very specific about which words were recorded as revelation, initially forbidding his own words to be recorded in any form whatsoever with the commandment to his companions, "Do not write anything from me except the Qur'an. Whoever writes anything besides the Qur'an should burn it."[260] Even later, when Muhammad began to permit the recording of hadith, his words and those of the revelation were never mixed, and there is no confusion over the fact that the words of Muhammad never approached the Divine eloquence of the Qur'an. A person can easily verify this language difference by comparing any book of hadith with the Holy Qur'an. The traditions of Muhammad were recorded in scores of volumes of hadith, preserving the language of Muhammad in a multitude of sources which give the reader extraordinary insight into the character and literary abilities of the man. Yet the rhyme and rhythm, the emotionally evocative essence of the message, the unique beauty of the Qur'an is nowhere to be found in the ordinary speech of Muhammad. As Dr. Laura Vaglieri questioned,

> "How could this marvelous book be the work of Muhammad, an illiterate Arab who in all his life composed only two or three verses, none of which reveals the least poetic quality; e.g., 'I am the Prophet and do not lie. I am the son of Abd el-Muttalib.'?"[261]

---

260. Narrated by *Muslim*.
261. Vaglieri, Dr. Laura Veccia. pp. 40-41.

(SECTION 3) BOOKS OF SCRIPTURE

Professor A. J. Arberry elaborates as follows:

"We know quite well how Mohammed spoke in his normal, everyday moods; for his *obiter dicta* have been preserved in great abundance. It is simply untrue therefore to say, as Margoliouth said, that 'it would be difficult to find another case in which there is such a complete identity between the literary work and the mind of the man who produced it.' Accepting, as we have good reason to accept, the sayings of Mohammed recorded in the books of Traditions as substantially authentic, and supposing, as Margoliouth supposed, that the Koran was Mohammed's conscious production, it would be more reasonable to say that it would be difficult to find another case in which the literary expression of a man differed so fundamentally from his ordinary speech."[262]

The point is that the difference between the language of Muhammad and that of the Qur'an is so readily identifiable that detractors of Islam have driven their imaginations great distances in order to deny the Qur'an as revelation. Many non-Muslims, such as the above-referenced Margoliouth, have gone so far as to allow religious prejudice to override scholastic perception, and so disingenuously express denial of what, to those accomplished in the Arabic language, is a clear reality. Such individuals throw themselves into direct conflict with the large body of more objective, equally non-Muslim, scholars of the Arabic language (of which Professor A. J. Arberry is a prime example*) who readily appreciate the huge difference between the speech of Muhammad and the literary miracle of the Qur'an.

Among those who deny the Qur'an as revelation, the difference

---

262. Arberry, A. J. *The Holy Koran – An Introduction with Selections.* pp. 31-32.

* On the same page as the preceding quote (i.e., p. 31), Professor Arberry wrote, "As for the faithful, I will not conceal from them, what they will not in any case imagine, that I am no Muslim, nor could ever be."

(3.C4) The Holy Qur'an / Evidences–2

between Muhammad's speech and the literary miracle of the Qur'an demands explanation. For if not from the mind of Muhammad, and if not from revelation, what was the source?

In the contest to provide an explanation which does not force the ultimate sacrifice, being that of religion, some scholars have even gone so far as to suggest that Muhammad must have had a teacher who tutored the composition of the Qur'an. This, they propose, would explain the difference. And indeed it would. However, whether asserting that Muhammad was just a very accomplished poet or that he had a teacher, one additional stumbling block to such claims is that the contemporaries of Muhammad pointed out that the form of the Qur'an was, and remains to this day, completely foreign to all lexical forms of Arabic poetry.[263] Furthermore, if there ever had existed such an accomplished tutor, who and where was he, and what happened to his other works, which common sense would dictate to have been equally glorious and distinct in style and literary impact? Treasures worthy of preservation one would think, and all the more so by a people who so prized their literature.

To expand the argument, the content of the Holy Qur'an broke many, if not most or even all, of the pre-existing literary rules. For one thing, poetry is most frequently focused on matters of common interest, the Western parallel being customarily bracketed within the boundaries of wine, women and song, with infrequent excursions into the esoteric at the pens of the masters. Arabic poetry in the period of Muhammad, like its Western parallel, reveled in the romantic and hedonistic delights of body and soul. However, issues of tribal superiority, the virtues of people and animals of noble breeding or notable qualities, contests of strength and wit, local heroes and history were also frequently the subject of commentary. As can be imagined, much of this poetry was inclined to extol the virtues of one's own person,

---

263. Said Qutub, *Fi Thilal Al-Qur'an*.

(Section 3) Books of Scripture

kin, and tribe, while at the same time denigrating all others. Excesses in exaggeration to the extreme of obscuration of reality was the rule, and the impact of the written word was such that wars were literally initiated, fought, and decided on the basis of the eloquence of authors. The Qur'an broke that mold in that exaggeration was gracefully avoided, descriptions never wavering from faithfulness to reality, and chosen topics strayed far from those of common interest into the fields of law and legislation, manners and morals, social and civil responsibilities, beliefs and practices of the religion. The combination of ostensibly dry topics, ranging from dietary restrictions to inheritance law, with an unembellished accounting, fails to fulfill what most people would imagine to be the list of essential ingredients for a literary masterpiece, much less the most eloquent and moving expression of a language of poets that the world has ever seen.

Though repetitive, it is not monotonous; though conveyed through a human vehicle, it does not betray the fluctuations of mood, and hence tone, so prevalent and pronounced amongst poets; though revealed over a period of 23 years, it hints at not the slightest refinement or evolution in style from beginning to end. In defiance of human variability, the Qur'an remained consistent in its expression, superlative in its eloquence, from topic to topic and from beginning to end.

Muslims point out that one of the many cherries on the top of the superlative beauty of the Holy Qur'an is that it was not revealed in chronological order. Muhammad was commanded to place each newly revealed verse in a specific spot in the framework of previous revelation – usually sandwiched between two previously revealed verses in the body of what had been revealed up to that point in time. The new verses may have been added anywhere from the beginning to the end of the work, inserted at a Divinely ordained locus in the scripture. As a preface to his own translation of the meaning of the

(3.C4) The Holy Qur'an / Evidences–2

Holy Qur'an, Professor A. J. Arberry commented on just this structure as follows:

> "...I have followed the traditional arrangement for all its admitted perplexities. The Suras themselves are in many instances—and this has been recognized by Muslim students from the earliest times—of a composite character, holding embedded in them fragments received by Muhammad at widely differing dates..." [264]

Again, Muslims assert that this simply does not approach human methodology. People tell stories and relate historical accounts, and attempt to link them all together if at all possible. Whether a person examines a history book or the Bible, the same pattern is evident – a string of stories placed end-to-end in an effort to achieve some degree of continuity. Constructing the Qur'an piecemeal, as was done, appears to be beyond human capacity, and certainly transgresses human methodology. Furthermore, should a person be faking revelation, it is just not necessary! History has shown that a false messiah doesn't have to perform such literary contortionism in order to mislead the masses.

Consequently, to be fair, for those who believe that they have come up with three verses which rival those of the Qur'an, now they have to do it backwards! Now they have to conceive and write the last line first (without having previously conceived the first two lines), the middle of the first line next, then the second line, then the beginning and end of the first line. Or something like that. Now they have to do it in such a way that each stage (the last line by itself, then the middle of the first line and the last line only, etc.) stands by itself. Then they have to do it in such a way that each stage of verse-evolution bears an

---

264. Arberry, A. J. 1996. *The Koran Interpreted.* A Touchstone book: Simon & Schuster. Preface, p. 25.

intelligent message and achieves a literary eloquence to remain unrivaled by the remainder of mankind. Additionally, the teachings have to foretell a future event, address a current concern, or teach a scientific fact that will not be known for the next 1,400 years. Ten different readings in seven different dialects at each stage of passage construction are required – each one complementary in meaning, each one embodying the above qualities. If the concept sounds crazy and the fulfillment impossible, the Muslim claim is that, from a human perspective, it is!

Yet the Qur'an was recorded in just this fashion over a period of 23 years, with the revelation passing across the lips of an illiterate man -- Muhammad. If construction of just three lines in this manner would seem impossible, consideration of how an illiterate person could possibly have written a complete book in his or her mind, without the luxury of reference to a written template, and then fill in the framework of such a project over the following two decades is baffling. Each stage of the work bore a comprehensible message of such practicality and incomparable beauty that no human being could match so little as three lines. There were no demonstrable errors, inconsistencies, or disruptions in flow. Can a person imagine all of the above, at *each* of the hundreds, if not thousands, of stages of revelation of the Qur'an, having been accomplished by a human being? Most of mankind can't hook up a surround sound system or assemble a do-it-yourself wall unit without misplacing leads, putting the long bolt in the short hole or vice versa, or misplacing shelves and partitions, all of which necessitate tearing down of the errors and reconstruction in anticipation of similar mistakes, before getting it near-right once and for all. And all that despite having a manual in hand.

So could a human being construct a book of the complexity described above? Muslims assert that the revelation and content of the Qur'an defy both human ability *and* methodology. After just a few

(3.C4) THE HOLY QUR'AN / EVIDENCES–2

years, if not just a couple months, of such an effort at piecemeal construction, the plan to put such-and-such a verse here or there would have been forgotten, or events would have conspired to negate planned verses and the whole thing would have degenerated into a soggy, uncohesive mess of literary kimchee. If nothing else, no human could even predict that they would live long enough to complete the task; an early demise would have left the work with visible holes where passages were still under construction. 1,400 years ago and in the desert, a man of 40 could have reasonably expected, in worldly terms, to be at the end of his life expectancy, and to have had a good run of it. To have expected to live yet another 23 years in that time and under conditions of persecution and warfare against overwhelming odds would have seemed grossly unrealistic, at best. An even greater breach from reality would have been to imagine that any human being could foresee the events around which future passages of the Qur'an would be revealed.

One of the first things a confidence artist learns is that in order to be a good liar, a person has to have a great memory. But the Islamic view is that no human has ever lived with the memory necessary to complete the above-described task. And yet, this is how the Qur'an was revealed. Verse by verse, over a period of 23 years, the Qur'an was pieced together and filled out in such a manner that it was, at all points in time and all stages of revelation, an incomparable, eloquent revelation of such sublime force and beauty as to change the hearts of man and the direction of mankind.

The decision as to Who the author was, in the mind of the Muslim, does not entertain a human candidate.

There are those who would agree that no human could write such a book, but who would follow such acknowledgement with the assertion that it must be the work of Satan. Such assertions are disappointing, at best, for the Bible relates that many of the disbelieving

(Section 3) Books of Scripture

Jews made the same claim about Jesus — that his works were not of God, but of Satan, the prince of devils (Matthew 12:24, Mark 3:22, Luke 11:15). On one hand, Christian hearts melt at the stories of the miracles of Jesus, wondering how the disbelieving Jews could possibly have denied the miracles as evidence of his prophethood. Reading the Biblical stories of the miracles of Jesus with tears in their eyes, thinking that had they been there, they wouldn't have been so blind — they would have believed — it is frequently the same Christians who slander the miracle of the Qur'an as the work of the Devil. Such Christians begin to look very much like the disbelieving Jews in the day of Jesus, of whom they themselves are so critical, for despite the predictors of the expected last prophet in both Old and New Testaments, and despite the weight of the evidences (miracles included), they not only adopt elaborate excuses by which to dismiss the Muslim Scripture, but they also frequently advance the same reflexive claim — that it is the work of the 'prince of devils.'

Even that challenge has an answer, though, as Muslims are quick to point out that the teachings of the Holy Qur'an preclude such a possibility. *Surah* 16, *ayah* 98 directs the Muslim, "When you do read the Qur'an, seek Allah's protection from Shaytan the Rejected One." (Yusuf Ali translation). The Muhammad Al-Hilali and Muhammad Khan translation is even more explicit — "So when you want to recite the Qur'an, seek refuge with Allah from Shaitan (Satan), the outcast (the cursed one)." The common sense realization is that Satan would not write a book which directs a person to take refuge from himself with Almighty God. Some might stretch their imaginations far enough to assert that Satan is just that tricky, and there even may be those who present such viewpoints without appearing hypocritical. But it is not possible for Christians to be amongst them, for the Bible reads,

(3.C4) The Holy Qur'an / Evidences–2

"But Jesus knew their thoughts, and said to them: "Every kingdom divided against itself is brought to desolation, and every city or house divided against itself will not stand. If Satan casts out Satan, he is divided against himself. How then will his kingdom stand?" (Matthew 12:25-26).

The teaching is repeated in Mark 3:23-27 and Luke 11:17. To deny the argument is to deny not only Jesus, but the authors of all three of the above-referenced gospels. Not to mention, for those who consider the Bible to be the word of God, denial of God Himself. The point? That the above is not just a Muslim argument, it is, in fact, a Biblical argument!

The Islamic world thus presents the challenge that if man and Satan are excluded as authors, exactly Whom then does that leave?

(3.C) The Holy Qur'an

(3.C5) Evidences – 3: Relation of Revelation to Preceding Events

"The past is a foreign country; they do things differently there."
– L.P. Hartley, *The Go-Between, Prologue*

Many Biblical stories are retold in the Qur'an, but with significant differences. A frequent challenge to the authenticity of the Qur'an is the assertion that the Qur'an was copied from previously revealed scriptures. There are many difficulties with this proposal, the first being that Muhammad was illiterate, and could not have read previous scriptures had he tried. A second difficulty is that even the Arabian Jews and Christians could not have read their scriptures, even had they tried. Why? Simply because the evidence suggests that there was no such thing as an Arabic Bible during the lifetime of Muhammad.

The lack of an Arabic Bible in the time of Muhammad is, and has been, very disturbing to those who would propose that Muhammad copied Biblical stories into the Qur'an. Consequently, the discovery of an Arabic Bible predating the time of Muhammad would go a long way towards bringing joy to such claimants. However, the result of such a search has proved disappointing. *The Encyclopedia of Religion and Ethics*, a series of voluminous tomes filled with slanders and poison for Islam, nonetheless admits that "there is no evidence of any parts of the Bible having been translated into Arabic before Islam."[265] Hasting's *Dictionary of the Bible* attributes the first Arabic translation of the Bible to the tenth century,[266] while *Encyclopedia Judaica* attributes the first Arabic translation of the Old Testament either to Hunayn Ibn Ishaq (800-873 CE) or to Saadiah b. Joseph Gaon (882-942 CE).[267]

Thus, a person wonders what Jewish and Christian resources existed in the time of Muhammad. If there was no Arabic Bible 200 years after the life of Muhammad, what was available to Muhammad? Copying something that didn't exist would be, well, tough — even tougher for the illiterate.

The presence of Jews and Christians in the Arabian Peninsula during the time of Muhammad is well known, and so the existence of oral traditions would be a reasonable expectation. Khadijah (Muhammad's first wife) had an aged cousin, Waraqah Ibn Nawfal, who was a Christian. Furthermore, Muhammad came into contact with Bahira-Sergius, a Nestorian monk of Syria, at a young age. Contact with the Jews of his community, and the opportunity for instruction in their religion, can be expected to have been no less likely. Thus, a case can be made for Muhammad having learned the basics of the Jewish and Christian religions by the oral route. As the Jews and Christians passed the teachings and traditions of their religions to one another, so they could have conveyed them to Muhammad. Such a case can be made. And such a case can be destroyed.

---

265. Hastings, James. *The Encyclopedia of Religion and Ethics*. Vol X, p. 540.
266. Hastings, James. *Dictionary of The Bible*. p. 105.
267. *Encyclopaedia Judaica*. Vol 4, p. 863.

(SECTION 3) BOOKS OF SCRIPTURE

The problem with the proposal that Muhammad copied Jewish and Christian teachings from the route of oral transmission is not that such teachings were unavailable, for no doubt they were readily available. The problem relates to exactly *what* Jewish and Christian teachings were circulated in the Arabian peninsula during and preceding the time of Muhammad, for the evidence suggests that the mainstream views of the Jewish and Christian religions were not exemplified amongst the Arabs of the Period of Ignorance, as acknowledged in the following statement regarding the period of Muhammad's prophethood:

> "Neither Arabian Jews nor Arabian Christians, unfortunately, were to be classed among the better representatives of their faiths at the time. The former had lived in comparative isolation possibly since the middle of the 1st millennium B.C., although they had been mildly successful in proselytism, and the latter were mainly heretical Monophysites, remote in every sense from the centers of Christian learning."[268]

Paul Wegner contributes:

> "The Scriptures do not seem to have been extant in an Arabic version before the time of Muhammad (570-632), who knew the gospel story only in oral form, and mainly from Syriac sources. These Syriac sources were marked by Docetism (believed that Jesus had only a divine nature and only appeared to be incarnate—they thought the material world and thus one's body was inherently evil)..."[269]

The point should be obvious – if the proposal is put fourth that

---

268. *New Catholic Encyclopedia.* Vol 9, p. 1001.
269. Wegner, Paul D. *The Journey from Texts to Translations.* 1999. Grand Rapids: Baker Books. p. 250.

(3.C5) The Holy Qur'an / Evidences–3

Muhammad copied from Jewish and Christian sources, and if the only sources of Judaism and Christianity available were those of the poorer "representatives of their faiths," meaning the heretical Monophysites, Docetists, and Nestorians (such as the above-mentioned Bahira-Sergius), then why does the Qur'an not copy the dogma peculiar to those heretical sects? Why does the Qur'an condemn association of Christ Jesus with divinity, rather than endorse belief in a union of godhead and manhood as one nature in the one person of Christ Jesus, as the Monophysites proposed? Why does the Qur'an validate Christ Jesus as a man in all aspects of human nature, and not advocate the Docetist concept of Jesus having been a phantasm? Had Muhammad appreciated the Nestorian faith, why does the Qur'an reject the Nestorian claim to union of God (the son) with Jesus (the man) as well as the doctrine of the crucifixion? If the Qur'an was copied from oral traditions, and the Jewish and Christian Arabs were themselves poor representatives of their faiths, why, then, are the heresies of the Arabs of Muhammad's exposure not argued in the Holy Qur'an? Why does the Qur'an address the valid beliefs of the Jewish orthodoxy, the commonly accepted historical accounts of both Old and New Testaments, and the mainstream issues of the Trinitarian Christianity of Constantinople, rather than the peculiar and unorthodox concepts of the Jews and Christians of the Arabia of Muhammad?

Related is the simple fact that the message of the Qur'an repeats, over and over again, the claim to revelation of historical details previously unknown to the Arabs – Jews and Christians included. An example includes details in the story of Noah, which is followed by the statement,

> "Such are some of the stories of the Unseen, which We have revealed to you: before this, neither you nor your people knew them." (TMQ 11:49).

(Section 3) Books of Scripture

And yet history does not record anyone, whether well-traveled Pagan, scholarly Jew, contemplative Christian, or Muslim, ever having stood up and laid claim to previous knowledge of the details of such stories. Nobody ran to the front of the congregation yelling, "Wait a minute, I knew that!" Once again, copying Jewish or Christian traditions which were nonexistent both on paper and in memory would be, well, troublesome. What could possibly be the source of such information if the authorities of the religions themselves drew cognitive blanks?

The most significant point, however, is that regardless of the scriptural information base available to Muhammad, if any at all, the stories of the Qur'an correct, rather than repeat, errors of the Bible. What should people think of a book which, instead of repeating errors which were unrecognized and thus popularly accepted as 'gospel truth' during the lifetime of Muhammad, presents corrections which were unknown at the time of revelation, and the validity of which would only be recognized by future generations? Here is something unusual. A man-made book designed to appeal to the masses would be expected to agree with, rather than confront, popular opinion. True revelation, however, would be expected to be designed to accomplish the exact opposite – i.e., to correct the errors of mankind, no matter how distasteful the truth may at first seem in the face of more appealing falsehoods. After all, is that not the point of revelation? And such is the case with the Holy Qur'an – correct beliefs were reinforced, commonly accepted errors were *not* repeated, and specific mistakes were corrected.

The most important and dramatic corrections relate to elements of belief, as discussed in previous chapters. The Holy Qur'an challenges Christians by telling them to look in their book, for they will find therein that Jesus never called himself 'Son of God' (see Section 2.B.6.). A person may well wonder how Muhammad could have known that; as pointed out above, he couldn't read their book. For that matter, even *they* couldn't read their book – it was 250 years from the pen of a translator. So what were Muhammad's sources? The most he could have heard were snippets of oral traditions from Christian clergy. Regardless of how complete such traditions may have been, how could he have known that he had heard them all, and that there weren't others in which Jesus *had* called himself 'Son of God?' Without a Bible for reference, he could not have known that some Gospel foreign to his experience would not be canonized and destroy the assertion of the Qur'an.

Examples of more tangible, objectively verifiable corrections include scientific evidences (see Section 3.C.8.). But consideration can also be given to such simple elements as the age of Jesus when he started his ministry.

According to the Bible, "Now Jesus himself began his ministry at about thirty years of age..." (Luke 3:23). Ask any Christian the age of Jesus when he started his ministry, and to this day the majority of those who produce an answer will claim something around the age of 30. However, any serious examination of surrounding historical facts reveals that Jesus could not have been a year less than 38 years old, and he was most likely older, perhaps as old as 46, but *at least* 38.[270] So Luke 3:23 should read "about forty." Where does the age of 38-46 come from? Jesus' age can be accurately determined by measuring the known time-span between his birth during the reign of King Herod the Great of Judaea (who died shortly after a lunar eclipse dated by astronomers to 12-13 March, 4 BC) and the beginning of his ministry following the imprisonment of John the Baptist. Why was John the Baptist imprisoned? For rebuking Antipas (King Herod the Great's son, also known as Herod the tetrarch [governor] of Galilee and

---

270. Fox, Robin Lane. 1991. *The Unauthorized Version; Truth and Fiction in the Bible*. Viking Press. pp. 28-34.

(SECTION 3) BOOKS OF SCRIPTURE

Perea), for marrying his own niece and sister-in-law. It is a fair assumption that most people understand that a man cannot marry his sister-in-law unless his brother is, by one means or another, out of the picture. Some small degree of sibling rivalry might otherwise ensue. Well, Josephus documents in his *Jewish Antiquities* that dear brother Philip died "...in the twentieth year of the reign of Tiberius..." and following a reign of 37 years himself, all of which corresponds with 33-34 CE.[271] A soap opera here, a battle there, a journey to fetch the questionably grieving widow, a marriage, a public rebuke, and John the Baptist finds himself in jail waiting for the manipulative step-daughter to dance. The timing works out to Jesus starting his ministry in 34 CE, following the imprisonment of John the Baptist, as supported by the gospels of Mark and Luke – "Now after John was put in prison, Jesus came to Galilee, preaching the gospel of the kingdom of God" (Mark 1:14).

So, the minimum age for Jesus at the onset of his ministry was 38 (the time span from 4 BC to 34 CE).

Assuming that Jesus was not born on the day King Herod the Great died, and allowing a more reasonable period of time for Antipas to have acquired his sister-in-law, Christ Jesus was more likely to have been well into his 40's. Such assumptions are not unreasonable. For example, a person can consider the following sequence of events:

(1) Christ Jesus was born during the reign of King Herod the Great. (Matthew 2:1)

(2) Following the birth of Jesus, Magi (wise men), having seen the star signaling his miraculous birth, came to Jerusalem from the east. (Matthew 2:1)

-----That's one major trip. In a period of history when first class transportation meant a donkey which didn't bite or a camel which

---

271. Whiston, William, A.M. 1998. *Josephus, The Complete Works.* Nashville: Thomas Nelson Publishers. 18.4.6., p. 580.

(3.C5) THE HOLY QUR'AN / EVIDENCES–3

didn't spit, such things took time.

(3) Herod sent the Magi on a reconnaissance trip to Bethlehem. (Matthew 2:8)

-----That's a second trip.

(4) The Magi returned to their own countries, unbeknownst to Herod. (Matthew 2:12)

-----That's a third trip.

(5) An angel of God directed Joseph to 'arise,' and flee the persecution of King Herod. (Matthew 2:13)

(6) Joseph arose (Matthew 2:14)

-----That may only have taken a minute or so.

(7) And took the family to Egypt for an indefinite leave of absence (Matthew 2:14)

-----That probably took slightly longer. A fourth trip.

(8) Herod found out about the deception. (Matthew 2:16)

-----That probably took some time too. A fifth trip (by the messenger).

(9) Herod, being a man of such possessiveness of position as to have executed his beloved wife Mariamne and, on separate occasions, three sons thought to threaten his throne, sent his flunkies in tyranny to kill all the male children two years old and less in Bethlehem and the vicinity. (Matthew 2:16)

-----Why two years old and younger? "...according to the time which he had determined from the wise men" (Matthew 2:16). In other words, Christ Jesus was getting on in infancy by this time.

(10) After some unspecified time – maybe long, maybe short – Herod died. (Matthew 2:19)

-----And not a moment too soon.

Some consider that Jesus could have been born as early as 8 BC. Whether or not he was born that early, nobody can say for sure. However, given the above scenario, a person can reasonably expect

367

(SECTION 3) BOOKS OF SCRIPTURE

Jesus to have been born at least two years prior to the demise of King Herod the Great, or in other words, in 6 BC. Similarly, it is not unreasonable to expect that events surrounding the shady marriage of Antipas unfolded slightly slower than the speed of time travel. Suddenly the seldom read and less often quoted, "You are not yet fifty years old, and have you seen Abraham?" (John 8:57) makes sense. A person would logically expect that, had Jesus been in his thirties, the challenge would read along the lines of, "You are not yet forty years old..."

Illustrating yet another difficulty in the Bible is not the point. The take home message is that to this day Christians assert that Jesus started his ministry around the age of 30. Had Muhammad asked, this is almost certainly what he would have been told. Now, what does the Qur'an say? The translation of the meaning of the Qur'an, *surah* 5:110, specifies that Jesus spoke to the people in childhood and when he was "*kahlan*." The word '*kahlan*' describes a man aged between 30 and 50.[272] Had the Bible been copied, a person would expect the claim that Jesus was 'about thirty' to be repeated. On the contrary, the Qur'an has a degree of accuracy over the Bible in this regard, and does not paint itself into a corner with sticky claims discredited by known history. Whereas hard evidence defies the Biblical record, the Qur'anic description conforms to what is known of history -- correcting, rather than repeating, this Biblical error.

Another point which stands out in the Biblical record of history is that the title 'Pharaoh' was historically used only during the time of, and following, the Egyptian rulers of the 14th century BC. To be specific, the term was only used during the years 1,539-1,292 BC and *circa* 945-c. 730 BC.[273] Another reference voices, "Originally referring

---

272. Wehr, Hans. *A Dictionary of Modern Written Arabic*. 3rd printing. Beirut: Librairie Du Liban; London: MacDonald & Evans Ltd. 1980.

273. *Encyclopaedia Britannica*. CD-ROM.

(3.C5) THE HOLY QUR'AN / EVIDENCES-3

only to the palace, the Egyptian term became a title of respect for the king during the 18th dynasty....Any use of "Pharaoh" for kings preceding Thutmose III is an anachronism."[274] The same source identifies Thutmose III as an Egyptian pharaoh of the 18th dynasty, who lived *circa* 1490-1436 BC.[275] Any use of the term 'Pharaoh' prior to the 1490's BC would therefore be an anachronism – "an attribution of a custom, event, etc., to the wrong period."[276] In other words, it would be out of time and out of place – a blatant stain in the fabric of history, rendering the garment in which it is recorded unsuitable for wear.

Now, during the time of Joseph (around 1700 BC), Egypt was ruled by a different line of monarchy. And had been for some time. The Hyksos dynasty were ethnic Arabs who usurped the Egyptian throne *circa* 2000 BC, and who ruled Egypt to the end of the 15th century BC. The title of 'Pharaoh' was never applied to any kings of the Hyksos dynasty, and did not breach the surface of history for another couple hundred years after the time of Joseph, for Joseph lived in the 1700's BC, smack-dab in the middle of the Hyksos dynasty. The time frame, plainly and simply, is wrong. Yet the Bible labels both the kings of Joseph (See Genesis, chapters 39-50) and of Moses (See Exodus 2-18) as 'Pharaoh'. Well, one out of two isn't bad, if that is the standard of accuracy a person seeks in a book of revelation.

Now, what about the Qur'an?

The Qur'an correctly acknowledges the king of Moses as 'Pharaoh,' but identifies the king of Egypt in the time of Joseph as just that – the 'King' – thereby avoiding repetition of the Biblical error (See *Surah* Yusuf [*surah* 12] of the Holy Qur'an). Yet the content of

---

274. *The Encyclopedia Americana International Edition*. 1998. Grolier Inc. Vol 21. p. 848.
275. *The Encyclopedia Americana International Edition*. Vol 26. p. 714.
276. Thompson, Della (editor). *The Oxford Dictionary of Current English* 1993. Second Edition. Oxford University Press. p. 26.

(SECTION 3) BOOKS OF SCRIPTURE

the Qur'an is not short on mention of the title, 'Pharaoh.' The term, in fact, is encountered over seventy times in the Qur'an, but in each case in reference to the monarch of Egypt during the historical period when the title of 'Pharaoh' was actually in use. Hence, the conspicuous avoidance of this term in reference to the Egyptian monarch of the time of Joseph appears to be statistically significant.

Speaking of Egypt, the Holy Qur'an records Pharaoh ordering a man entitled 'Haman' to bake bricks for the purpose of construction (TMQ 28:38). The word 'Haman' is a title from the lost hieroglyphic language of the ancient Egyptians, now believed to mean, "The Chief of the workers in the stone-quarries."[277] In other words, in a time and place where construction was largely tantamount to stacking blocks, 'Haman' was the foreman in charge of construction supplies. The meaning of the hieroglyphics was lost centuries before the time of Muhammad, and only relearned with the discovery of the Rosetta Stone in 1,799 CE. History records that after the death of Marcus Antonius (Marc Antony) and the subsequent suicide of Cleopatra in August of the year 30 BC, the Egyptian dynastic system came to an end, and Roman Governorship was established with Latin employed as the language of the realm. Greek continued to enjoy infrequent exercise, but the language of the hieroglyphics died out within the next century. It came to be neither utilized nor understood. And likely would have remained so, had the Rosetta Stone not been discovered. Resuscitating the asystolic, flat-line language of the hieroglyphics was by no means easy, even with the Rosetta Stone in hand. Completion of the effort demanded time (more than twenty years), inspiration, and some of the most brilliant minds of Europe. All of which leads a person to question how the author of the Qur'an knew

---

277. Hermann Ranke. *Die Ägyptischen Personennamen (Dictionary of Personal Names of the New Kingdom)*. Verzeichnis der Namen, Verlag Von J J Augustin in Glückstadt, Band I (1935); Band II (1952).

(3.C5) THE HOLY QUR'AN / EVIDENCES–3

to entitle the man in charge of construction supplies 'Haman.' With the language of the hieroglyphics dead and gone for over 500 years, and such titles presumed to have been extinct as well, what was the source of such knowledge in the day of Muhammad?

A similar example may emphasize the point. The fact that the followers of Jesus were labeled 'Christian' long after the ministry of Jesus was discussed above in Section 1.B. Jesus never identified his followers as 'Christians.' However, once the term was later invented and applied, it stuck – the term caught on and was adopted throughout the world of Christianity. Had Muhammad asked the Christians of his time what they called themselves, they would have identified themselves as 'Christian' (*Masihiyyun* in Arabic). *Masihiyyun* describes the followers (*-iyyun*) of Christ ('*Messiah*' in Hebrew, '*Masih*' in Arabic). To this day the Christian Arabs identify themselves as *Masihiyyun* (followers of Christ), just as their Western counterparts graft the label 'Christian' off the same stalk of faith. How, then, would Muhammad have known the followers of Jesus? As *Masihiyyun*. Why, then, is this word not mentioned once in the Qur'an? Not one, single, solitary time? Christians are spoken of repeatedly in the Qur'an, not as 'Christians' or '*Masihiyyun*,' but as '*Nasara*' (Nazarenes). This faithful description of the followers of Jesus was largely lost to the tongue of man, yet is congruous with the Biblical identity of Jesus not as a Christian, but as a Nazarene. A person wonders who whispered that tidbit into Muhammad's ear. Who told him that although virtually every Christian in the world identifies with the label 'Christian,' the correct term is '*Nasara*?' Maybe one Christian in a thousand knows that the label 'Christian' was a nickname and a derogatory one at that. Maybe. Maybe not even one in a thousand. The popular opinion, from the first century CE to the present day, has been to identify, whether in Aramaic or in Arabic, the followers of Jesus by the nickname '*Masihiyyun*' in preference to the faithful Biblical term of

(Section 3) Books of Scripture

'Nasara.' So why would Muhammad swim against such an overwhelmingly strong current of public opinion; unless, that is, he was only conveying words given to him – words which corrected his own opinion as well as that of most of the rest of mankind?

The above issues, while addressing relatively small details of historical accuracy, are highly significant, for it is just these minute details which exist as the tiny, largely unrecognized tripwires upon which false phophethood would be expected to snag a toe. Nobody trips over a building – it is always the small, seemingly insignificant irregularities in the pavement which a person stumbles over. And yet, rather than painting a new coat of gloss over old errors of popular misunderstanding, it is just these small points of detail which the Qur'an corrects with exquisite accuracy.

Whereas the unsteady gait of man is inclined to stumble into such traps of popularized inaccuracy, a book of God would be expected to gracefully conform to reality, passing all tests of critical analysis down to the most trivial of details. Furthermore, the Bible teaches, "He who is faithful in what is least is faithful also in much; and he who is unjust in what is least is unjust also in much" (Luke 16:10). If this teaching is applied to the Bible and the authors thereof, the significance of even the smallest error (unfaithfulness to detail) becomes apparent. Even so little as a copying error should sound the siren of alert to the fact that "he who is unjust in what is least is unjust also in much." So details are important, for they serve as signal flags of those scriptural ships which harbor the plague of unfaithfulness. Unfaithfulness to detail, to truth, and in the extreme, to God.

And then there is Iram.

The 89th chapter of the Holy Qur'an makes passing mention of a city of Iram (TMQ 89:7). The city of Iram was lost to history for over 3,500 years. As such, Qur'anic mention of Iram was a point of discomfort for many Muslim exegetes over the preceding 1,400 years.

(3.C5) The Holy Qur'an / Evidences–3

Here was a city mentioned in the Holy Qur'an, but with no evidence for existence. The accuracy of the Qur'an is beyond question in the minds of believers, but external evidence supportive of even the smallest of Qur'anic details is reassuring – especially to those who are tired of the "You just have to believe" methodology of faith construction. Hence, discovery of historical evidence of the city of Iram would have been considered a blessing to those seeking confirmation of the scriptural teaching.

The archeological roadmap to Iram passes through the ancient city of Ebla, as discussed in the December, 1978 issue of *National Geographic*. The article, "Ebla, Splendor of an Unknown Empire" outlines one of the greatest archeological finds of the present epoch -- the discovery of the city of Ebla, in Northwest Syria. Those with deeper interest may wish to research *Atlantis of the Sands*, by Ranulph Frennes, *Ebla – A Revelation in Archeology*, by Chaim Bermant and Michael Weitzman, and *Lost Civilizations*, by Bill Harris.

The magnitude of the Ebla find is related in the *National Geographic* article as follows:

> "...in 1975, Matthiae hit an archeological jackpot. In the ruins of a palace apparently destroyed in the 23rd century B.C., he came upon the greatest third-millennium archive ever unearthed. More than 15,000 cuneiform tablets and fragments – commercial records, treaties, chronicles – whispered, through the mists of ancient and ambiguous syntax, of an unknown Semitic empire, with Ebla as its seat, that once dominated much of the Middle East....this find struck the scholarly world like a thunderbolt."[278]

How big is this find? To quote Dr. Ignace J. Gelb, "Ebla was a mighty kingdom, treated on an equal footing with the most powerful

---

278. *National Geographic*. December, 1978. pp. 731-5.

(SECTION 3) BOOKS OF SCRIPTURE

states of the time."[279] How important are the cuneiform tablets? To quote Dr. Giovanni Pettinato, "*All* the other texts of this period recovered to date do not total a fourth of those from Ebla."[280]

This, the world's largest collection of cuneiform plates (clay tablets inscribed with wedge-shaped writing) lifts the veil of obscurity from the face of history to reveal an image contrary to many classical preconceptions. These tablets were written in the oldest Semitic language yet discovered, revealing a rich culture suffusing a thriving community – so much so that, following examination of the records of the palace library, archeological experts conclude, "…Ebla rivaled Egypt and Mesopotamia as a major power of the ancient world."[281] So what happened to so great a culture? Sometime around 2300 BC Ebla was defeated by Sargon. Much of Ebla was apparently razed. The burning of the palace converted the library into a kiln, baking the clay tablets into ceramic preservation. Layers to the ruins reveal that Ebla was destroyed again around 2000 BC, most likely following siege by the Amorites. Rebuilt upon the ruins once more, "Ebla flourished briefly once again, but around 1800 B.C. the city began to decline, and within two hundred years finally disappeared from history."[282]

What does all this have to do with Iram? Ebla, like all major world powers, maintained historical records of previously known populaces, comprehensive lists of the limits of known civilization, and catalogues of all cities from which tribute was exacted, and with which business was transacted. Prior to donning the sand-dune cloak of obscurity, such records were deposited in the palace library. What does a person find there? Mention of Beirut, Damascus, Gaza, Sodom, Gomorrah, among others. What else? "Also included is Iram, an

---

279. *National Geographic*. December, 1978. p. 735.
280. *National Geographic*. December, 1978. p. 735.
281. *National Geographic*. December, 1978. p. 731.
282. *National Geographic*. December, 1978. p. 748.

(3.C5) The Holy Qur'an / Evidences–3

obscure city referred to in *Surah* 89 of the Koran."[283] So in 1975, the city of Iram became historically identified. Also found in the records are the cities of 'Ad' and 'Shamutu' (believed to be the city of the 'Thamud') – two other lost civilizations mentioned in the Qur'an.[284] As a matter of fact, five short Qur'anic verses (89:6-10) mention four lost civilizations, all of which are now historically identified – Iram, Ad, Shamutu, and the people of Pharaoh.

Could Muhammad possibly have known of Iram? Ad? The people of Pharaoh almost certainly, and Shamutu very likely (in structure if not in name, for the ruins of Shamutu exist to this day as a popular attraction in the Saudi Arabian city of '*Mada-in Salih*')...but these other two lost cities? Could Muhammad possibly have known of cultures which ceased to exist thousands of years before the sun rose on his first day in his mother's arms? Did he know the names of lost cities in a time and place where the closest thing to an information superhighway was a level trail and a fast camel? Not likely. The average American can't name the first three settlements in the United States, and might miss the correct answer even if offered in the form of a multiple-choice question. And those settlements are not only known to history, but are only a scant few centuries old. So what hat did Muhammad pull the names 'Iram,' 'Ad,' and 'Thamud' out of? To put an obscure and unidentified name in your book is risky – unless, that is, you're God. And that, Muslims assert, is the point. If the book were from a man, a person would expect something very different. However, if the author were God, the book truly revelation, with man serving only to convey (but not conceive) the message, then there is no problem with finding obscure knowledge and lost civilizations in the revelation.

---

283. *National Geographic*. December, 1978. p. 736.
284. Bermant, Chaim and Michael Weitzman. 1979. *Ebla: A Revelation in Archaeology*. Times Books. p. 191.

(SECTION 3) BOOKS OF SCRIPTURE

Should a person attempt to conjure up a mental image of a false prophet, certain characteristics are common to average expectation. To begin with, should a false prophet attempt to build faith among followers, he would be foolish to deal in any currency other than that which is commonly accepted, whether valid or not. For example, why go out on a limb by naming lost civilizations when a person could limit his comments to known cities, like Nazareth? The Christians around Muhammad must have filled his ears with tales of Nazareth, so those who presume Muhammad to have been a false prophet should be challenged to explain why Nazareth isn't mentioned in the Qur'an. Mention of Nazareth would have fostered considerable favorable opinion amongst Christians, and a person is hard-pressed to find the harm in mentioning Nazareth at least once. Unless, that is, Nazareth didn't exist. And, as a matter of fact, the existence of Nazareth is yet another popular myth which lacks substantiation.

Nazareth is mentioned 29 times in the New Testament, but no city or town by that name can be proven to have existed in the time of Jesus. In fact, there is strong evidence to suggest that Nazareth did *not* exist in the time of Jesus. Now, whether or not Nazareth did in fact exist is not of any great importance, but it is interesting to note that the Romans had comprehensive mercantile and tax records of all the towns in Palestine. The Romans were methodical about their records, for they didn't want to have to aimlessly 'Rome' the countryside looking for pockets of peasants to beat the taxes out of. No mention of Nazareth, though. All kinds of Roman records from 2,000 years ago - - no Nazareth. Nazareth "...is not among the places mentioned in Joshua 19:10 f., nor is it referred to by Josephus, who gives the names of forty-five Galilaean towns, nor by the Talmud which names sixty-three."[285] Some scholars speculate, and *acknowledge* their discussion as

---

285. Kraeling, Emil G. Ph. D. 1952. *Rand McNally Bible Atlas*. Rand McNally & Co. p. 358.

speculation, that Nazareth and modern day *en Nasira* are one and the same. But no one knows for sure. Then why was Christ Jesus called the Nazarene? Hard to say, and in the end the reason is not very important. However, worthy of note is that 'Nazarene' is the English translation of the Greek '*Nazoraios*,' both of which appear to derive from the Hebrew '*Nozrim*,' which itself stems from '*Nozrei ha-Brit*,' the ancient Hebrew name by which the Qumran community identified themselves as 'Keepers of the Covenant.'[286] If the extraction seems strained, a person might consider that the modern day 'Tsar' derives from 'Kaiser,' itself derived from 'Caesar,' and bearing no relation to either seeded hamburger rolls or gourmet salads. Words separated by 2,000 years wrinkle with age. Returning to 'Nazarene,' the comment is offered that,

> "Contrary to the assumptions of later tradition, it has nothing whatever to do with Jesus' alleged upbringing in Nazareth, which, the evidence (or lack of it) suggests, did not even exist at the time. Indeed, it seems to have been the very perplexity of early commentators encountering the unfamiliar term 'Nazorean' that led them to conclude Jesus' family came from Nazareth, which by then had appeared on the map."[287]

Search Palestine now, and a person finds Nazareth in lower Galilee (Northern Palestine). The problem is, the city by this name appears not to have existed in Biblical times. History seems to indicate that a town was named Nazareth to satisfy Biblical interpretation, rather than the Bible mentioning a pre-existing town. In other words, present-day Nazareth appears to have derived its name as a result of the perceived need to back-fill a scriptural deficiency. This, then,

---

286. Baigent, Michael and Richard Leigh. 1991. *The Dead Sea Scrolls Deception.* New York: Summit Books/Simon & Schuster Inc. p. 174.

287. Baigent, Michael and Richard Leigh. p. 174.

(SECTION 3) BOOKS OF SCRIPTURE

constitutes one more point of accuracy. The Bible mentions a place which appears never to have existed in the lifetime of the prophet Jesus, whereas the Qur'an makes no such mention, once again gracefully avoiding repetition of a little-known, but nonetheless apparent error. Not only that, but 'Nazareth' is just the kind of commonly accepted scriptural currency, the mention of which would be expected to have appealed to the Christians of the time of Muhammad. Yet it bears no mention in the Holy Qur'an.

Back to Iram. To propose a passage which defied explanation during the lifetime of the prophet, not to mention for the next 14 centuries, is pretty bold for a man. Even bolder would be the mention of not just one, but three such cities, in succession. That's…that's…well, that's pretty unlikely. Muhammad would have had to have been both foolish and historically fortunate. In addition, a person might question the motivation, for there was nothing to be won and a great deal to be lost from such a mention.

On the other hand, imagining God to do such a thing poses no such problem. God, with His infinite knowledge, would have known that for roughly 1,400 years such an unexplained element of revelation might test the faith of those on the spiritual edge of commitment. God would also have known that 1,400 years later Iram, Ad, and the civilization of the people of Thamud would become identified realities, strengthening the faith of future generations, and providing signs for the people of this present age. One of the miracles of the Qur'an is held to be just this – it is timeless. Although the revelation was completed roughly 1,400 years ago, the miracles continue to surface even to the present day.

(3.C) THE HOLY QUR'AN

(3.C6) Evidences – 4: Relation of Revelation to Contemporaneous Events

"Truth would become more popular if it were not always stating ugly facts."

– Henry H. Haskins

The fact that specific passages of the Qur'an were revealed at the time of, or in proximity to, events contemporary to the life of Muhammad is not particularly surprising. What is extraordinary to note, however, is the content.

Anybody who reads the Qur'an for the first time may be struck not only by what the revelation contains, but also by that which is conspicuously absent. For example, Muhammad outlived his first wife, his first love, his only wife of twenty-five years, and the companion with whom he spent his youth, Khadijah. She died after two long, painful years during which the Meccan pagans ostracized, persecuted and starved Muhammad and his followers. And living in the desert adds a new dimension to starvation. All those years of love, support, caring and kindness – gone. His first wife, so loved by him that he remained faithful to her and her alone throughout their marriage and throughout his youth – gone. The first person to believe in his prophethood, the wife who bore all but one of his eight children – gone. So devoted was she that she exhausted her wealth and tribal relationships in support of him. Following which, she was gone.

Musicians croon endlessly over their lost loves; artists immortalize their infatuations in marble and on canvas, photographers fill albums with glossy memorials and poets pour their hearts onto paper with the inky stain of liquid lamentation. Yet despite what a person might expect, nowhere does the Qur'an record the name of Khadijah. She is not mentioned once. The wives of Pharaoh, Noah and Lot are alluded to, but Khadijah is not even given passing mention. Why? Because she wasn't loved? When Muhammad later had several wives, his then favorite wife, A'ishah, was known to comment that she was never as jealous of any woman as much as she was of Khadijah, for Muhammad remembered her frequently with love and respect, once commenting,

> "She believed in me when no one else did. She embraced Islam when people disbelieved in me. And she helped and comforted me in her person and wealth when there was none else to lend me a helping hand. I had children only from her."[288]

And yet the woman who so filled the life and mind of Muhammad was never mentioned in the Qur'an. For that matter, neither his father (who died before his birth), his mother (who died while Muhammad was a child), his wife Khadijah, nor any of his sons or daughters are mentioned – they are not even hinted at. Many orientalists claim that the Qur'an is from the mind of a man and not

---

288. *Musnad Ahmad.*

(3.C6) The Holy Qur'an / Evidences–4

true revelation. Compounding the peculiarity of this claim is the startling fact that the *only* woman mentioned by name in the Qur'an is Mary, an Israelite and the mother of Jesus – and she is mentioned in glowing terms. As a matter of fact, a whole *surah* bears her name. The Muslim questions if this could be the product of the mind of a man. To propose Muhammad a false prophet, claiming that he could have been so conscious of the women who filled his life and memory, and yet that he excluded them from the revelation he claimed in favor of focusing attention upon an Israelite woman and the mother of an Israelite prophet, drives recklessly against the flow of reasonable expectations.

During the life of Muhammad, he saw every one of his four sons die. All but one of his four daughters predeceased him. His favored uncle, Hamzah, was killed in battle and mutilated in a horrific manner. Muhammad and his followers were regularly insulted, humiliated, beaten, and on occasion murdered. One time Muhammad was stoned to the point that his shoes filled with blood, and another time the offal of a slaughtered camel was dumped on his back while he was praying in prostration – the sheer weight of which pinned him to the ground until his daughter uncovered him. Camels smell bad enough while they are living – a person should try to imagine the smell of their guts decomposing in the tropical sun once they're dead. If the uninitiated can (and they almost certainly cannot), they can also begin to imagine the assault being buried in the tangled mass of their slimy offense, so heavy that a person cannot straighten up, and dripping rivulets of rotting camel juice down exposed arms, cheeks, and behind the ears would have upon the sensitivities. And all that with a refreshing massage-head shower a couple thousand calendar pages away, and soap not yet in the patent office. Such events must have plagued the mind of Muhammad and tortured his memory. Yet they are described nowhere in the Qur'an.

(SECTION 3) BOOKS OF SCRIPTURE

On a more positive note, Muhammad was known to have been very concerned about oral hygiene and breath-odor. He brushed his teeth at least five times a day (before every prayer) and taught his companions to brush the tongue as well (over 1,300 years before the primary source of halitosis came to be recognized as the tongue). This was his passion of cleanliness, and a practice associated with one of the main rituals of any religion – prayer. Mentioned in the Qur'an? Not once.

Muhammad taught that every illness had a cure. Whether true or not, reliable traditions relate that he firmly believed this. Why, then, doesn't a person find the Qur'an filled with home remedies? The only mention of any product of medicinal value is in reference to honey, about which it is stated that therein "…is healing for men" (TMQ 16:69). Nobody disputes this point, most especially the throat lozenge and viral cold and flu medicine companies.

The Qur'an is remarkable in that the content does *not* appear to reflect the thoughts of the messenger. Whereas a person can reasonably expect that the mind of Muhammad was deeply affected by the above-mentioned events and considerations, the Qur'an does not reflect these same concerns. Most anybody who examines the life of Muhammad in parallel with the revelation of the Qur'an is quick to recognize that the Qur'an does not echo the thoughts and actions of Muhammad. In fact, in some cases the Qur'an does the exact opposite, correcting errors in the prophet's judgement.

For example, many of the passages define issues with which Muhammad and his companions were immediately concerned, or delivered lessons regarding contemporaneous events. Such passages are legion. Startling though it may be, just as the Qur'an admonishes the faults of certain of the believers, Muhammad himself is corrected on occasion. In *surah* 80, Allah admonished Muhammad for frowning and turning his back on a blind Muslim who, in seeking guidance, interrupted a conversation to which Muhammad gave priority. The error in judgement was understandable. Muhammad was trying to convey the message of Islam to certain leaders of Quraysh, the dominant tribe of Makkah, during a time when the Muslims were suffering greatly at their oppressive hands. However, the admonition of Allah conveyed the teaching that a simple blind man of low position, but sincere religion, is more worthy of the attention of the prophet (and by extension, all Muslims) than wealthy and powerful disbelievers who could not care less for the message.

On other occasions, Muhammad was admonished in revelation for forbidding himself the use of honey (after being deceived into believing that it gave his breath a bad odor [TMQ 66:1]), for directing his adopted son to keep his marriage when divorce was preferable (TMQ 33:37), and for praying for forgiveness of the Hypocrites (men who were denied the mercy of Allah due to their obstinate rebellion [TMQ 9:80]). The admonishment for his error of judgement with regard to his adopted son, Zaid, and his unhappy marriage to Zainab, was of such extreme embarrassment that Muhammad's wife, A'ishah, later commented to the effect that, "Were Muhammad to have concealed anything from the revelation, he would have concealed this verse"[289] (Referring to verse 33:37 – full discussion of which is deferred to section 4.D.5. of this book).

In one case Muhammad was corrected for being harsh of heart – when he saw his beloved uncle Hamzah slain in battle and horribly mutilated, his emotions were stirred to the point that he promised to do the same to 70 of the best of the enemy. He was corrected in *surah* Nahl, 16:126-128, in which he was commanded to no greater than equal punishment, and patience and restraint. Years later, Makkah was conquered by the Muslims and the woman who commissioned the murder of Hamzah presented herself to Muhammad. She had not

---

289. Narrated by *Al-Bukhari*

only ordered Hamzah killed, but was known to have cut out and chewed the liver of his corpse. Yet Muhammad forgave her. On yet another occasion, Muhammad was corrected for being soft of heart and ransoming a group of captives -- men who were clear and aggressive enemies of God, and who were captured while fighting to kill the Muslims for no other reason than their declaration of faith (TMQ 8:67). So not all situations were the same – some demanded patience and restraint, others strength and harshness. The lesson in the context of this chapter, however, is that Muhammad, albeit rarely, was subject to human errors of judgement.* However, unlike a false prophet who would be expected to have concealed such errors in an attempt at damage control, the Qur'an immortalized the admonition of Muhammad for his mistakes. Muslims point out that, as one would expect of a true messenger of God, the errors of Muhammad demanded correction by The One Whom Muhammad represented, lest they be taken as an example of acceptable conduct.

---

* A point needs to be made in this regard. Orthodox (Sunni) Muslims are sensitive to the fact that because Muhammad is recognized as having suffered the rare error of human judgement, certain 'Muslims' have misinterpreted this fact, and have sought to discredit whichever of his statements and actions are to their personal distaste. Such people take what they want from the *sunnah* of the prophet, and selectively disavow all that which goes against their preference, manufacturing the excuse that perhaps Muhammad's judgement with regard to specific matters was faulty. The essential element of Islamic faith which is compromised by such suggestions is that the Islamic religion teaches that any error of the prophet was corrected within his lifetime, for Allah would not allow the words or actions of His messenger to convey an error. Hence, whereas the rare fault of judgement was consistent with the humanity of the messenger, the prompt correction of those errors is consistent with the perfection of The Creator, and with the perfection of the message He chose to transmit, both in revelation and in the living example of the prophet. Islamically speaking, it is an article of faith to believe that any error committed by the prophet, Muhammad, was corrected within his lifetime, so that nothing improper or incorrect would be transmitted to future generations. To claim otherwise is to assert that Allah left the example set by His final prophet to some degree deficient, which is regarded by Sunni Muslims to be a deviant belief of such a grave nature as to threaten a person's religion.

(3.C6) The Holy Qur'an / Evidences–4

Such admonitions would constitute an extremely peculiar approach to inspiring confidence in the ranks of followers, should a person be a false prophet. On the other hand, should a man be a true prophet, the above examples would serve as timeless reminders of the prophet's humanity, thereby circumventing the apotheosis which has corrupted so many other religions. Was Muhammad a false prophet building a following through the unconventional and peculiar pathway of reporting his own misjudgements, or a true prophet whose errors of judgement necessitated correction, lest they be misperceived as bearing the approval of God?

Here is a man who held up a revelation claiming every letter and punctuation was from God, including the passages which corrected his own actions and instructed him to repent. A person should have great difficulty imagining a false prophet standing up and saying, "Here...this book is from God. As God is infallible, every word is true. So you must believe every word, sentence, and passage. Oh, and by the way, this book says that I, the prophet, am not perfect, that I made these mistakes, that I should repent and seek forgiveness." A very strange scenario, if a person imagines the Qur'an to have been authored by a man. False messiahs are either liars or deluded, and both attempt to build confidence in order to market the polluted products of misaligned minds. The author of the Qur'an, however, fails to fit this profile. If not a man, Who, then, authored the Qur'an?

(3.C) THE HOLY QUR'AN

(3.C7) Evidences – 5: Relation of Revelation to Subsequent Events

"The future? Like unwritten books and unborn children, you don't talk about it."

– Dietrich Fischer-Dieskau,
Daily Telegraph (London, 14 Oct. 1988)

To attempt to predict the future is to risk condemnation by events contrary to those predicted. As Albert Einstein wisely commented, "I never think of the future. It comes soon enough." The ultimate authority on the future can only be The One Whose dominion encompasses providence; the fallible predictions of all others are too easily exposed when the spotlight of truth scans the field of history.

In consideration of the above, books have been written regarding predictions encountered in the Bible. The validity of certain of those predictions comes as no surprise to those who presume much of the Bible to be from God. What *is* problematic, however, is all that which has been added without God's authority, and all that which is the stretch of peculiar imaginations. That which is obviously of human origin is easily exposed. That which is not dog-eared by the

(3.C7) THE HOLY QUR'AN / EVIDENCES–5

weathered hands of human fallibility may be even more dangerous, for divine origin can be claimed for teachings which lack the certainty of higher-than-human heritage. And for much of mankind, coming to know the truth of such cases may occur too late.

The Qur'an contains many predictions as well but Muslims assert that, unlike the Bible, there is not a single prediction made within the Qur'an which is assailable from a historic or scientific point of view. A weak link in Qur'anic prophesies has been sought for nearly 1,400 years by those who desire to disprove the divine origin of the work as a whole. To date this goal has not been achieved, and it is interesting to note that detractors of the Islamic religion mainly focus criticisms upon emotional issues, such as Islamic practices which seem distasteful when passed across the tongue of permissive Western society, rather than upon the evidences which are offered by way of Divine challenge. The fact that evidences such as those discussed herein repulse attempts at criticism provides humanity with relatively solid food for religious thought.

Early in the history of the Qur'an, while the Muslims were still an oppressed minority living in Makkah, a verse was revealed which promised victory (in battle) to the Muslims over the pagans, as follows:

> Are you Unbelievers (O Quraysh) better than they?
> Or do you have an immunity in the Sacred Books?
> Or do they say: "We, acting together, can defend ourselves?
> Soon will their multitude be put to flight, and they will
> show their backs. (TMQ 54:43-45)

The Muslims at that time were few, weak, and regularly beaten and killed by the pagan majority. Five years later, when emigrating to Medina, the Muslims were still so weak that the main tribe of Makkah, the Quraysh, were able to confiscate their land, property and

(SECTION 3) BOOKS OF SCRIPTURE

wealth, detain their wives, and torture and kill those unfortunate few who lacked tribal protection. Not only were the Muslims no force to contend with during that period of time, but they did not have sufficient numbers to anticipate anything but a life of persecution, much less independence and superiority over the overwhelmingly more populous and powerful Quraysh. The honey on the *kanafa* was that the Muslims had not yet even received the commandment to fight oppression and tyranny. Furthermore, amongst a people whose family ties were virtually tight enough to chafe, the concept of waging war on one's own tribe – one's own kin – was simply foreign to the most wildly sociopathic of imaginations. So seemingly out of place was this Qur'anic revelation that Umar Ibn al-Khattab (later to be the second caliph), upon hearing the passage recited, questioned, "Which group will we defeat?"[290] Only later were the Muslims commanded to fight tyranny and oppression, and only later were their numbers sufficient to actually do so. The following verse was subsequently revealed in Makkah, prior to the Muslim emigration to Medina:

> "Allah has promised, to those among you who believe and work righteous deeds, that He will, of a surety, grant them in the land, inheritance (of power), as He granted it to those before them; that He will establish in authority their religion – the one which He has chosen for them; and that He will change (their state), after the fear in which they (lived), to one of security and peace: 'They will worship Me (alone) and not associate anything with Me.' If any do reject Faith after this, they are rebellious and wicked." (TMQ 24:55)

As predicted in *surah* 54, *ayat* 43-45, as quoted above, the unbelieving Quraysh, despite a "multitude" which outnumbered the

---

290. Sa'eid Hawwa. 1990. *Ar-Rasool, Salallahu Alayhi Wa Salam*. Second Edition. Cairo: Dar As-Salaam Publishing. pp. 282-3.

Muslims by more than four to one, were "put to flight" and "show(ed) their backs" at the Battle of Badr.

Subsequently, in fulfillment of *surah* 24, *ayah* 55, the Muslims were decisively victorious when they peacefully retook Makkah in the year 8 AH (*A*fter *H*ijra – the Islamic calendar taking reference from the Prophet's migration from Makkah to Medina in July of the year 622 CE), and the fear and insecurity in which they had lived was replaced by security and peace, due to their establishment in authority both in power and religion.

The peace and security encountered in Makkah is itself a fulfillment of separate revelation, as follows:

> "Have We not established for them a secure sanctuary (Makkah), to which are brought fruits of all kinds, a provision from Ourselves…" (TMQ – Muhammad Al-Hilali and Muhammad Khan translation – 28:57)

And

> "Have they not seen that We have made (Makkah) a secure sanctuary, while men are being snatched away from all around them?" (TMQ – Muhammad Al-Hilali and Muhammad Khan translation – 29:67)

Remarkably, as foretold, Makkah has not only remained a "secure sanctuary" to this day, but despite the barren land and harsh desert climate, the plethora of food and fruit stores stands testimony to the promise of "…fruits of all kinds, a provision from Ourselves…" The mention of fruits and provision in revelation may at first seem peculiar, for to what purpose would such a mention be made? Speculation aside, however, the fact is that such a mention *was* made, and despite the barren land, harsh climate, and geographic isolation, this holy city of Makkah has since enjoyed a most unlikely and ample provision.

(Section 3) Books of Scripture

One more note of significance with regard to the conquest of Makkah: while still in Makkah, the following verse was revealed:

> "When comes the Help of Allah, and Victory, and you see the people enter Allah's Religion in crowds, celebrate the praises of your Lord, and pray for His Forgiveness: for He is Oft-Returning (in Grace and Mercy)." (TMQ 110:1-3)

Of note is the prediction of the people entering "Allah's religion in crowds." Following the conquest of Makkah, the conversion of the majority of the Meccan population was followed by numerous delegates from all over the Arabian peninsula, bearing the pledge of allegiance of entire tribes and communities. Such history of *en-masse* voluntary conversions stands in defiance of religious norms. And yet, it was foretold.

Prior to the conquest of Makkah, however, the Muslims faced many trials and much insecurity, being sandwiched, as they were, between the opposition of the disbelievers and the treachery of the Hypocrites. While in Medina, the Jewish tribe of Bani Nadir proved treacherous to their treaty with the Muslims, and were ordered to leave the city within ten days. Abdullah Ibn Ubayy, the head of the Hypocrites in Medina, pledged support to the Bani Nadir in the form of an army of 2,000 men, and promised to follow the Jews if they left or were expelled. The following days were a tense period for the Muslims, who took solace from their fears in the revelation,

> "Have you not observed the Hypocrites say to their misbelieving brethren among the People of the Book (i.e., the Christians and/or Jews)? – "If you are expelled, we too will go out with you, and we will never hearken to anyone in your affair; and if you are attacked (in fight) we will help you." But Allah is Witness that they are indeed liars. If they are expelled, never will they go out with them; and if they are attacked (in fight), they will never help them..." (TMQ 59:11-12)

Any fears vanished with the expulsion of the Bani Nadir within the timeframe of the ultimatum. True to the Qur'anic prediction, the Hypocrites neither accompanied nor defended them. At a time when the Muslims were still weak and vulnerable, all predictions such as the above could accurately be considered to have been supremely optimistic, if not frankly foolish, had they been from a man.

A prediction which must have seemed similarly rash, given the circumstances, was as follows:

"Say to the desert Arabs who lagged behind: "You shall be summoned (to fight) against a people given to vehement war; then you shall fight, or they shall submit." (TMQ 48:16)

Putting oneself in the circumstance, a person can reasonably question how he or she would have felt as a new convert to the ranks of the Muslims, only to be told the somewhat less than encouraging news that they would be called upon to fight "a people given to vehement war." At a time when normal converts would be struggling to refine and confirm their faith, this harsh prediction must have proved discouraging for many. To imagine revelation of such verses to be from the mind of a man set upon encouraging a following, and not from a Creator Who, by station of being the designer of all fates, need not consider such concerns, necessarily assumes a certain deviation from normal, human methodology on the part of the prophet. However, the prediction *was* made, and served to mentally and psychologically prepare the Muslims for the great trial which arose when Musailimah 'the liar' declared himself a prophet (as discussed in section 4.D.3. below). The ensuing conflict revealed the followers of Musailimah to be "given to vehement war," and in the resulting battle the enemy were either killed or conquered, and forced to submit (i.e., to relinquish their claim of false prophethood). The events in fulfillment of the above prophecy are doubly impressive in that they were realized following the death of Muhammad, and not during his lifetime, when he could have been accused of manipulating events to fulfill the predictions of the revelation he served to transmit.

One of the more interesting predictions of the Holy Qur'an is to be found in *surah* 111. This *surah* states that Abu Lahab (one of the uncles of Muhammad) and his wife would be occupants of the Hellfire. The point is not that this condemnation is verifiable fact, for witness of the final disposition of the couple is obviously lacking. Rather, Muslims point out that the Islamic understanding is that when a person accepts Islam, all his or her previous sins are forgiven. Furthermore, the religion teaches that all Muslims will eventually enter paradise. A Muslim dying with sins for which he or she did not repent falls upon the mercy of Allah – Allah may choose to punish or to forgive, according to His justice, wisdom and mercy. But the Islamic understanding is that even the Muslim with the greatest number of sins will eventually be rescued from the punishment of the fire of Hell and placed in paradise. Why this promise of salvation? Because Muslims believe that although a period in Hell is fair punishment for transgressing the laws of Allah, in the end even the sinful Muslim accepts the one greatest tenet of faith – the first and final commandment without which all other works are dead – even the sinful Muslim accepts belief in Allah, as Allah himself prescribes. And it is the judgement of The Creator that all those who submit themselves to His will are deserving of paradise, even if unable to refrain from transgressing His laws. Come the Day of Judgement, Allah, being fair and just, rewards the faithful with a lasting bliss in proportion to their piety and good deeds. The transgressors from amongst the believers may receive punishment commensurate with their evil deeds, though they do not deserve eternal damnation for reason of their faith. That is what Muslims believe, and it is a cornerstone of their faith with regard to the afterlife.

How does this pertain to the above-mentioned verses? Simple.

(3.C7) The Holy Qur'an / Evidences–5

Abu Lahab was one of the greatest antagonists of Muhammad. He hated the man, and wished death upon him. So much did Abu Lahab hate Muhammad that his animosity drove him to contradict virtually everything Muhammad said with regard to revelation. He used to follow the prophet for no other reason than to contradict his teachings. So a person can fairly wonder why it is that when a *surah* was revealed that implied that Abu Lahab would never repent, he didn't just stand up and say, "I repent." After all, that was his nature – whatever Muhammad said, he would contradict. Whether in sincerity or hypocrisy, loudly and publicly or in quiet semi-privacy, all he had to do was to come forth, say the *shahada* (testimony of faith), and pretend to become Muslim. Had he done so, Abu Lahab would have created a conflict sufficient to destroy the religion. In other words, either *surah* 111 of the Qur'an would have had to have been wrong, or the teaching that all Muslims would eventually be forgiven and blessed with paradise would have been contradicted by his conversion. In either case, the teachings of the Islamic religion would have been invalidated by the inconsistency.

Surah 111 was revealed in 3-4 BH (Before Hijra), and Abu Lahab died shortly following the Battle of Badr, in 2 AH.[291] His wife died roughly 6 years later, before the opening of Makkah.[292] So Abu Lahab and his wife had over five and ten years, respectively, to figure it out. No doubt there were Muslims who pressed them on the issue, repeating the *surah* in their faces or pointing out, "You know, we have been told through revelation that you will never repent, and never convert." All either one of them had to say was, "Well, I repent. As a matter of fact, I convert. What does your book say now?" So why didn't either Abu Lahab or his wife do it? Because ten years is not enough time to

---

291. Hammad, Ahmad Zaki. 1997. *Father of Flame, Commentary & Vocabulary Reference of Surat al-Masad.* Bridgeview, Illinois: Quranic Literacy Institute. p. 42.
292. Hammad, Ahmad Zaki. p. 42.

(SECTION 3) BOOKS OF SCRIPTURE

think it over? Because their polytheist friends didn't try to goad them into it? Because these vile antagonists had a code of ethics which permitted indecency, lying, and physical abuse of the believers, but not deception or hypocrisy as to faith and repentance?

What held the two of them back? Muslims maintain that only one thing held them back – they didn't have permission. The One who makes the rules of this life, The One who has lent mankind minds and bodies and Who will eventually demand their return, The One who can open or close the mouths of man, reverse thoughts, seal hearts (or open them wide), grant strength against adversity or paralyze to inaction in the face of insignificant dangers, this One can make the boldest of claims, the most assured of predictions. Why? Because He not only knows the future; He *determines* the future. And if He chooses to decree that such-and-such words will not be allowed to pass the lips of so-and-so, well, that's all there is to it. The Muslim claim is that no human can make promises such as that found in *surah* 111. That promise can only be made by The One who has the Divine confidence to know that He will not allow His book to be contradicted.

The above example is doubly impressive, not only because of the boldness of the claim, but also due to the fact that the example is repeated – *surah* 74:11-26 similarly condemns Al-Walid Ibn Al-Mughirah Al-Makhzumi.[293] Al-Walid was an early antagonist, who found himself hard-put to find an explanation of the revelation claimed by Muhammad. Heading up a convention of antagonists, Al-Walid attempted to harmonize the claims of the detractors of Islam, so as to present a united front with regard to their criticism of the revelation. The story of the conflict between his inner, private

---

293. Al-Hilali, Muhammad, Ph.D. and Dr. Muhammad Muhsin Khan, M.D. *Interpretation of the Meanings of The Noble Qur'an in the English Language; A Summarized Version of At-Tabari, Al-Qurtubi and Ibn Kathir with comments from Sahih Al-Bukhari. Surah* 74, *Ayah* 11.

(3.C7) The Holy Qur'an / Evidences–5

realization and outer, public profession beautifully exemplifies the derailing of logic which defines the duality of man, when caught in a conflict between opposing factions of prideful emotions and rational thought, as follows:

> Al-Walid heard Muhammad reciting the Qur'an and seemed to be affected by it. He stated that the recitation was not poetry, not magic, and not craziness, but could only be the speech of Allah. When Abu Jahl heard of this he went to Al-Walid and accused him of trying to get close to the prophet, and said that Quraysh was talking about the rumor. Al-Walid, succumbing to pride, became upset and responded, "Quraysh knows that I am the richest of them and do not need anything from Muhammad." Abu Jahl said, "Then you should let your position be known. Tell them what you think of Muhammad." Al-Walid responded by saying, "What should I say of him? By Allah there is none amongst you more knowledgeable of Arabic poetry and its scales than me, nor of the poetry of the Jinn. What he (Muhammad) says does not resemble any of that. By Allah, it is a beautiful speech and it crushes that which is below it and it surpasses that which is above it." Abu Jahl stated, "People will not be pleased with this. You must think of something to say." Al-Walid offered, "Leave me to think." When he returned to commune with the leaders of Quraysh over what they should say about Muhammad, some said Muhammad was a magician, others said a sorcerer, others said he was crazy. Al-Walid stated, "All of these things that you are saying I know are untrue, but the closest of these sayings is that he is a magician, because magic breaks apart a son from his father, a person from his brother, a husband from his wife, or a person from his

tribe."²⁹⁴ (As an aside, such also is the effect of revelation, for as Christ Jesus is recorded as having taught, "Do you suppose that I came to give peace on earth? I tell you, not at all, but rather division. For from now on five in one house will be divided: three against two, and two against three. Father will be divided against son and son against father, mother against daughter and daughter against mother, mother-in-law against her daughter-in-law and daughter-in-law against her mother-in-law." [Luke 12:51-53])

Shortly thereafter the following verses were revealed:

"Leave Me alone, (to deal) with the (creature) whom I created (bare and) alone!
To whom I granted resources in abundance,
And sons to be by his side!
To whom I made (life) smooth and comfortable!
Yet is he greedy – that I should add (yet more)
By no means! For to Our Signs he has been refractory!
Soon will I visit him with a mount of calamities!
For he thought and he plotted;
And woe to him! How he plotted!
Yes, woe to him: how he plotted!
Then he looked round;
Then he frowned and he scowled;
Then he turned back and was haughty;
Then he said: "This is nothing but magic, derived from of old;
This is nothing but the word of a mortal!"
Soon will I cast him into Hell-Fire!"
(TMQ 74:11-26)

These verses were revealed amongst the earliest of revelations, roughly 10 years before the death of the subject of these verses (Al-

---

294. *Tafseer Ibn Kathir*

Walid Ibn Al-Mughirah Al-Makhzumi), in the first year A.H.[295] So once again, the same obstacle to the boldness of the Qur'anic prediction presents itself for examination. How could the author of these verses have known the unseen future well enough to predict that Al-Walid would never break down and say the right words? For that matter, how could the author have known that Al-Walid would not state the Islamic testimony of faith hypocritically, for the sole purpose of nullifying the teachings of Islam? And would a mortal man, if a charlatan, have risked his entire claim to prophethood on such an easily refuted prediction?

An added point of interest is that the above example was one of a convention of men who hated and opposed Muhammad and his teachings. These were men who, in many cases, stooped to the lowest of tactics and the most vile of deeds in attempting to undermine the growth of Islam. Yet, although they would not refrain from lying about Muhammad when they could get away with it, they were reticent to propagate lies which, by nature of being too obvious, would have invited condemnation by their people. For the community of the Meccan Arabs were a people who, whether in favor of or opposed to the message of Islam, knew the character of Muhammad and would have readily rejected obvious slanders upon his person. Unlike those who slander Muhammad in the present day, all the while knowing little or nothing about him, those who knew him best, those who lived with him, walked with him, talked with him, dealt with him, managed affairs with him and, in short, knew the man through intimate and life-long relations, refused to call him a liar, a poet, a soothsayer, an epileptic, or even to claim the excuse that he was just an exceptionally intelligent man.

Surah Ar-Rum (The Romans – *surah* 30) similarly presents an interesting *entrée* on the banquet of 'food for thought.' Verses 2-4

---

295. Ibn Hisham, *As-Seerah An-Nabiwwiyyah,* and Azzirikly, *Al-Aa'lam.*

(SECTION 3) BOOKS OF SCRIPTURE

were revealed at the time of a victory (in battle) of Persia over Rome, *prior* to news of the battle reaching Makkah by normal channels (i.e., travelers, caravans, etc.). Furthermore, a reversal of fortunes, with Rome visiting victory over Persia within 3 to 9 years, was predicted in the same verses. As history records such events, Persia celebrated victory over Rome at Antioch in 613 CE, and the Byzantines were subsequently defeated in Damascus, driven out of Armenia, and overrun in their cherished city of Jerusalem.[296] Chalcedon was taken by the Persians in 617 CE, and Egypt conquered in 619.[297, 298] The situation was beginning to look pretty bleak for the Roman empire, right up to the time Heraclius launched his historic campaign of 622-627 CE. Decisively pounding the Persian forces, led by the famous general Shahr-Baraz, on Armenian soil in the year 622 CE, the Romans defeated a major Persian force for the first time in three years since losing Egypt, nine years since the defeat at Antioch, and bracketing the remainder of the above-mentioned list of defeats within the time period of three to nine years.[299, 300] *Surah* 30:2-4 reads:

"The Romans have been defeated.
In the nearest land (Syria, Iraq, Jordan, and Palestine),
and they, after their defeat, will be victorious.
Within three to nine years. The decision of the matter,
before and after (these events) is only with Allah.
And on that Day, the believers (i.e. Muslims) will rejoice."
(TMQ – Muhammad Al-Hilali and Muhammad Khan translation – 30:2-4)

---

296. Ostrogorsky, George. 1969. *History of the Byzantine State.* (Translated from the German by Joan Hussey). New Brunswick: Rutgers University Press. p. 95.
297. Sykes, Sir Percy Molesworth. 1951. *A History of Persia.* 3rd edition. Vol 1. London: Macmillan & Co., Ltd. p. 483.
298. Ostrogorsky, George. p. 95.
299. Ostrogorsky, George. pp. 100-101.
300. Sykes, Sir Percy Molesworth. Vol 1. pp. 483-484.

(3.C7) THE HOLY QUR'AN / EVIDENCES–5

The history is remarkable, for the reason that by the time of Muhammad, Rome was an empire in decay. The period of 395-476 CE is described in scholastic works as the fall of the Western Empire. Alaric, chief of the Visigoths, led the army which sacked Rome in August, 410 CE. Gaiseric, king of the Vandals and the Alani, sacked Rome in the summer of 455 CE. Attila the Hun overran the area in the mid-400's, and the last emperor of the intact and undivided Roman empire was deposed in the late 5th century. So a prediction which surfaced nearly two centuries later, stating that the already disintegrating Roman empire would gain a victory over the huge and seemingly superior Persian army, would have seemed rash on a human level. And so it appears to have been judged by those who denied the revelation – men such as Ubay Ibn Khalf.

The story is narrated in many historical accounts of Arabian history. The Arabs did not perceive the conflict to be limited to one of Persia versus Rome, but rather a contest between paganism and people of a scripture. The pagan Arabs conceived the fire-worshiping Persians to be brothers in paganism whereas the Muslims viewed the Romans to be people of a scripture. Hence the interest in one side prevailing, reflecting the superiority of the god of the winner. When the Persians were victorious over Rome, the pagan Arabs celebrated. Following this, the above *ayat* (verses) were revealed, strengthening the hearts of the believers. When Abu Bakr As-Siddiq (the closest companion and the future first Caliph following the prophet's demise) learned the revelation, he interrupted the pagans from their celebration and told them that they should not be so happy, because the victory was destined to be overturned with the help of Allah. Upon hearing this, Ubay Ibn Khalf called Abu Bakr a liar, prompting Abu Bakr to return the charge by saying, "You are the liar, O enemy of Allah." Ubay then challenged Abu Bakr by betting 10 camels that Rome would not be victorious in 3 years. When Abu Bakr informed

(SECTION 3) BOOKS OF SCRIPTURE

Muhammad of the wager (which was made before the prohibition of gambling was revealed), Muhammad reminded him that the Arabic word '*Bid'i*' in the revealed verses means between three and nine years, and so the time period should be extended to that foretold in the revelation. When Abu Bakr returned to Ubay, Ubay asked if Abu Bakr regretted the wager, to which Abu Bakr responded in the negative, following which he stated that he wanted to increase the wager to 100 camels and the time to 9 years. Ubay agreed. 9 years later Abu Bakr gained a herd of camels, and the encyclopedia of Islamic evidences gained yet one more entry.[301]

An odd prediction in completion of the above prophecy is the final line, "And on that Day, the believers (i.e., Muslims) will rejoice." In the absence of microwave and satellite relays, radios, CNN, etc., news of such events took days to weeks, sometimes even months (if weather forbade travel) to achieve transmission. How, then, could the prediction that the Muslims would be rejoicing on the very day the Persians were defeated be made with such confidence? Yet, such was precisely the case, for the predicted defeat of the Persians occurred on the exact same day that the Muslims celebrated their own victory over the disbelievers at the Battle of Badr. Worldly coincidence or divine plan?

Mention of *surah* 15, *ayah* number 9 has already been alluded to above. This verse presents the promise of Allah to be: "We have, without doubt, sent down the Message; and We will assuredly guard it (from corruption)." (TMQ 15:9) The statement is remarkable on several levels. The first is simply that the promise, to date, has been fulfilled – the Holy Qur'an of this day is unchanged from the original revelation, as discussed above. The extent of this miracle is apparent when comparison is made with all other world religions, for Islam is not the only religion which cherishes its revealed message. However,

---

301. *Tafseer Ibn Kathir, Musnad Ahmad, Sunan Tirmithee and An-Nisa'ee*

(3.C7) THE HOLY QUR'AN / EVIDENCES–5

no matter how many billions of followers, and no matter the level of their devotion and love of The Creator, and no matter the magnitude of their reverence of the revealed message, neither Judaism nor Christianity can produce the original and unadulterated revelation as revealed to the prophets Moses and Jesus.

The second level of interest is simply that the above statement would have been both foolish and unnecessary had Muhammad been an imposter. He could have gained nothing, in his lifetime, from such a statement; certainly he would have lost everything had a single letter of revelation been misplaced or forgotten – and there were over 300,000 letters at stake.

Examination of world history casts an interesting light on *surah* 5, *ayah* 82, the translation of the meaning of which reads,

> "Strongest among men in enmity to the Believers will you find the Jews and Pagans; and nearest among them in love to the Believers will you find those who say, 'We are *Nasara*'*: because amongst these are men devoted to learning and men who have renounced the world, and they are not arrogant."

Taken in the context of the life of Muhammad, the above is a strikingly bizarre comment, not just because 1,400 years of history have testified to the truth of the statement, but because the life of Muhammad was punctuated by several cooperative treaties with different Jewish tribes. Consequently, the above *ayah* is just one of many which left room to be disproved within the lifetime of Muhammad. However, such was not to be the case. Despite reasonable expectation for the Jews to have sided with the increasingly powerful Muslims, treachery and violation of treaty statutes became the rule rather than the exception. The fact that the Jews (as a nation) have not, at any

---

* i.e., Nazarenes – see discussion in section 4 regarding the selective Qur'anic description of the followers of Jesus as Nazarenes rather than as Christians.

(Section 3) Books of Scripture

point in history, maintained a benevolent posture to the Muslims affirms the 1,400 year-old assertion. Current events in Palestine serve to do nothing but underline the truth of the statement.

A wonder it is, then, that Muhammad released his bodyguards from duty. Living amongst so much hatred from the pagan Quraysh, Jewish clans, and disbelievers in general, and in a time and place where most who knew him wished death upon him, Muhammad survived multiple attempts upon his life. Muhammad was severely beaten by his people, choked with his own mantle, stoned until blood filled his shoes, an attempt was made to drop a boulder upon him while he sat in conversation with a Jewish tribe, his food was poisoned (so effectively that his dining companion died from a single mouthful), different people at different times took up swords to kill him, and not just in battle. Umar, one of the most feared men of the Quraysh, set out one day with the declared intention to kill the prophet, but ended up diverted to the house of his sister, challenged by a passage of Qur'an, and converting to Islam before fulfilling his evil intention. Twice Bedouins pulled Muhammad's own sword [once while he was sleeping in the desert and once while sitting at a well] with the intention of killing him in a defenseless state. Both times the men dropped the sword, finding themselves physically unable to hold it. On the evening of emigrating to Medina, virtually every tribe in Makkah sent a representative to kill Muhammad in a unified effort to share the deed while escaping the blame. The list goes on. And so, not unreasonably, hadith traditions record Muhammad as having utilized guards (including Saad Ibn Malik, Ali Ibn Abu Talib, and Al-Abass) while he slept. Yet when the following verse was revealed, things changed:

> "O Messenger! Proclaim the (Message) which has been sent to you from your Lord. If you did not, you would not have

(3.C7) THE HOLY QUR'AN / EVIDENCES—5

fulfilled and proclaimed His Mission. And Allah will defend you from men (who mean mischief). For Allah guides not those who reject faith." (TMQ 5:67)

Muhammad understood the above verse to be a promise of divine protection from the hand of man, and immediately announced to those who were guarding his tent and person, "Oh people, leave me for Allah the most High has protected me."[302]

And so it happened. Following the discharge of the guard, attempts upon the life of Muhammad continued, but were always frustrated, and in the end Muhammad's soul departed within the walls of his own home, his head cradled in the arms of his favorite wife, A'ishah, after suffering a brief but fatal illness. Point of the story? In a time and place where a person might reasonably feel the whole world was out to get him, Muhammad discharged his bodyguards on the promise of revelation, and that promise was fulfilled.

The bizarreness of the scenario is inescapable. False prophets are rightfully paranoid. As attempts upon their lives increase in number and narrowness of escape, they raise their guard. To release the guard in a time of war and with a past history of serial assassination attempts defies worldly reason. If the Qur'an came from the mind of a false prophet, the exact opposite would have been expected, to the tune of exhorting the believers to protect their prophet from the evil of those who seek to kill him. But it didn't happen that way, once again challenging a person to consider the source of the Qur'an, if not from the mind of a man. Who, exactly, has the power to fulfill such bold promises of lifelong protection, if not a man?

The final entry of this chapter involves the Old Testament story which is known to all. Pharaoh was a tyrant who oppressed a nation, killed upon whim, and slaughtered the children of the Jews out of fear

---

302. Narrated by *At-Tirmithi* and *Al-Haakim*

of the multitude of their race. As everyone knows, while Pharaoh's soldiers were rationing out infanticide in the village, Moses washed up in a gift-basket on the riverbank of Pharaoh's palatial estate. So while the big stones were being hoisted off the mangled corpses of the squashed serfs and stacked into pointy piles according to royal decree, the child grew up to set a historical record with regard to surrogate-filial ingratitude, if such is to be measured in terms of disobedience and defiance. On the other hand, Moses also stunned the world with his God-fear and loyalty, showing devotion where it was truly due.

A couple heated court conversations, a few ignored divine signs, some several periods of pestilence and misery, and Moses took his people on a divinely-ordained nature walk, the end of which is well known. The point is that no matter how the story is told, everybody knows the beginning, the middle, and especially the end – Pharaoh's Olympic-class dog paddle didn't stand up to the boiling torrent of two walls of water clapping its unforgiving hands over his mis-commanding mouth.

The story is so well known, in fact, that it is difficult to imagine that it missed Muhammad's ears. However, the common impression of this history, to this day, is that Pharaoh was buried beneath a couple million tons of seawater, where he eventually became bacteriologically bloated fish bait. It is not a common conception that the body of Pharaoh was preserved. And yet the Qur'an records a promise of Allah to Pharaoh at the time of his death, which reads:

> "This day shall we save you in your body, that you may be a sign to those who come after you! But verily, many among mankind are heedless of Our signs!" (TMQ 10:92)

Only in 1898 CE was the mummified body of Merneptah, successor to Rameses II and the most likely candidate to the title of 'Pharaoh of the Exodus,' according to Biblical history and archae-

(3.C7) The Holy Qur'an / Evidences–5

ological evidence, discovered at Thebes in the King's Valley.[303] The body is on display, along with various other royal mummies (including monkeys, cats, dogs, crocodiles, and even fish), in the Cairo Museum. Hence, over 1,200 years following the life of Muhammad, the Qur'anic promise of the body of Pharaoh being preserved as a sign to future generations appears to be satisfied. But over 1,200 years ago, how could Muhammad have foretold such a find, and why would he have gone out on the thin limb of speculation over such a detail? Unless, that is, the words were not his own.

---

303. Bucaille, Maurice. p. 239.

(3.C) THE HOLY QUR'AN

(3.C8) Evidences – 6: Revelation of the Unknown
(i.e., that which was beyond the experience of the Prophet)

"No one ever approaches perfection
except by stealth, and unknown to themselves."
– William Hazlitt, *Sketches and Essays,* "On Taste"

Perhaps a better title to this chapter would be that of 'Scientific Evidences.' Such a title, however, may strike the Western audience as overly bizarre, for the realms of scientific knowledge and religious thought are well recognized to have been antagonistic entities in the historical archives of Western civilization. The examples of Giordano Bruno (convicted of heresy and burned at the stake in the year 1600 CE) and Galileo (who escaped similar punishment in 1633 only through issuing a retraction) are oft-cited. Both were persecuted on the grounds of supporting the 'heretical,' but correct, Copernican theory of heliocentrism (i.e. the theory of the sun being the center of the planetary group now known as the solar system) in rejection of the officially sanctioned, though incorrect, Ptolemaic theory of

(3.C8) The Holy Qur'an / Evidences–6

geocentrism (i.e. planet Earth being the center). And hence the perception, in the West, that the entities of accurate scientific analysis and religious thought constitute incompatible apartment-mates. In fact, in view of the many Church policies which ran contrary to what are now known to be evident truths, a more odd couple is difficult to imagine. The voices of those who dared to oppose such Church policies, lost in the vapors of the fires which consumed the cords of their origin, or silenced of their gargled pleas in the waters in which the accused were tortured and drowned, would be expected to have agreed.

The horrors perpetuated by a rigid, intolerant, and oppressive Church over views contrary to those which bore official sanction, even when such 'deviant' views were correct, won sufficient societal condemnation in the recent past to eventually force a separation of Church and State. The process was bloody, as usual, and incalculable suffering occurred in the process. The end result has left the present generation with a tradition, now over two hundred years old, in which religion and science remain shy to dabble in one another's affairs. For many, no other system can be imagined.

On the other hand, separation of Church and State has no place in Islam. The Islamic revelation has long been recognized to be exhaustively comprehensive, entering and influencing all areas of human life. Protagonists argue that a revelation which defines the will of The Creator in all spheres of human existence is consistent with what should be expected of a final guidance to mankind. Antagonists often criticize such comprehensive guidance on the basis of holding preference for the *'laissez-faire'* lifestyle offered by the more permissive religions which took origin either entirely from human construction or from scriptural manipulation.

The Islamic revelation defines not only the tenets of faith and articles of worship enveloped in the oft-isolated bubble known as

(SECTION 3) BOOKS OF SCRIPTURE

'religion,' but the will of The Creator is also expressed with regard to politics, personal conduct, family and social structure, economic principles, civil and criminal law, and many other practicalities of human existence. Science and the study of the reality of man, his environment, and nature as a whole are nurtured by a revelation which encourages expansion of knowledge, while condemning close-mindedness. Multiple passages of the Holy Qur'an reference signs for those who reflect or for men and women of knowledge. The question is issued over and over again, both implicitly and explicitly, "Do they not think?" or "Do they not see?" Customs and traditions are criticized when lacking foundation upon knowledge, and the strongest of terms are used to condemn those who choose a path in conflict with God-given rational thought, an example of which is the directive to teach that amongst the things the Lord and Creator has forbidden are, "...sins and trespasses against truth or reason..." (TMQ 7:33)

The Muslim world witnessed an explosion of intellectual advances following the time of Muhammad, in no small part due to a revelation which made knowledge, of those sciences necessary for the fulfillment of tenets of Islamic faith, incumbent upon the Muslims. A religion which enjoins prayer within set times of the day and fasting in a particular month of the year can be expected to have stimulated advances in timekeeping and calendar computation. Similarly, a religion which requires payment of varying percentages of wealth according to category (e.g. agricultural products versus gold) as a poor-due can be expected to have led to advancements in methods of estimation and calculation (i.e., weights & measures, and mathematics). The institution of Arabic numerals along with the mathematically revolutionary number '0,' the development of algebra into a science, algorithms, and the development of the balance can all be traced to Muslims. Modern Western adoption of Arabic numerals can be

(3.C8) The Holy Qur'an / Evidences–6

traced to their assumption into European mathematics in the 12th century. The Arabic system replaced the troublesome and 'zero-less' Roman numerals and the laborious system of writing numbers longhand.

The Islamic religion forbade representational art, so many artists of the Islamic world channeled their skills to the geometrically-based Arabesque arts of masonry, inlay, weaving, and carpentry. Whether cause or effect, the fields of geometry and trigonometry gained significant contributions from Muslims. Sine and cosine tables were constructed, cubic equations defined, the roots of quadratic equations determined, spherical, analytical and plane trigonometry expanded, and geometry advanced.

Muslims were bidden to spread the word of revelation, and so a new breed of travelers and merchants was born. Furthermore, the command to direct prayer toward the *Kaba* (the house built by Abraham) in Makkah gave rise to the need for accurate directional determination. Consequently, a need for improvements in navigation and map-making arose. Such advancements as the use of the magnetic compass, calculation of latitude and longitudes, construction of star maps, and Astrolabes came into play. Observatories were constructed and astronomy developed as a science. Geographic maps were produced which remained unrivaled for centuries.

With an emphasis laid upon learning and transmission of knowledge, literacy and paper became critical commodities. The Kufic letters, the foundation of the modern alphabet, were invented on the banks of the Euphrates. First invented by the Chinese, who used the cocoon of the silk-worm, Muslims adopted and further refined the manufacture of paper using cotton, wood and rags in addition to silk. The process was sophisticated and demanded the development of several chemical processes.

Similar advancements were made in fields of Mechanical, Optical

(SECTION 3) BOOKS OF SCRIPTURE

and Theoretical Physics, Organic and Inorganic Chemistry, Medicine, Geography, Botany and Agriculture, and various other disciplines. Technological improvements included such instruments as the axle, lever, pulley, windmill, waterwheel and toothed wheel, and such processes as calcination (method of extracting metals from ore), reduction, distillation, and crystallization. Theories such as those of gravity and the elasticity of air were advanced. Hospitals were built, and great advancements were made in the field of medicine, including the development of new medicines and surgical techniques, one prominent example of which has now come to be relabeled the 'Cesarean' operation for childbirth.

The magnitude and significance of such advancements are best known to scholars in the respective fields, but the short and easily readable treatise entitled *Islam and Science** is a good starting point for many who wish to research further.

Lest the reader misunderstand, no attempt is made herein to carry such history over into an attempt to validate the Holy Qur'an based upon such 'fruits' of revelation. Rather, the simple observation is offered that a separation between Church and State was never an element of the Islamic religion. The observation is also offered, to those who conceive Muslims to be a backward people, that Muslims were, at least during the pre-Renaissance period, at the technological forefront of civilization. As Victor Robinson noted in his book *The Story of Medicine,*

> "Europe was darkened at sunset, Cordova shone with public lamps; Europe was dirty, Cordova built a thousand baths; Europe was covered with vermin, Cordova changed its undergarments daily; Europe lay in mud, Cordova's streets

---

* Authored by Shabir Ahmed, Anas Abdul Muntaqim, and Abdul-Sattar Siddiq, and published by the Islamic Cultural Workshop, P.O. Box 1932, Walnut, CA 91789; (909) 399-4708.

(3.C8) The Holy Qur'an / Evidences-6

were paved; Europe's palaces had smoke-holes in the ceiling, Cordova's arabesques were exquisite; Europe's nobility could not sign its name, Cordova's children went to school; Europe's monks could not read the baptismal service, Cordova's teachers created a library of Alexandrian dimensions."[304]

Other supportive comments include the following:

"The Arabs, in their turn, knew how to consolidate their rule. They were no bloodthirsty savages, bent solely on loot and destruction. On the contrary, they were an innately gifted race, eager to learn and appreciative of the cultural gifts which older civilizations had to bestow. Intermarrying freely and professing a common belief, conquerors and conquered rapidly fused, and from this fusion arose a new civilization—the Saracenic civilization, in which the ancient cultures of Greece, Rome, and Persia were revitalized by Arab vigour and synthesized by the Arab genius and the Islamic spirit. For the first three centuries of its existence (circ. A.D. 650-1000) the realm of Islam was the most civilized and progressive portion of the world. Studded with splendid cities, gracious mosques, and quiet universities where the wisdom of the ancient world was preserved and appreciated, the Moslem world offered a striking contrast to the Christian West, then sunk in the night of the Dark Ages."[305]

"From a new angle and with a fresh vigour it (the Arab mind) took up that systematic development of positive knowledge which the Greeks had begun and relinquished. If the Greek

---

304. Robinson, Victor, M.D. 1943. *The Story of Medicine*. New York: The New Home Library. p. 164.
305. Stoddard, Lothrop, Ph.D. 1922. *The New World of Islam*. Second Impression. London: Chapman and Hall, Ltd. p. 3.

(SECTION 3) BOOKS OF SCRIPTURE

was the father, then the Arab was the foster-father of the scientific method of dealing with reality, that is to say, by absolute frankness, the utmost simplicity of statement and explanation, exact record and exhaustive criticism. Through the Arabs it was and not by the Latin route that the modern world received that gift of light and power....And a century or so in advance of the west, there grew up in the Moslem world at a number of centers, at Basra, at Kufa, at Bagdad and Cairo, and at Cordoba, out of what were at first religious schools dependent upon mosques, a series of great universities. The light of these universities shone far beyond the Moslem world, and drew students to them from east and west. At Cordoba in particular there were great numbers of Christian students, and the influence of Arab philosophy coming by way of Spain upon the universities of Paris, Oxford, and North Italy and upon Western European thought generally, was very considerable indeed."[306]

"Many Westerners, accustomed by their history books to believe that Muslims were barbarous infidels, find it difficult to comprehend how profoundly our intellectual life has been influenced by Muslim scholars in the field of science, medicine, mathematics, geography and philosophy. Crusaders who invaded the Holy Land to fight Muslims returned to Europe with new ideas of love, poetry, chivalry, warfare and government. Our concept of what a university should be was deeply modified by Muslim scholars, who perfected the writing of history and who brought to Europe much Greek learning."[307]

And,

---

306. Wells, H. G. Volume 2, pp. 708-710.
307. Michener, James A. p. 74.

(3.C8) The Holy Qur'an / Evidences–6

"We must not be surprised to find the Qoran regarded as the fountain-head of the sciences. Every subject connected with heaven or earth, human life, commerce and various trades are occasionally touched upon, and this gave rise to the production of numerous monographs forming commentaries on parts of the holy book. In this way the Qoran was responsible for great discussions, and to it was indirectly due the marvelous development of all branches of science in the Muslim world."[308]

The list of endorsements is long, and downregulates the mental taste buds by sheer monotony of positive opinion. All the same, one last quote is perhaps worthy, for the great historian, H. G. Wells, so valued the truth of the passage as to have quoted from *A General History of Europe*, by Thatcher and Schwill, as follows:

"The origin of the so-called Arabic numerals is obscure. Under Theodoric the Great, Boethius made use of certain signs which were in part very like the nine digits which we now use. One of the pupils of Gerbert also used signs which were still more like ours, but the zero was unknown till the twelfth century, when it was invented by an Arab mathematician named Muhammad-Ibn-Musa, who also was the first to use the decimal notation, and who gave the digits the value of position. In geometry the Arabs did not add much to Euclid, but algebra is practically their creation; also they developed spherical trigonometry, inventing the sine, tangent, and cotangent. In physics they invented the pendulum, and produced work on optics. They made progress in the science of astronomy. They built several observatories, and constructed many astronomical instruments which are still in use. They calculated the angle of the ecliptic and the precession of the

---

308. Hirschfeld, Hartwig. p. 9.

(SECTION 3) BOOKS OF SCRIPTURE

equinoxes. Their knowledge of astronomy was undoubtedly considerable.

In medicine they made great advances over the work of the Greeks. They studied physiology and hygiene, and their *materia medica* was practically the same as ours to-day. Many of their methods of treatment are still in use among us. Their surgeons understood the use of anaesthetics, and performed some of the most difficult operations known. At the time when in Europe the practice of medicine was forbidden by the Church, which expected cures to be effected by religious rites performed by the clergy, the Arabs had a real science of medicine. In chemistry they made a good beginning. They discovered many new substances, such as alcohol, potash, nitrate of silver, corrosive sublimate, and nitric and sulphuric acid....In manufactures they out-did the world in variety and beauty of design and perfection of workmanship. They worked in all the metals—gold, silver, copper, bronze, iron, and steel. In textile fabrics they have never been surpassed. They made glass and pottery of the finest quality. They knew the secrets of dyeing, and they manufactured paper. They had many processes of dressing leather, and their work was famous throughout Europe. They made tinctures, essences, and syrups. They made sugar from cane, and grew many fine kinds of wine.* They practiced farming in a

---

* The authors (Thatcher and Schwill, as quoted by H. G. Wells) must be excused from any charge of inaccuracy on this point. The fact of the matter is that from the time of revelation to the present, there have always been Muslims who willfully persisted upon the forbidden. Most acted as individuals, but deviant practices grew to engulf entire societies far more often than most Muslims would like to admit. The common example of Muslim owners/operators of liquor-based businesses such as convenience stores, restaurants, and off-licenses illustrates that the hypocritical practice persists to the present day – openly in non-Muslim lands, underground in those few countries where Islamic law is enforced.

scientific way, and had good systems of irrigation. They knew the value of fertilizers, and adapted their crops to the quality of the ground. They excelled in horticulture, knowing how to graft and how to produce new varieties of fruit and flowers. They introduced into the west many trees and plants from the east, and wrote scientific treatises on farming."

One item in this account must be underlined here because of its importance in the intellectual life of mankind, the manufacture of paper. This the Arabs seem to have learnt from the Chinese by way of Central Asia. The Europeans acquired it from the Arabs. Until that time books had to be written upon parchment or papyrus, and after the Arab conquest of Egypt Europe was cut off from the papyrus supply. Until paper became abundant, the art of printing was of little use, and newspapers and popular education by means of books was impossible. This was probably a much more important factor in the relative backwardness of Europe during the dark ages than historians seem disposed to admit...[309]

Having presented the above as a foundation to the history of sciences in Islam, the subject of this chapter deserves to be addressed. The evidences which Muslims are fond of citing in support of the divine origin of the Holy Qur'an involve the many passages which comment on the nature of man and the universe in which he lives. Many such verses survived as unsubstantiated mysteries for nearly 1,400 years, only to achieve verification in light of modern knowledge.

The Holy Qur'an contains such a wealth of intriguing comments on man and nature that books have been written on the subject. Most oft-cited, in the English language, is Dr. Maurice Bucaille's

---

309. Wells, H. G. Volume 2, pp. 710-712.

comparative work, *The Bible, The Qur'an and Science*.* Many more readable books have surfaced on the shelves of Islamic bookstores, and most recently discussion of such evidences has made its way to the Internet.

When presented with such scientific evidences, many whose uncompromising doctrinal ties batten the mental hatches against the intrusion of objective discussion, turn to face the perceived enemy with claims of divine predictions within their own books of guidance. Two factors must then be taken into consideration. The first is to question whether such claims are true; the second is to consider the consequences of being forced to answer the stunningly simple question, 'So what?'

For example, should the Bible be considered to be filled with scientific evidences of Divine origin, one wonders why God is described as having bestowed light upon His creation three days before creating the stars (compare Genesis 1:3-5 with Genesis 1:14-19). Possibilities within the realm of Divine decree are beyond human imagination, but a basic scientific premise with regard to the nature of light is that before light can exist, a source of photon emission must assume some degree of responsibility. Similarly, a person can fairly ask how an evening and a morning occurred (Genesis 1:3-5) two days before the creation of the Earth (Genesis 1:9-13) and three days preceding creation of the Sun (Genesis 1:14-19). Without a horizon upon which the Sun could rise and set, and without a Sun in the first place, exactly how could an evening and a morning be? The Bible describes birds as having been created on the fifth day (Genesis 1:20-23), one day prior to the creation of the beasts of the Earth (Genesis 1:24-25), whereas the exact opposite order is indicated by the fossil record.

---

* While very useful in the field of scientific-religious correlates, Dr. Bucaille betrays a lack of familiarity with certain of the disciplines of Islamic knowledge. In specific, his views regarding the validity of hadith and the status of Muhammad are, in places, frankly incorrect.

(3.C8) The Holy Qur'an / Evidences–6

Biblical genealogies are the basis of the Jewish calendar, which claims the world to be 5,761 years old (as of the year 2,000 CE). With a solar system estimated at 4.5 billion years old, and the origin of man on Earth measured in hundreds of thousands, if not millions of years (e.g. the fossil remains of Peking man, Java man, and Lantian man date between 400,000 and 1,000,000 years old), this estimate falls somewhat short of the scientific evidence. A global flood, as dated in the Bible at approximately three hundred years before the time of Abraham, would have corresponded with the twenty-first to twenty-second centuries BC. As such the flood, as described in the Bible, failed to wash away both the Third Dynasty at Ur in Babylonia and the First Intermediate Period before the Eleventh Dynasty in Egypt. These were two civilizations which history testifies to have been uninterrupted. So the period to which the Biblical narratives attribute the global flood could stand revision.

However, putting all that aside and assuming, for the sake of discussion, that the Bible reads like the synthesis of a science library and a twenty-fifth century Farmer's Almanac, the 'So what?' challenge remains. The Islamic religion acknowledges both Judaism and Christianity to have taken origin from revelation, and points out that both worlds constructed around the Old and New Testaments are awaiting the final prophet, as predicted by their scriptures. The question then becomes not one of defining which religion takes origin from Divine revelation, but which religion was the *last* to be revealed, and which religion has been spared the corruption of time and man. For if that is not the religion of choice, what is?

The challenge, then, is for Christians and Jews to disqualify the Qur'an from the competition. Attempts have been made, but like the challenge to write just one *surah* like that of the Qur'an, no attempt has yet approached success. According to Muslims, no attempt ever will.

(SECTION 3) BOOKS OF SCRIPTURE

A word of caution is necessary at this point, for religious zeal leads many people to overstep the bounds of reason in attempting to support their position. Many passages from the Holy Qur'an are unclear in meaning, and as such the significance of such passages is speculative. To attempt to assign more meaning than actually exists, whether to support or refute the Qur'an, would be unreasonable. The best that can be said of such passages is that they are unclear in meaning, and as such can neither be held to be scientific evidences nor examples of inconsistency. Perhaps with time and advancement in human knowledge, such passages will gain explanation. Until then, such verses speak of things which remain undefined by the sciences. An example is the following: the fourth *ayah* of the seventieth *surah* (TMQ 70:4) is translated:

> "The angels and the spirit ascend unto Him in a day the measure whereof is (as) fifty thousand years."

Some Muslims have remarked that this verse can be related to the Special Theory of Relativity, and in fact it might. Then again, it might not. But, to pursue the hypothesis, according to the 'Special Theory of Relativity' the perception of time, size, and mass vary between two differing inertial frames of reference in motion relative to one another. In other words, a stationary and a moving observer will perceive time, size, and mass to be different. At speeds such as those traveled by humans in the present age, such differences in perception are negligible. However, should a person shift their Ford 2,800 year-model intergalactic positron-harvesting star-skipper into one-millionth gear and approach the speed of light, such differences are expected to become increasingly large. The space traveler and the stationary observer will then see two very different views of the same one world.

According to this Special Theory of Relativity, as speed approaches that of light (5.88×10^{12} miles/year) perception of time slows,

(3.C8) The Holy Qur'an / Evidences–6

size becomes reduced, and mass increases. Should Max Planck have hijacked a bunch of his theoretical quanta, pulled in the reins a tad, and screamed past Martha's Vineyard at near the speed of light, his bedside alarm clock would have been expected to have run imperceptibly slow, appeared infinitesimally small, and possessed an infinitely heavy mass. The concept is a little rough on most intellects, so the world has Albert Einstein to thank for the Lorentz transformations -- mathematical equations by which the differential perception of space and time by two observers, one stationary and one moving, can be related to one another. With regard to time, the equation is as follows:

$t' = (1-v^2/c^2)^{-1/2} (t-vx/c^2)$

where v = speed traveled

c = the speed of light (5.88×10^{12} miles/year)

x = position in space (defined by the equation $x^2 = c^2 t^2$)

t' and t are the two differing time perspectives

Plug the numbers from the above *ayah* into the equation, with 't' equaling 50,000 years and 't'' being a single day (2.7397×10^{-3} years) and 'v' calculates out to be, in gross scientific terms, a billionth of a hair of a balding smidgen less than the speed of light. The difference is small. So close is the value of 'v' to the speed of light, indeed, that the last decimal point in the chain of '9's' resulting from the fraction of (v/c) cannot be reached with a common calculator.

How does this relate to the Holy Qur'an? Well, according to Qur'an and hadith, man was made from clay, jinn (devils) from fire, and angels from light. So here is a passage of the Holy Qur'an which not only presents the differing perceptions of time defined as 'time dilation' by the theory of relativity, but the values presented describe the angels as traveling at the speed of that from which they were reported as having been created – i.e., light. The analysis is nice and neat, and may even be correct. But to assert that this is what

419

the above passage actually means is to make some bold assumptions. Far better, perhaps, would be to note the amazing correlation, but not go past discussion of the theory of 'time dilation.' The simple fact that differing perceptions of time were mentioned in a century and place where the fastest movement witnessed by the eye of man might have been the swoop of a hawk or the flight of an arrow is enough, especially considering that Sir Isaac Newton and his foundational ideas were over ten centuries away. To analyze any further seems speculative to an unacceptable extreme.

Similarly, detractors of Islam often chase their preconceptions so far out on the limb of speculation that the weight of their unbalanced conclusions either snap the branch from the trunk of logic, or destabilize the argument. Citing the above example, some detractors have claimed that the above passage conflicts with *surah* 32, *ayah* 5, which reads:

> "He rules (all) affairs from the heavens to the earth: in the end (all affairs) will go up to Him, on a day, the space whereof will be (as) a thousand years of your reckoning." (TMQ 32:5)

To claim that these two verses conflict with one another is to invite an updated Lithium prescription, for the two verses speak of completely different entities and circumstances. The common understanding amongst Muslims is that the first of the above-quoted verses speaks of the ascent of the angels and spirit, whereas the second refers to the Day of Judgement, being the day when all affairs will return to Allah for judgement.[310]

To analyze scientific evidences, then, requires a person to remain objective and firm on the path of that which is concrete, and not to deviate therefrom in either direction. Muslim analysts should not trespass into the realm of speculation, and non-Muslim detractors

---

310. Related by Ibn Abbas.

(3.C8) The Holy Qur'an / Evidences–6

should abandon superfluous arguments. Furthermore, detractors of Islam should recognize that illustrating a particular passage to lack scientific proof does not invalidate that passage; many passages of the Holy Qur'an endured 1,300 years devoid of substantiating evidence, only to achieve validation by the maturity of scientific knowledge in the 19th and 20th centuries. Lack of substantiating evidence equates to lack of proof, not lack of truth. Consequently, any given claim can only be disproven by that which proves a contradictory reality. All else is speculation and prejudice. And this is what is conspicuously absent from the Holy Qur'an – one or more passages, such as those cited above in reference to the Old and New Testaments, which are provably inconsistent either with the world as we know it or with other passages of the same text, either scenario of which would suggest a less than Divine author. Lack of such an inconsistency would suggest a very different possibility. And, in fact, the Qur'an itself offers the following challenge:

> "Do they not consider the Qur'an (with care)? Had it been from any other than Allah they would have found therein many a discrepancy." (TMQ 4:82)

Such a discrepancy could either be internal (i.e., passages which contradict one another) or external (i.e., passages contradicted by reality, such as asserting that the sky is not blue, or that trees are made of candy). Given the wealth of information presented in the Qur'an, the lack of one such discrepancy should be considered significant.

Addressing the issues discussed above in relation to the Bible, the Qur'an does not imitate the Bible by assigning dates or disorder to the sequence of Creation. Considering the number and primacy of such Biblical narratives, the assertion that the Qur'an was in part copied from previous scriptures, once again, looks sadly suspect. Were

(SECTION 3) BOOKS OF SCRIPTURE

Biblical scriptures recited or read from the beginning of the collection of books, no doubt the first scriptural encounter would have been the early chapters of the book of Genesis. The fact that these entries are not carried over into the Qur'an speaks strongly against such a theory of copying.

To search the Qur'an for statements which, like those of the Bible, conflict with archeological, historical, or scientific evidence, proves frustrating. Muslims hold that no such conflicts exist, for the claim is that the Qur'an conforms perfectly not only with the sciences, but with all fields of human knowledge, as would be expected of a book of God. That claim begins to look pretty good when examination is made of the list of scientific evidences proposed by different authors. And while a full discussion of such claims is beyond the scope of this book, a small sample is in order. Those with deeper interests can examine the books: *The Bible, The Qur'an and Science,* by Dr. Maurice Bucaille, *The Universe Seen Through The Quran* (Scientific Findings Confirmed), by Mir Anees-u-din M.Sc, Ph.D., and a variety of smaller treatises available through Islamic bookstores. An especially good primer on this subject is to be found in the small manual of Islamic invitation, *A Brief Illustrated Guide to Understanding Islam.**

Geology:

-----Beginning with the subject of mountains, then, a person might imagine that a mountain, to a desert Bedouin (or to anyone else for that matter), might appear to be nothing more than a rough and inconvenient beauty mark on the otherwise smooth complexion of the face of this Earth. To the caravan crews, farmers, travelers, and sheepherders of the time of Muhammad, mountains would likely have presented more difficulties than benefits. To have stopped and

---

* Available on the Internet at *http://www.islam-brief-guide.org*, and through *The Islamic Foundation of America*, P.O. Box 3415, Merrifield, VA 22116, USA, Tel.: (703) 914-4982, e-mail: ifam@erols.com

(3.C8) THE HOLY QUR'AN / EVIDENCES–6

thought about them would have seemed odd, and to have found something good to say about them, odder. Even in the present day few of mankind ever contemplate, much less write about mountains beyond the benefits gained thereupon. A nice hike, an exhilarating ski, a peaceful picnic in a gently sloping glade – mountains appear to present few material benefits past the pleasantries of the recreation they offer. No doubt mountains also offer a pleasing break from the otherwise monotonously flat terrain, but such pleasures can be diminished in the eyes of a Bedouin once faced with the inconvenience of having to detour a caravan around one, plow an agricultural field uphill, or climb an incline to retrieve a wayward sheep.

Only recently has modern geology recognized the greatest significance of mountains to the world as humankind knows it – mountains possess roots. To quote Tarbuck and Lutgens, "The existence of these roots has been confirmed by seismic and gravitational data."[311] A three or four mile-high mountain might project a root structure of continental crust thirty or forty miles deep into the surrounding mantle of the Earth.[312] This shaft of mountain-root serves to support the weight of the overlying mountain, thereby establishing an equilibrium or, in the language of the geologist, an isostasy.[313] The eye of man sees nothing more than the relatively small nubbin of a mountain, while a forty mile shaft of Earth's crust lies invisibly imbedded in the deeper, plastic asthenosphere, much like the head of a nail peeking above the surface of a block of wood, riding upon an imperceptible shaft of steel. Or like a peg. It is of interest, then, to

---

311. Tarbuck, Edward J. and Frederick K. Lutgens. 1982. *Earth Science*. 3rd ed. Columbus: Charles E. Merrill Publishing Company. p. 157.
312. Press, Frank and Raymond Siever. 1982. *Earth*. 3rd ed. San Francisco: W. H. Freeman and Co. p. 435; Cailleux, Andre. 1968. *Anatomy of the Earth*. New York: McGraw-Hill Book Company. Translated by J. Moody Stuart. pp. 218-222; Tarbuck, Edward J. and Frederick K. Lutgens. 1982. *Earth Science*. 3rd ed. Columbus: Charles E. Merrill Publishing Company. p. 158.
313. Cailleux, Andre. p. 222.

note the description of mountains in the Holy Qur'an as just this -- 'pegs:'

"Have We not made the earth as a wide expanse, and the mountains as pegs?" (TMQ 78:6-7)

Geological experts have also surmised in recent years that mountains play a role of stabilization, for mountains arise at collision points between continental plates. As such, they represent a weld between two colliding continental plates. In the absence of such a weld, the colliding plates of lithosphere would override one another, resulting in periodic earthquakes with the inevitable shifts which episodically occur along such fault lines, due to accumulated strain mandating periodic release. As all mountains represent such collision points, the complete absence of mountains would destabilize the Earth's surface, resulting in a tremulous world. Such knowledge has only surfaced since the study of plate tectonics in the late 20th century, the relevant conclusion being that without the stabilizing influence of mountains the Earth's surface would be in a frequent, if not continuous, quake. Such information is considered revolutionary in the field of geology, but invites a 1,400 year-old yawn from a revelation which records,

"And He has set up on the earth mountains standing firm, lest it should shake with you..." (TMQ 16:15)

Creation of the Universe

-----One of the most undisputed and concrete principles of cosmology is the understanding that the entire universe, as we know it today, was formed out of a hot, smoky mixture of gases and particulate matter.[314] The formation of stars can still be observed in the hearts

---

314. Weinberg, Steven. 1988. *The First Three Minutes, A Modern View of the Origin of the Universe.* Basic Books; Harper Collins Publishers. pp. 101-121.

(3.C8) THE HOLY QUR'AN / EVIDENCES–6

of nebula (presumed to be either remnants or imitators of the primordial dust-cloud) to this day.

Relevant mention in the Qur'an is made as follows:

> "Moreover He comprehended in His design the sky, and it had been (as) smoke. He said to it and to the earth: "You come together, willingly or unwillingly..." (TMQ 41:11)

The heavens having been 'as smoke' is a very accurate description of the primordial dust cloud – 'smoke' being a more apt description than 'cloud' for that matter, for whereas clouds usually evoke the image of a cool, relatively static mist, 'smoke' describes a swirling, hot gaseous mass choked with suspended particles. Such is the precise picture astronomers encounter in the present day evaluation of galaxies under formation in space. The second line of the above quote mentions the 'coming together,' which is a remarkable comment considering the necessary step of union of particle elements into a central core of condensed matter. It is from the rupture of this super-dense central mass that the 'Big Bang' emanated, following which the universe expanded (and continues to expand). Once again, reference to the Qur'an can be made:

> "Do not the unbelievers see that the heavens and the earth were joined together (as one unit of Creation), before We clove them asunder?" (TMQ 21:30)

The origins of the universe, and in particular the concept of a common origin of the heavens and earth have only been derived in the twentieth century. An additional point worthy of mention is that the main opposition to the 'Big Bang' theory, when first proposed in 1920 by Alexander Friedmann and Abbé Georges Lemaître, persisting until and past the popularization of the theory in the 1940s by George Gamow and colleagues, was the creationist theory. This observation drags a number of opponents onto the challenge court of analysis, the first of which is the thought that if the theory of creation was all that was on the mind of man up until 1920, what an extraordinary coincidence it would have been for a man to have conceived such a revolutionary concept as the Big Bang 1300 years previous. More striking, however, is the complexity of the knowledge and technology required to derive, or even to suggest, the theory of the Big Bang (or the Hot Big Bang, as it is now known, given that the temperature at 0.0001 seconds has been calculated to have been a cozy 10^{12} degrees Kelvin).

Development of the theory of the Big Bang required two major assumptions, the first being that Einstein's general theory of relativity accurately defined the gravitational interaction of matter, and the second being the cosmological principle, which is of such complexity as to be beyond the scope of this book. Validation of the theory became dependant upon the ability to measure and quantitate hydrogen, helium and lithium levels, as well as remnant microwave radiation (which itself was only discovered in 1965). The knowledge and technology necessary to even stimulate such thoughts as the Big Bang were absent from the highest institutions of human learning up until the late 20th century. What was available in the time of Muhammad, other than revelation, can only have been limited to a contemplative view of the night-time sky.

-----The theory of continental drift is similarly of recent proposal, having taken origin in the early 1800's. Around the year 1800, Alexander von Humboldt noted the near-perfect fit of the bulge of South America into the bright of Africa. He offered the suggestion that the landmasses bordering the opposite sides of the Atlantic were at one time joined.

Roughly fifty years later, Antonio Snider-Pellegrini noted the consistency between Baron von Humboldt's suggestion and the fossil record, which presented identical fossil plants in the coal deposits of North America and Europe.

The year 1912 entertained the proposal of continental drift by the German meteorologist, Alfred Wegener. Noting the geologic and paleontologic evidence, he suggested that all of the landmasses were at one time joined together in one continent. He called this one continent 'Pangaea,' and suggested that fragmentation occurred in the Triassic period (245 to 208 million years ago, give or take a long weekend). Separation and drift occurred, with the result being the present position of the world's landmasses.

In 1937 Alexander L. Du Toit favored the concept of two original landmasses, Laurasia in the north and Gondwanaland in the south.

Congruency of continental shelves, evidence of shared glaciation, shared similarity of rocks and geologic structures, the paleontologic record (which, in addition to the evidence cited above, shows the earliest marine deposits on the Atlantic coast of Africa and South America to date from the Jurassic period of 208-144 million years ago, suggesting the lack of an ocean before that time), the theory of seafloor spreading, and remnant magnetism (ferromagnetic materials crystallize with orientation along the Earth's magnetic field. Subsequent liberation of crystals, reorientation, and redeposition in sedimentary deposits provides a layered record of each continent's changing orientation through time) all support what has now become the accepted theory of continental drift. So...the concept of continental drift appears to have been figured out. In the 20th century. 1,400 years after the Holy Qur'an recorded the following verse:

"And it is He Who spread out the earth..." (TMQ 13:33)

Heavenly Bodies

-----*Surah* 10, *ayah* 5 describes the sun and moon by two different words, both of which mean 'light' in the Arabic language. However, the word *'Dhi-yaa-an,'* describes the sun as a source of light while the word *'noo-ran'* describes the moon as giving light which comes from a source other than itself. Lane's *Arabic-English Lexicon* comments, "...it is said that (*dui-yaa-an*) is essential, but (*noo-ran*) is accidental [light]..."[315] The Qur'anic and Biblical descriptions (Genesis 1:16 -- "Then God made two great lights: the greater light to rule the day, and the lesser light to rule the night.") differ in exactness of detail, with the Qur'anic description differentiating between, rather than equating, the light of the two heavenly bodies.

-----Rounded orbits of the celestial bodies are described, as are the rounded orbits of day and night ("It is He Who created the Night and the Day, and the sun and the moon: all [the celestial bodies] swim along, each in its rounded course." -- TMQ 21:33). Complementing the above with the Qur'anic verse of 39:5, in which the day and night are described by the verb *'kaw-wa-ra,'* which means to wind or coil, like wrapping a turban around the head (or, as per Lane's *Arabic-English Lexicon*, "he wound the thing in a round form") the description comes to be understood to include not only the rounded orbits of the planets and moon, but the roundness of the Earth itself. Furthermore, the teaching, "And the Sun runs his course for a period determined for him..." (TMQ 36:38) hints at the fact that the entire solar system moves. And in fact, such is precisely the case. Although a stationary center relative to the planetary group of our local solar system, the sun orbits in space around the axis of the Milky Way galaxy.

At a time when Western explorers were afraid to seek the horizon for fear of falling off, Qur'anic descriptions such as those above did not make sense in the framework of common perceptions for centuries, if not for more than a millennia.

---

315. Lane, Edward William. 1980. *An Arabic-English Lexicon Derived From the Best and the Most Copious Eastern Sources.* Beirut, Lebanon: Librairie Du Liban. Book I, Part 8, p. 2865, column 3.

(3.C8) The Holy Qur'an / Evidences–6

-----*Surah* 36, *ayah* 40 reads: "It is not permitted to the Sun to catch up the Moon, nor can the Night outstrip the Day: each (just) swims along in (its own) orbit (according to Law). This description of separate, rounded orbits is unusual enough. What really conflicts with expectations is the comment that the Sun and Moon are not permitted to catch up to one another, for the common perception amongst ancient man, viewing a solar eclipse, was that the sun and the moon did just that – catch up to one another. Yet, even though a solar eclipse occurred during the life of Muhammad, this verse corrects the error of such primitive thinking.

Physiology

-----Cells are the building blocks of all living things, and the majority component of cellular cytoplasm is water, to the tune of 80-85%. Life, as known to man, cannot exist without water, for a dry cell is a dead cell. And while these facts did not surface until the cell theory of the early 19th century, the Holy Qur'an contains the statement, "We made from water every living thing." (TMQ 21:30)

-----Only with electrophysiologic testing, intracellular recording, and sophisticated staining, fixation, sectioning and microscopy techniques did man learn that pain and temperature (thermo-) receptors are restricted to the dermal layer of the skin. Now, every religion which teaches 'heaven and hell' dangles the reward of paradise in front of the faithful, while attempting to flush the religiously negligent out of the bushes of spiritual demotivation by waving the threat of hellfire. How bad is hellfire? The Qur'anic description emphasizes the never-ending suffering of the occupants of Hell by stating that, "...as soon as their skins are roasted through, We shall change them for fresh skins, that they may taste the penalty: for Allah is Exalted in Power, Wise." (TMQ 4:56) What has become well known in this present century is presented as having been dictated to Muhammad

1,400 years ago, in a time and place where research into human physiology had not even progressed to the stage of bodily dissection. Those who wonder who had the power to effect such a punishment, and the wisdom to know such detail in the time of Muhammad are informed that "...Allah is Exalted in Power, Wise."

-----The frontal lobes of the brain are located at the most anterior (i.e. the most forward) aspect of the brain. They are called 'frontal' lobes for a reason — they ride up front. If a person were to tap the forehead, the closest aspect of the brain to the finger of annoyance would be the frontal lobes. Now, the pre-frontal region of the frontal lobes is the area of the brain concerned with personality — motivation, planning, initiation of deeds which are pooled under the label of 'behavior' all take place in the prefrontal (the most forward aspect of the frontal lobes themselves) area. To quote a reputable source, "The motivation and the foresight to plan and initiate movements occur in the anterior portion of the frontal lobes, the prefrontal area."[316] Surprising it is, then, to find mention in the Qur'an in association with this fact, as follows:

> "Let him beware! If he does not desist, We will drag him by the *naa-se-yah*, a lying, sinful *naa-se-ya-tin*!" (TMQ 96: 15-16)

The word '*naa-se-yah*' (or '*naa-se-ya-tin*' — different pronunciations of the identical same word), while often translated as 'forelock,' in fact deserves the longer and more accurate description of "fore part of the head."[317]

There is the amusing anecdote of the person who wanted to know which part of the body was concerned with thought. He decided that if he exercised his thought, the first part of his body to ache from

---

316. Seeley, Rod R., Trent D. Stephens and Philip Tate. 1996. *Essentials of Anatomy and Physiology.* 2nd edition. St. Louis: Mosby-Year Book, Inc. p. 211.
317. Wehr, Hans.

fatigue would have to be his brain. So he sat down and thought and thought and thought. After a while, the hard wooden stool that he had chosen to sit upon began to take its toll, leading the man to focus his conclusion on the area of his ache. It is a funny story, but it is not just for kids. The point is that a Bedouin of the desert from 1,400 years ago can hardly have been expected to have known what modern medicine has only figured out in the present century. A far fairer assumption would be that an illiterate Arab shepherd and desert caravan-leader of a thousand years ago would talk in terms of the shifty, give-the-truth-away 'lying eyes' which betray a liar, the 'lying lips' over which deceitful discourse passes, or the 'cheating heart' thought to generate such an illness of words. The person who comments, "What part of the body would a Bedouin of twelve centuries ago, even two centuries ago for that matter, have considered to be associated with conceiving sins and lies? Why, the prefrontal region of the frontal lobes of the cerebral cortex, of course!" should be suspected of harboring a personal agenda which obstructs cognitive reason.

-----600 years before Ibn Nafis described the circulation of blood, and 1,000 years before William Harvey took the credit following publication of his book entitled, *Exercitatio Anatomica de Motu Cordis et Sanguinis in Animalibus* (The Anatomical Exercises Concerning the Motion of the Heart and Blood in Animals) in 1628, the Holy Qur'an alluded to the processes of digestion, absorption, blood circulation, and excretion as follows:

> "And verily in cattle (too) will you find an instructive sign. From what is within their bodies, between excretions and blood, We produce, for your drink, milk, pure and agreeable to those who drink it." (TMQ 16:66)

Similar to the science of blood circulation, knowledge of the processes of digestion, intestinal absorption, and glandular secretion remained mysteries up until the past few centuries. To encounter one verse which links all such processes together is to encounter a complex scientific anachronism.

Bodies of Water

-----The Holy Qur'an glorifies The Creator by mentioning some of the unique and unexpected characteristics of His creation. For example,

> "It is He Who has let free the two bodies of flowing water: one palatable and sweet, and the other salt and bitter; yet He has made a barrier between them, a partition that is forbidden to be passed." (TMQ 25:53)

And,

> "He has let free the two bodies of flowing water, meeting together: between them is a barrier which they do not transgress: then which of the favors of your Lord will you deny?" (TMQ 55:19-21)

The first quote appears to refer to the barrier of brackish water encountered in an estuary. This zone of brackish water, which separates the sweet water of an emptying river from the salt water of the receiving sea, is well known. In the present day, that is. Whether it was known in a time and place where rivers were scarce and before the development of sensitive salinity equipment is hard to guess. A person can easily imagine that 1,400 years ago water was categorized as drinkable or not, with no room or practical need for subcategories. Furthermore, well water in the Middle East, to the present day, is frequently salty to begin with, so brackish water by the standards of modern developed nations was very likely to have been considered potable in the time and country of Muhammad.

(3.C8) The Holy Qur'an / Evidences–6

In any case, should a person contemplate a river emptying into a sea, even in the present day, the mind is filled with wonder that one day one of the two great bodies of water will not win out over the other. In the simple mind of seventh century man, whose salinity gauge was limited to the tip of the tongue, and whose ability to explore was restricted to the most basic of water transport, contemplation would no doubt have been simplified. Witnessing an estuary, seventh century man would likely have expected the force and volume of a major river such as the Nile or the Tigris-Euphrates to expand the region of brackish water, and eventually dilute the entire sea. To say that such would never be allowed to happen seems to go against what can be imagined to have been reasonable seventh century expectations. To bring up the point at all seems odd amongst a desert dwelling, and not a seagoing, people, but most vehemently defies explanation if one imagines Muhammad to have been anything other than genuine. For what would be the point of such a statement to a charlatan?

-----The second of the above quotes may relate to the fact that oceans and seas vary in salinity, temperature, and density, and where they meet is delimited by well-defined borders.[318] For example, the Mediterranean Sea meets the Atlantic Ocean in a stable and distinct border. The Mediterranean extends a several hundred kilometer long, dripping wet tongue of water of higher temperature, higher salinity, and lower density over the Gibraltar Sill at a depth of 1000 meters.[319] The border with the more cold, less saline, more dense Atlantic Ocean is relatively fixed and sharp, despite the strong currents, constant waves and regular tides which would be expected to blend these two bodies of water, or at least mix them where they meet. This

---

318. Davis, Richard A., Jr. 1972. *Principles of Oceanography*. Reading, Massachusetts: Addison-Wesley Publishing Co. pp. 92-93.
319. Kuenen, Philip H. 1960. *Marine Geology*. New York: John Wiley & Sons, Inc. p. 43.

has been held to be an example of the 'barrier which they do not transgress,' mentioned in the second of the above quotes, and, if so, is remarkable not only in and of itself, but all the more so because the example is repeated in the borders of other seas and oceans.

-----Another point with regard to seas is the mention of internal, deep waves. Such a mention may sound odd at first, and reasonably so, for it is in fact a recent discovery. Modern oceanography teaches that deep, internal waves "...are found at an interface between water layers of different densities—for example, the pycnocline."[320] Internal waves behave just like surface waves, and may even break. However, unlike surface waves, they cannot be seen or studied without complex equipment, and certainly this was not the work of a desert people for whom the simple act of swimming was an odd ability.

Of interest is the diagram which M. Grant Gross chooses for his book on oceanography to illustrate deep waves. His diagram shows two levels of waves, one at the surface and one internal, at the interface between the hyper-dense deep water and the less dense surface layer.[321] This illustration corresponds perfectly with the Qur'anic passage,

> "Or (the state of a disbeliever) is like the darkness in a vast deep sea, overwhelmed with waves topped by waves, topped by dark clouds, (layers of) darkness upon darkness: if a man stretches out his hand, he can hardly see it! And he for whom Allah has not appointed light, for him there is no light." (TMQ 24:40 – Muhammad Al-Hilali and Muhammad Khan translation)

Not only are the layers of both superficial and deep waves described, but the odd reference is made to "darkness in a vast deep

---

320. Gross, M. Grant. 1993. *Oceanography, a View of Earth*. 4th ed. Englewood Cliffs: Prentice-Hall, Inc. p. 223.
321. Gross, M. Grant. p. 224.

sea," to the point where a person can barely see. The absence of light at the ocean depth of 1000 meters is recent knowledge, and could only be gained with the use of special equipment, for the human chest has the annoying habit of imploding at such depths.[322] Appreciation of any significant darkness requires a dive in excess of 50 meters, where an unequipped surface dive of more than 15 meters is beyond all but the most rare of human capabilities. Among a people who can swim in the first place, that is.

The Atmosphere

-----Anyone who has climbed a mountain knows that air thins at altitude. The sensation of mountain sickness, or altitudinal shortness of breath, can develop after *rapid* ascent from sea level to altitudes in excess of 8,000 feet. Two factors deserve consideration in this regard, the first being that such altitudes are rarely to be encountered in the Middle East. A more relevant thought with regard to the time of Muhammad is that altitudinal shortness of breath was most likely unknown in the period prior to the late 1800's, and was clinically defined only as late as 1937.[323] For one thing there was little, if any, motivation to those living in lowlands to trouble themselves with climbing mountains, and especially to a vertical scale of 8,000 feet or more. Recreational exploration was virtually unknown amongst a people who exerted themselves to the fullest just to squeeze a bare existence out of an unsympathetic land. Equally important, prior to modern methods of rapid transportation, mountain folk acclimatized to the rarity of the atmosphere in which they lived. Those who sought higher altitudes in the process of pasturing their herds experienced such a slow transition from one elevation to another as to allow the body to adjust. The likelihood of any Arab possessing motivation,

322. Elder, Danny; and John Pernetta. 1991. *Oceans*. London: Mitchell Beazley Publishers. p. 27.
323. *Encyclopaedia Britannica*. CD-ROM. Under "Altitude Sickness."

interest, and equipment to seek a lofty summit in the range of 8-10,000 feet is slim to none. The availability of such a mountain to begin with was rare, and that of rapid transportation nonexistent. Yet mention is made of the closed and constricted breathing experienced by those who venture into the higher altitudes in the following passage:

> "Those whom Allah (in His plan) wills to guide, – He opens their breast to Islam; those whom He wills to leave straying, He makes their breast closed and constricted, as if they had to climb up to the skies: thus Allah (heaps) the penalty on those who refuse to believe." (TMQ 6:125)

-----Meteorologists have only recently described the formation of rain-generating cumulus clouds. In a nutshell, small cumulus clouds have been found to migrate and join together; updrafts develop as a cloud increases in size, with the result that the mass of vapor grows vertically, like a haystack.[324, 325] When the cloud extends sufficiently high vertically, the coolness of the higher atmosphere leads to condensation, which falls as rain. While meteorologists have required satellite photography, airplanes, weather balloons, computers for analysis, and other sophisticated equipment to determine the above, the Qur'an mentions,

> "Don't you see that Allah makes the clouds move gently, then joins them together, then makes them into a heap? Then you will see rain issue forth from their midst. And He sends down from the sky mountain masses (of clouds) wherein is hail..." (TMQ 24:43)

---

324. Anthes, Richard A., John J. Cahir, Alistair B. Fraser, and Hans A. Panofsky. 1981. *The Atmosphere*. 3rd ed. Columbus: Charles E. Merrill Publishing Co. pp. 268-269.

325. Miller, Albert and Jack C. Thompson. 1975. *Elements of Meteorology*. 2nd ed. Columbus: Charles E. Merrill Publishing Co. p. 141.

(3.C8) The Holy Qur'an / Evidences–6

"Mountain masses (of cloud) wherein is hail?" Interesting that the clouds which generate rain are described as heaps, but those which generate hail are described as being tall like mountains. And, in fact, such a description is accurate, for only when cumulonimbus clouds blossom from their altitudinal roots of 3-4,000 feet to a 25-30,000 ft ceiling (like mountains) are the upper layers exposed to atmospheric conditions which generate hail through both condensation and freezing.[326]

-----The following passage of the Holy Qur'an gives a respectable description of the rain cycle:

"Don't you see that Allah sends down rain from the sky, and leads it through springs in the earth? Then He causes to grow, therewith, produce of various colors..." (TMQ 39:21)

The rain cycle seems like a no-brainer for most people, but once again a person has to step out of their 21st century cone of silence to hear what people were saying a thousand years ago – or just a couple hundred years ago, for that matter.

René Descartes, the famous seventeenth century philosopher, proposed that seawater seeped through underground channels into reservoirs underneath the tops of mountains -- something like a natural water tower. Athanasius Kircher wrote that seawater was driven by the force of tides into subterranean rifts, and eventually to outlets at springs (see *Mundus subterraneus* [Subterranean World], 1664). Some even endorsed the concept of a huge underground sea in communication with the oceans and providing water through springs and rivers, exemplified in John Woodward's *'Essay Towards a Natural History of the Earth and Terrestrial Bodies,'* 1695.

Bernard Palissy laid the foundation for the truth of the situation, however, in 1580, with his *Discours Admirables* (Admirable

---

326. Miller, Albert; and Jack C. Thompson. p. 141.

Discourses). Therein he described rainfall as the sole source of springs and rivers.

Neither the people of Mount Waialeale, Hawaii, (despite having the World's highest average annual rainfall, at 11,700 mm/yr) nor the Bedouins of the desert (despite having the greatest *need* for rain) ever seemed to have figured out the rain cycle on their own. The first experiments which proved rainfall to be sufficient to provide for annual runoff were conducted in the basin of the Seine River by Pierre Perrault and Edmé Mariotte towards the end of the seventeenth century.[327] The Qur'anic passage, hence, presented the reality of the case over a thousand years before such opinions were either popularized or tested.

Anatomy and Embryology

Correlation between Qur'anic statements and embryology are so accurate and fascinating as to have stimulated books devoted solely to this topic. Complete summary in the format of this chapter, therefore, is doomed to inadequacy. However, some of the more salient features may be mentioned in brief, with a reference to more comprehensive books, should the reader desire to examine the topic in greater depth.

-----Conception. The concept of biparental inheritance was largely unknown to the Western world, until proposed by Pierre-Louis Moreau de Maupertuis in his *Système de la Nature* in 1751. Prior to this suggestion, the prevailing concepts of conception took root in Aristotle's Fourth Century BC suggestion that the embryo developed out of coagulation, or curdling, of menstrual blood, with 'vapors' of semen acting as catalyst. Such popular views may have made their way into the thoughts of at least one Bible author, for Job 10:10 records, "Did You not pour me out like milk, and curdle me like cheese..." Even when discovered under the microscope by Antonie van

---

327. *Encyclopaedia Britannica.*CD-ROM.

(3.C8) THE HOLY QUR'AN / EVIDENCES-6

Leewenhoek, spermatozoa were 'proven' by the experiments of Lazzaro Spallanzani to be nothing more than parasites in the semen. The theories of spontaneous generation (which means exactly what it says) and preformation (which proposed that a preformed fetus known as a 'homunculus' lived as a diminutive human form encased in the head of the sperm [Jan Swammerdam, 1637-1680] or in the ovum [DeGraaf, 1641-1693]), began to give way to the theory of biparental inheritance in the 18th century, eventually losing the battle and giving up a death rattle following the experiments of Driesch around the beginning of the 20th century. Yet, for the previous twelve centuries, lay Muslims were aware of the teaching of the Holy Qur'an that,

"O mankind! We created you from a single (pair) of a male and a female..." (TMQ 49:13)

and

"Verily, We created man from *Nutfah* (drops) of mixed semen (sexual discharge of man and woman)..." (TMQ 76:2)

In the 14th century, Ibn Hajar Al Asqalani recorded this conflict between the fallacious opinions of the anatomists of his day and the revelation of the Holy Qur'an:

"Many of the anatomists claim that the semen of the male has no role in creation of the baby. Its role, they claim, is limited to curdling the menstrual blood from which man is born. The sayings of the Prophet deny what they say. The semen of the male actually participates equally to that of female in formation of the embryo."[328]

An example of one such teaching is that when Muhammad was

---

328. *Fateh Al Bari Shareh Sahih Al Bukhari*. Ibn Hajar Al Asqualani, Bab Alqadar. Cairo: Al Mat'ba Assalafiyah. Vol II, Page 480.

(SECTION 3) BOOKS OF SCRIPTURE

questioned by a Jew, "O Muhammad! What is man created from?" he was recorded to have answered, "He is created from both: from the man's *Nutfah* (sperm) and the woman's *Nutfah* (ovum)."[329]

The plot thickens when a person also finds mention of the fact that only a tiny part of semen plays a role in conception, as found in both the Qur'an ("God made man's progeny from a quintessence of despised liquid." [TMQ 32:8]), and hadith (Muhammad is recorded as having said, "Not from the whole fluid [ejaculated], man is created, but only from a small portion of it."[330]). One more tidbit unknown to the scientific world until the last two centuries, for the first to scientifically describe the fertilization of an egg by a sperm was Hertwig, in 1875.

-----The embryo and fetus develop within the 'bouncy castle' of the amnio-chorionic sac, suspended within the muscular uterus, itself encased within the ballooning abdominal wall. These three layers of seclusion appear to be referenced in the passage,

> "He makes you, in the wombs of your mothers, in stages, one after another, in three veils of darkness." (TMQ 39:6)

One additional element of interest is simply that consideration of the development of the human embryo/fetus "in stages" was not recorded in scientific literature before the 15th century. And there should be no surprise. According to the theories of preformation and spontaneous generation, the human was created complete, and just grew in proportion. The refutation of such popular theories appears to have developed as a consequence of the realization that all was not what it was at first believed to be. First, the staging of fetal development was discussed and illustrated in the 15th century. Following that, thanks to Van Leeuwenhook's invention of the microscope in

---

329. *Musnad Ahmad.*
330. Narrated by *Muslim.*

(3.C8) The Holy Qur'an / Evidences–6

the 17th century, scientists were able to stage the development of chick embryos. Staging of human embryos had to wait a few years, and only boarded the subway of scientific archives when first described in the 20th century by Streeter. By that time, the Qur'anic concept of epigenesis (fetal development in stages) was 13 centuries old and sporting a beard that would have put Rumplestiltskin to shame. How complete are the Qur'anic descriptions of embryological staging? That question, in and of itself, deserves discussion.

-----The initial stages of embryogenesis involve the formation of a zygote from the union of sperm and ovum. The zygote then divides to form a blastocyst, which implants in the uterus. The zygote is a pale, drop-like structure, whereas the blastocyst develops chorionic villi which invade the uterine wall, resulting in adhesion as well as nutrition, for the chorionic villi become surrounded by microscopic lacunae (i.e., lakes) of blood. At this stage the blood is stagnant, and there is no arterial-venous pathway of exchange, for the blastocyst is small enough to derive nutrition from seepage of nutrients from the tiny blood lakes. Hence, the blastocyst appears under the microscope to be a tiny blood clot. Again, twentieth century scientific knowledge. Again, predated by 1400 years by the Qur'anic descriptions:

> "Then We placed him as (a drop of) *nutfah* (mixed drops of the male and female sexual discharge) in a place of rest, firmly fixed;
>
> Then We made the *nutfah* into a clot of congealed blood; then of that clot We made a (foetus) lump; then We made out of that lump bones and clothed the bones with flesh; then We developed out of it another creature. So blessed be Allah, the Best to create!" (TMQ 23:13-14).

Everything about the above passage is twentieth century scientific knowledge – the drop-like appearance of the first stage, the firmly-fixed adhesion of the blastocyst integrated into the uterine wall by interdigitating Chorionic villi, the clot-like appearance of the microscopic blastocyst. Even the development of the fetus is described in a note-worthy manner, for the Arabic word '*alaqah*' (translated 'clot' in the above passage) in fact describes three qualities – the first being a clot of blood, the second being leech-like in appearance, the third being the property of clinging.[331] And, in fact, the appearance of the embryo at this stage of development is so similar to that of a leech, both in form and physiology, as to be commented upon in the scientific literature.

Dr. Keith L. Moore is a man many would like to discredit for his work in this field. However, discrediting one of the world's foremost anatomists and embryologists is not particularly easy. Dr. Keith Moore, Professor Emeritus of Anatomy and Cell Biology at the University of Toronto, past Associate Dean of Basic Sciences at the Faculty of Medicine and Chairman of the Department of Anatomy for eight years, 1984 recipient of the J.C.B. Grant Award from the Canadian Association of Anatomists (the most distinguished award in the field of anatomy in Canada), and past director of the international associations known as the Canadian and American Association of Anatomists and the Council of the Union of Biological Sciences, authored a book on embryology entitled *The Developing Human*. The work is of such authority as to have been translated into eight languages. The third edition was published with Islamic additions in 1983. Within this edition, Dr. Moore comments on the correlation of the Qur'anic passages discussed herein, for he was "astonished by the accuracy of the statements that were recorded in the 7th century AD, before the science of embryology was established."[332]

---

331. Lane, Edward William. Book I, Part 5, p. 2134, column 3.
332. Moore, Keith L. 1983. *The Developing Human, Clinically Oriented Embryology, With Islamic Additions*. 3rd ed. Jeddah: Dar Al-Qiblah with permission of W.B. Saunders Co. Foreword.

(3.C8) The Holy Qur'an / Evidences–6

Dr. Moore points out that the word '*mudghah*,' described in *surah* 23:14, actually means a 'chewed lump.' He correlates this with the fact that the curved sequence of segmental somites at this stage of development looks very much like the curved sequence of 'segmented' teeth marks encountered when a person bites into a mold.

The mention of "...then We made out of that lump bones and clothed the bones with flesh" (TMQ 23:14) correlates precisely with the sequential development of the cartilaginous skeleton prior to development of the muscles, as occurs in embryogenesis.

The passage, "...then We developed out of it another creature" (TMQ 23:14) may refer to the transformation of the embryo in the eighth week of development from an indistinct embryo to a fetus bearing distinctive human characteristics. The verse of 22:5 mentions, "...then out of a leech-like clot, then out of a morsel of flesh, partly formed and partly unformed..." may refer to the fact that some of the tissues at this stage are differentiated, whereas others are not. The analysis goes on, and as mentioned above, is too lengthy for adequate discussion within a book not devoted to the subject. In addition to Dr. Moore's book, another excellent reference is Dr. Mohammed Ali Albar's book entitled, *Human Development, As Revealed in the Holy Quran and Hadith*, available through many Islamic bookstores.

In the end of the analysis, none of the above was known to the field of science prior to the invention of the microscope in the 17th century. Antonie van Leewenhoek's invention invited the first peeks at what had been, until that time, a world hidden from the inquiring eye of man by virtue of microscopic size. And while various religious groups may attempt to discredit authorities such as Dr. Keith Moore, for no other reason than the fact that he presents evidence contrary to what such groups would like to hear, it is very difficult to conceive of such an eminent authority compromising his reputation on such a matter. All the more so, considering that the book in question was published in English, which would severely limit marketability in Arabic speaking countries. What Dr. Moore's motivation could possibly have been, other than an academic pursuit of truth, is hard to fathom.

Miscellaneous

-----Honey. It's great stuff. And, as the Qur'an states, honey is a substance, "...wherein is healing for men" (TMQ 16:69). As per the *Encyclopaedia Britannica,*

> "Somewhat acid, it has mild antiseptic properties and has been used in the treatment of burns and lacerations. One of the most easily assimilated foods, it is widely used in baked goods, candies, prepared fruits, cereals, and medicines."[333]

A common ingredient in cold and allergy medicines, indeed honey does possess medicinal value. Of added interest is the fact that Muhammad was recorded in hadith to have said that all illnesses have a cure, as follows: "There is no disease that Allah has sent down except that He also has sent down its treatment."[334] Whether true or not, this is what he believed, so a person would rightfully expect to find a cookbook of home remedies in the Qur'an if, that is, Muhammad were the author. But such is not the case. Mention of medicinal treatments are conspicuously absent. The chapter on medicine in the seventh volume of Dr. Muhammad Muhsin Khan's translation of Sahih Al-Bukhari *alone* contains no less than fifty eight entries. So voluminous is the hadith record of the homeopathic and naturopathic remedies prescribed by Muhammad, that numerous books

---

333. *Encyclopaedia Britannica.* CD-ROM.
334. *Al-Bukhari,* Muhammed Ibn Ismaiel; translated by Dr. Muhammad Muhsin Khan. 1997. *Sahih Al-Bukhari.* Riyadh: Darussalam. Volume 7, hadith #5678, p. 326.

(3.C8) THE HOLY QUR'AN / EVIDENCES–6

have been written devoted solely to the subject. Hence, it would be unreasonable for a person to propose that the subject of medicine was not on Muhammad's mind – it appears to have been very much on his mind. The point remains that although frequently occupied with the subject, the Qur'an does not reflect Muhammad's interest in this regard, as one would expect, were he the author. Quite the contrary, the only Qur'anic reference to a healing agent is to honey, and it is interesting to note that, in the face of what Muhammad believed, the only mention of a therapeutic agent in the Holy Qur'an happens to be correct.

-----Fingerprinting was developed into a science in the late 19th century. The British scientific journal '*Nature*' published observation of the uniqueness of fingerprints in 1880. The observations were tried and tested, following which Sir Francis Galton suggested a classification system on the basis of pattern analysis, to include arches, loops, and whorls. The Galton-Henry system of fingerprint classification was subsequently developed, published in June 1900, and adopted by Scotland Yard in the early 1900's. Subsequent modification and improvements led to the adoption of the fingerprint system of identification around the world. The entire concept rests upon the individual variability of fingerprint pattern, for no two are alike. Yet, the intricate uniqueness of the fingertips was alluded to in the Holy Qur'an 1300 years before British detectives started dusting-down crime scenes. The relevant passage discusses the resurrection of mankind on the Day of Judgement, and emphasizes the creative abilities of Allah by questioning,

> "Does man think that We cannot assemble his bones? Nay, We are able to put together in perfect order the very tips of his fingers." (TMQ 75:3-4)

(3.C) THE HOLY QUR'AN
(3.C9) Summary of Evidences

"Knowledge is what we get when an observer,
preferably a scientifically trained observer,
provides us with a copy of reality
that we can all recognize."
— Christopher Lasch, "The Lost Art of Political Argument,"
Harper's, Sept. 1990

With regard to the message of the revealed book of Islam, the Qur'an states,

"No falsehood can approach it from before or behind it: it is sent down by One full of Wisdom, Worthy of all praise." (TMQ 41:42)

The Qur'an states that it is infallible, and lays the message open for all to examine, challenging non-believers to find one single falsehood. Even a little one. Some may conclude that Muhammad was just a very smart man, but, as Dr. Maurice Bucaille points out

"...it is easy to put forward the hypothesis of Muhammad as being a brilliant thinker, who was supposed to have imagined

(3.C9) The Holy Qur'an / Summary of Evidences

all on his own what modern science was to discover centuries later. In so doing however, people quite simply forget to mention the other aspect of what these geniuses of philosophical reasoning produced, i.e., the colossal blunders that litter their work."[335]

Not only is the Qur'an *not* littered with "colossal blunders," but it appears to be devoid of the smallest of errors. This purity is interesting in consideration of the fact that such a wealth of information, spanning a diversity of disciplines, is presented. Many of the statements found in the Qur'an would have seemed peculiar mysteries in the time of their revelation, and unnecessary in consideration of the prevailing level of ignorance with regard to history and science. Many of the concepts presented confronted established thought, and remained items of bitter contention within the scientific community for centuries, if not in excess of a millennia. Should Muhammad be proposed an imposter, the question as to why he projected such a large number of diverse and revolutionary claims, including predictions of future events, demands an answer. Should Muhammad be imagined a charlatan, the follow-on question of how he got all the predictions right 1,400 years in advance of scientific proof is equally thought-provoking.

In the words of Dr. Maurice Bucaille,

"How could a man living fourteen hundred years ago have made corrections to the existing description to such an extent that he eliminated scientifically inaccurate material and, on his own initiative, made statements that science has been able to verify only in the present day? This hypothesis is completely untenable."[336]

---

335. Bucaille, Maurice. p. 162.
336. Bucaille, Maurice. p. 148.

(Section 3) Books of Scripture

In self-defense, non-Muslims often present 'our book against yours' arguments, presenting differences along the lines of 'our book says this and your book says that, therefore if I take my book to be correct yours is wrong.' The argument only has validity if both books have the same authority, and the choice of which book is to be considered a more reliable resource is left to the reader.

Non-Muslims also present many emotionally charged arguments against a wide variety of practices associated with the Islamic religion. Many such issues are, in fact, social customs or unfounded traditions, and so bear no relation to the analysis of religion. Other issues, such as the permissibility of polygamy, the requirement of *hijab* (the female headscarf), family roles and food restrictions *are* religiously based, but peculiar to Western lifestyle. As such, these are not points of proof, but of preference, which is a dangerous basis for choice, for Allah is recorded as having cautioned mankind, "But it is possible that you dislike a thing which is good for you, and that you love a thing which is bad for you. But Allah knows, and you know not." (TMQ 2:216). Personal preference, in other words, may be distracting from the path of His design.

Despite all philosophical arguments, the challenges remain to find a single falsehood or to compose a ten word, three-line chapter better than that of the Qur'an. Should such a contest remain unsatisfied the challenge of the Qur'an deserves respect.

Statistical analysis may have some application, for a person who 'plays the odds' will note that many of the predictions made in the Holy Qur'an would have been thought to have been bad bets in their day. Predictions such as those involving the battles of Rome versus Persia and the condemnation of Abu Lahab and his wife would certainly fall into this category. The odds of such predictions are incalculable, but even if each event were assigned a likelihood of 50%, the sheer number of such predictions calculates out to an astronomically

(3.C9) The Holy Qur'an / Summary of Evidences

small likelihood of being correct in each and every instance. For example, the likelihood of two such predictions, each having a probability of one out of two, both being correct is one out of four. In essence, there are three combinations of error (the first prediction is right and the second wrong, or the first is wrong and the second right, or both are wrong), and only one chance of both predictions being correct – one chance out of four. The chance of three such predictions all being correct is one in eight, and with each additional prediction the probability halves once again. Added all together, the cumulative likelihood of correctness in each and every instance is staggeringly small. For example, there are well over 60 such evidences cited above – and these represent only a fraction of the total number of evidences cited by scholars of the religion. Yet, if each one of these sixty evidences were assigned the conservative probability of 50%, the likelihood of all 60 evidences proving correct on the basis of sheer chance would be $(1/2)^{60}$, which translates to less than one chance in 1,000,000,000,000,000,000. The fact that a popular religion surrounds a revelation which has such a vanishingly small possibility of coincidental correctness is hardly surprising. Indeed, the fact that so many stand in denial of such odds is the true wonder.

Despite all of the evidences mentioned above, many Westerners may complain that the language of the Qur'an does not inspire them in the manner of the familiar verses and style of the Bible. Two main themes need to be considered in this regard. The first is simply that the opinions of those who have mastered the Arabic language should be respected. A few such authors comment,

> "All those who are acquainted with the Quran in Arabic agree in praising the beauty of this religious book; its grandeur of form is so sublime that no translation into any European language can allow us to appreciate it."[337]

---

337. Montet, Edward. 1929. *Traduction Francaise du Couran*. Paris. Introduction, p. 53.

(SECTION 3) BOOKS OF SCRIPTURE

"The truth is, I do not find any understanding author who controverts the elegance of the Alcoran, it being generally esteemed as the standard of the Arabic language and eloquence..."[338]

"The Quran, in its original Arabic dress, has a seductive beauty and charm of its own. Couched in concise and exalted style, its brief pregnant sentences, often rhymed, possess an expressive force and explosive energy which it is extremely difficult to convey by literal word for word translation."[339]

Many Westerners may then despair over ever being able to fully appreciate the eloquence of the Qur'an in the full beauty of the revealed Arabic. This difficulty can be compounded by the plethora of poor translations freely available through Western bookstores. The Abdullah Yusuf Ali translation of meaning (*The Holy Qur'an*), that of Saheeh International (*The Qur'an*), of the combined effort of Muhammad Al-Hilali and Muhammad Khan (*The Noble Qur'an*), and of Marmaduke Pickthall (*The Glorious Qur'an*) are amongst the most respected. Other respected translations exist, but most of these lack the same level of endorsement by the community of Islamic scholarship, and those of Alexander Ross, George Sale, Rev. J. M. Rodwell, Edward Henry Palmer, and Richard Bell are certainly to be avoided if a person seeks the most modern and objective scholarship.

What remains, then, is for a person to read expecting the emotive and evocative qualities of the Arabic to be compromised in translation. Having said that, the message and the messenger are an integrated unit, and many may first wish to consider the profile of the man who bore the message in synchrony with examination of the scripture itself.

---

338. Stubbe, Dr. Henry, M.A. 1975. *An Account of the Rise and Progress of Mohomedanism, with the Life of Mahomet.* Lahore: Oxford and Cambridge Press. p. 158.

339. Naish, John, M.A. 1937. *The Wisdom of the Qur'an.* Oxford. Preface, p. viii.

Section 4
Messengers

"All cats are gray in the dark."

– Old Proverb

(SECTION 4) MESSENGERS

And so it is with the messengers. Those who live in the darkness of disbelief tend to see all prophets as charlatans. Those who believe in the process of revelation, however, will evaluate those who claim prophethood with more discrimination.

To begin with, we must define what we mean when we speak of a prophet. For the purposes of this book, the word 'prophet' is taken to refer to one who received and transmited divine revelation. It is important to distinguish this definition from the more colloquial sense of one who possesses greater than normal spiritual insight, or in other words, one who claims divine inspiration. To take an easy example, should Christ Jesus be considered a prophet by the first definition, Paul would have to be considered a man who professed to be categorized in the second.

Which leads to a critical issue. One fact, which quickly becomes apparent to students of religion, is that Judaism, Christianity, and Islam all evolved from an original core message of remarkable consistency to a kaleidoscope of sects founded upon bizarre creeds of mystical transformation. What is interesting to note in each such case is not only the remarkable consistency of the shared foundation (being strict monotheistic creed), but also the critical role 'inspired prophets' played in corrupting these religions from the orthodoxy of the original.

(SECTION 4) MESSENGERS

Hence, strict, literalistic Orthodox Judaism largely succumbed to the more permissive and relaxed Reform Judaism; the monotheism and commitment to Old Testament law which characterized Christianity at the period of origins lost over to the Trinitarian formula and the lawless concept of justification by faith; and oxthodox Islam similarly has been compromised by the corruptions of 'reform' and 'modernization' movements which have attempted to rewrite the laws of Islam. At the head of each of these sectarian divisions is a man, woman or group claiming heightened spiritual insight, by which they seduce followers to a religious construct of greater permissiveness. But as with all seductions, nobody follows unless deep down they really want to. The fact of the matter is that the world is divided into two kinds of people on this issue. Just as some people prefer cats and others dogs, some cars and others trucks, some sweet and others savory, well, in similar manner some trust scripture and the prophets who conveyed it; others mold guidance around a core of mysticism, typically trusting to the promise of an easy, if not effortless, salvation, as offered by those who claim divine inspiration and heightened spiritual insight.

The fact that the teachings of these 'reform' groups typically contradict the teachings of the true prophets should serve as a warning to those enamored with the leaders' sanctimonious professions of holiness – sufficient holiness, that is, to overrule the teachings of the prophets, and of revelation itself. The true prophets called to something quite different, namely to worship God as one God and to keep the commandments of revelation.

Should criteria for distinguishing prophets from false claimants be derived, the above would have to weigh heavily into the formula. Those who contradict the teachings of the true prophets stand to be instantly disqualified. Those expressing bizarre ideology are close cousins. In addition, the evidence of divine condemnation is frequently manifest not only in how false claimants lived, which is commonly in high style, but also in how they died, which is typically horrific. Suicide and violent death, not infrequently by burning, is so common as to be striking.

Should we think of the true prophets, however, we discover a different pattern. True prophets typically lived lives of persecution and suffering, but bore the evidence of divine protection. Hence, although they did not live like kings or, in even higher style, like televangelists, and although they may have suffered severe trials in worldly terms, they always received relief and reward within their lifetimes. And in the end, they passed from this world in a peaceful, if not unremarkable, manner. One thinks of the enslaving and imprisonment of Joseph, followed by liberation and elevation in position; the suffering of Job, followed by the return of his health, wealth and, again, elevation in position; the rejection and ridicule of Noah, followed by salvation from the flood and from the disbelieving people accompanied by, yes, that's right, elevation in position; the trials and suffering of Moses, followed by the establishment of authority amongst the Jews. The list goes on, and the pattern is consistent. False prophets may enjoy high style in this worldly life in anticipation of a significantly less delightful decree in the hereafter, but true prophets tend to prove their sincerity through forebearance of trial, with an end result which carries the implication of divine approval.

Some might then ask, "But what about Jesus Christ? What about his crucifixion and suffering? What about his *passion*?" Yes, well, if Christ Jesus was not crucified, then there *was no passion*. Should such have been the case (as discussed in Section 2.B.10. above), the raising up of Jesus followed by his expected return combines to conform perfectly with the formula of relief from trial and establishment in authority.

Another feature of the true prophets was that they endorsed the

(Section 4) Messengers

unity of God and taught that there is only one religion, the worship in which is most pleasing to God. All other religions are either corruptions of an original revelation or man-made to begin with. Hence, each prophet was sent to correct those transgressing against previous revelation. At each stage of revelation up to and including the most recent and final revelation, some embraced while others refused, some sought to live the purity of the guidance and others were only partially-compliant, some attempted to pervert the message, and others denied it outright. Such a construct is easily believable -- it explains the diversity of religious schools and matches the collage of human nature. It explains what happened at each stage of revelation both with regard to the consistency of core revelation and the equally consistent degeneration into sectarian strife and mysticism. The concept of One God spreading out a myriad of divergent paths to all those who claim personal guidance (whether through divine inspiration or the guidance of the 'holy spirit')? That is considerably more difficult to accept, even though it may be appealing to those who gain satisfaction and a feeling of personal exclusivity thereby.

Those who revere scripture and the men appointed with transmission of God's revelation are challenged, then, to differentiate the true prophets from the charlatans, and true revelation from imitation (or, in the case of the Old and New Testaments, the truth from the adulterations).

Most people consider themselves capable of such discrimination, but it is a fact that for every prophet there have been those who considered him deluded, and for every deluded babbler there have been those who considered him a prophet. Not that critical defining features fail to exist for those who can look at such things with a mind devoid of prejudice – such defining indicators most certainly do exist. And it is through examination of the objective indicators of divine appointment that the truth of each claimant's case may be known.

(4.A)
Adam to Moses

"One man with courage is a majority."

– Andrew Jackson

Judaism, Christianity and Islam all describe the chain of prophethood from Adam to Moses, and recognize each prophet to have stood relatively alone in the field of righteousness during his day. The Bibles of the Jews and Christians, as well as The Holy Qur'an, all mention the following (with the Arabic names, where different, in parentheses): Adam, Noah (Nuh), Lot (Lut), Abraham (Ibrahim), Ishmael (Isma'il), Isaac (Ishaq), Jacob (Yaqoub), Joseph (Yusuf), Aaron (Harun), Moses (Musa), David (Dawood), Solomon (Sulaiman), Job (Ayyub), Ezekiel (Zulkifl), Jonah (Yunus), Elias (Ilyas), Elisha (Al-Yasa').

In addition, the Holy Qur'an mentions others, identified as prophets sent to small communities of their day. Examples include Hud, sent to the people of 'Ad (TMQ 7:65), and Salih, sent to the people of Thamud (TMQ 7:73) – two lost civilizations referenced in the library records of the Ebla dig, as previously mentioned (see Section 3.C.5.).

While many prophets are unanimously agreed upon, reported details of the lives of specific prophets differ. For example, Jews, Christians and Muslims all affirm the people of Lot to have perished

(4.A) Adam to Moses

as punishment for their 'backward' ways; the prophet Jonah is acknowledged as having traveled both directions on the slick waterslide somewhere south of a whale's seawater sifter; and everybody seems to agree that David made a stunning first (and last) impression on Goliath. However, significant differences are frequently encountered. The Islamic religion records Adam and his wife as having been forgiven for their sin, closing the door on the possibility of a concept such as that of 'Original Sin.' Incest, drunkenness, contracting prostitution, and murder are *not* attributed to the prophets in the Holy Qur'an, in contrast to Old Testament descriptions of Lot, Noah, Judah, and David. The Islamic religion, rather than struggling to explain impious behavior, asserts that the lives of the prophets exemplified, rather than contradicted, the righteous conduct they were sent to convey.

While continuity can be found in the chain of the major prophets, the pattern of prophethood remains somewhat elusive in the Jewish and Christian religions. Certainly, the genealogy of the human race appears to have been agreed upon: Adam had a wife, they had children, and from them the race known as mankind arose. The two sons of Adam established the tradition of sibling rivalry to no small degree, while also exemplifying the opposite poles of piety and unrighteous behavior. And men have been beating each other's brains out ever since.

A series of defined prophets followed in well-spaced sequence, with other prophets as off-shoots from the main lineage, and having been sent to specific communities by the command of the All-Mighty. But what is the overall scheme? Certainly, some prophets are recorded as having followed in the footsteps of others, such as the seemingly endless succession of prophets sent to the rebellious and wayward Jews. However, what about those cultures which grew, prospered, and died off without ever having a Moses or Christ in their midst in order

(SECTION 4) MESSENGERS

to direct the religion of the people? What is the fate of such a populace? The only resource for resolution of such questions, within the confines of Judeo-Christian teachings, lies in speculation.

The Islamic religion, on the other hand, teaches a framework of Divine methodology which is filled out by the stories of the prophets. The Islamic understanding, as previously mentioned, is that messengers were sent throughout time to bear the essential teachings of God to mankind. The first prophet/messenger was Adam, who bore the truth of God to his wife and offspring. Mankind soon spread out into villages, tribes, etc., but no population was ever left without guidance. As per the Holy Qur'an,

> "Verily, We have sent you (i.e., Muhammad) in truth, as a bearer of glad tidings, and as a warner: and there never was a people, without a warner having lived among them (in the past)" (TMQ 35:24).

Somewhere in time, God bestowed the blessing of written language upon mankind, and subsequent revelation was recorded in hard copy. In specific, the Suhuf (Sheets) were revealed to Abraham, the Zaboor (Psalms) to David, the Tawraat (Torah) to Moses, the Injeel (Gospel) to Jesus and the Qur'an to Muhammad.

With the advent of written records, each revelation enjoyed greater duration and circulation, with reduced need for human reminders. However, scripture came to be manipulated and corrupted, with each scriptural perversion demanding a renewed revelation to set the record straight. The Islamic religion claims the chain of prophethood and revelation culminated in the disclosure of a final revelation which was endowed with Divine protection until the end of time. That final revelation was sent with proofs and promises, as discussed above, and through a final prophet. Who that final prophet was, and what is the revelation with which he was sent, according to Islamic faith, is no mystery.

(4.B)
Moses

"What matters is not how far you fall, but how high you bounce."
— Anonymous

Who was the Moses of the Old Testament? A human 'Trojan Horse' in the house of Pharaoh, a murderer in self-imposed exile, a man of honor and integrity returning to the land of his crime fearless of consequences in order to satisfy the command of his Lord and Creator, and a prophet struggling against all levels of adversity, both from without and within the rebellious body of refugees rescued from slavery by the will of God – this was the man Moses. He was a prophet rejected by the majority of the people of his homeland, repeatedly defied by those he was sent to save, who struggled, to the end, to instill some vague sense of unity and God-fear in a people who, time and again, openly flouted their disobedience.

And yet he persisted. He fell from a lofty royal office to the lowest position of anonymity, only to hit the trampoline of revelation strung between a series of supportive miracles, from which he bounced to the highest human appointment known in this life.

(SECTION 4) MESSENGERS

And in this he appears to have succeeded, for he is understood to have left this earth having satisfied what was commanded of him. From amongst his followers there grew a few who remained upon the strictness of Old Testament law, and a large number who diverged therefrom. Most peculiar, however, is that while the revelation transmitted through Moses admonished the Jews for their transgressions, over and again, the only message many of them seem to have retained is the concept of having been 'chosen.' The importance of fidelity to the mandates of God became secondary, in many minds, to the simplistic concept of racial elitism. This despite the number of Old Testament verses which criticize or condemn the Jews.

For example, Moses went through some pretty thick hieroglyphics for the sake of those to whom he bore his message of revelation. Yet he couldn't even take a leave of absence to commune with The Creator for 40 days without those followers who were closest to the revelation reverting to paganism. Even though they had witnessed the miracles – having walked between the walls of water, been shaded by a pillar of cloud during the day and warmed by a pillar of fire at night, been sustained on manna and quail and watered from the rock of twelve springs, all by the grace of God – when Moses stepped out of the picture for a little communion with The One who saved and protected them all, they set about making a useless idol of an impotent flop-dropping quadraped! (Neh 9:9-18) God's reaction? To advise Moses:

> " 'Arise, go down quickly from here, for your people whom you brought out of Egypt have acted corruptly; they have quickly turned aside from the way which I commanded them; they have made themselves a molded image...I have seen this people, and indeed they are a stiff-necked people. Let Me alone, that I may destroy them and blot out their name from under heaven...'" (Deuteronomy 9:12-14)

(4.B) MOSES

The Old Testament continues by recounting the Jews' rebellion against the commandments (e.g. Deuteronomy 9:22-24), their stubbornness and wickedness (e.g. Deuteronomy 9:27), their breaking of their covenant with God and his anger against them (e.g. Deuteronomy 31:16-21), with Moses effectively summing up,

> "Take this Book of the Law, and put it beside the ark of the covenant of the LORD your God, that it may be there as a witness against you; for I know your rebellion and your stiff neck. If today, while I am yet alive with you, you have been rebellious against the LORD, then how much more after my death? Gather to me all the elders of your tribes, and your officers, that I may speak these words in their hearing and call heaven and earth to witness against them. For I know that after my death you will become utterly corrupt, and turn aside from the way which I have commanded you. And evil will befall you in the latter days, because you will do evil in the sight of the LORD, to provoke Him to anger through the work of your hands." (Deuteronomy 31:26-29)

See also Deuteronomy 32:16-21, wherein God is recorded as having said,

> "They have provoked Me to jealousy by what is not God;
> They have moved Me to anger by their foolish idols.
> But I will provoke them to jealousy by those
> who are not a nation;
> I will move them to anger by a foolish nation."

This last line concerning '...who are not a nation....a foolish nation' may strike a cord of interest, for which group of people in the land of the Israelites were more divided than the Ishmaelites, i.e., the Arabs? An uneducated and ignorant, 'foolish,' if you will,

(SECTION 4) MESSENGERS

disparate and divided group of desert-dwellers in the pre-Islamic Period of Ignorance, they were so much 'not a nation' that Alexander the Great, the Persian empire, the Roman empire, and the Egyptians all passed them by. Why? Because there was no Arabian nation to conquer. They were so divided and spread out, so unorganized and tribal, that there was no national identity to address and no crown jewels to covet. Yet, following the revelation of the Holy Qur'an, these people became united for the first time in history, rose up to develop the greatest intellectual institutes of their day, spread their territorial boundaries from Spain to the edge of China, establishing, in the short span of 25 years, an empire which held dominion over more kingdoms and countries than ever the Roman Empire did in eight hundred. In addition to which they subjugated the Jews, effectively 'move(ing) them to anger by a foolish nation.'

And God foretold of even greater punishment:

"I will heap disasters on them;
I will spend My arrows on them.
They shall be wasted with hunger,
Devoured by pestilence and bitter destruction;
I will also send against them the teeth of beasts,
With the poison of serpents of the dust.
The sword shall destroy outside;
There shall be terror within
For the young man and virgin
The nursing child with the man of gray hairs…
Vengeance is Mine, and recompense
Their foot shall slip in due time
For the day of their calamity is at hand
And the things to come hasten upon them."
(Deuteronomy 32:23-35)

(4.B) Moses

And yet, despite God's repeated punishments, chastisements, curses and condemnation, how often does a person encounter a member of the Jewish religion contemplating the significance of such harsh statements of censure, as opposed to boastfully parroting the phrase of 'chosen people'? The error is regrettable, for it misguides many to consider themselves above the law, and beyond the need of recognizing the prophets predicted to follow. For Moses conveyed more than a law – he transmitted a message of hope with the prediction of three prophets to follow in the line of Divinely-appointed messengers. The Jews understood this. A person could reasonably conclude that it was for this reason that the Pharisees inquired into the identity of John the Baptist. To quote John 1:19-21:

> Now this is the testimony of John, when the Jews sent priests and Levites from Jerusalem to ask him, "Who are you?" He confessed, and did not deny, but confessed, "I am not the Christ." And they asked him, "What then? Are you Elijah?" He said, "I am not." "Are you the Prophet?" And he answered, "No."

After John the Baptist identified himself in evasive terms, the Pharisees persisted by inquiring, "Why then do you baptize if you are not the Christ, nor Elijah, nor the Prophet?" (John 1:25).

Christ, Elijah, and 'the Prophet' – clearly enumerated not just once, but twice. By the scripture, John the Baptist wasn't the Christ, of that a person can be reasonably certain. John the Baptist is also recorded as having denied being Elijah (although Christ Jesus identified him as Elijah in Matthew 17:11-13). Inconsistencies aside, the real question is who this third messenger is. Who is 'the Prophet?'

Since the Jewish scholars of the time of John the Baptist lived in anticipation of three messengers to follow, a person can reasonably expect the Old Testament to bear evidence; for from what other source would the Pharisees have known to expect guests?

(SECTION 4) MESSENGERS

The Old Testament teems with predictions and descriptors of messengers to follow. Those passages aligned with predictions of John the Baptist and Christ Jesus are well known, as previously discussed. Predictably, however, several passages simply do not fit the description of Christ Jesus or John the Baptist, as might be expected considering the fact that the Jews anticipated a third, – one whom they identified as 'the Prophet.' Amongst these predictors is the chapter of Isaiah 42. The prophet spoken of in Isaiah 42 is twice referred to as a messenger to the Gentiles (Isaiah 42:1 and 42:6), unlike Christ Jesus, who was an ethnic prophet, not having been sent, '…except to the lost sheep of the house of Israel.' (Matthew 15:24)

Furthermore, the prophet predicted in Isaiah 42 (see verse 11) is suggested to be an Ishmaelite prophet in the line of Kedar (through which the ancestry of Muhammad is to be traced), consistent with other Old Testament predictors of an Ishmaelite prophet (see, for example, Genesis 17:20 ["And as for Ishmael, I have heard you. Behold, I have blessed him, and will make him fruitful, and will multiply him exceedingly. He shall beget twelve princes, and I will make him a great nation."], Genesis 21:13 ["Yet I will also make a nation of the son of the bondwoman, because he *is* your seed."], and Genesis 21:18 ["Arise, lift up the lad and hold him with your hand, for I will make him a great nation."].

Relevant to this topic, discussion was offered above in Section 3.A (item number 12 in the list of Old Testament contradictions) to the effect that the names of Isaac and Ishmael may have been switched where it served a purpose. The suggestion is not unreasonable, for other elements of the story fit together no better than a square peg in a round hole. A very large square peg in a very small round hole, to be sure. (see item number 4 of the same list, Section 3.A).

The aforementioned Isaiah 42 is not the only passage of the Old Testament which suggests a prophet other than John the Baptist or

(4.B) MOSES

Christ Jesus. Jeremiah 28:9 states, "As for the prophet who prophesies of peace, when the word of the prophet comes to pass, the prophet will be known *as* one whom the LORD has truly sent." Should a person accept this verse as a criterion by which to judge one who claims prophethood, Muslims would be quick to point out that Muhammad satisfies the verse. Not only did Muhammad prophesy peace, but, as discussed in the sections on Qur'anic evidences, every prediction found within the Holy Qur'an has either come to pass or, at the very least, remains unassailable. An interesting thought to ponder is that the word translated to 'peace' in the above quote of Jeremiah 28:9 is the Hebrew word, 'shalom,' the Arabic equivalent of which is *'salam,'* or 'Islam.' Hence, should the above verse be translated into Arabic, it would read, "As for the prophet who prophesies of *salam*..." or "As for the prophet who prophesies of Islam..."

Most significant, however, is the point that because Jeremiah 28:9 speaks of a prophet who would prophesy peace, John the Baptist and Christ Jesus are likely to be excluded. While most Christians associate Christ Jesus with a religion of peace, history presents the reality of the case to be nothing if not the opposite. The many evils which have been committed in the name of God by Christian believers, as well as the numerous horrific Christian campaigns for religious domination, can be held up as evidence. Furthermore, a person notes with interest that Christ Jesus did not claim to have been a messenger of peace. On the contrary, Jesus is recorded to have stated, "Do not think that I came to bring peace on earth. I did not come to bring peace but a sword." (Matthew 10:34) and "Do *you* suppose that I came to give peace on earth? I tell you, not at all, but rather division." (Luke 12:51). So who is the predicted prophet who would prophesy peace (*salam*, or Islam), if not Jesus?

Jacob, in Genesis 49:10, stated that,

(Section 4) Messengers

> "The scepter shall not depart from Judah,
> Nor a lawgiver from between his feet,
> Until Shiloh comes;
> And to Him *shall be* the obedience of the people."

Who, or what, is this 'Shiloh?' A person, a place, a town, an ideology? It doesn't much matter. Could 'Shiloh' refer to Christ Jesus? Most certainly not, for he was born in the bloodline of Judah, from which this verse predicts the scepter to depart. Could 'Shiloh' refer to Islam, since (as Muslims point out) both Shiloh and Islam mean peace? Well, maybe. But maybe not. Again, it doesn't much matter. What does matter is that the loss of the power of legislation and prophethood in the line of Isaac is foretold. It's a done deal. If the Old Testament is to be respected, it either has happened, or will happen. After all, what is the entire book of 'Malachi' about, if not the transfer of revelation from the wayward Israelites to the line of the Gentiles?

Attempting to navigate the somewhat tangled forest of the Old Testament, then, a person discovers the ancient ruins of a thriving, though seldom recognized and less often discussed, concept. Eroded by the whims of human speculation and lying nearly concealed beneath the overgrowth of ancient prejudice, the solid substructure of Old Testament teachings suggest not only a third messenger to follow Moses, but one predicted in the line of the Ishmaelites.

Should a person recognize that the Old Testament speaks of a prophet to follow Jesus, identified to be within the line of Ishmael, and sought by those Jews in the know, a person can reasonably return to the focus of this chapter. In other words, if such a great prophet were to arise, would not the books of Moses be expected to have some few words of import on the subject? The suggestion is offered that they did. In Deuteronomy 18:18-22, God is recorded as having informed Moses of the following:

(4.B) MOSES

"I will raise up for them a Prophet like you from among their brethren, and will put My words in His mouth, and He shall speak to them all that I command Him. And it shall be *that* whoever will not hear My words, which He speaks in My name, I will require *it* of him. But the prophet who presumes to speak a word in My name, which I have not commanded him to speak, or who speaks in the name of other gods, that prophet shall die.' And if you say in your heart, 'How shall we know the word which the LORD has not spoken?'— when a prophet speaks in the name of the LORD, if the thing does not happen or come to pass, that *is* the thing which the LORD has not spoken; the prophet has spoken it presumptuously; you shall not be afraid of him.

The above verses deserve to be broken down.

To begin with, the predicted prophet was foretold to be a prophet like Moses. Secondly, the oral transmission of revelation was described. Thirdly, those who refuse to entertain the message will bear responsibility for their rejection. Lastly, some criteria by which the prophet can be recognized are defined.

Taken in order, a person has to question who, amongst the candidates, might be the prophet 'like Moses.' Christ Jesus does not appear to have been a likely candidate, for his lineage was through the line of Isaac, and the prophet in question was foretold to arise from among the brethren of the Israelites, which a person could not be faulted for understanding to mean the Ishmaelites. Opinions in the available literature waft back and forth on this subject, so an authoritative reference which removes all doubt would soothe the convictions, for too many religious reference works are slanted to one degree or another. The definitive reference in this case is to be found in the Bible itself, for the Ishmaelites are identified as brethren of the Israelites in Genesis 16:12. This verse states of Ishmael, "...and he shall dwell in the presence of all his brethren." One wonders how this could be when, at the time of this revelation, Ishmael did not even have offspring? For that matter he, himself, wasn't even born yet. An average of 14 years to maturity, nine months for the first child, another 15 years for the first child to mature and blend bloodlines with those of an outsider, another 15 years to maturity – nearly fifty years would have had to have passed before the bloodline could be diluted to 25%. So who could the brethren, in whose presence Ishmael would dwell, be, if the only other Ishmaelites, for the next fifty or so years, would be his very own children and grandchildren? If the passage meant to speak of his offspring, a person would expect them to be described as such, for to call a person's own offspring 'brethren' is to snap and splice a few branches off the old family tree. The only remaining candidates for brethren to Ishmael, then, were his brothers, the Israelites.

Recognition of the above focuses inquiry upon the question of who 'the prophet' in the line of the Ishmaelites might then be.

(a) To begin with, Moses was born of both father and mother, whereas Jesus was born by immaculate conception, which is to say, without a father

(b) Moses married and had children while Jesus was unmarried and celibate

(c) Moses, though initially rejected by his people, was eventually accepted, while Jesus to this day is rejected by the people to whom he was sent – i.e., the Israelites

(d) Moses was a king to his people, holding the power to assign capital punishment, as found in Numbers 15:35-36, while Jesus held that "...My kingdom is not of this world..." (John 18:36) and refused to assign capital punishment, as recorded in the story of the adulterous woman (John 8:3-7)

(e) Moses conveyed a new law to the people whereas Jesus professed, "Do not think that I came to destroy the Law or the Prophets.

(4.B) Moses

I did not come to destroy but to fulfill." (Matthew 5:17). The role of Jesus was to confirm and remind the Israelites of the law they already had—the Mosaic Law—and not to introduce a new covenant

(f) Moses led his people to freedom in a mass exodus from the land of their persecution. There is no such parallel in the historical record of Jesus

(g) Moses was victorious over his enemies whereas the Biblical record claims that Jesus was the opposite—a victim to his enemies

(h) Moses died a natural death, and was buried in the ground. The Christian claim is that Jesus was crucified and his body raised up to heaven

(i) Moses was held by his people to have been a prophet, but a mortal man. Jesus was and is held by Christians to be God, a son of God, and/or partner with God.

(j) Once dead, Moses stayed dead, whereas Christians claim Jesus to have been resurrected.

On the other hand, Muhammad was born in the line of Ishmael, with genealogy traced through the second son Kedar. And, to revisit the above points of comparison, both Moses and Muhammad were born of both a father and a mother. Both Moses and Muhammad married and had children. Both, though initially rejected by their people, were eventually accepted and elevated to hold the power of kings, including the power to assign capital punishment, direct the people to warfare, etc. Both conveyed a new law to the people, while maintaining unchanged the essential elements of monotheistic creed. Moses led his people to freedom in a mass exodus from the land of their persecution; Muhammad did the same in directing his people from Makkah to Medina in the hijra (migration). Both Moses and Muhammad were victorious over their enemies. Both died natural deaths, and were buried. Both were held by their people to be prophets, but mortal men. Neither suffered apotheosis, and neither

(SECTION 4) MESSENGERS

were resurrected. In fact, whereas attempts to define parallels between Jesus and Moses, whether with regard to their worldly lives or prophetic missions, prove frustrating, it is a challenge to find one single element of importance in the life of either Muhammad or Moses which does not have a close parallel in the life of the other.

Jesus, unlike Muhammad, can hardly be said to have been 'like Moses,' as is the description of the foretold prophet in this passage of Deuteronomy 18:18-22.

In satisfaction of the remainder of the above verses of Deuteronomy, Muhammad conveyed an oral revelation claimed to have been transmitted by the angel of revelation. He conveyed this revelation over a period of 23 years, without suffering the death promised to false prophets. And there was no doubt in whose name Muhammad claimed to speak, for all but one of the 114 surahs of the Holy Qur'an begin with the dedication, "In the name of Allah, most Gracious, most Merciful." Nothing in the revelation has ever failed to come true, and nothing has ever been proven false, contrary to the promised fate of false prophecies, as per the above verses.

So who believes the predicted prophet in Old Testament Deuteronomy 18:18-22 bears association with "…the prophet" foretold in New Testament John 1:21? Well, Christians, for one. Pick up any Bible bearing cross-references, such as the *New International Version Study Bible,* and a person will find that John 1:21 cross-references Deuteronomy 18:18. Christian scholars believe these two passages link together in description of the same final messenger.

Muslims claim that firmly fixing the above stanchions of comparison limits the sway in the field of historical possibilities. Muslims assert that Muhammad fulfills all the Old Testament predictors of the foretold prophet, and wonder why the commandment, "Him you shall hear…" is so oft-ignored by the body of those who claim to keep the commandments of God. Most Christians, however, continue to

(4.B) Moses

assert that the Biblical prediction of a prophet to follow Jesus remains unfulfilled, prompting Muslims to compare the Christian denial of Muhammad with the obstinate Jewish denial of Jesus. The argument is advanced that both cases seem to defy fairly conclusive evidence in the context of revelation and history, and both postures reveal more devotion to doctrine than divinity. But to be fair to the Christians, a person is forced to consider what Jesus had to say on the subject.

(4.C)
Christ Jesus

"Pressed into service means pressed out of shape."
— Robert Frost, "The Self-Seeker"

Who was Christ Jesus? That question has plagued the world of Christianity for two millennia. The historical Jesus is so shrouded in mystery as to have invited thousands of books on the subject, with no resultant clear consensus of opinion. Many authors have stitched together comfortable pillows of conjecture upon which popular opinion reclines, whereas others rip the seams open and pull out the stuffing with polished tongs of conflicting evidences and rational argument. Heinz Zahrnt builds one such convincing argument, which concludes:

> "Once the Biblical history had been divested of dogma, the Christ proclaimed by the Church seemed in unavoidable conflict with Jesus himself. There was a manifest contradiction between what historical investigation discovered about Jesus of Nazareth and what the Church said of him in its preaching, between what Jesus himself originally proclaimed and did and what the Church afterwards made of him."[340]

340. Zahrnt, Heinz. p. 43.

(4.C) Christ Jesus

Regarding the deficiencies of the historical record, he comments:

"This was the reason why those who studied the life of Jesus could never escape from their predicament. How are the gaps to be filled in? In the worst instances this was done with clichés, in the best with historical fantasy....

The image of the historical Jesus which was now being developed was not in fact simply drawn from the historical sources. It was largely governed by the presuppositions entertained by the writers themselves."[341]

Martin Kähler concluded the following:

"The Jesus of the "Lives of Jesus" is nothing but a modern variation of the products of human inventive art, no better than the discredited dogmatic Christ of Byzantine Christology; both are equally far removed from the real Christ."[342]

The shock in review of such literature is not in discovering how little is known of the *private* life of this great messenger of God, but in learning how little is known of his *public* person, and just how free people are in speculation thereupon. Scant knowledge exists of the man who taught in the synagogues, lectured on the mount, and organized the guidance and feeding of the masses. Touring the countryside, reportedly turning water into wine, calming storms, walking on water, exorcising demons, healing lepers, curing blind, raising dead, he must have attracted a lot of attention, he must have made quite an impression. Why, then, is his historical person so inadequately described? More importantly, why has the little which *has* been passed down in the historical record been buried beneath

---
341. Zahrnt, Heinz. pp. 47-48.
342. Kähler, Martin. 1953. *Der sogennante historische Jesus und der geschichtliche, biblische Christus*. Munich: New edn by Ernst Wolf. p. 16, as quoted by H. Zahrnt.

conflicting dogmas, to the point that, "...the discontinuity between the historical Jesus and the Christ of the Church became so great that it was almost impossible to recognize any unity between the two figures"?[343]

The critical question, then, becomes whether Jesus was the Christ of scripture or the Christ of Pauline Theology. The Christ of scripture spoke of a final prophet to follow, but Pauline theology pushed the primacy of seeking the final prophet from the forefront of Christian consciouness with the promise of salvation based on faith alone – the Christian analogue of the Jewish concept of having been 'chosen.' The Jews consider themselves chosen, the Christians consider themselves forgiven. Neither viewpoint was endorsed by the prophets of scripture, and both prove destructive through inviting a false sense of spiritual security, religious elitism, and closed-mindedness.

Similarly, the Christ of scripture spoke of himself as a 'son of man,' yet Pauline theology painted him to be 'son of God.' The Christ of scripture spoke of One God; the religious reformers proposed to partition the One God into three metaphysical plots. Jesus focused on God, the Christians of Pauline theology focus on Jesus, or even more oddly, on his mother. Jesus spoke of not changing the law; they discarded it. Jesus spoke of the final prophet and the angel of revelation; they transmuted his words to imply some intangible, esoteric 'holy spirit,' to the point where instead of seeking the final prophet as foretold by Jesus, Pauline 'Christians' focus their priorities on embodying some mystical 'holy spirit,' of whom their preachers claim to possess exclusive distribution rights.

Previous chapters have addressed the above issues by chipping away the fractured amber of Christian mysticism, within which the reality of the man Jesus remains frozen and obscured. The stark conflict between the Christ of scripture and the Christ of Pauline theology clearly exposed, people have to realize that they can have one,

---

343. Zahrnt, Heinz. p. 61.

(4.C) Christ Jesus

but not both. Moving on to more worldly issues, the average person expects certain qualities from a prophet, including modesty and humility, honesty, benevolence, gentleness and kindness, and the best of manners. A prophet is expected to be preoccupied with worship, rather than to focus on material benefits of worldly pursuits. And, for the most part, the brief Biblical sketch of the man, Christ Jesus, satisfies these expectations. But not always.

Cursing a fig tree for not bearing fruit (Matthew 21:19, Mark 11:20-21), likening Gentiles (and don't look now, but that is most of mankind, most of this book's audience, and most of those of the Christian faith) to dogs (Matthew 15:26, Mark 7:27) or swine (Matthew 7:6), and rebuffing his very own mother, as if she were not of those who "...does the will of my Father in heaven..." or who "...hear God's word and put it into practice..." (Matthew 12:48-50, Mark 3:31-35, Luke 8:20-21), a person encounters accounts which drag one wheel on the soft shoulder of the road of lofty expectations. The resultant dust cloud is slightly off-putting, especially when pelted by the loose gravel of the claim that Christ Jesus lost faith in his Creator, questioning Divine Decree with the sacrilegious words, "My God, my God, why have you forsaken me?" (Matthew 27:46). History boils over with examples of righteous men and women who endured equal or greater suffering, persecution, and death in the path of what they believed to be obedience to Almighty God. The tales of such martyrs dying with staunch and intact faith are copious. Yet a person is to believe that Christ Jesus died questioning, with his last words, the decree of his Creator? Socrates died without a word of impatience or despair.[344] Michael Servetus and Joan of Arc were burned to death with more honor and dignity, and with more intact faith than Christ Jesus? Once again, either the words attributed to Jesus had to have been wrong, or the authors quoted the wrong man.

---

344. Gibbon, Edward, Esq. Vol. 5, Chapter XLVII, p. 206.

(SECTION 4) MESSENGERS

So what should we make of the above quotes? If they are to be believed, a more human and less 'divine' impression of the man, Jesus, emerges. And perhaps that is precisely the point. On the other hand, if the above quotes are not to believed, we return to questioning what part of the Bible is to be trusted.

Having said that, the thrust of this work is to derive conclusions based upon a chain of accepted evidences, and not to throw one more straw of opinion onto the mountainous haystack of speculation. If the needle of truth with regard to the historical person of Christ Jesus has not been discovered and laid bare for analysis by the present age, it likely will remain buried until such time as he returns. And in any case, the vast majority of mankind reject any one man's opinion on the subject. One person's scholar is another's totem of ridicule, and frequently for good reason.

Yet Christians, for the most part, at least agree to accept most of what Christ Jesus was recorded as having said in the Bible. And it is from this perspective that the seekers of the foretold final prophet analyze the scripture, wondering, as the Jews did with Moses, what Christ Jesus had to say on the subject.

With regard to the assertion that the final prophet would be from the line of Ishmael, Jesus is quoted as having taught the parable of the vineyard, the lesson of which is that those who fail in keeping their covenant, and who defy and kill the messengers, will be destroyed by God and replaced by those who would "...render to (God) the fruits in their seasons." (Matthew 21:41). Following this parable, Jesus was recorded to have said:

"Have you never read in the Scriptures
'The stone which the builders rejected
Has become the chief cornerstone
This was the LORD's doing
And it is marvelous in our eyes'?*
"Therefore I say to you, the kingdom of God will be taken

(4.C) CHRIST JESUS

from you and given to a nation bearing the fruits of it."
*(Psalm 118:22-23)

The reaction of the chief priests and Pharisees? They "...perceived that He was speaking of them" (Matthew 21:45). Of note is that Christ Jesus was not quoted as *threatening* that the kingdom of God would be taken away. A threat, by definition, is conditional, along the lines of, "If you don't do this, then such-and-such will happen." That is a threat. But the above is not a conditional threat – it is an unconditional decree. It was over. The decision had been made. It was going to happen.

So here is a passage which references the transfer of "...the kingdom of God..." from the Israelites to a "...nation bearing the fruits of it." Not only a faithful nation, but one which would "...become the chief cornerstone." Exactly who this passage refers to is the subject of great and unrelenting debate. However, what defies debate is the simple and undeniable fact that the above passage predicts transfer of revelation outside the line of the Israelites. So who are referenced as "The stone which the builders rejected?" Who are those slated to receive this revelation? Ask a hundred Christians. Ask a thousand Jews. Ask Paul of Tarsus. The answer is always the same. The 'rejected' are the Ishmaelites.

Analysis was made of the *'paraclete'* Christ Jesus predicted to follow the period of his ministry in section 2.B.9. Repetition is unnecessary. Suffice it to say that the four passages of the Gospel according to John (14:16, 14:26, 15:26, and 16:7), foretell the coming of **another** *'paraclete,'* where Christ Jesus was himself described as a *'paraclete'* in the 1st epistle of John 2:1. The foretold prophet is expected to be "...the Spirit of truth...," and to "...abide with you forever..." (John 14:16-17), to convey a comprehensive revelation, remind the people of the message of Christ Jesus, reverence Christ Jesus (John 14:26 and 15:26), and yet, be rejected by the majority of

477

mankind (John 14:17). One renown author, after listing the evidences, concluded,

> "The Paraclete therefore is a parallel figure to Jesus himself; and this conclusion is confirmed by the fact that the title is suitable for both. It is clear from 14.16 that the source taught that there were two sendings of two Paracletes, Jesus and his successor, the one following the other."[345]

This concept of an unfulfilled prophecy leaves the Christian world with a blank scriptural check – the prediction remains unfulfilled, in their view, and awaits the account holder to come and fill in the blanks. Muslims claim that the final prophet *has* come, and point out that Muhammad's honesty was unchallenged even by his enemies, and that he bore the distinctive reputation of telling the truth even when joking. His historical person is preserved in exquisite detail within extensive hadith records, which 'abide' with mankind to the present day. The Holy Qur'an reverences Christ Jesus and claims to correct misunderstandings over his teachings, thereby registering a reminder of his true message. At the same time, the Holy Qur'an is a comprehensive revelation which suffuses the spirituality and directs the exercise of the essential elements of a believer's life. Accepted by over a billion Muslims, both the Holy Qur'an and the messenger Muhammad are nonetheless rejected by the majority of mankind.

Why? What is so appealing to some, and so distasteful to others about this man, Muhammad? And do those who pass opinion upon him actually know the man? Commonly, a person finds that those who reject Muhammad do so based upon personal dislike of the message with which he was sent, or based upon unfounded propaganda to which they are exposed (which, in non-Muslim countries, is overwhelmingly negative). Conclusions of non-Muslims based upon objective study of the character of the man himself are rare.

---

345. Bultmann, Rudolf. 1971. *The Gospel of John, a Commentary.* Translated by G. R. Beasley-Murray. Oxford: Basil Blackwell. p. 567.

(4.D)
Muhammad

"In matters of style, swim with the current;
In matters of principle, stand like a rock."

– Thomas Jefferson

So who was this man Muhammad? Prospecting for resolution to this question demands the ages-old process of passing the waters of history over the heterogeneous soil of the opinions of humankind. Once the worthless dirt of prejudiced or politically/doctrinally motivated editorials (both positive and negative) are washed away by the pure current of verifiable historical fact, the truth of the personage of Muhammad has a chance to settle out for clear inspection.

Several good biographies have been written upon this subject, the most excellent and highly acclaimed being *Muhammad, His Life Based on the Earliest Sources*, by Martin Lings and *When the Moon Split* by Safi-ur-Rahman al-Mubarakpuri.* There is insufficient

---

* Few works, including those of excellence, are without error, and the biography by Martin Lings proves this point. The two errors which are significant enough to warrant mention are the assertion that Muhammad preserved icons of Jesus and Mary, as well as a picture of Abraham, when he destroyed the idols of the Kaaba, and that Muhammad sought Zainab in marriage due to physical attraction. Neither of these

(contd. on page 480)

(SECTION 4) MESSENGERS

room in such a work as this for a full biography, and a biography equal to those of the above books would be difficult, at best. However, some salient points can be introduced.

Muhammad, the son of Abdullah Ibn 'Abdul-Muttalib Ibn Hashim and Amina bint Wahb, was born in Makkah into the powerful tribe of Quraysh in or about the year 570 CE – a time, place and culture dominated by idol worship and heathen practices. Muhammad's father died before he was born, and his mother passed away when he was only 6 years old. He was raised an orphan by a Bedouin family, where he gained the essential skills necessary for shepherding and caravan trading. Over time he became well regarded for high ethics and honesty, gentleness, fairness, sobriety and a deep, contemplative spirituality. With time he rose to wealth and high social position upon marriage to one of the most eligible widows of Quraysh, Khadijah, at the age of 25. She was 15 years his senior, yet he remained faithful to her throughout their loving marriage, unto her death. By the age of 40 he had secured a successful life, having been happily married with children, wealth and high social position. Yet it was at this point that he began receiving revelation in a traumatic and terrifying upset to the peace and tranquility to which he had become accustomed. Subsequently, he went on to sacrifice virtually everything of this world for the sake of conveying the message revealed through him. It was at the conclusion of that purpose that he passed from this worldly life in the year 632 CE.

(contd. from page 479)

assertions is supported by the textual evidences (i.e., the hadith), and both are condemned by the scholars of the Sunni orthodoxy. The biography is otherwise comprehensive, well-researched, beautifully written, inspirational, and highly regarded amongst Muslims and Orientalists alike. Consequently, the common opinion amongst the members of the educated Islamic community is that despite the few errors encountered therein, there is probably no better biography of Muhammad available in the English language, at the present time, than that of Martin Lings.

(4.D) Muhammad

Forced to face enemies to the monotheism of the revelation, Muhammad initially found himself confined between the hatred of his tribesmen, whose religion required many idols, and the malevolence of those Jews and pagans who rejected his message and sought his death. Forced first to flee, and later to fight, the small band of Muslims who joined Muhammad in faith succeeded and grew against remarkable odds. With time Islam revolutionized life throughout the Arabian Peninsula. Idol worship and the practices of the period of pagan ignorance were abolished, women liberated from the oppression of tribal custom, and a code of conduct, morality and social justice established from that day to this. More profound than any other accomplishment, a religion was established wherein worship was directed to the One God, and a revelation conveyed which has grown to be guidance and inspiration to one fifth of the world's population.

Alexander Ross, though no friend of the Islamic religion, nonetheless neatly outlines the purpose of Muhammad as follows:

"He did not pretend to deliver any new religion to them, but to revive the old one, which God gave first to Adam; and when lost in the corruption of the old world, restored it again by revelation to Abraham, who taught it his son Ismael their ancestor, and then he, when he settled first in Arabia, instructed men in the same; but their posterity degenerating into idolatry, God sent him now to destroy it, and restore the religion of Ismael. He allow'd both of the Old and New Testament, and that Moses and Christ were prophets sent from God; but that the Jews and Christians had corrupted these Holy Writings, and that he was sent to purge them from those corruptions, and to restore the Law of God to that purity in which it was first deliver'd..."[346]

---

346. Ross, Alexander. 1718. *The Life of Mahomet: Together with The Alcoran at Large.* London. p. 7.

(Section 4) Messengers

During his lifetime, Muhammad came to be known and described with regard to his roles as child, father, friend, husband, neighbor, merchant, teacher, preacher, judge and law-giver, commanding general, statesman, ruler, and gentleman. Above all, he was a poor man by choice and a social and religious reformer. Perhaps the most influential man of history, yet he was illiterate throughout his life.

His person is well documented, from descriptions of physical appearance to traits and habits, teachings and endorsements. For example, from the late 1800's, in a time and place where such compliments were of scant popularity, if not frankly condemned by an oppressive Anglican Church, a person finds,

> "Mohammad was of middle height, rather thin, but broad of shoulders, wide of chest, strong of bone and muscle. His head was massive, strongly developed. Dark hair, slightly curled, flowed in a dense mass almost to his shoulders; even in advanced age it was sprinkled with only about twenty gray hairs, produced by the agonies of his 'Revelations.' His face was oval-shaped, slightly tawny of colour. Fine long arched eye-brows were divided by a vein, which throbbed visibly in moments of passion. Great black restless eyes shone out from under long heavy eyelashes. His nose was large, slightly acquiline. His teeth, upon which he bestowed great care, were well set, dazzling white. A full beard framed his manly face. His skin was clear and soft, his complexion 'red and white,' his hands were as 'silk and satin,' even as those of a woman. His step was quick and elastic, yet firm as that of one who steps 'from a high to a low place.' In turning his face he would also turn his whole body. His whole gait and presence was dignified and imposing. His countenance was mild and pensive. His laugh was rarely more than a smile.

(4.D) Muhammad

In his habits he was extremely simple, though he bestowed great care on his person. His eating and drinking, his dress and his furniture retained, even when he had reached the fullness of power, their almost primitive nature. The only luxuries he indulged in were, besides arms, which he highly prized, a pair of yellow boots, a present from the Negus of Abyssinia. Perfumes, however, he loved passionately, being most sensitive to smells. Strong drink he abhorred.

….He was gifted with mighty powers of imagination, elevation of mind, delicacy and refinement of feeling. 'He is more modest than a virgin behind her curtain,' it was said of him. He was most indulgent to his inferiors, and would never allow his awkward little page to be scolded whatever he did. 'Ten years,' said Anas his servant, 'was I about the Prophet, and he never said as much as "uff" to me.' He was very affectionate towards his family. One of his boys died on his breast in the smoky house of the nurse, a blacksmith's wife. He was very fond of children; he would stop them in the streets and pat their little heads. He never struck anyone in his life. The worst expression he ever made use of in conversation was, "What has come to him? May his forehead be darkened with mud!' When asked to curse someone, he replied, 'I have not been sent to curse, but to be a mercy to mankind.' 'He visited the sick, followed any bier he met, accepted the invitation of a slave to dinner, mended his own clothes, milked the goats, and waited upon himself,' related summarily another tradition. He never first withdrew his hand out of another man's palm, and turned not before the other had turned.

He was the most faithful protector of those he protected, the sweetest and most agreeable in conversation. Those who saw

(SECTION 4) MESSENGERS

him were suddenly filled with reverence; those who came near him loved him; they who described him would say, 'I have never seen his like either before or after.' He was of great taciturnity, but when he spoke it was with emphasis and deliberation, and no one could forget what he said."[347]

Even his greatest enemies admitted his virtues, from the period of his life to contemporary times. George Sale filed a statement which documented abject hatred buffered by admiration of Muhammad's personal virtues. In Sale's address 'To the Reader' of his translation of the Holy Qur'an, he stated,

"...for how criminal forever Mohammed may have been in imposing a false religion on mankind, the praises due to his real virtues ought not to be denied him; nor can I do otherwise than applaud the candour of the pious and learned Spanhemius, who, tho' he owned him to have been a wicked impostor, yet acknowledged him to have been richly furnished with natural endowments, beautiful in his person, of a subtle wit, agreeable behaviour, showing liberality to the poor, courtesy to every one, fortitude against his enemies, and above all a high reverence for the name of God; severe against the perjured, adulterers, murderers, flanderers, prodigals, covetous, false witnesses, etc. a great preacher of patience, charity, mercy, beneficence, gratitude, honouring of parents and superiors, and a frequent celebrator of the divine praises."[348]

Islamic history records a hadith in which Hind Ibn Abi Hala, the son (by previous marriage) of Muhammad's wife Khadijah, noted the following:

---

347. Lane-Poole, Stanley. 1882. *The Speeches and Table-Talk of the Prophet Mohammad.* London: MacMillan and Co. Introduction, pp. xxvii-xxix.
348. Sale, George. Address 'To the Reader,' page v.

(4.D) MUHAMMAD

"The Messenger of Allah was of consecutive sorrows, continuous thought, never finding rest, long in silence. He did not speak without cause. He spoke with his full mouth (was not arrogant), and spoke concisely. His speech was just, with neither excess nor deficiency. He was not pompous, nor denigrating. He exalted all blessings no matter how small and never belittled a single one. He would never praise his food nor criticize it. He was never angered by matters of this life nor that which was associated with it. However, if justice was transgressed nothing could stand up to his anger until justice was established. He never became angry for his own self nor sought retribution for himself. If he gestured, he did so with his whole palm. If he was amazed, he overturned it. If he spoke, he struck with his right palm the inside of his left thumb. If he became angry he turned away, and when he was happy he lowered his gaze. The majority of his laughter was (restricted to) smiling."[349]

Similarly, Ali Ibn Abi Talib, cousin to the prophet, described:

"He was not vulgar nor did he condone vulgarity, and he was not one to shout in the market place. He did not reward evil with evil, rather, he would forgive and overlook. He never in his life struck anything with his hand except when he was fighting in the name of Allah. He never struck a servant nor a woman, and I never saw him taking revenge for an injustice dealt him, except if the prohibitions of Allah were transgressed. For if the prohibitions of Allah were transgressed he was among the strongest of them in anger. He was never given a choice between two matters but he chose the simplest of the

---

349. Narrated by At-Tabarani in *Mu'ajm Al-Kabeer*.

two. If he entered into his home he was a man like any other, cleaning his own garment, milking his own goat, and serving himself."

"He was continually smiling, gentle in manners, soft in nature. He was not severe, harsh-hearted, loud, abusive, or miserly. He would disregard that which he disliked, and no one ever despaired of him. He never responded to disparagement or evil words. He forbade himself three things: argument, arrogance, and that which did not concern him. And he relieved the people of three: He would not degrade any among them or abuse them, he would not search after their honor or private matters, and he would not speak except in matters which he hoped to be rewarded for. When he spoke his attendees would lower their heads as if birds had alighted upon them. Once he finished they would speak. They would not vie with one-another in his presence to speak, but when one would talk in his presence the rest would listen until he finished. Speech in his presence was that of the first among them. He would laugh with them, and wonder with them. He had patience with the strangers when they were gruff in speech and requests, to a degree that his companions would fetch them to him. He would say: 'If you see someone in need, fetch him to me.' He would not accept praise except from those who were balanced and not excessive. He would not interject into someone's speech unless they transgressed, in which case he would either rebuke them or else leave."[350]

One of the most beautiful and succinct comments recorded in the hadith literature simply reads:

---

350. *Mukhtasar Ash-Shama'el Al Muhammadiyyah* by Imam At-Tirmithi, pg 18, hadith No. 6. Second paragraph also narrated by *At-Tabarani* in *Mu'ajm Al-Kabeer*.

(4.D) MUHAMMAD

"He was the most generous of heart, truthful of tongue, softest in disposition, and noble in relationship."[351]

The above quotes provide brief peeks through a small window through which the life and character of the man Muhammad can be viewed. In striking contrast to the fuzzy profile of the historical Abraham, Noah, Moses and Jesus, the personage of Muhammad is brought into focus in startling detail by the preservation of volumes of authenticated hadith cataloging the most intimate descriptors of appearance and manners, character and conduct. As a consequence, those Muslims who choose to do so can view Muhammad's life in fine focus of the historical man, and live in emulation of the many beautiful qualities he exemplified. In this regard, D.G. Hogarth wrote:

"Serious or trivial, his daily behaviour has instituted a canon which millions observe at this day with conscious mimicry. No one regarded by any section of the human race as Perfect Man has been imitated so minutely. The conduct of the Founder of Christianity has not so governed the ordinary life of his followers. Moreover, no founder of a religion has been left on so solitary an eminence as the Muslim Apostle."[352]

Acknowledgment of the truth of the above is forced by recognition that those who claim the title of 'Christian' most commonly defy, if not flaunt defiance, of the little that is known from the life and example of Christ Jesus, as listed in section 2.B.8. Whether looking at the example of modesty in dress, avoidance of pork and usury, wearing of a beard, praying in prostration, etc, the example of Christ Jesus has rarely been preserved in the practices of those who claim the title of 'Christian' followers. In fact, the living example of not

---

351. Narrated by *Al-Bukhari* and *Muslim*.
352. Hogarth, D.G. 1922. *Arabia*. Oxford: Clarendon Press. p. 52.

(Section 4) Messengers

only Muhammad, but of Jesus as well, is best visited in the practices of Muslims rather than Christians, with the most important example being respect of the commandment to worship God as One, alone and without partner.

To return to the man Muhammad, however, he has further been described as follows:

> "He was sober and abstemious in his diet, and a rigorous observer of fasts. He indulged in no magnificence of apparel, the ostentation of a petty mind; neither was his simplicity in dress affected; but the result of a real disregard to distinction from so trivial a source....
>
> His military triumphs awakened no pride, no vainglory, as they would have done had they been effected for selfish purposes. In the time of his greatest power, he maintained the same simplicity of manners and appearance as in the days of his adversity. So far from affecting regal state, he was displeased if, on entering a room, any unusual testimonial of respect were shown him. If he aimed at universal dominion, it was the dominion of the faith: as to the temporal rule which grew up in his hands, as he used it without ostentation, so he took no step to perpetuate it in his family.
>
> The riches which poured in upon him from tribute and the spoils of war, were expended in promoting the victories of the faith, and in relieving the poor among its votaries; insomuch that his treasury was often drained of its last coin. Omar Ibn Al Hareth declares that Mahomet, at his death, did not leave a golden dinar nor a silver dirhem, a slave nor a slave girl, nor anything but his gray mule Daldal, his arms, and the ground which he bestowed upon his wives, his children, and the poor.

(4.D) Muhammad

"Allah," says an Arabian writer, "offered him the keys of all the treasures of the earth, but he refused to accept them."[353]

The relevant question, however, is not how perfectly historical records preserve a profile of the man, but whether or not Muhammad was the prophet he claimed to be.

In order to evaluate the man Muhammad, several challenges arise. Certainly a person need overlook barriers of slander erected on impiety and fixed in place by the mortar of prejudiced hatred. Equally important, a person is best to deny admission of loving testimonies by the uneducated devout. Of course, were Muhammad a true prophet, no depth of love could reasonably be considered too great. However, were Muhammad a false prophet, the love of his followers would be nothing if not misdirected. Therefore, the call to establish the reality of the case must necessarily precede the emotions assigned thereupon. The foundation of such conclusions should properly rest upon facts, and little else, for even Satan has opinions – opinions, for that matter, of such effective seduction as to have misguided many of those presumed by men to have been amongst the very elect.

All positions in life have qualifying criteria, and the same is true of the station of prophethood. The example of the Biblical prophets is one of a number of men, each of whose claims of divine appointment was, sooner or later, supported by one or more of the following banquet of evidences.

---

353. Irving, Washington. 1973. *Mahomet and His Successors*. Vol 1. New York: G. P. Putnam's Sons. pp. 342-4.

(4.D) MUHAMMAD

(4.D1) Predictions in Previous Scripture

> The best way to suppose what may come,
> is to remember what is past"
>
> – George Savile, Marquis of Halifax

The person, life and circumstances of the prophets often conformed to prior scriptural predictions. Christian scholars link John the Baptist with the book of Malachi, and Christ Jesus with multiple predictions found in the Old Testament. Old and New Testament predictors, as discussed in several sections above (most specifically Sections 2.B.9., 4.B. and 4.C.) can easily be linked with the man, Muhammad, with equal or greater congruency. No wonder, then, that the *New Catholic Encyclopedia* remarks, "...there is reason to believe that many Jews, expecting the imminent advent of a messiah in Arabia, showed special interest in him (Muhammad)."[354]

---

354. *New Catholic Encyclopedia.* Vol 7, p. 677.

(4.D) MUHAMMAD

(4.D2) Miraculous Signs

"A miracle is not the breaking of the laws of the fallen world. It is the re-establishment of the laws of the kingdom."

--André Borisovich Bloom, *Living Prayer*

Miraculous circumstances surrounded the personage of many of the prophets, but while attributed to God, were not channeled through the prophets themselves. Examples include the flood during the time of Noah, Daniel being saved from the lions, Jonah from the whale, Abraham from the fire, baby Moses from Pharaoh and his army, the immaculate conception of Jesus and the miracle of the star in the East. Similarly, a popular tradition amongst Muslims relates that when Muhammad was born the 'eternal' flame of the fire-worshiping Zoroastrians in Persia was miraculously extinguished. Perhaps more impressive is that Hassan Ibn Thabit was recorded as having related that, on the day of Muhammad's birth in Makkah, he heard a Jew screaming at the top of his voice on a hill in Madina (over two hundred miles, and several days journey, distant), "O my Jewish community, tonight the star of Ahmad (the foretold prophet,

(Section 4) Messengers

Muhammad) in which he was born upon, has arisen."[355] This hadith is substantiated by a narration that Zaid Ibn Amr Ibn Nufa'il said that a respected Jewish scholar told him while he was in Syria, on the day of Muhammad's birth, "A prophet has appeared in your country, or he is going to appear, because his star has arisen. Go back (to your country)! Believe in him, and follow him."[356]

Of greater interest, perhaps, is that many events suggesting divine protection are recorded surrounding the life of Muhammad, to include several incidents of Muhammad having been saved from murderous disbelievers. In one case, a disbeliever accosted Muhammad when unarmed for his afternoon rest. Threatening him with his own sword, which he had taken from the tree where Muhammad had hung it, the disbeliever asked Muhammad "Who will save you now?" When Muhammad replied, "Allah," the disbeliever's hand became paralyzed, and he was unable to keep ahold of the sword.[357] Abu Jahl intended to crush the prophet's head with a boulder while he was in prostration, but when he approached the praying Muhammad he was repelled by a vision of a vicious camel, which none of his companions could see.[358] Umm Jameel bint Harb, the wife of Abu Lahab, once went looking for Muhammad with the intention of stoning him. When she found and questioned Abu Bakr about the whereabouts of Muhammad, her eyes were blinded to his presence, for he was sitting immediately next to Abu Bakr.[359] On other occasions, Muhammad claimed to have been informed, either by miracle or by the angel of revelation, of plots to kill him by dropping a stone

---

355. Ibn Hisham. *As-Seerah An-Nabiwwiyyah*.
356. Abu Nu'aem. *Dala'el An-Noobowah*.
357. *Al-Bukhari* and *Muslim*.
358. Ibn Hisham. *As-Seerah An-Nabiwwiyyah*.
359. Ibn Hisham. *As-Seerah An-Nabiwwiyyah*.

(4.D2) MUHAMMAD / MIRACULOUS SIGNS

upon him from a height,[360] by pushing him off a mountainside,[361] and by poisoning him in his food.[362] So he left the invitation where the stone was to be dropped, took a companion who averted the threat of the murderous Hypocrites on the mountainside, and begged off from the poisoned meal. What is compelling about all of these circumstances is not only that they did indeed prove to be true plots, but that there were no incidents in which Muhammad claimed a plot which did *not* prove true. He was not in the habit of suddenly reversing social plans, unexpectedly changing his travel route, or refusing food out of suspicion. His example was that of a man who boldly forged forward upon his purpose, without what most people would view to be normal precautions. Only on occasion was his otherwise incautious schedule interrupted by a premonition, or actual revelation, of a planned attempt upon his life. And in the few instances in which he perceived danger, he was never wrong.

Muhammad, as previously mentioned, released his bodyguards from duty upon receiving the revelation "...Allah will defend you from men (who mean mischief)...", by which he understood Allah's promise to protect him. He did not even have a food taster, despite the fact that poisoning was a common threat to rulers and prominent men of his time. He did not live a life plagued by suspicions and paranoia, but rather, calmly approached each day and each circumstance with confidence that 'God was with him.' His behavior, in fact, displayed a confidence which speaks of the depth of his trust in divine protection. Faced with the most hazardous of circumstances, he cultivated a virtually superhuman calm and control.

For example, on the night of his emigration from Makkah to Medina, Muhammad's house was surrounded by a veritable

---

360. Ibn Hisham. *As-Seerah An-Nabiwwiyyah.*
361. *Musnad Ahmad.*
362. *Musnad Ahmad* and *As-Seerah An-Nabiwwiyyah*, by Ibn Hisham.

(SECTION 4) MESSENGERS

mob of murderers, representing every tribe of Makkah, excepting Muhammad's small subtribe of the Quraysh, *bani Hashim*. All the same, Muhammad supplicated Allah, and left his residence with confidence that Allah had blinded the eyes of his would-be assassins to his presence. Instead of furtively keeping to shadows, ducking corners, attempting to slyly creep past or to make a mad dash for freedom, he simply trusted in the protection of his Creator, recited from the Holy Qur'an, and calmly walked out of his home and through the midst of his enemies, whom he found, mystically, to be lacking their senses, and out of Makkah. Later, when evading his pursuers en route to Medina, he and his companion, Abu Bakr, hid in a small cave on Mount Thawr. When the murderous pursuers approached the mouth of the cave intent on searching it for their objective, Muhammad stilled Abu Bakr's fears with the soothing reminder that Allah was their protector. Although Muhammad and Abu Bakr were no more than a few steps beyond the mouth of the cave, the pursuers left without entering. When Muhammad and Abu Bakr investigated, they found the entrance to the cave partially obstructed by an acacia tree the height of a man, a large spider's web spun across the remainder of the opening, and a dove upon a newly-built nest, positioned where someone entering the cave would almost certainly have disturbed either the nest, its occupants, or both. The pursuers had turned back, confident that no one could have entered the cave without destroying such delicately woven wonders balanced upon, and obstructing, the entrance. Yet none of the three – the tree, web and nest – had been there when Muhammad and Abu Bakr had entered the cave to begin with. Muslims advance the question, "But how did they get there in the first place, if not from Allah?"

Similarly, when Suraqah Ibn Malik caught up with the two on open ground, Abu Bakr recognized the great warrior. However, Muhammad's calm remained undisturbed, and confidence unshaken.

(4.D2) MUHAMMAD / MIRACULOUS SIGNS

Muhammad calmed Abu Bakr's fears with the teaching, "Don't be downcast, verily, Allah is with us."[363] As discussed in the following pages, Suraqah's attempts to apprehend the two were frustrated by similarly 'supernatural' events, and Muhammad and Abu Bakr were able to continue to their planned destination.

At the Battle of Badr, the Muslim army of between 300 and 317 men faced a force of 1,300 Quraysh. The Muslims had two horsemen, the Quraysh, 100. The Muslims had few weapons and little equipment; 600 of the Quraysh wore mail. What did Muhammad do? Order retreat with intent to seek reinforcements and come back another day? Organize guerrilla warfare? No. He threw a handful of gravel and dust at the distant enemy in a symbolic gesture and supplicated, "Confusion seize their faces!" Immediately, a violent sandstorm sprung up in the faces of the enemy Quraysh, and Allah revealed, "...when you threw (a handful of dust), it was not your act, but Allah's..." (TMQ 8:17). The end of the battle saw seventy of the Quraysh dead, a like number captured, and a scant fourteen Muslims killed in battle, despite the fact that the Muslims were underequipped and outnumbered more than four-to-one. Following the battle, both sides testified to having seen angels fighting in the ranks of the Muslims.[364]

The above were only a few of the incidents in which forces of nature were recruited to serve the man, Muhammad. On one occasion, the Meccan pagans drafted a pact to impose a boycott upon Muhammad and his followers. The proclamation forbade social relations (including talking), marriage, and business transactions, to include sale or even charitable provision of food. The proclamation declared that the boycott would not end until Muhammad

---
363. *Sahih Al-Bukhari*
364. Al-Mubarakpuri, Safi-ur-Rahman.1995. *Ar-Raheeq Al-Makhtum (The Sealed Nectar)*. Riyadh: Maktaba Dar-us-Salam. pp. 210-226.

(SECTION 4) MESSENGERS

was ostracized by his clan of *Hashim*, or until Muhammad renounced his claim to prophethood. However, after three years of lethal starvation, certain blood relatives became anxious for an end to the suffering and death of their Muslim relatives. With debate ongoing amongst the pagan Quraysh, Muhammad had a revelation that the original parchment upon which the unholy pact had been written had been eaten by ants, save for the words glorifying Allah. Muhammad's uncle, Abu Talib, conveyed the message of the revelation to the pagans, promising to turn Muhammad over to them if not true. When the pagans retrieved the proclamation from the Kaba they found the revelation to be true, for ants had eaten everything but the words, "In the name of Allah". Thus, the pagans were able to cancel the boycott without losing face, for the proclamation appeared to have been definitively cancelled by Higher Authority, using ants as His agents, and revelation as the mode of notification.[365]

Additionally, Muhammad's caravan companion, Maisara, reportedly observed Muhammad to have been followed by clouds in the desert, providing shade. Bahira, the afore-mentioned Nestorian monk of Syria, noted the same phenomena when Muhammad was a child of twelve, passing through the Bosra market in attendance of the 'Bilad as-sham' caravan of his uncle, Abu Talib. Bahira questioned Muhammad and, becoming increasingly certain that Muhammad was the 'expected prophet,' physically examined him. Finding what he was looking for, he noted a birthmark which he claimed to be the seal of prophethood described in scriptures of old as a mark of the final prophet.[366]

Most Muslims regard the most dramatic example of this class of miracle to be the night-time transportation of Muhammad from Makkah to Jerusalem, followed by ascension through the heavens,

---

365. Al-Mubarakpuri, Safi-ur-Rahman. pp. 117-119.
366. Ibn Hisham. *As-Seerah An-Nabiwwiyyah*.

(4.D2) Muhammad / Miraculous Signs

described by Muslims as "Al-Isra' w'al-Mir'raj" (The journey and ascension). When Muhammad reported this miracle to the people of Makkah on the morning of his return, his claim met with understandable consternation. How could Muhammad possibly have journeyed to Jerusalem – a distance of not less than twenty days travel by caravan (one way)[367] – ascended through the seven heavens (an odyssey of considerably more complex dimensions, one would think), and returned to Makkah all in one night? And yet, when challenged, Muhammad described Jerusalem in exquisite and accurate detail to those of knowledge, even though he had never been there.[368] Furthermore, the famous second century (AH) Islamic historian, Ibn Hisham, narrated that while upon his journey to Jerusalem, Muhammad reported having seen a Bedouin on caravan seeking a lost camel, and having directed him from his vantage point in the sky to the camel visible from his lofty perspective. Muhammad described the approaching caravan as two days distant, and included in his description the distinctive markings of the lead camel. He described how one camel had broken its leg, and the features of the camels of all other riders. Pretty wild claims, a person might have been inclined to think. And yet, not only did the caravan predicted to have been two days away in fact arrive in two days, complete with the distinctive lead camel and all other riders outfitted as described, but one of the Bedouins confirmed having been guided to his lost camel by a voice from the night-time sky.[369]

---

367. Gibbon, Edward, Esq. Vol. 5, Chapter L, p. 442.
368. *Musnad Ahmad.*
369. Ibn Hisham. *As-Seerah An-Nabawwiyyah.*

(4.D) MUHAMMAD

(4.D3)
Miracles Performed

"A miracle is an event which creates faith.
That is the purpose and nature of miracles."

–George Bernard Shaw, *Saint Joan*

That miraculous events and circumstances peppered the lives of the prophets appears to have been a common scenario, and emerges as an accepted indicator of divine favor. In addition, miracles attributed to God but performed through the persons of the prophets are commonly understood to convey the assignment of some significant degree of not only divine favor, but actual authority. Those miracles associated with Moses and Jesus have been previously discussed, and are well known in any case. Those associated with Muhammad are so numerous as to warrant another book entirely.

This point is not an exaggeration. Many books have been written, in English as well as in Arabic, upon just this subject.* The listed miracles include everything from predictions to physical feats, but by

---

* See al-Waada'ee, Muqbil ibn Haadee, *Saheeh al-Musnad min Dalaa'il an-Nubuwwah*, Kuwait: Dar al-Arqam, 1987 for one of the best references in this category.

(4.D3) MUHAMMAD / MIRACLES PERFORMED

far the greatest such miracle is the Qur'an itself. The unmatched eloquence, consistency with prior revelation (in conflict with prevailing popular opinion during the time of Muhammad), confirmation of previously unknown history, statements of scientific fact over a thousand years in advance of validation, predictions, assurances, unconquered challenges, and much more, have all been discussed above. When taken in total, a person is left with a revelation of unmatched perfection. And if that is not a miracle, a person should be dared to define what is.

However, considering that not every prophet flung little stones into Goliath-sized brains, teased snakes out of walking sticks, parted seas, tumbled the ailing off their deathbeds and onto their feet, fed thousands with a few sardines and dinner rolls, and raised the dead, people nonetheless have reason to question what Muhammad is recorded as having done. The answer is, "A lot." Exhaustive disclosure is not possible in such a book as this, but those interested can find more comprehensive discussion in such books as the aforementioned biographies of Muhammad, *Ash-Shifa*, by Al-Qadi 'Ayad (now available in English translation), and certainly in the many collections of *hadith*. The books of *hadith* of highest reliability are commonly acknowledged to be those of *Sahih Al-Bukhari* and *Sahih Muslim*, named after the famous third century AH (ninth century CE) Imams bearing those respective names. Anyone reading such books encounters a wealth of miracles beyond easy cataloging. Anyone reading such books also confronts a methodology of historical authentication and accuracy of record keeping which puts Western archives of similar period, and for many centuries to follow, to shame.

Within such books a person finds stories of Muhammad, through prayer or invoking blessings from Allah, bringing milk to the udders of dry sheep, transforming camels virtually too weary to walk into the fastest and most energetic of the bunch, transforming a stick of wood

499

(SECTION 4) MESSENGERS

into a sword for a soldier whose sword had broken (Ukashah Ibn Mihsan Al-Asdi at the Battle of Badr), and feeding and watering the masses from miniscule quantities. Scores of hungry poor were fed from a bowl of milk which appeared sufficient for only one. An entire army numbering more than a thousand were fed from a measure of flour and pot of meat so small as to be thought sufficient for only ten persons at the 'Battle of the Trench,' after which the flour and the meat seemed undiminished. So much was left over that a gift of food was made to the neighbor of the house in which the meal was prepared. Another army of 1,400, headed for the Battle of Tabuk, was fed from a few handfuls of mixed foodstuffs, over which Muhammad invoked blessings, and the increase was sufficient to fill not only the stomachs of the army, but their depleted saddlebags as well.

An expedition group numbering around 80 on one occasion, and an army of fourteen hundred (this time en route to settle the Treaty of Hudaibiya) on another, were watered (both for drinking and making ablution) from handfuls of water appearing less than sufficient for one.

Evil spirits (Jinn) were exorcised, the broken leg of Abdullah Ibn 'Ateeq and the war-wounded leg of Salama Ibn Aqua'a were healed on the spot (each on their own separate occasion), the eye inflammation of Ali Ibn Talib cured, the bleeding wound of Al-Harith Ibn Aws cauterized and healed instantly, the poisonous sting of Abu Bakr's foot quieted, and the vision of a blind man restored. On a separate occasion, Qutadah Ibn An-Nu'man was wounded, in the Battle of Badr, so severely that his eye prolapsed onto his cheek. His companions wanted to cut off the remaining attachments, but Muhammad supplicated over the eye, replaced it, and from that day on Qutadah could not tell which was the injured eye, and which not. Until the Battle of Uhud, that is. At the Battle of Uhud an arrow struck him in the socket while he was defending the person of Muhammad, and

(4.D3) MUHAMMAD / MIRACLES PERFORMED

upon removal of the arrow, the eye came with it. But Muhammad is recorded as having supplicated to the effect, 'Allah protect his eye as he protected my face, and make this eye the best eye he has, and the strongest eye he can see with.' Muhammad replaced the orphan eye in the socket, and thereafter it became the man's strongest eye.[370]

Muhammad is reported as having called for rain from a cloudless sky in a time of drought, whereupon the sky filled with clouds and the earth painted with rain until he was requested to supplicate for an end to the deluge, one week later, due to the damaging effects of the prolonged downpour. In response, Muhammad prayed for the rain to be 'around us, but not upon us,' whereupon the city of Medina became surrounded by rain and its runoff, but the melting earthen houses, soaked crops and drenched animals were spared the direct damage of the profuse precipitation.

Many times Muhammad conveyed information which, though not revealed in the Holy Qur'an, bears all the earmarks of having been transmitted via revelation, as claimed. All such information proved to be transmitted by other than temporal means. On one occasion Muhammad advised messengers from Persia, upon arrival in Madina, that the emperor for whom they were emissaries had been murdered, necessitating their return. With no mode of communication of such information other than that of revelation, the Persian governor of Yemen and his subjects accepted Islam when the messengers returned, bearing the above story in confirmation of a letter just received from the new ruler of Persia. The two sources of knowledge met in Yemen, triangulating a place and point in time where it was impossible for Muhammad to have known, by temporal means, that which he conveyed of the Persian monarch's assassination.[371] Similarly, Muhammad predicted, "Yamama is bound to give rise to a liar who

---

370. Sa'eid Hawwa. p. 322.
371. *Fath Al-Bari*

501

(SECTION 4) MESSENGERS

will arrogate prophethood to himself but he will subsequently be killed."[372] The prediction came true when Musailimah claimed prophethood in Yamama, rising to be considered by his followers in the light of his claims. Though advised by Muhammad, "You are doomed. Even if you repented and stopped what you were doing, Allah appointed that you would be slain,"[373] Musailimah persisted and, true to the promise, was slain in Yamama during the caliphate of Abu Bakr, following the death of Muhammad.[374] Another false claimant to prophethood, Al-Aswad Al-'Ansi, was killed in the distant land of Yemen only a day and a night before Muhammad's own demise. Yet Muhammad informed Al-Aswad's delegates that news of his death had reached him through divine revelation. Following Muhammad's demise, the veracity of his statement was confirmed from sources in Yemen.[375] The martyrdom of 'Amir at the battle of Khaibar was foretold, as was the condemnation of one of the soldiers of the Muslim army, who later was witnessed committing the unforgivable sin of suicide.[376] In one of the boldest predictions ever, Muhammad was recorded to have commented,

> "When Khusraw (Chosroes) is ruined, there will be no Khusraw after him; and when Caesar is ruined, there will be no Caesar after him. By Him in Whose Hands my life is, you will spend their treasures in Allah's cause."[377]

As Heraclius had so accurately predicted (see quote of Heraclius, following section), the Muslims did indeed capture the land under his very feet, as well as that of the Chosroes (the ruler of Persia), for,

---

372. *Zad Al-Ma'ad*
373. *Sahih Al-Bukhari*
374. Al-Mubarakpuri, Safi-ur-Rahman. p. 454.
375. Al-Mubarakpuri, Safi-ur-Rahman. p. 454.
376. Sahih Muslim and Sahih Al-Bukhari.
377. Sahih Al-Bukhari, narrated by Jabir ibn Samurah

(4.D3) Muhammad / Miracles Performed

"...in the last eight years of his reign, Heraclius lost to the Arabs the same provinces which he had rescued from the Persians."[378] The lines and traditions of the two emperors did indeed come to an end and the wealth of their treasuries was spent in the Muslim cause.

When asked by the Quraysh to provide a miracle, Muhammad is recorded as having directed their vision to the sky and having shown them the moon split in two. The moon split in two? Pretty far-fetched, to the minds of most. However, others acknowledge that any element of creation is subject to the command of The Creator and so anything, in a human frame of reference, can happen. If a sea could be ordered to split for Moses, so too could the moon be divided for Muhammad.

When called to wrestle Rukanah, an unbeaten champion, Muhammad won miraculously. Merely touching Rukanah on the shoulder, he fell down, defeated. In rematch, the miracle was repeated. A third challenge brought the same result.

When asked to call for rain, he did, and rain fell. When requested to feed the people his supplications brought sustenance, from where, the people did not know. When interceding as a healer, wounds and injuries disappeared.

In short, the prayers and supplications of Muhammad brought relief and blessings to the believers. And yet, whether being stoned in Ta'if, starved in Makkah, beaten in front of the Kaba, or humiliated amidst his tribe and loved ones, Muhammad's example appears to have been one of facing personal trials, of which there was an abundance, by relying upon internal patience in preference to calling for divine intervention.

His character was one of selfless persistence and forbearance. His character was one of patience and constancy. His character was one of...well, was one of which many people would like to know more.

---

378. Gibbon, Edward, Esq. Vol. 5, Chapter XLVI, p. 197.

(4.D) MUHAMMAD
(4.D4) Character

"Some people strengthen the society
just by being the kind of people they are."

– John W. Gardner

Exemplary character was the predictable pattern of all the prophets. What else would a person expect of a messenger of God? A Noah who strips naked and passes out drunk, a Lot of incest (a lot of incest?), a murdering David, a Judah of fornication, a Jesus of cursing the fig tree, degrading the Gentiles and rebuking his mother? The poverty of information regarding the Biblical prophets, speckled with unseemly inconsistencies, presents a conglomerate of blurred, Picasso-like portraits. The curve of one concept skirts the shadow of another, less seemly, design. Essential details necessary to focus the cubist conflict into accurate and appealing portraits are largely lacking. What was Abraham like? Well, you know, he was a prophet. Yes, but I want details. Oh, sorry, can't help you there.

As previously discussed, similar difficulties with the description of the prophet Muhammad, both in books of history and in *hadith*, are not encountered. The image which is rendered from the efforts of any serious and objective research is remarkably consistent. With regard to the subject of this section, for a person to claim Muhammad to have been anything less than an example of piety is to thrash against a very strong current of scholastic opinion. Scanning opinions of the past, a person finds such comments as,

> "...the essential sincerity of his (Muhammad's) nature cannot be questioned; and an historical criticism that blinks no fact, yields nothing to credulity, weighs every testimony, has no partisan interest, and seeks only the truth, must acknowledge his claim to belong to that order of prophets who, whatever the nature of their physical experience may have been, in diverse times and in diverse manners, have admonished, taught, uttered austere and sublime thoughts, laid down principles of conduct nobler than those they found, and devoted themselves fearlessly to their high calling, being irresistibly impelled to their ministry by a power within."[379]

And:

> "His readiness to undergo persecution for his beliefs, the high moral character of the men who believed in him and looked up to him as leader, and the greatness of his ultimate achievement—all argue his fundamental integrity. To suppose Muhammad an impostor raises more problems than it solves. Moreover, none of the great figures of history is so poorly appreciated in the West as Muhammad. Western writers have mostly been prone to believe the worst of Muhammad, and, wherever an objectionable interpretation of an act seemed plausible, have tended to accept it as fact. Thus, not merely must we credit Muhammad with essential honesty and

---

379. *The New International Encyclopaedia.* 1917. 2nd Ed. Vol XVI. New York: Dodd, Mead and Company. p. 72.

(SECTION 4) MESSENGERS

integrity of purpose, if we are to understand him at all; if we are to correct the errors we have inherited from the past, we must in every particular case hold firmly to the belief in his sincerity until the opposite is conclusively proved..."[380]

Muhammad lived a life, acknowledged by both Muslims and non-Muslims alike, devoted to the delivery of the message he claimed to be that of revelation. Worldly comforts were of little or no concern to him. He is recorded as having lived a life which many people would consider so abstentious as to overload tolerances and trip the circuit-breaker of the unbearable. History relates him having housed in single room, dirt-walled apartments similar in size to that of a small bedroom of modern dimensions. He slept on a rough leather mat stuffed with the stiff fiber of date-palm trees, dressed in common clothing, ate whatever was available during times of hardship (and even then sharing with his companions from whatever little he had), and yet he partook of simple and unrefined foods, in restraint, during times of plenty. Months went by during which Muhammad survived on naught but dates and water, with an occasional treat of camel's milk. From the time he first received revelation until the day he died, he did not partake of such simple luxuries as bread made from fine flour, or roast mutton (a luxury since the fat from roasting is lost into the fire). He routinely prayed two thirds of the night while most of the rest of his world was sleeping, fasted in all seasons, and never held wealth for himself, ultimately distributing all gains of his office to the various categories of need defined by the revelation he transmitted. He was described as having been more shy than a virgin in her boudoir, yet he was the most determined and stalwart of fighters in battle. Ali, himself famous for combat bravery and prowess, related,

---

380. Watt, W. Montgomery. p. 52.

(4.D4) Muhammad / Character

"Whenever the fight grew fierce and the eyes of fighters went red, we used to resort to the Prophet for succor. He was always the closest to the enemy."[381]

Muhammad's generosity was legendary, his manners exemplary, his comportment inspiring. He died, as he lived, a pauper, having given his weapons to the Muslims and the last seven dinars in his possession to charity the day preceding his demise. Muhammad left behind, at the height of his success and power, a treasure consisting of nothing more than his riding mule, his armor (which was mortgaged to a wealthy Jew), and a piece of land designated for charity. To the nine wives and one daughter who outlived him, Muhammad left behind the promise of Allah to provide for His servants – a promise which history discloses to have been handsomely fulfilled. To his one surviving daughter, Fatimah, he left the glad tidings that she would be the first of his family to follow him in death, and to join him in the afterlife – news in which she rejoiced. Six months later, and despite the youth of Fatimah compared with the more advanced age of most of the surviving wives, the word of Muhammad was proven to hold true, even after death.

Anything but a self-centered sample of pampered royalty, Muhammad used to milk his own goat, mend his own clothes and shoes, serve his family in the home, and attend the poor when taken ill. When manual labor was called for, he was the first to lay bricks and stones in raising the Quba mosque in Medina. At the 'Battle of the Trench,' he was found digging right amidst his followers, in one instance clearing a boulder over which the other companions, working together, had been unable to prevail. When stones were to be hauled, he carried two when all others were carrying one. Allowing no one to accept challenges in his place, at the Battle of Badr, when a charging horseman by the name of Ubai Ibn Khalaf swore either to

---

381. *Ash-Shifa*

(Section 4) Messengers

kill Muhammad or be killed, Muhammad refused the offers of his companions to combat the man in his stead, and facing the horseman on foot, dealt him a mortal wound.

Aristotle defined the doctrine of the golden mean as the existence of virtue at the middle point between the opposite extremes of self-indulgence and self-renunciation. While such philosophy is not precisely consistent with the teachings of Islam, the Islamic religion does stress, over and over again, the virtue of taking the 'middle path' with regard to licit items and issues. There is a time for work and a time for play, but then again there is a time for prayer and contemplation – acts which demand some physical and psychological effort, but which bring the oft-felt immediate reward of some varying degree of inner peace. A person is denied food and drink when fasting, but may graze a buffet at the time of breaking fast. At most other times, it is considered commendable to take food in moderation. Money is not to be hoarded (as is the way of the miser), but is to be spent on self, family, and others in need, but not to the point of excess (as is the way of the spendthrift). For those whose means exceed needs, the virtues of charity are frequently recounted, but there is no compulsion to spend a penny more than the required *zakat* (poor-due). Worldly pleasures are not denied and reclusiveness is not condemned, but excesses in both sensuality and self-denial are considered offensive. The ideal Muslim may be considered to be neither Epicurean nor ascetic. However, there is nothing wrong, and actually a great deal to be admired, in achieving the state of a *zahid*.

The Arabic word '*zahid*' has no English equivalent, but is probably best translated 'stoic,' for the philosophical doctrine of stoicism is one which asserts that happiness is dependant upon inner peace rather than outward circumstance. Thus, a *zahid* may live rich or poor, sick or healthy, and yet maintain happiness through inner peace rather than through material comforts. The world is full of such people –

(4.D4) MUHAMMAD / CHARACTER

admirable souls who, for reasons poorly understood by materialistic others, have deserted the race to accumulate worldly goods and sensual pleasures for the simple reason that they have their pleasure, and it is within. Once such an internal and over-riding peace is discovered, material comforts tarnish into insignificance.

Sometimes an item is best understood not by direct definition, but rather by its opposite. Pleasure is a friend of those in pain, light a welcome guest to those in darkness. If the world is peppered with *zahids*, or stoics, the opposite is surely more prevalent. How many people live with adequate food and housing for their needs, sufficient comforts and recreations, but little or no peace and satisfaction? The bored, dissatisfied wealthy have become a maladjusted, neurotic, and frequently suicidal cliché. Money can't buy happiness, so they say, and yet, in the absence of recognizing any more appealing alternative, most people are anxious to see if they can break the old rule. The *zahid* has a different focus, and so if money, materials, and sensual pleasures enter life, well, that's great. But if such enjoyments are lacking, well, life is still good, and the pursuit of such objectives is not worth the compromise of an inner peace and satisfaction independent of such fleeting pleasures.

So, to make a long story short, Muhammad was *zahid*. Whether suffering the humiliations, beatings, and abuse of the disbelievers, whether starving in exile from Makkah or surrounded by the wealth of a rapidly expanding empire, he appears to have remained constant in his convictions, and hence, in his inner peace and satisfaction. Although his living conditions were outwardly those of an ascetic, the fact is that he was not an ascetic at all, for he did not practice self-denial as a spiritual discipline. Rather, his indifference to wealth and material goods was such that he gave priority to the needs and desires of others over those of himself. Furthermore, he preferred to divest himself of anything which served to distract from the source of

(SECTION 4) MESSENGERS

his greatest pleasure – i.e., the practice of his religion. Thus, a person encounters stories of Muhammad giving away a colorful garment on one occasion, and the last of his money on another, simply to rid himself of material goods which distracted his concentration while in prayer.

A religious leader who shunned self-glorification, an emperor who toiled beside his followers, a general who eschewed finery and distinction, Muhammad was a man who reformed a nation, established a state, and carried the message of a religion destined to be the choice of over one fifth of humankind in the present day. And yet, his sober affect, admirable humility, and sedate character cast a cloak of commonality over the completely uncommon man sufficient to awaken the uncompromising love of his followers.

> "'I have seen,' said the ambassador sent by the triumphant Kuraish to the despised exile at Medina; 'I have seen the Persian Chosroes and the Greek Heraclius sitting upon their thrones, but never did I see a man ruling his equals as does Muhammad.
>
> Head of the State as well as of the Church, he was Caesar and Pope in one; but he was Pope without the Pope's pretensions, and Caesar without the legions of Caesar. Without a standing army, without a body-guard, without a palace, without a fixed revenue, if ever any man had the right to say that he ruled by a right Divine, it was Mohammad; for he had all the power without its instruments and without its supports."[382]

As previously mentioned, Muhammad's honesty was unquestioned, to the point where even non-believers accepted his word of promise. One notable example is that of Suraqah Ibn Malik Ibn Ju'sham. Suraqah was a noted warrior and horseman who was enticed

---

382. Smith, R. Bosworth. pp. 288-289.

(4.D4) Muhammad / Character

by the reward of 100 camels, offered by the pagan Quraysh, for the return of Muhammad when he was attempting to emigrate from Makkah to Medina. Chasing after Muhammad and Abu Bakr, Suraqah was the only Qurayshite warrior to intercept the two *en route* to Medina. However, Suraqah ran into a slight difficulty. Upon approaching the pair, his one horsepower vehicle of conveyance stumbled and he fell off. The event was peculiar enough to this noted horseman to caution his consciousness, and so he stopped and drew lots in order to divine whether or not to continue, as was the habit of the pagan Arabs in such circumstances. He found the divination unfavorable, but nonetheless allowed his caution to be trampled by lust for the hundred fuzzy humps of reward, and so returned to the chase. His horse stumbled again, and he fell. He mounted. Stumbled and fell. Mounted. The combination of the unpropitious divination and the repeated insults to his horse, body, and pride served to awaken him to the peculiarity of the chain of events. With considerably more prudence, he approached close enough for Muhammad to call out and promise Suraqah that he would one day wear the bracelets and crown of the Chosroes (the emperor of Persia), if he would abandon his pursuit. Even though then a non-Muslim, upon hearing such a promise from a man known to him as 'As-Saadiq Al-Ameen' (the truthful; the trustworthy), he gave up the chase and returned to Makkah confident that one day the promise would be fulfilled.

The circumstance teases the imagination. A non-Muslim accepted the promise of a man who was, at that time, the spiritual leader of a tiny group of followers, numbering in the hundreds, and running for their lives from the persecution of the Quraysh. Suraqah trusted a man emigrating from persecution, attended by only one faithful follower, and escaping a town in which he had failed to establish authority amongst the ruling class. And yet Suraqah accepted the assurance that one day this meager group of outcasts would grow to overcome the major world power of Persia and that he, Suraqah,

(SECTION 4) MESSENGERS

would wear the crown and bracelets of the monarch. To accept such a covenant demanded conviction, if not in the divine role of the messenger, then in the honesty of the man to begin with.

And there is a startling incongruity – Many of Muhammad's contemporaries refused the message of Islam, but nonetheless trusted him to the letter of his speech in all things but religion. Dramatic examples from the words and actions of such people speak for themselves, beginning with the unanimous consensus of the entire population of Muhammad's native city of Makkah. Muhammad first declared his appointment to prophethood by assembling the people of Makkah, and announcing the fact. However, prior to announcing his calling to prophethood, Muhammad tested the trust of those who had known him for the first forty years of his life by questioning if they would believe him, should he state that an army was approaching from the other side of the mountain. One of the audience responded, "We have never caught you out lying," and not a single person differed or objected. When Muhammad followed this vote of confidence by proclaiming his messengership, the people responded by refusing the message, but not his honesty.[383]

Similarly, Abu Jahl, one of the greatest enemies to Muhammad and the message of Islam – a man who once swore to kill Muhammad by crushing his head with a rock (and then failed in the attempt); a man who brutalized the followers of Muhammad, having gone so far as to have killed a defenseless woman, Sumaya bint Khibat, by the horrific brutality of thrusting a spear into her genitals; a man who fought (and was himself killed) in battle against the Muslims in the Battle of Badr – nonetheless was recorded to have repudiated Muhammad's correctness, but not his honesty, with the words, "We do not accuse you of being a liar, but verily we reject what you have come with."[384] It would appear that Abu Jahl's sense of honor would

---
383. Narrated by *Muslim* and *Al-Bukhari*
384. Narrated by *At-Tirmithi*

(4.D4) MUHAMMAD / CHARACTER

not allow him to advance a claim he could not substantiate, and so the only protest he could offer was that Muhammad, while not lying, was propagating a message that Abu Jahl nonetheless refused to accept. Following the record of this interaction with Abu Jahl, the verse was revealed, "We know that you, (O Muhammad), are saddened by what they say. And indeed, they do not call you untruthful, but it is the verses of Allah that the wrongdoers reject." (TMQ 6:33 – Saheeh International)[385] And nobody ever disputed the fact.

Ubai Ibn Khalaf once threatened Muhammad that he would kill him. In return, Muhammad corrected him, stating that surely he would kill Ubai instead. At the Battle of Uhud, when the two met in arms, Ubai was inflicted with a wound which appeared so insignificant as to be a small scratch on the neck. Nonetheless, Ubai's confidence in the honesty of a man from whom he had never heard a lie, and never witnessed a promise but that it came true, was such that he told his companions, "He (Muhammad) had already told me when we were in Makkah: 'I will kill you.' By Allah, had he spat on me, he would have killed me." Perhaps he died of unseen internal injury; perhaps he died of panic. Whichever was the case, two things are certain, the first being that Muhammad killed him, as promised. The second is that Ubai's conviction in the validity of Muhammad's vow was so great that the people ascribed the severity of his affliction not to his wound, but to the depth of his trust in Muhammad's promise, for they counseled Ubai, "By Allah you are scared to death." And die he did.[386]

On one occasion, a disbeliever named 'Utaibah Ibn Abi Lahab abused the prophet both verbally and physically, culminating in the poor career choice of grabbing him so severely as to tear his shirt, and attempting to spit in his face. Thereupon, Muhammad supplicated,

---

385. Ibn Hisham. *As-Seerah An-Nabiwwiyyah*.
386. *Tafheem-ul-Qur'an*

(SECTION 4) MESSENGERS

"O Allah! Set one of Your dogs on him." Some time later, when traveling in Syria, a lion was spotted near the group of travelers. Remembering Muhammad's words, 'Utaibah expressed his conviction in the supplication of Muhammad with the words, "Woe to my brother! This lion will surely devour me just as Muhammad supplicated. He has really killed me in Syria while he is in Makkah." When the lion rushed the group, even though forewarned and anticipating attack, it was 'Utaibah's head that was crushed by the beast.

Yet another tradition found in Sahih Al-Bukhari, the most respected and rigorously authenticated collection of hadith, relates the interrogation of Abu Sufyan by Heraclius, the monarch of Rome. Abu Sufyan was anything but a friend to Muhammad at the time, for prior to the Muslim conquest of Makkah, Abu Sufyan was a member of the elite alliance of wealthy and powerful Quraysh'ites devoted to the defamation of Muhammad and the destruction of the Islamic message. The tradition relates:

> "Allah's Messenger (peace be upon him) wrote to Caesar and invited him to Islam. Allah's Messenger (peace be upon him) sent Dihyah al-Kalbi with his letter and ordered him to hand it over to the Governor of Busrah who would forward it to Caesar, who as a sign of gratitude to Allah, had walked from Hims to Ilya (i.e., Jerusalem) when Allah had granted him victory over the Persian forces.
>
> So when the letter of Allah's Messenger (peace be upon him) reached Caesar, he said after reading it, "Seek for me any one of his people, if at present here, in order to ask him about Muhammad." At that time Abu Sufyan Ibn Harb was in Sha'm with some men from Quraysh who had come (to Sham) as merchants during the truce that had been concluded between Allah's Messenger (peace be upon him) and the pagans of Quraysh.

(4.D4) MUHAMMAD / CHARACTER

Abu Sufyan narrated, "Caesar's messenger found us somewhere in Sha'm so he took me and my companions to Ilya (Jerusalem). We were admitted into Caesar's court, to find him sitting in his royal court wearing a crown and surrounded by the senior dignitaries of the Byzantines.

He said to his interpreter, 'Ask them who among them is a close relation to the man who claims to be a prophet.'" Abu Sufyan said, "I replied, 'I am the nearest relative to him.' He asked, 'What degree of relationship do you have with him?' I replied, 'He is my cousin.' And there was none of Banu Abdul Manaf* in the caravan except myself. Caesar said, 'Let him come nearer.' He then ordered my companions to stand behind me near my shoulder and said to his interpreter, 'Tell his companions that I am going to ask this man about the man who claims to be a prophet. If he tells a lie, they should give me a sign.'"

Abu Sufyan added, "'By Allah! Had it not been shameful that my companions label me a liar, I should not have spoken the truth about Muhammad when Caesar asked me. But I considered it shameful to be labeled a liar by my companions. So I told the truth.'

Caesar then said to his interpreter, 'Ask him what kind of family does Muhammad belong to.' I replied, 'He belongs to a noble family among us.' He said, 'Has anybody else among you ever claimed the same before him?' I replied, 'No.' He said, 'Had you ever known him to tell lies before he claimed that which he claimed?' I replied, 'No.' He said, 'Was anybody amongst his ancestors a king?' I replied, 'No.' He said, 'Do the noble or the poor follow him?' I replied, 'It is the poor who

---

* Banu Abdul-Manaf (meaning the children of Abdul-Manaf) was the tribe of Muhammad.

follow him.' He said, 'Are they increasing or decreasing?' I replied, 'They are increasing.' He said, 'Does anybody among those who embrace his religion become displeased and then renounce his religion?' I replied, 'No.' He said, 'Does he break his promises?' I replied, 'No, but we have now a truce with him and we are afraid that he may betray us.'" Abu Sufyan added, "'Other than the last sentence, I could not work in a single word against him.' Caesar then asked, 'Have you ever waged war with him?' I replied, 'Yes.' He said, 'What was the outcome of your battles against him?' I replied, 'The result varied; sometimes he was victorious and sometimes we were.' He said, 'What does he order you to do?' I said, 'He tells us to worship Allah alone, not to worship others with Him, and to discard all that our forefathers used to worship. He orders us to pray, give in charity, be chaste, keep our promises and return that which is entrusted to us.'

When I had said that, Caesar said to his interpreter, 'Say to him: I asked you about his lineage and your reply was that he belonged to a noble family. In fact, all messengers of God came from the noblest lineage of their nations. Then I questioned you whether anybody else among you had claimed such a thing, and your reply was in the negative. If the answer had been in the affirmative, I should have thought that this man was following a claim that had been made before him. When I asked you whether he was ever known to tell lies, your reply was in the negative, so I took it for granted that a person who did not tell a lie about people could never tell a lie about God. Then I asked you whether any of his ancestors was a king. Your reply was in the negative, and if it had been in the affirmative, I should have thought that this man sought the return of his ancestral kingdom.

(4.D4) Muhammad / Character

When I asked you whether the rich or the poor people followed him, you replied that it was the poor who followed him. In fact, such are the followers of the messengers of God. Then I asked you whether his followers were increasing or decreasing. You replied that they were increasing. In fact, this is the result of true faith until it is complete (in all respects). I asked you whether there was anybody who, after embracing his religion, became displeased and renounced his religion; your reply was in the negative. In fact, this is the sign of true faith, for when its blessedness enters and mixes in the hearts completely, nobody will be displeased with it.

I asked you whether he had ever broken his promise. You replied in the negative. And such are the messengers of God; they never break their promises. When I asked you whether you fought with him and he fought with you, you replied that he did, and that sometimes he was victorious and sometimes you. Indeed, such are the messengers of God; they are put to trials and the final victory is always theirs.

Then I asked you what he commanded of you. You replied that he ordered you to worship Allah alone and not to worship others along with Him, to leave all that your forefathers used to worship, to offer prayers, to speak the truth, to be chaste, to keep promises, and to return what is entrusted to you. These are the qualities of a prophet who I knew (from the previous Scriptures) would appear, but I did not know that he would be from amongst you. If what you say is true, he will very soon capture the land under my feet, and if I knew that I would reach him definitely, I would go immediately to meet him; and were I with him, then I would have certainly washed his feet.' Caesar then collected his nobles

(Section 4) Messengers

and military leaders and asked them what would be their response if he were to accept Muhammad's request. The whole court was thrown into a great uproar, the officers became extremely restless raising their voices in objection and their eyes grew wild. When he saw this he quickly interjected and claimed that he had only asked that question in order to test their resolve and their firm stance. So he renounced his previous resolve and refused Muhammad's message."[387]

The above is a long tradition, with a great many morals. With regard to the present topic, two points stand clear, the first being, once again, that the enemies of Muhammad testified to his truthfulness. Not only did Abu Sufyan affirm Muhammad's honesty, but none of his disbelieving companions, standing behind him as directed by Heraclius, contradicted his claim. In effect the testimony was unanimous even though the situation, being one in which the ruler of one of the greatest of the world powers was being invited to the religion of their enemy, was one in which the pagan Quraysh would have been wont, if not desperate, to disparage the character of Muhammad.

The second interesting point is the resurfacing of the peculiar paradox of recognizing a man's honesty but refusing his message. On one hand Heraclius stated, "...I took it for granted that a person who did not tell a lie about people could never tell a lie about God" and, "...such are the messengers of God; they never break their promises." On the other hand, when he saw the seeds of sedition in his court, he "...renounced his previous resolve..." Here is a man who not only recognized the indicators of Muhammad's claim to prophethood, but who actually explained his reasoning and analysis to the audience. Yet, when the test of sincerity was offered him, he refused the message in deference to his worldly concerns, becoming victim to the very paradox he himself identified.

---

387. *Sahih Al-Bukhari*

(4.D4) Muhammad / Character

The above incongruity is witnessed on multiple occasions, one infamous such case being that of Safiyah, the daughter of Huyayi Ibn Akhtab, who related that her father and her uncle, Abu Yasir Ibn Akhtab, (two of the leaders of the Jews at that time) went to see Muhammad when he came to Quba, staying with Bani 'Amr Ibn 'Awf. Safiyah described that her father and uncle:

> "...did not return until sunset when they came back walking lazily and fully dejected. I, as usually, hurried to meet them smiling, but they would not turn to me for the grief that caught them. I heard my uncle Abu Yasir say to Ubai and Huyayi, "Is it really he (i.e., the foretold prophet)?" The former said, "It is he, I swear by Allah!" "Did you really recognize him?" they asked. He answered, "Yes, and my heart is burning with enmity towards him."[388]

There should be no surprise that some of those who recognize truth nonetheless refuse to act upon it. The all too-common reality is that what is right frequently falls sacrifice to what is convenient. The point is, however, that whatever the choice may have been of those who have lain in their graves for nearly fourteen centuries now, both believers and disbelievers alike testified to the honesty of Muhammad.

Mention is made in the Qur'an itself of the above paradox, for the disbelievers were reminded that they were living witnesses to Muhammad's life-long legacy of honesty, yet they denied the revelation he claimed. Translation of the relevant *ayah* reads, "A whole life-time before this I have tarried amongst you: will you not then understand?" (TMQ 10:16) Furthermore, as quoted above, Muhammad was consoled with the revelation: "We know indeed the grief which their words do cause you: it is not you they reject: it is the Signs of Allah which the wicked disdain." (TMQ 6:33) Of note is

---

388. Ibn Hisham. *As-Seerah An-Nabiwwiyyah.*

(SECTION 4) MESSENGERS

not so much what the Qur'an states, but rather the fact that none of the disbelievers were ever recorded as having stood up and disputed the claim. To quote the *New Catholic Encyclopedia* once again, "His adversaries, among whom were many Jews and Christians, watched eagerly for indications of fraud; and Mohammed was able successfully to assume a remarkable self-assured attitude toward any accusations of that sort."[389]

As for Suraqah, he came to accept Islam after some time, to outlive Muhammad by more than a decade, to survive multiple military campaigns against sizeable odds, to participate in the defeat of the Persian empire, and to wear the crown and bracelets of the Chosroes, albeit for such a short period of time as to count a symbolic gesture, perhaps, but without doubt a definite fulfillment of a most unlikely prophecy.

---

389. *New Catholic Encyclopedia*. Vol 7, p. 677.

(4.D) Muhammad

(4.D5) Persistence

"God Almighty hates a quitter."
– Samuel Fessenden, Republican National Convention, 1896

Selfless persistence against all levels of adversity was characteristic of the prophets. Whether ridiculed for constructing an Ark in a relatively waterless wasteland of desert, suffering the trials of facing Pharaoh and his malignant host, or being rejected, humiliated and beaten by those to whom the message was sent, the suffering incurred in the delivery of revelation was beyond that which an imposter could reasonably be expected to have endured. As such, the extraordinary persistence of the prophets casts a cloak of credibility over their claim to divinely appointed purpose.

Similar to the above examples, history shields Muhammad from the oft-flung accusation of insincerity. Over a span of 23 years he delivered a revelation which infuriated his antagonists to ostracize, humiliate, assault, torture, and even murder the believers. Muhammad was himself threatened, humiliated, beaten, stoned, and driven out of his home and city. His beloved wife died in exile

(SECTION 4) MESSENGERS

and starvation imposed by the leaders of Makkah. His followers were beaten and tortured in front of his eyes, and murdered when the opportunity arose. Attempts on his own life were numerous. Yet through all periods of stress and hardship, Muhammad stood in prayer at night until his body rebelled.[390]

On one occasion, a passage of the Qur'an was revealed stating that Muhammad was forgiven for his sins, past, present, and future (TMQ 48:2). Muhammad's response? To sit back and take it easy? Anything but. Despite the assurance of forgiveness and the implication of the guarantee of paradise, Muhammad nonetheless used to stand two thirds of the night in prayer, until his feet became swollen and cracked. When asked: 'Hasn't God forgiven you that which is before you and that which is behind you?' Muhammad replied: "Should I not be a thankful servant?"

Deceivers tend to adopt any excuse to escape from non-compulsory duties, while those suffering delusion typically excuse themselves from religious duties entirely, claiming divine dispensation. The example of Muhammad, like that of the other prophets, fails to fit either of these profiles.

---

390. Narrated by *Al Bukhari*

(4.D) Muhammad

(4.D6) Steadfastness

"An honest man's the noble work of God"
— Robert Burns

Just as the true prophets refrained from compromising the message of revelation in the face of adversity, so too did they refuse to manipulate the message for self-serving ends. For one thing, no true prophet ever claimed to be anything more than a man transmitting revelation. As discussed above, the apotheosis of Jesus was not of his construction, but of those who came after him. Being aware of the danger, Muhammad took every precaution to prevent such a deviation from developing in the minds of his followers. On one hand, Muhammad responded to token gestures of respect with humility uncharacteristic of those of high worldly office, exhibiting a dislike of preferential treatment. Anas related,

> "No one was more beloved to us than the Messenger of Allah (peace be upon him), [however], if we saw him we would not stand up for him for we knew how much he disliked [for us to do so]. And on one occasion someone called to him

saying: 'O best of mankind...' He replied: 'That is Abraham, peace be upon him.'"[391]

On another occasion, when a man stated, "God and You (O Muhammad) have willed this" in reference to a certain matter, Muhammad is recorded to have rebuked him with the question, 'Have you made me equal to God?'"[392] The distinction between God and His messenger was made clear. Muhammad was recorded as having taught, "Do not over-praise me as the Christians over-praised [Jesus] the son of Mary. For I am only His [God's] servant, so say: 'Allah's servant and messenger.'"[393] Consistent to the very end, even when suffering the final stages of his terminal illness, Muhammad reminded his companions to uphold their religious duties and warned them not to make his grave a focus of worship.[394]

During the lifetime of Muhammad, many significant events served to illustrate the humility and reserve of the man. In one dramatic example there was an eclipse of the sun on the day that Ibraheem, the son of Muhammad, died. The people observed the coincidence, and out of love for their prophet began to say, "The sun has eclipsed for the death of Ibraheem." Upon hearing this, Muhammad rebuked his followers with the words, "Verily, the sun and the moon are two signs of the signs of Allah; they do not eclipse for the death of anyone nor for his birth, so if you see that (an eclipse) then supplicate to God, reverence His name, pray and give charity."[395] Truthful, and accurate. Now, what would an imposter have said? What would a liar or a man of delusional thinking have done? Liars and confidence artists grasp hold of such opportunities and distort the

---

391. Narrated by *Muslim*
392. Narrated by *Al-Bukhari* and *Muslim*
393. Narrated by *Al-Bukhari* and *Muslim*
394. *Sahih Al-Bukhari* and *Muata'h Imam Malik*
395. Narrated by *Al-Bukhari* and *Muslim*

(4.D6) Muhammad / Steadfastness

significance to serve their purpose. A reasonable expectation would be for an imposter to review the situation (i.e., my son died, the Sun eclipsed, and the people think the two are related), and play up the misunderstanding of the masses for personal gain. But Muhammad didn't do that. If ever there was an opportunity for self-glorification during the life of Muhammad, that was it. Yet he seized the opportunity not for his own design, but rather to correct the thoughts of the people and redirect their astray focus from himself to reverence of God and fulfillment of religious duties.

Such was the character of the man, Muhammad. He repeatedly demoted his significance in the eyes of his followers, stressing the fact that, as revealed in the Holy Qur'an, "Muhammad is no more than a messenger…" (TMQ 3:144). In so doing, he not only maintained an appropriate modesty, but fulfilled the teachings of the very revelation he served to transmit, for yet another passage of the Holy Qur'an directed Muhammad as follows: "Say: 'I tell you not with me are the Treasures of Allah, nor do I know what is hidden, nor do I tell you I am an angel. I but follow what is revealed to me.'" (TMQ 6:50)

In addition to the above, a person encounters many circumstances which, but for the restraint of the messenger, could have been seized upon for self-serving ends. Even the simple act of retribution was forsaken when deemed a compromise to the example of Islamic virtues, as evidenced by the act of Muhammad granting clemency to Hind, the lady who had contracted the murder of Muhammad's uncle, Hamzah, and who had subsequently carved the liver from his corpse and chewed it. Despite a time of great physical and emotional trial, Muhammad maintained patience and forgiveness, gracefully avoiding the common trap of implementing inappropriate and self-serving policies which so frequently typify deceivers. When Muhammad had the 'high hand,' instead of exerting his power in an ignoble manner, he opened it and gave freely of that which people sought.

(Section 4) Messengers

Although firm and uncompromising in the imposition of revealed laws, as one would expect of a prophet, Muhammad demonstrated the greatest restraint and gentleness of character when the only rights violated were those of his own person. Thus, though fair and just, and at times strict in assigning punishment for the violation of the rights of others (and all the more so when addressing trespasses against the commandments and rights of Allah), Muhammad adopted the most gentle of responses to those affronts which typically tip the scale of most people's tempers. Disrespect, verbal, psychological, and even physical abuse failed to elicit what most people would consider to have been justifiable anger and retribution.

When Muhammad victoriously reoccupied the Makkah of his persecution, the conquest of his enemies and oppressors was highlighted by a peaceful and virtually bloodless takeover. When the populace requested clemency, it was granted. Despite the many previous crimes of oppression, no revenge was taken, no punitive measures implemented in excess of justice. A man acting upon passion would have been expected to have inclined towards teaching the transgressors a lesson. A 'my wife died under your imposition of starvation and exile, you killed my followers, stole our homes, and appropriated our possessions; well, the shoe is on the other foot now' attitude would in no way violate reasonable expectations. The evil which normally gushes from the sinister soul of wrathful man in the boil of emotions which accompanies such circumstances is easily understood, if not actually anticipated. However, conforming to the mold of men guided by passions and personal agendas was not to be the case. Completely the contrary, Muhammad exhibited a calm and generosity which spoke of the sincerity of his selfless campaign. Measuring the munificence of the conqueror against the 'rape and plunder, raze to the ground and stack the heads in the town square' manner of conquest with which they were so familiar, the population of Makkah embraced Islam in

(4.D6) Muhammad / Steadfastness

mass, and in the absence of the slightest compulsion. That the conversion of the population was sincere is witnessed by the fact that the people did not revert from their faith when Muhammad passed from this worldly life a scant few years later. Two classic comments on the event are as follows:

> "The day of Mohammad's greatest triumph over his enemies was also the day of his grandest victory over himself. He freely forgave the Koreysh all the years of sorrow and cruel scorn in which they had afflicted him, and gave an amnesty to the whole population of Mekka. Four criminals whom justice condemned made up Mohammad's proscription list when he entered as conqueror to the city of his bitterest enemies. The army followed his example, and entered quietly and peacefully; no house was robbed, no women insulted. One thing alone suffered destruction. Going to the Kaaba, Mohammad stood before each of the three hundred and sixty idols, and pointed to it with his staff, saying, "Truth is come, and falsehood is fled away!" and at these words his attendants hewed them down, and all the idols and household gods of Mekka and round about were destroyed.
>
> It was thus that Mohammad entered again his native city. Through all the annals of conquest there is no triumphant entry comparable to this one.
>
> The taking of Mekka was soon followed by the adhesion of all Arabia."[396]

and,

> "It is greatly to his (Muhammad's) praise that on this occasion, when his resentment for ill-usage in the past might

---

396. Lane-Poole, Stanley. Introduction, pp. xlvi-xlvii.

(SECTION 4) MESSENGERS

naturally have incited him to revenge, he restrained his army from all shedding of blood, and showed every sign of humility and thanksgiving to Allah for His goodness....

The prophet's first labor was the destruction of the idol-images in the Kaaba, and after that had been done he ordered his original muezzin to sound the call to prayer from the top of the Kaaba, and sent a crier through the streets to command all persons to break in pieces every image that they might possess.

Ten or twelve men who had on former occasion shown a barbarous spirit, were proscribed, and of them four were put to death, but this must be considered exceedingly humane, in comparison with the acts of other conquerors; in comparison for example, with the cruelty of the Crusaders, who, in 1099, put seventy-thousand Moslems, men, women and helpless children, to death when Jerusalem fell into their hands; or with that of the English army, also fighting under the cross, which, in the year of grace, 1874, burned an African capital, in its war on the Gold Coast. Mohammed's victory was in very truth one of religion and not of politics; he rejected every token of personal homage, and declined all regal authority; and when the haughty chiefs of the Koreishites appeared before him he asked,

"What can you expect at my hands?

'Mercy, O generous brother

"Be it so; you are free!" he exclaimed.[397]

---

397. Gilman, Arthur, M.A. 1908. *The Saracens*. New York: G. P. Putnam's Sons. pp. 184-5.

(4.D6) MUHAMMAD / STEADFASTNESS

Perhaps the greatest example of Muhammad's refusal to compromise his mission for self-gratification follows: Though fallen from wealth, power, and high social standing early in his period of prophethood, Muhammad refused reinstatement of his position when offered. At a time of persecution and humiliation, Muhammad's uncle, Abu Talib, appealed to him to leave his course of preaching, to which Muhammad replied, "O my uncle! By Allah if they put the sun in my right hand and the moon in my left on condition that I abandon this course, until Allah makes me victorious or I perish therein, I would not abandon it."[398] The test of such a statement came shortly thereafter, when 'Utbah Ibn Rabi'a, speaking for the leaders of the pagan Quraysh, virtually offered Muhammad just such a ransom, petitioning him with the words:

> "If you are doing all this with a view to getting wealth, we will join together to give you greater riches than any Qurayshite has possessed. If ambition moves you, we will make you our chief. If you desire kingship we will readily offer you that. If you are under the power of an evil spirit which seems to haunt and dominate you so that you cannot shake off its yoke, then we shall call in skilful physicians to cure you."[399]

Muhammad's refusal of the above offer not only testified to his selfless devotion, but also raised the uncomfortable question, when directed to those who choose to disbelieve, "For what, then, did Muhammad suffer such tortures and indignities, if not for wealth or kingship?" The answer, for Muslims, is that he strove not for the comforts of this world, but for the rewards of the next. Refusal of wealth, kingship, and all other offers of material comforts remained consistent with the profile of one seeking the pleasure of his Creator over those of his own self.

---

398. Ibn Hisham. *As-Seerah An-Nabiwwiyyah*.
399. *As-Seerah An-Nabiwwiyyah* by Ibn Hisham, and *Musnad Abu Ya'ala*.

(Section 4) Messengers

Years later, when at the height of success and power, Muhammad demonstrated remarkable restraint from the whims and fancies which assail the mind of average man. Having subdued the immediate enemy and established his position of authority, Muhammad then transmitted the following verse of revelation on the Day of 'Arafat, in the final *Haj* (pilgrimage), and in the final year, of his life:

"This day have I perfected your religion for you, completed My favor upon you, and have chosen for you Islam as your religion." (TMQ 5:3)

The message was one signaling completion. Completion, among other things, of "...My favor upon you..." At a time when any charlatan in the world would consider himself perfectly poised as the emperor of the realm to begin 'revealing' verses inclined to self-gratification, Muhammad transmitted a verse which spoke of an end – an end of Allah's favor upon him. Around a time when any confidence artist would be drafting a dream sheet of 'revealed' pay-backs, Muhammad not only transmitted revelation which closed the door upon such possibilities, but he also transmitted a verse commanding him to, "Celebrate the praises of your Lord, and pray for His forgiveness..." (TMQ 110:3). The last verse revealed was conveyed months following the *Haj*, and a short nine nights preceding Muhammad's death.[400] This last revelation brought emphasis to bear upon his sincerity, for rather than speaking of a legacy to his family and loved ones, rather than injecting some final passage of personal wisdom or timeless philosophy, rather than glorifying himself and pleading a promise of salvation, the final verse revealed in the Holy Qur'an counseled the messenger:

---

400. Qadhi, Abu Ammaar Yasir. 1999. *An Introduction to the Sciences of the Qur'an*. Birmingham: Al-Hidaayah Publishing. p. 94.

(4.D6) Muhammad / Steadfastness

"And fear the Day when you shall be brought back to Allah. Then shall every soul be paid what it earned, and none shall be dealt with unjustly." (TMQ 2:281)

Greatly in tribute to Muhammad's sincerity, not only did the above verses not call for any worldly gratification of the messenger, but they in fact encouraged, if not commanded, him to divert praise from himself to The Creator, and seek forgiveness rather than glorification. Where others would bask in the self-veneration so typical of conquerors, Muhammad revealed a series of verses which bade him to direct the praise of his success to The One from Whom all successes come and humble, rather than elevate, his own human self. His victory was marked not by the whim of self-glorification, by the satiation of long-suppressed lusts, or by the satisfaction of a thirst for revenge, but by the same piety and devotion to prayer, fasting, and self-imposed poverty which had been the trademark of his sincerity from the very beginning.

Muhammad's death followed shortly, about which the following authors commented:

> "Even to-day, with all the details of his early life and subsequent career laid bare by men of our own race, who have studied the whole extraordinary story of the noble Arabian, it is no easy matter to comprehend the character, or to account for the marvelous success of Mohammed in the early part of the seventh century. Never claiming divine powers at any period of his mission...this very human prophet of God made his first converts in his own family, was able, after almost hopeless failure, to obtain control in his own aristocratic *gens* (i.e., clan), and had such remarkable personal influence over all with whom he was brought into contact that, neither when a poverty-stricken and hunted fugitive, nor at the height of

(Section 4) Messengers

his prosperity, did he ever have to complain of treachery from those who had once embraced his faith. His confidence in himself, and in his inspiration from on high, was even greater when he was suffering under disappointment and defeat than when he was able to dictate his own terms to his conquered enemies. Mohammed died as he had lived, surrounded by his early followers, friends and votaries: his death as devoid of mystery as his life of disguise."[401]

And

"Even in his own dying hour, when there could be no longer a worldly motive for deceit, he still breathed the same religious devotion, and the same belief in his apostolic mission."[402]

To return to the impressions of Thomas Carlyle,

"His last words are a prayer; broken ejaculations of a heart struggling up, in trembling hope, towards its Maker... He went out for the last time into the mosque, two days before his death; asked, If he had injured any man? Let his own back bear the stripes. If he owed any man? A voice answered, "Yes, me, three drachms," borrowed on such an occasion. Mahomet ordered them to be paid: "Better be in shame now," said he, "than at the Day of Judgement"... Traits of that kind shew us the genuine man, the brother of us all, brought visible through twelve centuries..."[403]

The above portrait is that of a man who died as he lived, ever seeking the fulfillment of his religion and the reward of the hereafter.

---

401. Hyndman, H. M. 1919. *The Awakening of Asia*. New York: Boni and Liveright. p. 9.
402. Irving, Washington. Vol 1, p. 345.
403. Carlyle, Thomas. pp. 115-116.

(4.D) Muhammad
(4.D7) Lack of Disqualifiers

"A person searches coal for diamonds,
but searches diamonds for flaws."

– author

True prophets are more rare than diamonds, and like diamonds, not expected to be perfect. Certainly the profile of the prophets of the Bible allowed for sins and errors in judgement, as well as the common attributes of humanity. However, conspicuously absent were those traits which, though frequently encountered in average men, should reasonably be considered contrary to expectations of true prophets -- traits such as exploiting prophethood for personal gain, presenting oneself as more than a man given revelation (such as falsely claiming ties with divinity), or persisting on a recognized sin. Lying, in particular, was absent, as was even the hint of any of the mental afflictions or detiorations, for these qualities would suggest lack of trustworthiness and/or reliability in men sent by Almighty God with the specific design of being trustworthy and reliable. Muhammad having been cleared on all such counts, his detractors primarily focus on emotional issues possessing manipulative potential but which, on analysis, prove insignificant with regard to any man's claim to prophethood.

(SECTION 4) MESSENGERS

For example, as mentioned above, a passage of the Qur'an was revealed stating that Muhammad was forgiven for his sins, past, present, and future (TMQ 48:2). Many Christians have been trained to quote this *ayah* to stress the fact that Muhammad had sins. Christ Jesus, by comparison, is acknowledged by Christians and Muslims alike to have been sinless. Similar arguments, such as the Christian polemic that Abraham, Noah, Moses and Muhammad all died and were buried, but Christ Jesus was raised up alive, are constructed in a strained attempt to bolster Christian confidence that "My prophet is better than yours." However, such cake-rusk polemics fall apart when dunked in the warm milk of pure reason for three reasons, the first being there is no contest between Christ Jesus and Muhammad in the Islamic religion -- both men are recognized as prophets, with the former having predicted the coming of the latter, and with the pure teachings of both having been the teachings of Islam. Secondly, the Biblical parable of the lost sheep overrides the first of the above arguments, for the lesson is,

> "What do you think? If a man has a hundred sheep, and one of them goes astray, does he not leave the ninety-nine and go to the mountains to seek the one that is straying? And if he should find it, assuredly, I say to you, he rejoices more over that sheep than over the ninety-nine that did not go astray." (Matthew 18:12-13)

Or, as Luke 15:7 concludes the parable,

> "...there will be more joy in heaven over one sinner who repents than over ninety-nine just persons who need no repentance"

The parable of the lost coin conveys the similar lesson that "...there is joy in the presence of the angels of God over one sinner

(4.D7) Muhammad / Lack of Disqualifiers

who repents" (Luke 15:10). And is not the moral of the parable of the prodigal son the same – that there is more rejoicing over the repentance of the sinful son than over the one who never went astray to begin with? (Luke 15:11-32)

Finally, nowhere in the Bible is Jesus recorded as having foretold that the final prophet would be sinless or that he would not die and be buried in the manner of others of the prophets. Now, no doubt Christ Jesus was a hard act to follow, but the point is that if having sins or having died and been buried excludes a person from prophethood, then don't all other prophets (for example, Abraham, Noah, Moses, etc.) stand to be disqualified as well? And if not, what, then, is the point of the argument? One point that *can* be made, however, is that Muhammad persisted upon his mission despite his own human shortcomings. He neither attempted to excuse nor to conceal his sins, his weaknesses, his humanity. On the contrary, he conveyed a revelation which immortalized these facts, following which, he continued to persevere. In the manner, one would think, of a true prophet.

Just as Muhammad did not seek to define any one prophet as better than any other, he did not seek to elevate his own status above that of those who preceded him. Moses is considered by Jews to hold special rank for the miracles passed through his personage, and for the liberation of their race from the oppression of Pharaoh. Christ Jesus is held by Christians to have elevated status amongst the prophets for reason of his alleged link with divinity, atoning sacrifice, the fact that he was raised up and will some day be returned to complete his mission on earth, and the belief that he will ultimately stand as intercessor on the Day of Judgement. Muhammad could just as easily have claimed exclusive rank on the basis of having been the last of the prophets, having liberated his followers from the oppression of the Quraysh, and having been the vehicle through which a long list of miracles were conveyed. Had he claimed ties with divinity, a sector of the people were ready to stand in belief and support. Yet rather than do any of the above, he transmitted a revelation which proclaimed all the prophets to have been men, no one of whom is to be considered superior to the others. *Surah* 2:136 instructs Muhammad to teach:

> "We believe in Allah, and the revelation given to us, and to Abraham, Isma'il, Isaac, Jacob, and the Tribes, and that given to Moses and Jesus, and that given to (all) Prophets from their Lord: we make no difference between one and another of them, and we bow to Allah (in Islam.)" (TMQ 2:136)

Perhaps the most common claim against Muhammad is that he was a voluptuary. Of note is that this is a modern claim, for the disbelieving contemporaries of Muhammad, though eager to attack his character, refused to advance charges so clearly contrary to the reality. The preceding description is one of a man who, though not denying himself life's pleasures, lived a most frugal and austere existence. What wealth came his way was distributed; what food, shared; what gifts, passed on to others. Fame and prestige were denied and the finery of his position, once successful in his mission, rejected. Power was neither an objective nor, once gained, abused. In general Muhammad lived a selfless existence from beginning to end, characterized by placing the needs and desires of his followers ahead of his own. His own pleasures in life, such as perfumes and honey, were rarely in the offering, and when available were enjoyed sparingly.

The society to which Muhammad conveyed the revelation of the Qur'an was one which permitted prostitution, temporary marriage contracts, and limitless polygamy. Gambling and alcohol consumption were common and reckless social norms – alcohol consumption not infrequently to such an excess as to be fatal, gambling often with such abandon that a person would first lose his family and possessions, and next his own freedom, gambling himself into slavery on a single throw. Yet the revelation of the Holy Qur'an changed all that.

(4.D7) Muhammad / Lack of Disqualifiers

Alcohol, gambling, and all associated evils were out. Taking of interest? A parasitic practice whereby the strong get stronger at the expense of the poor and downtrodden -- forbidden. Countless number of wives, temporary marriage contracts and prostitution when the woman is only desired for temp duty? No more. The lazy had to face the prospect of ablution and prayer five times daily; the licentious encountered segregation of sexes and a dress code of modesty, and in a society which reveled in feasting a most rigorous fast was prescribed. Even sleep became an issue, for Muhammad routinely sacrificed his sleep for prayer. Most everything hedonistic man loves to do was curtailed or forbidden by the revelation of the Holy Qur'an, yet the charge of voluptuousness continues to flap in the breeze of unbalanced opinion. Islam, a man's religion? In which feasting, fighting, cursing, arguing, gambling, drinking, prostitution, fornication, licentiousness and laziness were either forbidden or curtailed? Not exactly a compatible formula.

Those who presume voluptuous appetites with regard to women have overlooked the forest of refutation in preference to placing focus upon one lone tree of assertion. Had Muhammad been a voluptuary with regard to women, a person would have thought such desires to have been manifest in his youth, when a young man's sexual drive is at its Himalayan hormonal peak. However, throughout Muhammad's youth he only had one wife, Khadijah. They were married for 25 years, and throughout that period he was unwaveringly faithful, despite the fact that his wife was 15 years his elder. Yet his detractors propose that Muhammad began, at the age of 50, with the fire of his youth behind him and the main effort of his life being the transmission of revelation, to set a flock of wives as goal in life. Were the assertion true, never in the history of humankind did a man suffer so much for something he could have had anyway. For had Muhammad wished, he could have had any number of wives, even from his youth, according to the laws of the society in which he lived. More to the

(SECTION 4) MESSENGERS

point, he could have fornicated freely, contracted marriages for time-specified periods of play, and let his lusts run wild in the pasture of sexual permissiveness of his time. But he didn't. Even in his youth, to the age of 25 and prior to marriage, he remained chaste despite the sexual freedoms which must have tempted any man of youth and vigor. Instead, he became known for his temperance and reserve, eventually transmitting a revelation which forbade the boundless abuse of women.

Restricting interactions between the sexes to marriage, for the first time in history revelation was recorded which demanded that women be respected and married with necessary formality. Thirteen centuries before women were awarded rights of inheritance, ownership of property, veto of marriage offers, and equality in education and religion in the developed West, the revelation of the Holy Qur'an commanded such rights. The most revolutionary concept, perhaps, was the open recognition of women possessing souls and equal prospects to those of men as regards the afterlife – two concepts openly debated in Christian circles up to the turn of the twentieth century, after which the debate of such issues was not extinguished, but rather cloistered behind closed doors for reason of political correctness.

True, polygamy is permitted in the Islamic religion, as it was permitted in the Old Testament (see Section 2.B.5.) and, although not explicitly condoned in the New Testament, a person can certainly argue that it was not forbidden either. The Christian cliché of monogamy with episodic lapses into adultery is all too commonplace for criticisms from that quarter to carry any weight, in any case. But the point is that evidence of voluptuousness on the part of Muhammad is lacking. If anything, the opposite is encountered, for the expectation of finding his house filled with a banquet of beauty pageant winners and nubile young things, of high social standing and financial position, is quickly dispelled. Most, if not all, of the wives of Muhammad were married not out of desire, but for practical

(4.D7) MUHAMMAD / LACK OF DISQUALIFIERS

reasons. Muhammad married two ladies (one from Kindah, the other from Bani Kilab) with whom he never consummated the marriage.[404] Only one wife (A'ishah) was a virgin,[405] and the rest were either old, divorced, widowed, or a combination of the above. On an opposite end of the scale from the youth of A'ishah, Muhammad married Mai'moona when she was 51 years old. Similarly, whereas Muhammad's first wife was Khadijah bint Khuwailid, one of the most eligible widows of Quraysh, Muhammad also married Zainab bint Jahsh, a woman who bore the social stigma of having been previously married to a freed slave.

For the most part, the wives of Muhammad were not known for beauty, wealth, or position. So what were the practical reasons for the multiple marriages of Muhammad? Inter-tribal ties were cemented, orphaned widows and divorcees were sheltered, and practical examples of accepted marital limits were exemplified. Hence most, if not all, of the marriages of Muhammad bore practical considerations. Certainly the objective analyst must deny the example of a powerful ruler handpicking the choicest maidens of the realm for his own personal enjoyment, casually discarding rejects in favor of new conquests whenever the whim arose.

Hence, the accusation that Muhammad died poor, but with a stable of wives as his object and satisfaction in life is an insult not only to the man, but to the very process of reason. The lusts of a voluptuary are readily apparent, yet the actions of Muhammad nowhere betrayed such an inclination. Spiritual leader, commander of the faithful, king of the realm, no law was beyond his position, had he been acting outside of divine constraints. Others have instituted manorial laws ranging from legalized prostitution to the infamous *droit du seigneur*, whereby feudal lords in medieval France and Italy

---

404. Al-Mubarakpuri, Safi-ur-Rahman. p. 485.
405. Al-Mubarakpuri, Safi-ur-Rahman. p. 483-485.

(SECTION 4) MESSENGERS

assumed first right to bed the bride of their vassals on the wedding night. And if nothing else, the example of Muhammad falls well within the limits of the stories related about accepted prophets of the Bible – with fewer wives that Solomon, less transgression than David (whose lust for Bathsheba, it is recorded, motivated him to send her husband to his death), and more restraint than Judah (who, it is recorded, contracted with Tamar, whom deceived him to believe she was a prostitute), Muhammad's claim to prophethood cannot be contested on this charge, unless the Biblical prophets are likewise challenged.

As expressed by Thomas Carlyle:

"Mahomet himself, after all that can be said about him, was not a sensual man. We shall err widely if we consider this man as a common voluptuary, intent mainly on base enjoyments,--nay on enjoyments of any kind. His household was of the frugalest; his common diet barley-bread and water: sometimes for months there was not a fire once lighted on his hearth. They record with just pride that he would mend his own shoes, patch his own cloak. A poor, hard-toiling, ill-provided man; careless of what vulgar men toil for. Not a bad man, I should say; something better in him than *hunger* of any sort, – or these wild Arab men, fighting and jostling three and twenty years at his hand, in close contact with him always, would not have reverenced him so! They were wild men, bursting ever and anon into quarrel, into all kinds of fierce sincerity; without right worth and manhood, no man could have commanded them."[406]

But command them he did. And it is the nature of what, exactly, Muhammad commanded that should be of central interest.

---

406. Carlyle, Thomas. pp. 114-115

(4.D) MUHAMMAD
(4.D8) Maintenance of The Message

"If you wish to preserve your secret,
wrap it up in frankness."

– Alexander Smith, *Dreamthorp*

The Islamic viewpoint, as discussed in the relevant sections above, is that the core message of revelation never changed – the Islamic monotheism of Adam was the same as the Islamic monotheism conveyed by all the prophets, Moses, Jesus and Muhammad included. And logically, it cannot be any other way -- unless a person believes in a Creator Who changes His mind, it is impossible to conceive of a Creator who changes the core values expressed through revelation. To say that 'God is One' gave way to 'God is One, but three in one and one in three' is to claim that God changed teachings with regard to such explicit fundamentals as Himself.

With regard to the Holy Qur'an, the Oneness of Allah is not the only teaching in common with the other two Abrahamic faiths of Judaism and Christianity. The Ten Commandments, with the exception of the commandment of the Sabbath, are preserved throughout

(Section 4) Messengers

all three religions. With regard to the Sabbath, Muslims hold that the restrictions of the Jewish Sabbath were a punishment upon the Jews for their repeated transgressions, and as such were lifted from less rebellious future generations. Would Allah do such a thing? Would Allah punish a people by ordering rigid and inconvenient mandates? Well...yes, apparently so. Or, at least, it sure looks that way. Why were the Jews left to wander in the wilderness for forty years after having been liberated from the oppression of Pharoah? It had something to do with disobedience, didn't it? And what about the story of the golden heifer? The Jews could have offered any heifer for sacrifice, when first commanded, but they resisted the command, and what did they get? A considerably more difficult command. Why didn't they ask again, just to see how much harder it could get?

Are the above scenarios unreasonable? If anything, they should be expected. Everybody knows that rebellion against authority invites punishment. Whether a parent ordering an obstreperous child, a boss commanding an insolent employee, or a government laying laws upon a rebellious populace, the natural consequence of disobedience is to have commandments tightened and penalties applied. The scenarios of such cases are too easy to imagine – the child who refuses one chore will be given two more, the troops who are dawdling will be ordered to double-time, the slack employee will be offered the option between picking up the performance or a pink slip.

Disobey The Creator, and what does a person expect, if lessons are to be learned from life? A pink slip from The Creator would be nothing to laugh at.

The Islamic understanding, then, is that many restrictive subsidiary laws served as punishments in one way or another, and were lifted from subsequent, less rebellious nations. Examples include the dietary restrictions of the Jews, needing to wash new cooking vessels in a river before first use, etc. The Islamic religion, like the Judaic, for-

(4.D8) MUHAMMAD / MAINTENANCE OF THE MESSAGE

bids eating pork, but many other Jewish dietary restrictions were eliminated in the law of the Holy Qur'an. On the other hand, certain new restrictions were added, such as the abolition of alcohol. According to the Islamic viewpoint, such new commandments were withheld from previous revelation, for Allah delayed certain restrictions until mankind developed the individual refinement and social maturity to be capable of satisfying the law. Earlier revelation of such commandments would have placed a burden upon mankind greater than it could have borne, practically assuring noncompliance. Knowing the weaknesses of creation as none but The Creator can, Allah was selective and gentle in weaning the human race onto the restrictions of revelation, revealing the essentials of creed with consistency from the very beginning, but imposing restrictive commandments in appropriate stages.

The Islamic religion, then, teaches that while the creed conveyed through revelation never changed, laws subsidiary to the creed may have been changed according to a Divine Plan which dictated progressive modification in prohibitions and commandments. Just as a child receives instruction in life appropriate to the various developmental stages of maturity and responsibility, mankind may not have been able to handle certain commandments and prohibitions at earlier stages in revelation. Thus, a person can readily conceive that The Almighty, possessing Divine wisdom surpassing all human cognition, always knew best when and where to command what.

Lest any objections be raised from Jewish or Christian quarters, this process of abrogation is not foreign to Judaic and Christian theology. In the Old Testament, the sons and daughters of Adam were initially allowed to marry. Only later was this incestuous practice forbidden. Noah and his people were allowed to eat all kinds of animals before boarding the ark, but later certain restrictions were applied. At one time, a man could marry two sisters – later this

(SECTION 4) MESSENGERS

practice was forbidden. It is true that Abraham was commanded to slaughter his son, but it is also true that he was later relieved of the duty. Many other examples exist. As regards Christianity, the claim of most modern Christians is not that one or two commandments have been abolished, but that the entire law has been repealed. Not only has the law been rescinded in Christian theology, displacing accountability for actions with justification by faith, but the nature of God Himself was transformed from a wrathful and harsh Lord to an all-forgiving God. It is hard to conceive a greater abrogation than that of the very nature of The Creator. And yet, the argument is often advanced, "We say the nature of God Himself is transformed and all previous laws are repealed. But you say alcohol is now forbidden? That's ridiculous!"

A slightly more logical conclusion is that whether a person likes it or not, what is certain is that abrogation is the right of The One Who decrees all matters of His creation, and has been exemplified in all previous scripture. So it is nothing new.

So if the restrictions of the Sabbath appear to have been recalled here, and the permissibility of alcohol annulled there, there should be no surprise. A person can imagine a lot of changes having been made in line with the plan of The One Who holds all creation at His command. But The Creator changing the message as regards Himself? A collective, "Enh, don't think so" issues from the minds of the faithful of mankind.

Hence, as mentioned above in section 2.B.7, the First Commandment of the Old Testament teaches the oneness and preeminence of God ("You shall have no other gods before Me." -- Exodus 20:3), and Christ Jesus reaffirms this teaching in the New Testament as follows: "Jesus answered him, 'The first of all the commandments is: "Hear, O Israel, the Lord our God, the Lord is One. And you shall love the Lord your God with all your heart, with all your soul, with all your mind, and with all your strength. This is the first commandment." (Mark 12:29-30), repeating and emphasizing the lesson in Matthew 22:37 and Luke 10:27. Consistent with this line of thought is the fact that Christ Jesus nowhere taught the Trinity (see Section 2.B.7.).

Now, what does the Holy Qur'an say? The same -- the dominant, focal teaching in the Holy Qur'an is the Oneness and preeminence of Almighty God, Allah.

This being the first and final commandment, the point needs little stress. Deceivers and false prophets characteristically adopt accepted religious conventions into their own teachings, to serve as springboards onto the stage of popular acceptance. Charlatans build off the foundation of what other people already believe. Hence, false prophets seeking to establish a following have historically tended to pledge themselves to be the fulfillment of religious expectations – claiming to be Christ returned, a saint, another in the chain of prophets, or whatever, but always something acceptable in the view of those they seek to deceive. In such cases the falsehood of a person's claim, sooner or later, is exposed when various inconsistencies or idiocies come to light. The annals of history are filled with examples of such charlatans, but whether knowing deceivers or suffering from delusional thinking, such impostors have frequently failed rich and successful, in worldly terms. So people keep trying. The retirement pay is good.

Did Muhammad conform to such a framework of falsehood? All indicators seem to settle centrally in the solid green 'No' box. Not only did the message transmitted through Muhammad correct popular misconceptions of both Jewish and Christian religions, but absolutely nothing can be identified as a worldly gain sought by this great messenger of Islam. As previously mentioned, his was a strange way to gather a following – to tell the pagans, Jews, and Christians that the popular opinions they held (and still hold) are wrong, and then set about teaching the Jews and Christians their own scripture. It is strange to face such an uphill battle with no apparent worldly incentive -- for all but a true prophet, that is.

So was Muhammad the final prophet as predicted in both Old and New Testaments? If so, one thing is certain, and that is that the message of revelation he transmitted upset a lot of people. Surprising? Maybe not. The only hatred which exceeds that held by a person of piety for a mis-commanding charlatan is the hatred conceived by those of impiety for a righteous good example. A man who preaches societal and religious reform will invariably face adversity issuing out of the dark alleyways of selfish desire and preconceived prejudice. Prophethood was never a popularity contest. Rather, it was always a test of sincerity and endurance, commitment and correctness. And it was always the minority who followed, in line with the parable of the wedding feast, which concludes, "For many are called, but few are chosen" (Matthew 22:14).

Muhammad's teachings can partially be appreciated through the testimonies of others. Ja'far (son of Abu-Talib) testified to the Christian King of Abyssinia as follows:

> "O King of Abyssinia, we used to be a people of ignorance, worshipping idols, eating dead animals, performing indecencies, casting off family bonds, doing evil to our neighbors, and the strong among us would eat the weak. This remained our common trait until God sent to us a messenger. We knew his ancestry, his truthfulness, his trustworthiness, and his chastity. He called us to Allah that we might worship Him alone and forsake all that which we had been worshipping other than Him of these stones and idols. He commanded us to be truthful in speech, to keep our trusts, to strengthen

(4.D8) MUHAMMAD / MAINTENANCE OF THE MESSAGE

our family bonds, to be good to our neighbors, to avoid the prohibitions and blood, and to avoid all indecencies, lying, theft of the orphan's money, and the slander of chaste women. He further commanded us to worship Allah alone, not associating anything in worship with Him. He commanded us to pray, pay charity, and fast (and he listed for him the requirements of Islam). So we believed him, accepted his message, and followed him in that which he received from Allah, worshipping Allah alone, not associating any partners with Him, refraining from all prohibitions, and accepting all that which was made permissible for us."[407]

Some will be impressed by the above, and follow. Others will view the bearer of such teachings with such distaste as to ignore, or even with such hatred as to seek to kill, the messenger, the message, or both. Much like the ungrateful invitees to the king's wedding feast in the above-referenced parable. And look what happened to them.

In conclusion, then, many people throughout history, and not just Muslims, find ample cause to attribute greatness to this man, Mohammad. Examples include:

"If greatness of purpose, smallness of means, and astounding results are the three criteria of human genius, who could dare to compare any great man in modern history with Muhammad? The most famous men created arms, laws and empires only. They founded, if anything at all, no more than material powers which often crumbled away before their eyes. This man moved not only armies, legislations, empires, peoples and dynasties, but millions of men in one-third of the then inhabited world; and more than that, he moved the altars, the gods, the religions, the ideas, the beliefs and souls.

---

407. *Musnad Ahmad*

(SECTION 4) MESSENGERS

On the basis of a Book, every letter of which has become law, he created a spiritual nationality which blended together peoples of every tongue and of every race. He has left us as the indelible characteristic of his Muslim nationality the hatred of false gods and the passion for the One and immaterial God. This avenging patriotism against the profanation of Heaven formed the virtue of the followers of Muhammad; the conquest of one-third of the earth to his dogma was his miracle; or rather it was not the miracle of a man but that of reason. The idea of the Unity of God, proclaimed amidst the exhaustion of fabulous theogonies, was in itself such a miracle that upon its utterance from his lips it destroyed all the ancient temples of idols and set on fire one-third of the world. His life, his meditations, his heroic revilings against the superstitions of his country and his boldness in defying the furies of idolatry, his firmness in enduring them for fifteen years at Mecca, his acceptance of the role of public scorn and almost of being a victim of his fellow countrymen; all these and, finally, his flight, his incessant preaching, his wars against odds, his faith in his success and his superhuman security in misfortune, his forbearance in victory, his ambition, which was entirely devoted to one idea and in no manner striving for an empire; his endless prayers, his mystic conversations with God, his death and his triumph after death; all these attest not to an imposture but to a firm conviction which gave him the power to restore a dogma. This dogma was twofold, the unity of God and the immateriality of God; the former telling what God is, the later telling what God is not; the one overthrowing false Gods with the sword, the other starting an idea with the words.

(4.D8) Muhammad / Maintenance of The Message

Philosopher, orator, apostle, legislator, warrior, conqueror of ideas, restorer of rational dogmas, of a cult without images; the founder of twenty terrestrial empires and of one spiritual empire, that is Muhammad. As regards all standards by which human greatness may be measured, we may well ask, is there any man greater than he?"[408]

---

408. De Lamartine, A. 1854. *Histoire de la Turquie*. Paris. Vol. II, pp. 276-277.

Section 5

The Unseen

"There is no good in arguing with the inevitable."

– James Russell Lowell, 1884

(SECTION 5) THE UNSEEN

Preceding chapters discuss the material reality of the prophets and the books of revelation. This present section shifts to examination of the unseen – intangible entities and/or concepts which have long been the object of classic comparative religious analysis. While preceding chapters expose corroborating evidences suggestive of continuity of revelation from Judaism to Christianity to Islam, this present section proves supportive through demonstration of commonality of concepts, as concerns the ethereal. Differences do exist, of course, but once the outer shell of dissenting opinion is exposed to have been molded of human caprice, the central core of belief can be seen to be remarkably harmonious.

(5.A)
Angels

"Man, proud man,
Drest in a little brief authority,
Most ignorant of what he's most assur'd,
His glassy essence, like an angry ape,
Plays such fantastic tricks before high heaven
As make the angels weep."
--Shakespeare, *Measure for Measure*

Angels They're there. Any questions?

At least, that is the view of all three Abrahamic faiths. Those who base belief upon the analytical may be frustrated to find that angels are not available for individual analysis, scientific research, or talk shows. They are one of the unseen creations of God, in addition to the devils, heaven, hell, and many other entities which mankind is to encounter as material realities in the next plane of existence.

Judaism and Islam both view angels in a very practical manner, silhouetting the existence of angels against the backdrop of the totality of God's creation. Humans, when distracted from spiritual reality by the arrogance of disbelief, conceive themselves to be the supreme

(SECTION 5) THE UNSEEN

being of planet Earth. Conversely, the mainstream understanding of all monotheistic religions is that no human being is more than a tiny dot of relatively insignificant protoplasm precariously perched on the brink of a frail mortality, occupying borrowed real estate on a pinhead-sized mud-ball called Earth, spun into orbit 150,000,000 kilometers from the nearest yellow dwarf of spectral class G2 solar hand warmer, largely ignorant of the immediate Milky Way Galaxy neighbors spanning a scant 80,000 light-years diameter, itself deeply buried in what is known as a "local group" of roughly 30 galaxies occupying a cylinder of space 5,000,000 light-years in diameter, which is *itself* only a speck of insignificance cloistered within the "local supercluster" of scores of "clusters," some containing close to 200 galaxies, and laying claim to yet another insignificantly small cylinder of space 150,000,000 light-years in diameter, neatly tucked into the heart of the known universe – a daunting 40,000,000,000 light-years in diameter (each light-year being roughly 6,000,000,000,000 miles).[409] All in all, it's a long drive, and many of mankind have just passed the last rest stop. The only human quality approaching 240,000,000,000,000,000,000,000 miles in diameter, containing 100 billion known galaxies, and expanding at greater than 90% the speed of light is some people's egos. As Rudyard Kipling wrote, "You haf too much Ego in your Cosmos."[410]

The Islamic understanding is that humankind is not alone, and certainly does not hold supremacy of power. God created Man, indeed, but He also created Angels and Jinn. Man takes origin from clay, Angels from light, and Jinn (spirits – and like mankind possessing free will; some are evil, some merely mischievous, some righteous and devout) from fire. Angels have no free will, are absolutely obedient, and are devoted to carrying out the commands of God.

409. *National Geographic Society.* "The Universe, Nature's Grandest Design." Cartographic division. 1995.
410. Kipling, Rudyard. *Life's Handicap.* 1891. "Bertran and Bimi."

(5.A) ANGELS

Their duties include, but are not limited to, the worship of God, conveying revelation to prophets, recording each person's good and bad deeds, protecting the righteous when Allah so decrees, collecting the souls of the dying, fighting on the side of the righteous in time of war, and directing elements of weather. The best known example of such angelic functionaries is Gabriel (also known as the 'holy spirit,' in the Islamic religion), the angel of revelation.

If the question arises as to why God didn't just make all mankind faithful and good, and grant every person paradise, one answer may be that He certainly could have, had He so desired. Allah acknowledges that He could have done so, for He questions mankind, "...Do not the Believers know, that, had Allah (so) willed, He could have guided all mankind (to the right)?" (TMQ 13:31) Furthermore, He teaches, "And to Allah leads straight the Way, but there are ways that turn aside: if Allah had willed, He could have guided all of you." (TMQ 16:9) So why didn't Allah create all mankind obedient and blessed? The reasons are best known to Him, but perhaps one piece of the puzzle is that prior to the creation of mankind, Allah had already made one element of creation (i.e., the angels) perfectly obedient to Him. We humans, however, are a separate element of creation, dedicated to a life of trial. In truth, humans have the opportunity to be *better* than angels by choosing to be obedient of our own free will. Angels have no choice in the matter. Of course, people can also choose to be worse; and therein is the test, and therefrom comes the reward or punishment.

In contrast to the Judaic and Islamic understanding of angels as functionaries of Allah, Christianity delves deeply into fanciful impressions of cupids, cherubs, guardian angels, and a huge host of imaginary angels whose existence is unsubstantiated by scripture. Most all of these angels are imagined to be female, once again in conflict with a scripture which makes no such claims. Such inaccuracies may seem to be of minor significance, but the religious purist is quick to point out the relevance of the commandment, "You shall not make for yourself any carved image, or *any* likeness of *anything* that is in heaven above, or that is in the earth beneath, or that is in the water under the earth..." (Exodus 20:4). The false images incubated in the minds of men would not lend themselves to such misunderstandings were they not immortalized in the artwork of those who violated this commandment.

Association testing will likely find the average person imagining angels to be rotund, pink little cherubs reminiscent of the artwork of Rubens. Portraits of Jesus need little discussion, save pointing out that he should be portrayed as he desired – that is to say, not at all. There are probably more icons of the iconoclast Jesus than of any other personage in the history of mankind. And even those images do not faithfully portray Jesus with the features described in the Bible – attributes such as bronze skin 'like fine brass,' eyes 'like a flame of fire' and curly hair 'like wool,' in color 'white as snow' (Revelation 1:14-15). Certainly not the tanned, blue-eyed, aquiline-nosed, straight-haired blond cast in the mold of the most refined Western European features. If a religion cannot even get the portrait of its own prophet correct, according to their *own* scripture, how much more fervently should sacrilegious images of the unseen God (including those commissioned for the Sistine chapel – the 'pope's own chapel') be cast out? The Renaissance frescoes of Michelangelo were commissioned by not just one, but two popes (Pope Julius II in 1508, and Pope Paul III in 1534) and have been condoned by papal authority to this day. When papal opinion abuts the commandments of God, who is more likely to be in need of reposturing?

Once again, the issue of the appearance and gender of angels may at first seem unimportant. Significance is noted only when taken in the context of the commandments of God. But that, of course, is what religion is all about.

(5.B)
Day of Judgement

"A person never gets a second chance
to make a good first impression"

— old proverb

True belief, by account of all the Abrahamic religions, has a reward in the hereafter. Disbelief faces a slightly less jolly judgement. Such has always been the message of the prophets — all of them.

Why believe in an afterlife? Where else can a person expect to find the full expression of God's infinite justice and mercy, if not in an afterlife? The apparent imbalances of justice in this worldly life would be a poor reflection upon God's sense of justice, if not offset by rewards and punishments in the hereafter. Those whom God loves, so they say, die young. Life plainly illustrates the misery and suffering of the just, with the prophets — being God's elect — presenting prime examples. Which prophet had an easy time of it? Which prophet lived a life of luxury to match that of a contemporary tyrant, mafia boss or modern day drug lord? Yet which prophet threw his hands up in the air in despair and deserted the efforts of his mission for the pleasures of this world? Clearly not Moses, certainly not Christ Jesus, and most definitely not Muhammad.

(Section 5) The Unseen

Should people conceive existence to end upon worldly death, they must necessarily deny the mercy and justice of The Creator, for the inequities of this life are too clearly evident to be missed. Those who trust worldly life to be only one small interval in a continuity of existence which passes from the worldly life of man, through the spiritual way-stations of death and judgement, and beyond to an afterworldly life of unimaginable dimensions, hold trust that in the end justice will be served, and served well.

How will mankind stand for judgement? Where and when? And by Whom? The answers to these questions are concepts dictated by creed. The common denominator of certainty, however, is that one day all mankind will face the reality, whether equating to personally preferred design or not.

Many choose to not even bother contemplating such issues as the how, where, and when of the Day of Judgement. The stark reality that sooner or later, come helium or high water, the day will come, is of sufficient concern. Given the clarity of such a realization and the horror of the consequences of condemnation, who, amongst those who truly believe and fear the wrath of their Lord, can be so confident as to postpone righteous conduct to a later moment, much less a later day?

And yet, most people choose not to believe.

For those who *do* choose to believe, the anxiety of the Day of Judgement, the pleasures of the gardens of paradise, and the horrors of the tortures of hell are realities described or alluded to in all three of the Abrahamic faiths of Judaism, Christianity, and Islam. Humankind will be sorted according to belief and deeds, the faithful and obedient vindicated, the unrighteous condemned, rewards and punishments assigned according to absolute justice. Some claim a purgatory, others either deny the concept or abstain from the vote.

(5.B) Day of Judgement

Differences exist in descriptions and concepts, but one common claim is that only the group of 'us' will bask in the pleasures of the gardens of paradise, and all the 'them' will burn in the eternal and unquenchable fire of hell. Some, such as the various sects of Judaism, claim paradise to be a birthright of the 'chosen people,' based upon previous covenant with God. Most Christians integrate salvation with certain physical (such as baptism) and spiritual (such as accepting specific tenets of faith) testimonies. The Islamic religion is considerably more flexible than others in this regard, for Islam teaches that all who die in submission to The Creator are eligible for redemption. However, submission is measured by specific criteria, and those who fail to accept the true teachings to which they have been exposed cannot be expected to be amongst the successful. Only those who truly submit, accepting revealed truth when made evident, can be considered Muslim – all others live in submission to whatever standard or concern distracts from obedience. Thus, those who followed the prophets, from the time of Adam, were successful, whereas those who forsook the message of their day did so to the compromise of their own souls.

According to Islamic ideology, if it can be imagined that there is a Jew in the world who has not received the news of the prophets who followed, he/she is not to be condemned for ignorance, but judged by the degree of submission to the revelation to which he/she was exposed. Should a Christian die in ignorance of Muhammad and the revelation of the Holy Qur'an, the same applies. Those who die ignorant of revealed truth will be judged based upon depth of sincerity and efforts of faith rather than upon acts of ignorance. The person who dies sincerely seeking the truth of revelation, and accepting it wherever it was found, has hope for salvation, even if ignorant of the perfection of the message of revelation. However, those of insincerity can have little or no such hope, even if educated.

(Section 5) The Unseen

In the end, people will be weighted in the balances according to their sincerity, faith, and commitment. Even then, the scales will be tipped to the side of favor only by the will and mercy of The Creator.

(5.C)
Divine Decree

"For man plans, but God arranges."

–Thomas Kempis

The concept of fate has been argued over and again, but the fact is that none of the various theories of predestination can be proven to the satisfaction of all individuals. Discussion of predestination in the context of this chapter, therefore, is limited to a clarification of the commonality of the concept. For, unknown to many who vocally deny such concepts from the unstable platform of personal opinion, theories of predestination run common through all three of the Abrahamic faiths.

There is no mystery that the dominant Jewish concept of predestination is one of societal salvation based upon selection as the 'chosen people' and the 'elect' of God. Aside from this supremely optimistic thought, very little is written in the Old Testament to solidify a theory of predestination. Regarding the concept of being the 'chosen people,' *Holman's Bible Dictionary* comments,

(SECTION 5) THE UNSEEN

> "From time to time the children of Israel were tempted to presume upon God's gracious favor, to assume, for example, that because the Lord had placed His temple at Jerusalem, they were exempt from judgement. Again and again the prophets tried to disabuse them of this false notion of security by pointing out the true meaning of the covenant and their mission among the nations (Jer. 7:1-14; Amos 3:2; Jonah)."[411]

Even Christ Jesus was recorded as having lamented,

> "O Jerusalem, Jerusalem, the one who kills the prophets and stones those who are sent to her! How often I wanted to gather your children together, as a hen gathers her chicks under *her* wings, but you were not willing!" (Matthew 23:37)

Which raises the question, "Chosen for what? To kill the prophets and stone the messengers?" Hardly a sensible formula for salvation, one would think. But then again, how often can rational argument penetrate the armor of elitist conceit? Surely the Israelites were the 'chosen people' in the time of revelation of the Old Testament. The relevant question amongst the Jews of today is, "How does that apply to us now?" The point has been made before that the Jews were to remain the 'chosen people' only so long as they were faithful to their scriptures and to the prophets predicted in their own books of revelation. Failing that, the covenant with God was broken, and all promises of salvation can reasonably be expected to have been rendered null and void. *Encyclopedia Judaica* comments on just this fact, as follows:

> "The covenant relationship defined in this manner carries with it responsibilities, in the same way that chosen individuals are responsible for certain tasks and are required to assume

---

411. Butler, Trent C. Under 'John, the Gospel of,' (subsection: 'Election').

(5.C) Divine Decree

particular roles....Israel is obligated by this choice to "keep His statutes, and observe His Laws (Ps. 105:45)."[412]

Not the least of which, of course, was to accept and honor the foretold prophets.

With regard to Christian theology a person encounters the theme of foreknowledge and predestination in Romans 8:29 – "For whom He foreknew, He also predestined..." Ephesians 1:3-14 either explicitly or implicitly describes predestination ten times, and Acts 4:27-28 reads, "For truly against Your holy Servant Jesus, whom You anointed, both Herod and Pontius Pilate, with the Gentiles and the people of Israel, were gathered together to do whatever Your hand and Your purpose determined before to be done." 1 Peter 1:1-2 contributes, "To the pilgrims of the Dispersion in Pontus, Galatia, Cappadocia, Asia, and Bithynia, elect according to the foreknowledge of God the Father..." with the fourth verse adding "...to an inheritance incorruptible and undefiled and that does not fade away, reserved in heaven for you..."

Christ Jesus is regarded to have taught predestination when he said, "Come, ye blessed of my Father, inherit the kingdom prepared for you from the foundation of the world" (Matthew 25:34) and, "...but rather rejoice, because your names are written in heaven" (Lk 10:20).[413]

And that's about it. From such minimal beginnings, a plethora of theories have sprouted, shooting off in a variety of disparate directions from the mixed scriptural seeds of a challenging concept.

Steadily balanced and strongly back-peddling on one end of the log-roll of thought, the world of Christianity resolutely defends the concept of God wishing salvation for all mankind, while refusing to

---

412. *Encyclopaedia Judaica*. Vol 5, p. 499 (under "chosen people").
413. *New Catholic Encyclopedia*. Vol 11, p. 713.

(SECTION 5) THE UNSEEN

knock off the somewhat less secure concept which feebly teeters on the opposite end, to the effect that the fate of every human being is predetermined. The answer to the paradox, "How can God wish the salvation of all humankind if He has already destined some for Hell?" rolls like the irritating stone it is in the heel of the shoe which transports the hypothesis. Between the two concepts, one proposal has to be thrown from the equation before an equilibrium of understanding can be established.

In addition, the fight to sustain some degree of belief in human free will is evident, even though many conceive every thought and action to be nothing more than fulfillment of preexisting divine decree. All of which tempts most religious adherents to toe whatever theory is sanctioned by their faith along the lines of, "Of course I can see the emperor's clothes. Smashing, aren't they? They're just so, so, so…well, words just can't describe them, can they?"

How true. Yet that doesn't stop people from trying. The various theories proposed over time are interesting, if not confusing to those seeking resolution on the issue. On one hand, Catholic theology proposes God's infallible foreknowledge of who will be saved, and who not (and why), combined with God's decree to save the blessed in precisely the manner He foreordained.[414]

On the other hand, there was the Protestant reform, and with it an invitation to intellectual rebellion against established religious thought. However, contrary to what a person might have expected, the theories of both Martin Luther and John Calvin were even more rigid and uncompromising than those of the Catholic Church concerning this issue. Whereas the common thinking amongst the theologians of the Catholic Church credited "…that predestination is in some way to be explained by God's foreknowledge of man's

---

414. *New Catholic Encyclopedia.* Vol 11, p. 714.

(5.C) Divine Decree

conduct,"[415] both Luther (in his treatise *De servo arbitrio – The Will Enslaved*) and Calvin (in his *Institutes of the Christian Religion*) claim each member of mankind to have been predestined by God either to eternal beatitude or everlasting perdition from the time of creation. Whereas Luther proposed belief in Christ to be the trademark of the elect, Calvin proposed that, as man was either saved or doomed from the time of creation, the elect were physically incapable of nullifying their salvation, and the doomed were incapable of committing acts sufficient for redemption. Hence, adopting correct belief was not possible for one doomed, as God had already willed such a person to die in disbelief.

Into such a fray walked Jacobus Arminius. Born in 1560 CE, fourteen years following Martin Luther's death and four years preceding John Calvin's demise, Arminius grew to contest Calvin's proposal of unconditional election and irrevocable grace. Arguing the incompatibility of the injustice of irrevocable condemnation with the absolute justice attributed to The Creator, Arminius proposed that God's comprehensive knowledge encompasses the will of man. Hence, though God neither wills man to specific actions nor predestines man to a particular fate, the spiritual design and moral substance of man is known from before the day he or she is born. By way of His infinite knowledge, God knows the path each element of humankind will tread in life, up to and including his or her end. Thus, Arminius proposed that man exists free to make alternative choices. The Creator, having comprehensive foreknowledge of the will of each element of His creation, also has foreknowledge of what each man, woman and child will choose, in thoughts, words, actions and deeds, at all decision points in life. Though the fate of man is foreknown by The Creator, no person is created for a specific predestined fate. Rather, he or she is created in a particular mold, from which the

---

415. *New Catholic Encyclopedia.* Vol 11, p. 719.

(SECTION 5) THE UNSEEN

human being lives life in fulfillment of his or her nature, arriving at the balance of scales foreknown to The Creator from before the time of conception. Man arrives at a foreknown fate, but as consequence of his or her own intrinsic nature and free will rather than the result of pre-assignment.

The theories of Arminius are of interest for two reasons. The first being that they were condemned by the Reformed Church at the Synod of Dort in 1618-19, with the resultant reinstatement of Calvinism as the accepted theory of predestination. Different branches of Protestant faith subsequently set their sails to the prevailing winds of popular theology, tacking back and forth between the rigid theories of Luther and Calvin to retrospective views sympathetic with those of the Catholics, with no resultant clear consensus of canon. In modern times, most Protestant sects have since drifted to the twentieth century weld of predestination and Christology. Although satisfying to those who seek easy salvation through simplistic formulas, the above chapters reveal nothing if not that acceptance of Christ Jesus dictates adherence to what he himself taught, and not to that which others taught about him – all the more so when the two are in direct conflict.

The second point of interest, regarding the theories of Arminius, concerns the simple fact that concepts of predestination, no matter how appealing in explanation, remain the subject of debate, and frequently, of condemnation. Yet the subject remains very much alive, if for no other reason, because it is by its very nature controversial, and inclined to intrigue the internal philosopher who insistently knocks at the door of human desire to explain all things.

The subject of predestination is perhaps less debated within the Islamic religion than within Judaism and Christianity, for the simple reason that the Islamic perspective at the outset is to accept, and not argue, the concept. All religions have their 'mysteries' of faith, with

(5.C) Divine Decree

the concept of predestination being one such mystery which runs common within all three of the Abrahamic religions. The Islamic religion, however, rather gracefully deals with the concept first by defining reasonable and believable elements of the 'mystery' of predestination, second by recognizing the mechanics and existing conditions of the concept to be one of the secrets of Allah, and third by discouraging debate over what is recognized to be a problematic topic given the limits of human intellect and experience.

Complete avoidance of the issue would be inappropriate, however, so a brief description is offered as follows: to begin with, the Islamic religion teaches predestination, while at the same time acknowledging free will of the individual. To deny predestination would be to deny the omnipotence and omniscience of Allah, whereas to deny the free will of mankind would be to negate a freedom of action which each and every element of mankind feels inherent to their humanity.

On one hand, Muslims believe that Allah ordered creation with comprehensive knowledge of the beginning, end, and all between, with each element of creation having a predetermined nature, and with all beings destined to live in fulfillment of their defined disposition. The exertion of free will is consistent with each person's substance and design, but restricted within those boundaries set by Allah. Good occurs only with the help of Allah whereas evil can be committed, though against the pleasure and commandments of Allah, within the limits of transgression He alone permits. All people arrive at a predestined end of which Allah had foreknowledge since the beginning of creation, having earned their judgement through the words, actions, and deeds consistent with their constitutions.

However, having said that, the Islamic religion teaches that all actions of Allah's creation are nonetheless predetermined.

(SECTION 5) THE UNSEEN

A relevant hadith in this regard concerns a Bedouin who asked Muhammad, "Has everything we do been preordained, or do we do it ourselves?" Muhammad replied, "Rather, it has been preordained." The Bedouin then responded, "In that case, why don't we give up doing any acts, and rely upon what has been preordained for us?" Muhammad then advised, "Nay, rather, act (i.e., do what you wish), for every person will find it easy to do what he was created for."[416]

One more tradition which may serve to clarify the Islamic understanding is the hadith in which Ali related Muhammad as having taught,

> "There is not one amongst you for whom a seat in Paradise or Hell has not been allotted and about whom it has not been written down whether he would be a miserable person or a happy one." A man said, "O Apostle of Allah, should we not then depend upon our destiny and abandon our deeds?" Thereupon the Messenger of Allah said, "Whoever belongs to the company of happiness, he will have good works made easier for him, and whoever belongs to the company of misery, he will have evil acts made easier for him." Then he recited, "So he who gives (in charity) and fears (Allah), and (in all sincerity) testifies to the Best, We will indeed make smooth for him the path to Bliss. But he who is a greedy miser and thinks himself self-sufficient, and gives the lie to the Best, We will indeed make smooth for him the path to Misery." (TMQ 92:5-10)[417]

Attempting to rectify concepts of human free will with the proposal of foreknowledge and predestination opens no end of doors to the spacious ballrooms of speculation and argument. It is for the very

---

416. Narrated by *Al- Bukhari*.
417. Narrated by *Muslim*.

(5.C) Divine Decree

reason that such speculation and argument frequently proves destructive that it is discouraged. People might just as well argue any number of the secrets of the unknown as to argue the concept of predestination, for exactly how many angels *can* dance on the head of a pin?

However, unlike arguments over the nature of angels, the spirit, the Day of Judgement, heaven, hell, etc., philosophy over the concept of predestination may lead a person to destruction – debates run the risk of beginning upon a foundation of faith, yet ending in disbelief. For this reason, if for no other, the Islamic religion teaches that discussion of the issue is best limited to definition of the concept, whereas debate is best avoided.

The opinion of Muhammad upon this matter is clear. Once, a group of his companions were debating the concept of predestination, with some of them quoting verses from the Qur'an which prove that Allah wills everything, while others quoted verses which prove the free will of man. Hearing the commotion, Muhammad investigated and inquired about the subject of the argument. When the Companions informed him, signs of anger became visible on his face, and he stated,

"Is this what you have been commanded to do? Is this why I have been sent to you? Verily, the people before you were destroyed when they argued amongst themselves regarding this matter. I caution you not to differ about it."[418]

Those who heed Muhammad's caution continue with their effort in life and religion, all the while accepting that, "The pens have been lifted and the pages have dried."[419] All of which boils down to a philosophy very much in line with the old proverb, "Pray to God, but keep hammering."

---

418. Narrated by *At-Tirmithi*
419. Narrated by *At-Tirmithi*

Section 6
Conclusions

"Wisdom is knowing what to do next. Virtue is doing it."

– David Starr Jordan

(SECTION 6) CONCLUSIONS

The greatest and most significant deductions in life usually culminate from a sequence of smaller steps of cognitive closure. The following three chapters represent the steps deemed necessary by this author to arrive at the most balanced and correct conclusion, as concerns the subject of this book.

(6.A)
The Deviant Religion

"What is truth? said jesting Pilate;
and would not stay for an answer."

— Francis Bacon, *Essays*

Many years ago a zealot of one of the three religions under discussion labeled one of the remaining Abrahamic faiths a 'deviant religion.' That challenge was the impetus for this book. Opinionated oratory can have fleeting emotional appeal, but discourse founded upon evidence argues a lasting truth.

The above-mentioned zealot parroted a common Western thought, targeted to achieve a slanderous persuasion. However, the goal of creating slanted prejudices to override what people directly perceive with their own senses and intellect fails against those who place greater value upon their own measured reason. Too many people of integrity and introspection have come to learn that once the veil of tightly woven slanders is lifted from the face of a much-maligned institution, a person frequently encounters a reality of such deep grace and exquisite appeal as to defeat all false preconceptions.

To return to the charge of deviancy, the analysis of deviancy requires certain steps, the most critical of which is to establish a

(Section 6) Conclusions

laser-straight level of reference, for until a standard for correctness is defined the question "Deviancy from what?" will have no foundation for an acceptable answer. With regard to religion, there simply can be no argument. The measure of religious correctness can have no other standard than that of compliance with the directives of Almighty God.

Should correctness be sought within a religion which rests predominantly upon the canonized creed of men, deviancy will be measured in reference to the wrong standard. Each group of soldiers standing out of rank and file will consider all others to deviate from their misaligned standard, if blinded to the possibility of being in the wrong themselves. Unfortunately, most religions foster just such a cognitive paralysis, instilling an uncompromising 'us against them' attitude of unquestioning superiority. Breaking through this barrier of committed ignorance, the building blocks of which are usually wishful thinking reinforced by pillars of unfounded teachings designed to support what adherents want to hear, is often not possible. However, this is the second ingredient necessary for the determination of deviancy – the ability to analyze objectively and remain receptive to truth, whether welcome or not, whether confirming previously held opinions or not.

Some may measure deviancy in reference to accepted norms, but this methodology is error-prone. If majority opinion is the standard by which correctness is to be measured, then the concepts of the planets orbiting around the sun, the earth being round, and the germ theory of disease were deviant opinions at their time of conception. Ditto the truth of revelation transmitted through Noah to the wayward majority of his time. And if the evidence cited in the body of this book is to be respected, the examples of the minority acceptance of the revelations conveyed through Moses and Jesus to their target populations are not far behind. So deviation from social norms and

(6.A) The Deviant Religion

deviation from absolute truth do not necessarily skip hand-in-hand down the avenue of actuality.

Those who consider themselves to be Muslims contend that they bow to the will of Allah in Islam, recognizing the decree of The Creator to be the ultimate standard of correctness. Those who claim to bow to the will of Allah in Judaism or Christianity must face the full force of the evidences enumerated above, the sum total of which prompts the question as to exactly which group is bowing to the word of God, and which to an error-ridden creed constructed by fallible and scripturally manipulative man.

The information presented above should be adequate to answer such a question, and to afford insight into which of the Abrahamic religions have inclined to deviancy and which not. Whether or not a person acts upon such insight is left to the fate of the individual, which itself largely depends upon a willingness to surrender to the presented evidences.

(6.B)
Surrender

"Swift gratitude is the sweetest"

— Greek Proverb

Those who dive into the effort of making sense of the lack of unity of opinion amongst Jewish and Christian schools of thought frequently emerge frustrated. The differences in understanding are so great as to lead a person to suspect that conflicting sects use different books of guidance. And, as it turns out, frequently they do. The Roman Catholic (Douay) Bible is comprised of 73 books, 7 more than the 66 books of the Protestant Bible and 7 less than the Orthodox version. The number of available versions within the Protestant faiths has become oppressive to those who attempt to catalog the variants. Differing groups endorse dissimilar versions, varying widely not only in emphasis upon specific teachings, but also in the degree of fidelity to the Hebraic and Greek manuscripts from which they are translated. The fact that few of the multitude of denominations agree upon one specific version of the Bible, much less the profile of God, is disturbing to many. The conclusion that the many disparate sects are suffering from a chronic, smoldering lack of

(6.B) Surrender

definitive guidance, and searching for a scriptural cure, is not uncommon, and not unreasonable.

Should a person share the understanding that there is only one God, the conclusion that there is only one approach to Him which is absolutely correct according to His design and most pleasing to Him in conformity with His revelation is likewise not unreasonable. Those sects which deviate therefrom are, well, deviant. Yet these deviant groups and their adherents have become so numerous, as was the case with the obstinate Jews who opposed the prophethood of Jesus in his day, as to be incorrectly perceived as an appropriate norm.

So where should a person look to find that one, most correct approach to God? No doubt the community of the religious agrees that the best a person can do is to submit completely and totally… but to what? Judaism is notorious for the reputation of prioritizing acquiescence to family and cultural tradition; Christianity has grown to teach surrender to indoctrination, whereas Islam teaches submission to the commandments of The Creator. The difference in focus is striking and yet, on the individual level, the value of differentiating the three religions on the above basis blurs when brushed by the consideration that *all* religious adherents consider themselves to be living in submission to The Creator. The relevant distinction subsequently becomes one of ideology rather than definition, for most people of religion, whether Jewish, Christian, Zoroastrian, Muslim, or whatever, believe themselves to be 'Muslim' by definition once they understand the textbook meaning of the word. Even fundamentalist 'give-me-the-power-and-I'll-start-another-Inquisition' Christians believe themselves to be living in submission to the will of God. For that matter, even the chicken-swinging, snake-draping voodoo cults profess worship in submission to God. But only one group of people can be right, leaving a whole lot wrong. So who and what should a person trust?

(Section 6) Conclusions

The faithful harmonize upon the answer, "God."

To surrender to God, on the face of it, should not be all that difficult, yet most people 'surrender' on conditional terms. The first condition in many cases is simply the presence of God, as found in the ill-conceived but frequently offered preface to prayer, "Oh, God, if you are there…" Other conditions include restricting guidance to being within the realm of that which a person has already chosen, such as asking to be guided to be a better Christian. Or a better Jew. Or a better chicken-swinger.

Many adherents of a variety of religions ranging from those based on revelation to those devoted to frank sacrilege adopt the cultist attitude of unquestioning certainty, and so pray for guidance within the confines of the chosen faith, whether in fact astray or not. But is that surrender? What happens if a person's firm confidence is not only unfounded, but wrong? "Well, that's just not possible," the closed-minded prisoners of unquestioning conviction respond. Those of greater humility may be drawn by the affront of such incautious opinion to question exactly who is presumed to be The All-Knowing, The Infallibile – the worshipper or The Worshipped? Some degree of modesty necessarily forces a person to recognize the capriciousness of human convictions, and the sensibility of entertaining all possibilities, including that of being wrong.

The suggestion is offered that surrender to God is only of value when complete and selfless. Whatever a person's religion may be, a person simply cannot go wrong by surrendering to God in search of the truth of Him. Those already on the correct path can expect to be confirmed thereupon, whereas those astray can expect a benevolent push in the right direction.

Surrender, in fact, is an easy word, an uneasy concept, and a challenging act, for in the minds of most the word is associated with giving in to an adversary. However, whereas surrender to an adversary

(6.B) Surrender

is a demoralizing product of defeat, surrender to The Creator is a joyful victory of faith. An adversary threatens abuse, humiliation, imprisonment, torture, even death. The Creator promises mercy and benevolence, peace and salvation.

Similar to an adversarial surrender, religious surrender demands a casting aside of the weapons and tools of self-defense, abandonment of social (and often family) ties, a rejection of the opinions and approval of friends and authorities who may know no better, and a forsaking of all those who feign support, but whose promises and fidelity will be found to be vacuous lies when faced with a supreme reality which tolerates no excuses and permits no resistance. Yet the sacrifices of a religious surrender are not extended in a gesture of disarming to a position of weakness, but rather are offerings tendered for the higher position of gaining the favor of The One Who commands creation.

Those who submit to an enemy seek to escape slaughter. Those who surrender to God flee from a world of persuasive lies and deceptive illusions, entangling hedonism and magnetic seductions, to One Whose mercy is guaranteed, Whose forgiveness is assured, Whose security is absolute.

He is One Who can be counted upon to receive His servants with loving grace.

He is One Who can be trusted to reward the patience and suffering of His servants.

He is One Who can be relied upon to welcome those who seek His pleasure with an incomparable hospitality.

He is The One Who made mankind
    The One Who sustains mankind
        The One Who awaits mankind.

And yet, He is The One Who is denied by the majority of mankind.

And He deserves better from us.

(Section 6) Conclusions

The sincere will open their hearts and minds and submit to the commands of The One to Whom all creation owes the sum total of everything. They will seek the truth, whether to their liking or not, and face their Creator with a desire to serve and worship Him in the manner most pleasing to Him. They will appeal to His mercy and seek His guidance with a depth of devotion sufficient to turn themselves over to His command, completely and totally.

Without compromise.
Without qualification.
Without resistance.
A total, unconditional surrender.
Anything less is just bargaining.

Unlike an adversarial surrender, the religious surrender demands work. A person must examine the religions to which they are exposed and sift through the various propagandized objections. A person who dismisses Judaism out of prejudice against the stereotypical avarice, or Christianity out of revulsion against the sensationalized pedophile priests and hypocritical congregations, has judged according to the impious actions of the adherents rather than by the tenets of faith. Similarly, the person who rejects Islamic ideology on the basis of popularized notions of oppression of women, terrorism, compulsion of religion, and harsh brutality will be surprised to learn that the above-mentioned slanders are not elements of the Islamic religion. They are elements of anti-Islamic propaganda and are found in the deviant example of a few impious people who make headlines by identifying their astray actions with Islam, but they are not a part of Islamic ideology.

Similarly, the customs and traditions of a people should not be allowed to obstruct cognitive analysis. As Suzanne LaFollette so accurately stated, "There is nothing more innately human than the tendency to transmute what has become customary into what has

(6.B) Surrender

been divinely ordained."[420] So whereas the average Christian household may unite upon Christmas trees and crucifixes, these practices represent traditions and not scriptural teachings. In fact, many would argue that such traditions are in fact condemned by Biblical scripture (See Jeremiah 10:2-4 regarding Christmas trees, the second commandment [Exodus 20:4-5] regarding statues) and by the pious examples of the apostolic fathers. Similarly, many of the customs and traditions of Jewish and Muslim communities are religiously distracting, and in certain cases combat the tenets of their respective religions as well.

Once a person can look past the human pollution of different religious beliefs, willingness to rely upon God for direction is complemented by the act of turning to Him in prayer for guidance. People of faith will readily rely upon The Almighty for direction, unburdening their fallible selves from the decision-making process, and trusting God to open the hearts and minds of all sincere supplicants to the truth.

Such individuals would do well to surrender their preconceptions and approach God in the manner of the prophets, many of whom are recorded as having purified themselves by washing prior to prayer (see Exodus 40:31-32 in reference to Moses and Aaron). Purification is a prerequisite for prayer faithfully practiced to this day by Orthodox Jews and Muslims around the world. This is one practice even Paul submitted to, as evidenced by his ritual purification in Acts 21:26.

Next, a person might wish to pray for guidance in the way of the prophets, assuming the posture of prostration (see Nehemiah 8:6 with regard to Ezra and the people, Joshua 5:14 for Joshua, Genesis 17:3 and 24:52 for Abraham, Exodus 34:8 and Numbers 20:6 for Moses and Aaron, and Matthew 26:39 for Jesus). All individuals can glorify God in their own words, but a reasonable suggestion might be

---

420. LaFollette, Suzanne. 1926. *Concerning Women*. "The Beginnings of Emancipation."

(Section 6) Conclusions

for the body of the prayer to include a request for guidance to the religion in which the servitude and worship of God is most pleasing to Him.

The Lord's Prayer (Matthew 6:9-13 and Luke 11:2-4) might be a good starting point for Christians, or for anybody else for that matter. The prayer is non-denominational and a person would have to be hard pressed to object to a request to be 'delivered from evil.' If any objection exists at all, it would have to address either the fact that guidance is not specifically requested or that the two recorded forms of the prayer differ, as follows:

Matthew 6:9-13	**Luke 11:2-4**
"Our Father which art in heaven Hallowed be thy name. Thy kingdom come.	"Our Father which art in heaven Hallowed be thy name. Thy kingdom come.
Thy will be done *in earth,* *as it is in heaven.*	Thy will be done, *as in heaven,* *so in earth*
Give us *this day* our daily bread. And forgive us our *debts,* *as we forgive our debtors.*	Give us *day by day* our daily bread. And forgive us our *sins;* *for we also forgive every one that is indebted to us.*
And lead us not into temptation,	And lead us not in temptation;
but deliver us from evil:	but deliver us from evil."
For thine is the kingdom, *and the power,* *and the glory, forever. Amen."*	

(6.B) Surrender

Which prayer, if either or both, was voiced by Jesus remains uncertain – all the more so considering that more than 1,500 variants to the over 500 sayings ascribed to Jesus are known to exist. The Jesus Seminar, the body of prominent Protestant and Roman Catholic Biblical scholars organized by the aforementioned Robert W. Funk, have gone public with the announcement that the only word of the Lord's Prayer which can be directly attributed to Jesus is "Father."[421] This conclusion is startling, for it not only shakes one of the most accepted trees in the forest of Christian faith, but in fact questions the validity of the tree's very existence.

Some modern translations attempt to hide the above inconsistency, but pretty much any Bible published prior to 1970 records a 2,000 year-old discrepancy, which raises questions regarding the provenance and content of one of the most famous of Christian prayers.

The following prayer is a completely acceptable alternative:

"In the name of Allah, Most Gracious, Most Merciful.
Praise be to Allah, The Cherisher and Sustainer of the Worlds:
Most Gracious, Most Merciful;
Master of the Day of Judgement.
You do we worship, and Your aide we seek.
Show us the straight way,
The way of those on whom You have bestowed Your grace,
those whose portion is not wrath, and who go not astray."

Simple, non-denominational and to the point, this is the Abdullah Yusuf Ali translation of the meaning of the first *surah* of the Holy Qur'an, and is recited a minimum of seventeen times a day by practicing Muslims the world over. But regardless of where it comes from, can any person of piety stand in reasonable criticism of a prayer

---

421. *Newsweek.* October 31, 1988. p. 80.

(SECTION 6) CONCLUSIONS

which glorifies God and unconditionally seeks His guidance? As is the case with the 'Lord's Prayer' of the Bible, no person of God is likely to object, unless it is to question the divine authority of the prayer to begin with. The relevance of such an objection is questionable, however, since the content of all three prayers (counting both versions of the 'Lord's Prayer') stand as beautiful appeals regardless of author.

(6.C)
Consequences of Logic

"Logical consequences are the scarecrows of fools
and the beacons of wise men."
– Thomas Henry Huxley, *Animal Automatism.*

The various world religions invite humankind to accept belief systems via acquiescence to a specific set of teachings—just give up, don't fight that which doesn't make sense, have faith in what a person is told, and be good. Judaism and Christianity command the acceptance of canonized doctrines, many of which not only lack support by, but are in fact contrary to, what are held to be foundational scriptures. The Islamic religion, on the other hand, demands submission to God with the expectation that Allah will guide those who are receptive to truth. Islamic teachings suggest, however, that this is the critical step where most of humankind fail, for, "…whoever seeks a religion other than Islam, it will never be accepted of him, and in the Hereafter he will be one of the losers." (TMQ, 3:85) Understanding the definition of Islam to be 'Submission to the will of Allah,' a person can hardly argue the point on lexical grounds, for who would be so bold as to claim that the focus of religion is other than submission to the will of The Creator?

(Section 6) Conclusions

Any remaining argument, then, must focus upon doctrinal grounds, which requires analysis of the foundational scriptures. Many Jews and Christians argue 'Submission to the will of Allah' in Judaism or Christianity, claiming that the following passage in the translation of the meaning of the Qur'an endorses their respective religions:

> "Say (O Muhammad): "We believe in Allah and in what has been sent down to us, and what was sent down to Ibrahim (Abraham), Isma'il (Ishmael), Ishaq (Isaac), Ya'qub (Jacob) and *Al-Asbat* [the offspring of the twelve sons of Ya'qub (Jacob)] and what was given to Musa (Moses), 'Isa (Jesus) and the Prophets from their Lord. We make no distinction between one another among them and to Him (Allah) we have submitted (in Islam)." (TMQ 2:136)

The above statement commits all Muslims to belief in the validity of the original revelation conveyed to each of the above-named prophets, Moses and Jesus included. One may wonder, then, why Muslims don't revere the Old and New Testaments as highly as they do the Holy Qur'an.

Two reasons.

Upon reading the above quote, many Jews and Christians argue with Muslims, "See, see...your book says my book is true and valid." Not so. The fundamental point of misunderstanding in this regard is that the Islamic religion testifies to the validity of all *true* revelation, meaning original, pure and uncorrupted. That the original Torah of Moses and Gospel of Christ Jesus are lost is no mystery. That what remains in the present day has been corrupted from the originals is supported by evidence taken from the books of Jewish and Christian scripture themselves, as discussed in the relevant sections above. Hence, although the Islamic religion testifies to the truth of all *original* revelation in the form and purity that "...was given to Musa

(6.C) The Consequences of Logic

(Moses), 'Isa (Jesus) and the Prophets from their Lord," that tenet does not equate to accepting the Jewish and Christian Bibles in their present, impure forms.

Secondly, even if the Old and New Testaments were presumed valid in their present forms, conclusions drawn from analysis of these scriptures are conflicting and diverse. Muslims contend that the teachings of the prophets encased within these scriptures nonetheless endorse the religion of Islam and the messengership of Muhammad more than they do the canonized creeds of Judaism and Christianity. Those who follow the teachings of the prophets will discover the religion of Islam in their own books. However, those who follow the writings of contrary authors (such as Paul) will be led astray.

The Islamic view, then, is that each stage of revelation prepared true believers for the next, with no differences in creed between any of the many stages. Those who follow the chain of revelation with sincerity will progress from one stepping stone in the path of revelation to the next, with the logical end-result being acceptance of the final prophet and the revelation with which he was sent, as foretold in the scriptures of both the Judaic and Christian religions.

Consequently, the entreaty is offered,

> "Say: "O People of the Book (i.e., Jews and Christians)! Come to common terms as between us and you: that we worship none but Allah; that we associate no partners with Him; that we erect not, from among ourselves, Lords and patrons other than Allah." If then they turn back, say you: "Bear witness that we (at least) are Muslims (bowing to Allah's Will)." (TMQ 3:64)

Will mankind establish such common terms? Will all of humankind purposefully unite in the worship of Allah and Allah alone? Associating no partners or co-sharers in His divinity? Well, it hasn't happened yet.

(Section 6) Conclusions

But it is not all of mankind with which a person need be concerned – it is only with regard to the self that each individual need assume responsibility.

And if every person were to make the right decision in *that* regard, the unity of mankind would be assured.

But either way, the message has been borne.

~

"In a time of universal deceit, telling the truth is a revolutionary act."

– George Orwell

APPENDIX

Recommended Reading

Translations of the Meaning of the Holy Qur'an

(1) *The Holy Qur'an* (King Fahd Holy Qur-an Printing Complex, Al-Madinah Al-Munawarah, Saudi Arabia) and *The Qur'an* (Tahrike Tarsile Qur'an Inc., Elmhurst, New York) both present the translation of Abdullah Yusuf Ali – an excellent translation, enhanced by the beauty of more classical English than that found in more modern translations. A major shortcoming, however, is that the translator's commentary contains multiple errors, and is best avoided in favor of more classic, and respected, *tafaseer* (explanations of the meanings of the Qur'an).

(2) *The Noble Qur'an* (King Fahd Holy Qur-an Printing Complex, Al-Madinah Al-Munawarah, Saudi Arabia) translated by Dr. Muhammad Al-Hilali and Dr. Muhammad Muhsin Khan. A more modern and literal translation than that of Abdullah Yusuf Ali, thoroughly researched and complemented by explanations from the *tafaseer* of Ibn Katheer, al-Qurtubee, and at-Tabaree, as well as quotations of authentic hadith, primarily from the collection of al-Bukhari. This is without a doubt the most error-free of the English

Recommended Reading

translations, yet this translation nonetheless suffers from a certain lack of fluency in the English language. Although an exceptional reference, dedicated reading can become tiresome due to the format and limitations of the language.

(3) *The Qur'an* (revised and edited by Saheeh International, Abul-Qasim Publishing House, Jeddah, Saudi Arabia). An excellent, modern, easily readable and highly respected translation, thought by many to be the overall best available in the English language. Highly recommended as the first book for those seeking an easy, accurate, and pleasing translation of meaning of the Qur'an.

Sciences of the Qur'an

(1) *An Introduction to the Sciences of the Qur'an* (Al-Hidaayah Publishing, Birmingham, England), by Abu Ammaar Yasir Qadhi.

History (of Islam)

(1) *Muhammad, His Life Based on the Earliest Sources* (The Islamic Texts Society, Cambridge, England) by Martin Lings. An excellent and comprehensive history of the life of Muhammad, only slightly marred by the few aforementioned errors (see relevant footnote, section 4.D.).

(2) *When the Moon Split* by Safi-ur-Rahman al-Mubarakpuri. Published by Maktaba Dar-us-Salam, Saudi Arabia. An excellent, award-winning history of the Prophet, translation in the English language is slightly disappointing, but still readable and highly informative.

History (of the Arabs)

(1) *A History of the Arab Peoples* (Warner Books) by Albert Hourani. Scholarly and comprehensive

Recommended Reading

Comparative Religion (from a Muslim perspective)

(1) *A Muslim Study of the Origins of the Christian Church* (Oxford University Press), by Ruqaiyyah Waris Maqsood. An extraordinary, and sadly neglected, treasure of theology written by this British scholar

(2) *The Mysteries of Jesus* (Sakina Books, Oxford), by Ruqaiyyah Waris Maqsood. Same book and author, different title.

Basic Information on Islam

(1) *What Everyone Should Know About Islam and Muslims* (Kazi Publications, Chicago, IL), by Suzanne Haneef. A comprehensive, beautifully written primer.

(2) *What Every Christian Should Know About Islam* (The Islamic Foundation, Markfield, England), by Ruqaiyyah Waris Maqsood. Shorter than Suzanne Haneef's book, but every bit as enjoyable and informative, with greater emphasis on theology, balanced by personal narrative.

Guidance to New Muslims

(1) *Bearing True Witness* (or, *Now That I've Found Islam, What Do I Do With It?*) -- see author's website, www.Leveltruth.com

Miscellaneous Treasures

(1) *The Road to Mecca* (Islamic Book Trust, Kuala Lumpur), by Muhammad Asad. A remarkable and heartwarming story of one man's journey, first to Islam, and then through the world of the Arabs.

Bibliography

Abu Nu'aem. *Dala'el An-Noobowah.*

Achtemeier, Paul J. (General Editor). *Harper's Bible Dictionary.* 1985. New York: Harper and Row.

Al-Bukhari, Muhammed Ibn Ismaiel; translated by Dr. Muhammad Muhsin Khan. 1997. *Sahih Al-Bukhari.* Riyadh: Darussalam.

Al-Haakim

Al-Hilali, Muhammad, Ph.D. and Dr. Muhammad Muhsin Khan, M.D. *Interpretation of the Meanings of The Noble Qur'an in the English Language; A Summarized Version of At-Tabari, Al-Qurtubi and Ibn Kathir with comments from Sahih Al-Bukhari.*

Al-Mubarakpuri, Safi-ur-Rahman. 1995. *Ar-Raheeq Al-Makhtum.* Riyadh: Maktaba Dar-us-Salam.

An-Nisa'ee

Anthes, Richard A., John J. Cahir, Alistair B. Fraser, and Hans A. Panofsky. 1981. *The Atmosphere.* 3rd ed. Columbus: Charles E. Merrill Publishing Co.

Arberry, A. J. 1953. *The Holy Koran – An Introduction with Selections.* London: George Allen & Unwin Ltd.

Arberry, A. J. 1964. *The Koran Interpreted.* London: Oxford University Press.

Arberry, A. J. 1996. *The Koran Interpreted.* A Touchstone book: Simon & Schuster.

Arbuthnot, F. F. 1885. *The Construction of the Bible and the Korân.* London: Watts & Co.

At-Tabarani, *Mu'ajm Al-Kabeer.*

Ayto, John. *Dictionary of Word Origins.* 1991. New York: Arcade Publishing, Inc.

Azzirikly, *Al-Aa'lam.*

BIBLIOGRAPHY

Baigent, Michael and Richard Leigh. 1991. *The Dead Sea Scrolls Deception*. New York: Summit Books/Simon & Schuster Inc.

Bermant, Chaim and Michael Weitzman. 1979. *Ebla: A Revelation in Archaeology*. Times Books.

The Bible, Revised Standard Version. 1977. New York: American Bible Society.

Bucaille, Maurice, M.D. 1977. *The Bible, the Qur'an and Science*. Lahore: Kazi publications.

Bultmann, Rudolf. 1971. *The Gospel of John, a Commentary*. Translated by G. R. Beasley-Murray. Oxford: Basil Blackwell.

Butler, Trent C. (General Editor). *Holman Bible Dictionary*. Nashville: Holman Bible Publishers.

Buttrick, George Arthur (Ed.). 1962 (1996 Print). *The Interpreter's Dictionary of the Bible*. Nashville: Abingdon Press.

Cadoux, Cecil John. 1948. *The Life of Jesus*. Middlesex: Penguin Books.

Cailleux, Andre. 1968. *Anatomy of the Earth*. New York: McGraw-Hill Book Company. Translated by J. Moody Stuart.

Carlyle, Thomas. 1841. *On Heros, Hero-Worship and the Heroic in History*. London: James Fraser, Regent Street

Carmichael, Joel, M.A. 1962. *The Death of Jesus*. New York: The Macmillan Company.

Carroll, Lewis. *Alice's Adventures in Wonderland*.

Catholic Encyclopedia. 1914 Edition, CD-Rom.

Chamberlin, E. R. 1993. *The Bad Popes*. Barnes & Noble, Inc.

Chapman, Dom John. 1907. *The Condemnation of Pope Honorius*. London: Catholic Truth Society.

Conybeare, Fred. C., M.A. 1898. *The Key of Truth*. Oxford: Clarendon Press.

Cross, F. L. and E. A. Livingstone (editors). 1974. *The Oxford Dictionary of the Christian Church*. London: Oxford University Press.

BIBLIOGRAPHY

Davis, Richard A., Jr. 1972. *Principles of Oceanography.* Reading, Massachusetts: Addison-Wesley Publishing Co.

Dawud, Abdul-Ahad (Formerly known as Reverend David Benjamin Keldani, Bishop of Uramiah).1992. *Muhammad in the Bible.* Jeddah: Abul-Qasim Publishing House.

De Lamartine, A. 1854. *Histoire de la Turquie.* Paris.

Denzinger, Henricus & Schonmetzer, Adolfus. 1973. *Enchiridion Symbolorum, Definitionum et Declarationum de Rebus Fidei et Morum.* Barcinone: Herder.

Douglas, J. D. (general editor). *The New International Dictionary of the Christian Church.* 1978. Grand Rapids, MI: Zondervan Publishing House.

Dow, Lorenzo. *Reflections on the Love of God.*

Dummelow, Rev. J. R. (editor). 1908. *A Commentary on the Holy Bible.* New York: Macmillan Publishing Co., Inc.

Easton, M. G., M.A., D.D. *Easton's Bible Dictionary.* Nashville: Thomas Nelson Publishers.

Elder, Danny; and John Pernetta. 1991. *Oceans.* London: Mitchell Beazley Publishers.

*The Encyclopedia Americana International Edition.*1998. Grolier Inc.

Encyclopaedia Britannica. 1994-1998. CD-ROM.

Encyclopaedia Judaica. 1971. Jerusalem: Keter Publishing House Ltd.

Fateh Al Bari Shareh Sahih Al Bukhari. Ibn Hajar Al Asqualani, Bab Alqadar. Cairo: Al Mat'ba Assalafiyah.

Findlay, Rev. Adam Fyfe, M.A., D.D. 1929. *The History of Christianity in the Light of Modern Knowledge.* London: Blackie & Son, Ltd.

Fossier, Robert (editor). 1986. *The Cambridge Illustrated History of The Middle Ages.*Cambridge: Cambridge University Press.

Bibliography

Fox, Robin Lane. 1991. *The Unauthorized Version; Truth and Fiction in the Bible.* Viking Press.

Funk, Robert Walter. 1996. *Honest to Jesus, Jesus for a New Millennium.* Polebridge Press.

Gehman, Henry Snyder (editor). *The New Westminster Dictionary of the Bible.* 1970. The Westminster Press.

Gibbon, Edward, Esq. 1854. *The History of the Decline and Fall of the Roman Empire.* London: Henry G. Bohn.

Gilbert, Arthur. 1968. *The Vatican Council and The Jews.* New York: The World Publishing Company.

Gilman, Arthur, M.A. 1908. *The Saracens.* New York: G. P. Putnam's Sons.

Goodspeed, Edgar J. 1946. *How to Read the Bible.* The John C. Winston Company.

Gross, M. Grant. 1993. *Oceanography, a View of Earth.* 4th ed. Englewood Cliffs: Prentice-Hall, Inc.

Guillaume, Alfred. 1990. *Islam.* Penguin Books.

Guinness Book of Knowledge. 1997. Guinness Publishing.

Gwatkin, H.M. 1898. *The Arian Controversy.* London: Longmans, Green, and Co.

Hammad, Ahmad Zaki. 1997. *Father of Flame, Commentary & Vocabulary Reference of Surat al-Masad.* Bridgeview, Illinois: Quranic Literacy Institute.

Hart, Michael H. *The 100, A Ranking of the Most Influential Persons in History.* p. 39 of the 1978 edition by Hart Publishing Co.; p. 9 of the 1998 edition my Citadel Press.

Hastings, James (editor). 1913. *The Encyclopedia of Religion and Ethics.* Charles Scribner's & Sons.

Hastings, James (editor); Revised edition by Frederick C. Grant and H. H. Rowley. 1963. *Dictionary of The Bible.* Second Edition. Charles Scribner's Sons.

Hermann Ranke. *Die Ägyptischen Personennamen (Dictionary of Personal Names of the New Kingdom).* Verzeichnis de Namen, Verlag Von J J Augustin in Glückstadt, Band I (1935); Band II (1952).

Hirschfeld, Hartwig, Ph.D. 1902. *New Researches into the Composition and Exegesis of the Qoran.* London: Royal Asiatic Society.

Hogarth, D.G. 1922. *Arabia.* Oxford: Clarendon Press.

The Holy Bible, New King James Version. 1982. Thomas Nelson Publishers.

The Holy Bible, New Revised Standard Version. Grand Rapids, MI: Zondervan Publishing House.

Huxley, Thomas H. 1870. *Discourse Touching The Method of Using One's Reason Rightly and of Seeking Scientific Truth.*

Hyndman, H. M. 1919. *The Awakening of Asia.* New York: Boni and Liveright.

Ibn Hisham. *As-Seerah An-Nabawwiyyah.*

Imam At-Tirmithi. *Mukhtasar Ash-Shama'el Al Muhammadiyyah.*

The Interpreter's Bible. 1957. Nashville: Abingdon Press.

Irving, Washington. 1973. *Mahomet and His Successors.* New York: G. P. Putnam's Sons.

Kähler, Martin. 1953. *Der sogemnante historische Jesus und der geschichtliche, biblische Christus.* Munich: New edn by Ernst Wolf.

Kee, Howard Clark (Notes and References by). 1993. *The Cambridge Annotated Study Bible, New Revised Standard Version.* Cambridge University Press.

Kelly, J. N. D. 1978. *Early Christian Doctrines.* San Francisco: Harper & Brothers Publishers.

Bibliography

Kipling, Rudyard. *Life's Handicap.* 1891. "Bertran and Bimi."

Kittel, Gerhard and Gerhard Friedrich (editors). 1985. *Theological Dictionary of the New Testament.* Translated by Geoffrey W. Bromiley. William B. Eerdmans Publishing Co., Paternoster Press Ltd.

Kraeling, Emil G. Ph. D. 1952. *Rand McNally Bible Atlas.* Rand McNally & Co.

Kuenen, Philip H. 1960. *Marine Geology.* New York: John Wiley & Sons, Inc.

LaFollette, Suzanne. 1926. *Concerning Women.*"The Beginnings of Emancipation."

Lane, Edward William. 1980. *An Arabic-English Lexicon Derived From the Best and the Most Copious Eastern Sources.* Beirut, Lebanon: Librairie Du Liban.

Lane-Poole, Stanley. 1882. *The Speeches and Table-Talk of the Prophet Mohammad.* London: MacMillan and Co.

Lea, Henry Charles.1958. *A History of The Inquisition of The Middle Ages.* New York: Russell & Russell.

Lehmann, Johannes. 1972. *The Jesus Report.* Translated by Michael Heron. London: Souvenir Press.

London *Daily News.* June 25, 1984.

Manaahil Al-Irfaan fi Uluum Al-Qur'an (Wells of Knowledge of the Sciences of the Qur'an). 1988. Muhammad Abdul-At-Theem Az-Zarqaani. Dar Al-Kutub Al-Ilmee'a.

McBrien, Richard P. (General Editor). 1995. *HarperCollins Encyclopedia of Catholicism.* New York: HarperCollins Publishers.

McManners, John (Editor). 1990. *The Oxford Illustrated History of Christianity.* Oxford University Press.

Meagher, Paul Kevin OP, S.T.M., Thomas C. O'Brien, Sister Consuelo Maria Aherne, SSJ (editors). 1979. *Encyclopedic Dictionary of Religion.* Philadelphia: Corpus Publications.

BIBLIOGRAPHY

Merriam-Webster's Collegiate Dictionary. 1997. Tenth edition. Merriam-Webster Inc.

Michener, James A. May, 1955. 'Islam: The Misunderstood Religion,' in Reader's Digest [American Edition].

Miller, Albert and Jack C. Thompson. 1975. *Elements of Meteorology.* 2nd ed. Columbus: Charles E. Merrill Publishing Co.

Montet, Edward. 1929. *Traduction Francaise du Couran.* Paris.

Moore, Keith L. 1983. *The Developing Human, Clinically Oriented Embryology, With Islamic Additions.* 3rd ed. Jeddah: Dar Al-Qiblah with permission of W.B. Saunders Co.

Motley, John Lothrop. 1884. *The Rise of the Dutch Republic: A History.* London: Bickers & Son.

Muata'h Imam Malik

Muhammad Ibn Ishaq Ibn Yasar. 1963. *Seerat An-Nabi.* Maydan Al Azhar (Cairo): Muhammad Ali Sabi'eh & Children.

Muir, Sir William. 1923. *The Life of Mohammad.* Edinburgh: John Grant.

Muslim.

Musnad Abu Ya'ala.

Musnad Ahmad.

Myers, Jacob M. 1966. *Invitation to the Old Testament.* New York: Doubleday & Company.

Naish, John, M.A. 1937. *The Wisdom of the Qur'an.* Oxford.

National Geographic Society. "The Universe, Nature's Grandest Design." Cartographic division. 1995.

National Geographic. December, 1978.

New Catholic Encyclopedia. 1967. Washington, D.C.: The Catholic University of America.

BIBLIOGRAPHY

The New International Encyclopaedia. 1917. 2nd Ed. New York: Dodd, Mead and Company.

Newsweek. October 31, 1988.

Nostra Aetate. 28 October 1965. Item #4. Official publication of the Vatican website, *www.vatican.va*

Ostrogorsky, George. 1969. *History of the Byzantine State.* (Translated from the German by Joan Hussey). New Brunswick: Rutgers University Press.

Parke, David B. 1957. *The Epic of Unitarianism.* Boston: Starr King Press.

Press, Frank and Raymond Siever. 1982. *Earth.* 3rd ed. San Francisco: W. H. Freeman and Co.

Qadhi, Abu Ammaar Yasir. 1999. *An Introduction to the Sciences of the Qur'an.* Birmingham: Al-Hidaayah Publishing.

Reumann, John. 1991. *Variety and Unity in New Testament Thought.* Oxford University Press.

Rippin, Andrew (editor). 1988. *Approaches to the History of the Interpretation of the Qur'an.* Chapter: 'Value of Hafs and Warsh Transmissions,' by Adrian Brockett. Oxford: Clarendon Press.

Robinson, Victor, M.D. 1943. *The Story of Medicine.* New York: The New Home Library.

Ross, Alexander. 1718. *The Life of Mahomet: Together with The Alcoran at Large.* London.

Roth, Cecil B. Litt., M.A., D. Phil. and Geoffrey Wigoder, D. Phil. (editors-in-chief). 1975. *The New Standard Jewish Encyclopedia.* W. H. Allen.

Sa'eid Hawwa. 1990. *Ar-Rasool, Salallahu Alayhi Wa Salam.* Second Edition. Cairo:Dar As-Salaam Publishing.

Sahih Al-Bukhari.

Sale, George. 1734. *The Koran.* London: C. Ackers.

BIBLIOGRAPHY

Sayed Qutub, *Fi Thilal Al-Qur'an.*

Scofield, C. I., D.D. (Editor). 1970. *The New Scofield Reference Bible.* New York: Oxford University Press.

Seeley, Rod R., Trent D. Stephens and Philip Tate. 1996. *Essentials of Anatomy and Physiology.* 2nd edition. St. Louis: Mosby-Year Book, Inc.

Shakespeare, William. *The Merchant of Venice.*

Shaw, George Bernard. 1944. *Everybody's Political What's What?*

Smith, R. Bosworth, M.A. 1986. *Mohammad and Mohammadanism.* London: Darf Publishers Ltd.

Stanton, Graham N. 1989. *The Gospels and Jesus.* Oxford University Press.

Stoddard, Lothrop, Ph.D. 1922. *The New World of Islam.* Second Impression. London: Chapman and Hall, Ltd.

Strong's Exhaustive Concordance of the Bible. 1980. World Bible Publishers.

Stubbe, Dr. Henry, M.A. 1975. *An Account of the Rise and Progress of Mohomedanism, with the Life of Mahomet.* Lahore: Oxford and Cambridge Press.

Sunan Tirmithee.

Sykes, Sir Percy Molesworth. 1951. *A History of Persia.* 3rd edition. London: Macmillan & Co., Ltd.

Tafheem-ul-Qur'an

Tafseer Ibn Kathir

Tarbuck, Edward J. and Frederick K. Lutgens. 1982. *Earth Science.* 3rd ed. Columbus: Charles E. Merrill Publishing Company.

Thompson, Della (editor). *The Oxford Dictionary of Current English.* 1993. Second Edition. Oxford University Press.

Toland, John. 1718. *Tetradymus; bound with, Nazarenus: or, Jewish, Gentile and Mahometan Christianity.* London.

BIBLIOGRAPHY

Tugwell, Simon OP. 1989. *The Apostolic Fathers.* Harrisburg, Pennsylvania: Morehouse Publishing.

Twain, Mark. *Following the Equator.* "Pudd'nhead Wilson's New Calendar."

Vaglieri, Dr. Laura Veccia. Translated from Italian by Dr. Aldo Caselli, Haverford College, Pennsylvania. Originally published in Italian under the title: *Apologia dell' Islamismo* (Rome, A. F. Formiggini, 1925). 1980. *An Interpretation of Islam.* Zurich: Islamic Foundation.

Wakefield, Gilbert, B.A. *An Enquiry into the Opinions of the Christian Writers of the Three First Centuries Concerning the Person of Jesus Christ.* 1824. Editor's dedication.

Wallace, Robert, F.G.S. 1850. *Antitrinitarian Biography.* London: E.T. Whitfield.

Watt, W. Montgomery. 1953. *Muhammad at Mecca.* Oxford: Clarendon Press.

Wegner, Paul D. *The Journey from Texts to Translations.* 1999. Grand Rapids: Baker Books.

Wehr, Hans. *A Dictionary of Modern Written Arabic.* 3rd printing. Beirut: Librairie Du Liban; London: MacDonald & Evans Ltd.1980.

Weinberg, Steven. 1988. *The First Three Minutes, A Modern View of the Origin of the Universe.* Basic Books; Harper Collins Publishers.

Weiss, Johannes. 1909. *Paul and Jesus.* (Translated by Rev. H. J. Chaytor). London and New York: Harper and Brothers.

Wells, H. G. 1922. *The Outline of History.* Fourth Edition. Vol. 2. Section XXXI- 'Muhammad and Islam.' New York: The Review of Reviews Company.

Werblowsky, R. J. Zwi and Geoffrey Wigoder (editors in chief). 1997. *The Oxford Dictionary of the Jewish Religion.* Oxford University Press.

BIBLIOGRAPHY

Whiston, William, A.M. 1998. *Josephus, The Complete Works.* Nashville: Thomas Nelson Publishers.

Wrede, William. 1962. *Paul.* Translated by Edward Lummis. Lexington, Kentucky: American Theological Library Association Committee on Reprinting.

Zad Al-Ma'ad.

Zahrnt, Heinz. 1817. *The Historical Jesus.* (Translated from the German by J. S. Bowden). New York: Harper and Row.

Glossary of Terms

AH – After Hijra. The zero point of the Islamic calendar corresponds to the Prophet Muhammad's Hijra (migration) from Makkah to Medina in July of the year 622 CE (AD). Subsequent dates were calculated according to the lunar calendar, which differs from the Julian calendar by roughly 10 days each year.

Ayah (Plural: Ayat) – Verse of the Holy Qur'an.

BH – Before Hijra. See 'AH' for explanation.

Bint – Daughter of.

CE – 'Common Era' or 'Christian Era,' corresponding to the same calendar and dates as 'AD.'

Fitrah – The innate nature instilled by Allah as human birthright. Fitrah includes the recognition and understanding of Allah as Lord and Creator, and the inborn ability to discriminate between good and evil.

Hadith – A tradition recording the words, actions, appearance, or implied consents of Muhammad Ibn Abdullah.

Hafith – A memorizer of the Holy Qur'an.

Haj – The annual Muslim pilgrimage to Makkah.

Hijra – Prophet Muhammad's migration from Makkah to Medina in July of the year 622 CE.

Ibn – Son of.

Imam – Leader of the prayer, being the one who goes out in front of the congregation.

Makkah – (aka Mecca, Bakka, Becca, Baca) – The holy city to which Muslims make pilgrimage. The Kaba, to which Muslims direct prayers, and the well of Zam-Zam is contained in the central, sacred mosque.

Glossary of Terms

Mecca – See Makkah.

Mushaf – Book.

Sahaba – The companions of the prophet Muhammad.

Sunni – Orthodox sect of Islam, accounting for 95% of all Muslims.

Surah – Chapter of the Holy Qur'an.

Tawheed – Islamic monotheism.

Zakat – The poor-due incumbent upon Muslims.